Opportunity Lost

Opportunity Lost
Race and Poverty
in the Memphis City Schools

Marcus D. Pohlmann

The University of Tennessee Press / Knoxville

Library of Congress Cataloging-in-Publication Data

Pohlmann, Marcus D., 1950–
Opportunity lost: race and poverty in the Memphis City schools / Marcus D.
Pohlmann — 1st ed.
    p. cm.
Includes bibliographical references and index.

ISBN-13: 978-1-57233-716-9
ISBN-10: 1-57233-716-8

1. De facto school segregation—Tennessee—Memphis.
2. Education—Tennessee—Memphis—Finance.
3. Memphis City Schools.
I. Title.

LC212.623.M45P64 2008
379.2'630976819—dc22
2008017197

To Melvin Hetland,
a consummate educator

Contents

Figures

Tables

Preface

The origins of this project actually go back to the late 1980s. At that time, my colleague Dr. Michael Kirby and I were contracted to do research that culminated in *Racial Politics at the Crossroads: Memphis Elects Dr. W. W. Herenton,* a book which focused on the evolution of white and black politics in Memphis. The project gave me a chance to carefully review the history of the city, including both its racial and economic histories. Among other things, I was struck by the extent of racial separation and the breadth and intensity of the poverty that existed in large segments of the city.

In the spring of 2001, Johnnie B. Watson, the superintendent of the Memphis City Schools, asked me to conduct a review of school consolidation efforts in Knoxville, Nashville, and Chattanooga. With the able assistance of colleagues Dr. Joy Clay and Dr. Kenneth Goings, we completed that task and reported to the Memphis City School Board in the summer of that year.

It was hard to conduct our study of educational reform in the state's other large cities without beginning to ponder what problems Memphis shared with those cities and how such reforms might benefit the Memphis public schools. Yet, given the conflicting passions surrounding the issue of school consolidation in the Memphis area, we had been explicitly asked not to address that question in our analysis. Meanwhile, bad reports continued to dominate the local news. Related in part to the federal policy of "No Child Left Behind," a sizable number of Memphis City Schools were struggling to make the grade in terms of state-mandated competency exams.

An interview I conducted in Knoxville continued to resonate in the back of my mind. An African American administrator candidly speculated that school success has far less to do with what actually goes on in school than many people believe. Specifically, the administrator speculated that you could take middle-class children from the wealthiest school in the area, transfer them to the most poorly funded school, and they would still do well. Conversely, you could take the lowest-income children from the latter school, transfer them to the best endowed school, and they would still struggle academically.

That politically incorrect thinking came from a young and otherwise quite liberal African American who had taught for several years before assuming a high-level administrative position. This led me back to a book that had been gathering dust on my shelves since I took a graduate course on the Politics of Education in the 1970s. It was Christopher Jencks et al., *Inequality: A Reassessment of the Effect of Family and Schooling in America*.[1] That 1966 book grew out of a seminar at Harvard University designed to reassess the findings of James Coleman and his colleagues, findings that suggested desegregating the schools could boost black students' educational performance.[2] In their book, Jencks et al. came to some relatively radical conclusions about the relationship between the socioeconomic position of parents, the likelihood of their children succeeding in school, and to what degree the school ever could be a realistic launching pad to larger economic equality in the United States.

I decided I would return to the alleged relationship between socioeconomic class and educational success as a starting point in my analysis of the struggling Memphis City Schools. To what degree could the city's racial divisions and levels of poverty help explain at least some of the specific problems holding back students in Memphis, Tennessee? Answers to these questions would have definite implications for proposals to improve educational performance.

Acknowledgments

I wish to express my deep appreciation to Scot Danforth and Stan Ivester for being terrific editors and for their invaluable help in steering this project to completion. I would like to thank Johnnie Watson, David Sojourner, Lee Garrity, Linda Sklar, Katie Stanton, Maura Black Sullivan, Nancy Richie, Yi Liu, Michael Cervetti, and Jimmie Covington for helping me collect the data for this study. I also would like to thank the many students who assisted me along the way, including David Goudie, Casey Hail, Charlie Patrick, Naomi Long, Becky Saleska, Alexandra Felgar, Stephanie Fox, and Elizabeth Holladay. In addition, Mike Kirby's contributions to our original analysis of racial politics in Memphis have continued to shape my understanding of the city and are no doubt embedded in much of my own subsequent analyses. Last, but certainly not least, I wish to thank Barbara Pohlmann, a lifelong elementary schoolteacher who was my main sounding board throughout this project and who made numerous substantive contributions. Beyond that, I remain eternally indebted to her for her patience and unquestioning love.

Chapter 1

Memphis Schools in Context

> The biggest challenge facing U.S. cities and their school systems is concentrated poverty. In poor neighborhoods, the deck is stacked against children from the moment they are born.
>
> —Virginia Edwards, *Quality Counts '98: The Urban Challenge and Public Education in the 50 States*, 1998

The nineteenth-century writings of Horatio Alger inspired generations of American youth with tales of penniless heroes gaining wealth and fame through a combination of goodness and courage. Essential to much of that success was an education system that prepared students to rise almost limitlessly, with enough talent, ambition, and perseverance.

What contemporary evidence demonstrates is that education does indeed affect one's economic position in life, especially in today's increasingly technological information age. Nevertheless, the economic circumstances into which one is born also appear to have a significant impact on the extent and quality of one's education. The socioeconomic circumstances into which most inner-city children are born today does not bode well for a twenty-first-century rags-to-riches metamorphosis. A combination of postindustrial economic changes and a history of racial exclusion have combined to make it harder than ever for children to rise from rags to riches in today's postindustrial information age.[1]

The American Educational System

To be sure, we have some control over our own economic fate. Financial success, for instance, is strongly correlated with educational attainment, and this has become especially true in recent years. The average college graduate now makes

$51,000, the high school grad $28,000 and the high school dropout less than $19,000. The high school dropout is twice as likely as the high school graduate to be unemployed, and he or she would have to work 109 hours per week to make what the college grad makes in 40 hours. The same is even truer for wealth accumulation, where the college graduate has more than seven times the financial assets of a high school graduate and some thirty-two times that of a grade-school graduate.[2] But who gets the higher levels of education?

A child's school advancement will depend to a significant degree on how that child scores on standardized achievement tests. To begin with, parents' income and education correlate well with how their children will do on standardized tests.[3] This is particularly true for poor children. They tend to start school at achievement levels that are roughly two years behind their nonpoor counterparts and are less than half as likely to achieve proficiency at designated junctures.[4] As Harry Miller put it, "There is a clear, consistent, and moderate relationship between social class position and both measured intelligence and school achievement."[5]

Correspondingly, higher academic achievement leads to more school years completed. Thus, the children of better-off parents also generally finish more school years. The high school graduation rate has remained well over 90 percent for those with parents in the top economic quartile, yet scarcely over 60 percent for those whose parents are in the bottom one. Meanwhile, the likelihood of completing a B.A. degree has become even more skewed in recent years, with those in the top group being four times more likely to receive such a degree in 1980 and nearly twelve times more likely today. Poverty, however, is the best predictor of a child's educational attainment, and it correlates negatively with high school graduation, college attendance, college grades, and school years completed.[6] As an Annie Casey Foundation study concluded, "nothing predicts bad outcomes for a kid more powerfully than growing up poor."[7]

Recent trend data suggest that the gap in educational attainment between the children of the haves and have-nots has increased significantly since the late 1970s, especially with rising tuition costs and a decline in governmental tuition assistance.[8] When the impediments of race and poverty come together, we find scarcely more than 1 percent of African American students from the poorest category of households attending college full time.[9] Not surprisingly, weak students from well-off families stand a better chance of attending college than better students coming from poorer backgrounds.[10]

Student academic success appears to have more to do with what the students bring to school than what they will get in the classroom. As Christopher Jencks et al. concluded, "Most differences in adult test scores are due to differences that schools do not control."[11] This is because "children seem to be far more influenced by what happens at home than by what happens at school.

They may also be more influenced by what happens on the streets."[12] Jencks et al. also found the achievement differences attributable to family background to be greatest for verbal ability and general information, tests highly correlated with one another as well as with IQ scores. The correlation was somewhat less strong in tests on reading, math, and nonverbal ability, possibly because "these skills are largely taught in school, so that differences between homes affect them less."[13] In addition, James Coleman found 1960s student achievement to be closely related to the educational backgrounds and aspirations of the other students in the school.[14] Eric Hanushek et al. found similar trends in American schools today.[15]

Underlying Causes

Educational attainment does seem to be linked both directly and indirectly to the socioeconomic position of a student's parents, and these advantages of birth play out in several different ways. To begin with, as nearly one-half of all school funding comes from local property taxes, there have been substantial discrepancies in the amount of money available to spend on local public schools. In the state of Texas, prior to judicial intervention, one district spent $2,337 per pupil, while another was able to spend more than $56,791 and still enjoy a much lower tax rate.[16] As a result, wealthy schools often were more apt to have the latest textbooks, full libraries, science laboratories, state-of-the-art computer equipment, and attract the better teachers. Meanwhile, at the other end of town, children often made do with out-of-date textbooks and other hand-me-down resources, and many teachers eschewed teaching there.[17]

Although the U.S. Supreme Court has refused to apply the Constitution's equal protection clause to school spending discrepancies, a good many state courts have ruled that such discrepancies do run afoul of the equality guaranteed by their state constitutions.[18] The California Supreme Court, for instance, found school spending discrepancies to violate their state's concept of equal protection. As they put it, "We have determined that [relying on local property taxes] invidiously discriminates against the poor because it makes the quality of a child's education a function of the wealth of his parents and neighbors. Recognizing as we must that the right to an education in our public schools is a fundamental interest which cannot be conditioned on wealth, we can discern no compelling state purpose necessitating the present method of financing. . . . [S]uch a system cannot withstand constitutional challenge and must fall before the equal protection clause."[19]

Even when courts intervene, however, they normally stop well short of guaranteeing full equality between the various public schools in the state. Consequently, considerable inequality remains between public school districts. This is only exaggerated by the fact that it normally costs proportionately more to teach underprivileged children, those coming to school with higher incidences of malnutrition, poor health, less caregiver involvement, less nurturing and stimulating home environments, frequent changes of residence, and more exposure to violence.[20]

Beyond disparities in school funding, parents and organizations in wealthier neighborhoods have been known to contribute additional private monies to their local public schools for items such as a weather station, a greenhouse, smart boards, television equipment, and a ropes course. Schools with a higher percentage of educated parents are also more likely to offer things like advanced placement courses. In addition, there is the contrast between public schools and their elite private counterparts. Elite private schools may well offer added educational opportunities and prestige, besides contacts they and their more affluent parents can provide after graduation. Beyond all that, wealthier and better educated parents are able to provide a more educationally enhanced home environment, utilizing tutors, educational camps and family trips, as well as a wide variety of books and electronic devices, and still have the time and confidence to more closely monitor their child's schoolteachers and administrators.[21]

Lastly, as an increasing proportion of the middle class has managed to work its way into college classrooms, a mere college degree is no longer enough to open many of the most desirable doors of employment. That now requires an advanced degree from a prestigious college. Not surprisingly, it is the wealthier who are more likely to attend the more expensive elite colleges given steep tuition increases and more systematic elite efforts to get their children admitted.[22]

The Black Educational Experience

The state of New Jersey provided schooling for black residents as early as 1777, and religious and humanitarian groups set up private schools for free blacks in several other states. Black slaves, on the other hand, were systematically denied most types of education. In many places, it was actually illegal to teach a slave to read. As a result, W. E. B. DuBois estimated that only about 5 percent of former slaves were literate as of 1865.[23] That would begin to change following the Civil War.

Freedmen's Bureaus were instrumental in helping pave the way for the creation of elementary, secondary, and college level schools for former slaves. This included assistance in the establishment of such well-known institutions as Howard, Fisk, and Atlanta universities and the Hampton Institute. By 1870, some 247,333 black students were attending 4,329 schools, and the cost to the Freedmen's Bureaus exceeded $5 million.[24] Various black and white religious denominations, as well as private foundations like the Peabody Educational

Fund, also became involved. Black schools continued to expand, and a few colleges like Oberlin and Berea were racially integrated despite strong social pressure to the contrary.

The school doors swung open even further with the series of Supreme Court decisions culminating in the *Brown v. Board of Education* school desegregation decision.[25] Thereafter, a combination of the growing civil rights and the black power movements paved the way for even more racially equal educational opportunities. Busing and affirmative action plans were implemented, and curricula began to include more black perspectives. Black history was taught in increasing numbers of high schools, and black studies programs emerged on a number of college campuses. In addition, where there was only one predominantly black college in 1854, there were more than 100 such schools by the early 1970s.

Nevertheless, educational opportunities were far from equal between the races.[26] Most blatant were the inequities in school funding. In the South, for instance, predominantly white schools outspent their predominantly black counterparts by a three-to-two ratio during the Jim Crow days at the turn of the century. Neighborhood funding formulas also meant that the poorest neighborhoods, where blacks disproportionately dwelled, had fewer taxable assets and consequently fewer tax dollars with which to fund their schools. The racial spending differential soon grew to three-to-one and beyond, before state and federal courts began providing some remedies.[27]

Black enrollment in majority white schools reached its peak in 1988; yet, it has been declining ever since. It has now returned to its pre-1971 levels. More than 97 percent of black students currently attend a public school, and two out of every three attend a public school that has a predominantly African American student body. Those student bodies also have a disproportionate concentration of intense poverty.[28] As journalist Anna Quindlen put it, "in America's cities we've met the future, and its past. Black families live in the urban equivalent of sharecroppers' shacks, and their children go to segregated schools."[29] This time, however, the courts have not been intervening because they are inclined to see today's school segregation as occurring by choice and not by law.

Despite all of that, education still represents an area of marked gains for African Americans. Whereas more than 80 percent of all blacks were completely illiterate in 1870, very few are today.[30] In addition, racial differentials in school years completed and college enrollment have been reduced considerably. The black high school dropout rate, for instance, has been reduced and is now only slightly higher than the corresponding white rate, especially for black women.[31] Black women with a B.A. degree now out-earn comparably educated white women.[32] Such indices of progress, however, mask some serious underlying problems.

Persistent Problems

Even though it has been reduced, black adult illiteracy remains nearly three times that of white adults, while more than 40 percent of all black teenagers have serious problems in terms of literacy.[33] Additionally, although the overall racial discrepancy in dropout rates has indeed declined, the high school dropout rate for inner-city black males now exceeds 50 percent.[34] Beyond that, the average dropout rate for the nation's largest urban school districts is 22 percent, twice the national average. The Memphis rate is roughly 50 percent, and cities like Chicago have districts with dropout rates exceeding 86 percent.[35] Black students also exhibit significantly higher failure rates.[36] And, although black women now out-earn comparably educated white women, white men earn roughly 50 percent more than comparably educated black men, black women, or white women.[37]

In addition, achievement test scores indicate that although they are in school and passing from grade to grade, black students are often modal years behind their white counterparts in both reading and writing skills and in actual knowledge.[38] The typical black student scores below 75 percent of the white students on standardized tests, and, that gap does not shrink unless they are in the same schools or have families with the same amount of schooling, income, and wealth.[39] To make matters worse, these deficiencies tend to increase the longer blacks are in school. By the twelfth grade, the average black student reads and does math at the level of the average white eighth grader.[40]

As for the school atmosphere in which they study, increased security measures and "zero tolerance" laws have helped make the black school experience less dangerous; but that also means that black students are seven times more likely than their white counterparts to have to pass through metal detectors on their way into school and more than four times as likely to sit in classrooms with bars on the windows. And despite all those measures, they are nearly twice as likely to report having gotten into a fight at school and are still twice as likely as whites to report feeling unsafe.[41]

For those who stick it out and graduate from high school, average black SAT scores remain some one hundred points behind those of whites in both the verbal and mathematics categories, although the gap has narrowed slightly in recent years.[42] The proportion of blacks attending college seems to have peaked in the mid-1970s and remains more than 25 percent lower than for whites. In addition, a third of all black college students are in two-year schools, and blacks are still badly underrepresented in graduate and professional programs.[43] Meanwhile, whites are nearly twice as likely to have graduated from college, and nearly twice as likely to have a graduate degree, numbers that would be far higher if it were not for the graduation rates of black women.[44]

For African Americans, the stakes are particularly high when it comes to educational attainment. As an example, one in four black men were unemployed all year long by 2002, but that number was 44 percent for high school dropouts, 26 percent for high school graduates, and 13 percent for those with at least a B.A. degree.[45] Even more dramatic is the fact that black high school dropouts in their late twenties are more likely to be in prison than working.[46] Meanwhile, there are three times as many blacks in prison as in college, and nearly one in four black males who did not go to college finds himself incarcerated.[47]

Causes

Research indicates that a variety of causes contribute to these academic problems. To begin with, E. Horace Fitchett and others have found semblances of a correlation between black literacy in nineteenth-century and twentieth-century black elites, further reinforcing the intergenerational value of education.[48] Disparities in family background may in fact account for up to two-thirds of the black-white test score gap, and four-fifths of the IQ gap, while the remainder can be ascribed to school-related variables.[49] In addition, these correlations appear to be even truer in today's contemporary inner cities.[50] Even where black and white parental education is similar, white parents often have attended better schools and colleges; and, grandparent backgrounds correlate as well.[51] It is also telling that more than three-quarters of white students have Internet access at home, but fewer than half of black students have such access.[52]

Racial analysts such as Orlando Patterson, John Ogbu, and Claude Steele have stirred controversy by suggesting several additional causes. Patterson looks at black men failing academically, while black women in those same environments are not nearly so likely to fail. He blames contemporary street culture, with its hanging out on the street, violence, sexual conquests, party drugs, and hip hop music.[53] Ogbu and others also discuss the possibility that a "black oppositional culture" has developed in opposition to the language and mores of whites, and when blacks try to cross over they are seen as traitors to the cause.[54] Steele adds that black males may "disidentify" with school success in order to maintain their self-esteem in the face of academic difficulties.[55]

There is disagreement about the value of racial integration in what have generally become highly resegregated urban schools. The 1966 Coleman Report and subsequent research indicated that desegregating the schools could boost black students' educational performance without harming white achievement.[56] These findings have been challenged, however, by other recent studies indicating that blacks do not necessarily perform any better when integrated with whites if key socioeconomic variables are controlled.[57] There is also some evidence that white schools cherry-pick top black students in order to help integrate themselves, both inflating the apparent value of integration and depriving predominantly black schools of high achieving role models.[58] Nonetheless, seg-regated schools do deny both races opportunities to interact as they will almost certainly have to do later in life.[59]

In the modern era, when advanced education has become more important than ever, today's least privileged African Americans appear to face long odds in their attempt to raise themselves from the poverty of the inner city.[60] Addressing the National Press Club in Washington, D.C., educator Ernest Boyer concluded that, "What we could be left with in our major cities is a kind of educational Third World. And it is here, in these schools, that the battle of American educa-tion will be won or lost. If urban schools do not become a national priority, the promise of excellence will remain sadly unfulfilled."[61]

Historical Context

To understand how race and poverty have come together to challenge the effec-tiveness of many urban educational systems, it is important to see how these two phenomena have developed across urban American history. What follows is a brief historical overview of postindustrial urban development, as well as the American racial dilemma identified by Gunnar Mydral and others. These two trends set the stage, indicating the economic and social milieu in which today's urban schools are compelled to operate. They also accentuate the ever increas-ing importance of advanced education if one is to succeed in today's increas-ingly technological information age.

Economic History

The postindustrial period can be distinguished by the introduction of such tech-nological developments as automated assembly lines, automobiles, airplanes, computers, and telecommunications. Among other things, these developments freed many companies from the necessity of locating near specific workers, markets, waterfronts, and related businesses. As a result, corporations have become mechanized and quite mobile, with serious implications for a society's workforces and the cities in which they reside.

Beginning in the 1930s, and really accelerating after the 1970s, veritable revolutions in transportation, communication, and manufacturing technology allowed owners of venture capital to invest their money virtually anywhere on the face of the earth. Individual businesses also would be far freer to move to more profitable locations without jeopardizing their production or distribution schemes. In addition, technological developments fundamentally altered the manufacturing process to the point where an ever larger portion of the work-force ended up working in the service sector of the economy instead of in the manufacturing sector. Then, such developments began altering the service sector as well. All of this had significant economic implications for large U.S. cities and the children trying to emerge from them.

Technological Change. Machines were developed that could accomplish many of the tasks previously done by human hands, such as cutting, canning, and labeling. With the development of robotics, even more specialized human tasks, such as painting and welding, could be performed mechanically. In addition, computers could be programmed to do much of the record keeping, billing, and other paperwork that once required large clerical staffs. Moreover, artificial intelligence programming now allows computers to randomly perform calculations until a problem is solved, reducing the need for some analytical positions.[62]

Meanwhile, the development of the automobile and the proliferation of highways significantly accelerated the decentralization of the nation and its individual metropolitan centers, and the growth of air travel and advanced telecommunications further fueled this dispersion. Soon it became increasingly possible to have access to the workforce, resources, and markets only cities had long been able to provide, without locating within the confines of a large waterfront city, or any city at all for that matter. In addition, the development of fiber-optic cable increased the capacity of the Internet to carry ever larger amounts of information. Combined with new software applications and work-form platforms, small segments of larger service jobs soon could be outsourced to virtually anywhere.

Many corporations rode this wave of technological change, allowing them to relocate all or portions of their operations where they could operate more cheaply. They moved first from the crowded center-city to the more spacious suburbs, then from the unionized Snow Belt to the less unionized Sun Belt, and ultimately from the United States to the Third World, where labor was far cheaper and where there were fewer environmental regulations adding to production costs. Such moves were facilitated in part by governmental reductions in tariffs on imported and exported goods, an attempt to encourage more "free trade" between nations.[63] In addition, American-based companies have been sending their managers to foreign countries in order to facilitate this movement, while American universities are also beginning to locate branch campuses in such locations.[64]

Employment Impact. Where manufacturing was still the most common form of employment as late as 1979, it was surpassed by trades and services by the mid-1980s. Today, only about one in ten American workers are employed in factories. More people have come to be employed by Wal-Mart and McDonald's than by General Motors and United States Steel. Thus, an ever-increasing proportion of

America's available postindustrial jobs are found in professional and personal services. These tend to be in fields as health care, finance, insurance, information technology, retail sales, and government. At the high end, educated and skilled employees operate sophisticated technological machinery and function as managers. Meanwhile, the lesser skilled are often either being replaced by machines or they are left working at the middle to lower end of the service sector.[65]

It was not long, however, before advanced telecommunications and the Internet allowed a variety of service positions to be "offshored" to less costly locales, including higher-end jobs in research and analysis, accounting, consulting, computer programming, and engineering. Even highly skilled positions in fields such as radiology and pathology were in jeopardy, as the Internet allowed tests and images to be analyzed and results reported from almost anyplace on Earth. Lower-end service jobs, those requiring the fewest skills and thus open to the largest number of Americans, also began to be outsourced overseas. Solicitations, customer service, clerical work, and some retail jobs could now be done far more cheaply in the Third World via telephone and Internet lines.[66]

American Express outsourced computer programming to India as early as 1993. General Electric began offshoring service jobs in 1998. International Business Machines (IBM) recently cut thirteen thousand jobs in the U.S. and Western Europe and added fourteen thousand in India. Such moves, where feasible, are nearly irresistible when one considers the wage differentials. A software programmer in the United States, for example, makes roughly five times what a comparably trained programmer in India is paid.[67] As IBM executive Harry Newman concluded, "[Globalization] is rapidly accelerating, and it means shifting a lot of jobs, opening a lot of locations in places we had never dreamt of before, going where there's low-cost labor, low-cost competition, shifting jobs offshore."[68] Back in the United States, however, Bob Herbert notes that American workers "can be ever so bright, well trained and hard working, and still lose [their] job to an Indian who works for [many] times less."[69]

Thomas Friedman and others remind us that offshoring also can create American jobs, as foreign workers may well be using American-made computers, telephones, and the like.[70] Nevertheless, there are still indications that offshoring will turn out to be a net loss for the United States workforce. Katherine Bradbury and others, for example, have warned that the number of "discouraged workers," those no longer even looking for work, appears to have risen to five million or more beyond the formal unemployment figures.[71] In what he refers to as "the next Industrial Revolution," Alan Blinder concludes that the offshoring has only just begun, and it will eventually cost Americans more than forty million jobs.[72] Economist Martin Kenney agrees, concluding that it "is going to be much, much bigger than we ever imagined."[73]

Wages and Benefits. People who lose jobs in manufacturing end up taking an average pay cut of between 13 and 14 percent if and when they find new work.[74] That pay cut runs about 11 percent for displaced service-sector workers.[75] Yet, as Steve Lohr warns, "the broader impact may be to put pressure on the wages of many technical workers in the United States, who increasingly live under the shadow of foreign competition."[76]

Nevertheless, despite all the corporate mechanization and mobility, a number of well-paying skilled positions remain in this nation's more service-oriented economy. That list includes jobs such as physical therapists, store managers, and legal litigators. Such work involves specialized training and knowledge as well as being geographically situated.[77] These jobs tend to generate the kind of wages, benefits, skill development, and opportunities for advancement that place workers in what economists refer to as the "primary labor market." They afford the kind of comfort and security normally associated with middle-class status. If enough wealth is accumulated, they even can elevate one into the corporate owning class.[78]

Unionized blue-collar workers in manufacturing industries also have been able to enter the primary labor market, earning a comfortable living and at the same time developing skills and advancing.[79] In addition, they helped create a standard that influenced the wage and benefit package offered by many nonunion employers trying to attract good workers and avoid union organizing. Unionization reached its peak in the late 1940s, when more than one-third of the American workforce belonged to a labor union, and the ranks and affluence of the middle class grew.

The unionized proportion of the American workforce, however, has declined to fewer than 8 percent of private-sector workers, and fewer than 13 percent of workers overall. Corporate mobility and the changing nature of much of the employment itself have left many workers hesitant to organize, while companies are becoming much less inhibited about firing striking union workers and replacing them with nonunion employees.[80] President Ronald Reagan's high profile firing of striking air traffic controllers further emboldened employers.[81] As a result, even many factory jobs no longer provide middle-class wages, benefits, and opportunities.[82]

One major exception has been governmental employees, a disproportionate number of whom are unionized. In 2005, for example, governments paid an average of $24.17 in wages and salaries and another $11.29 in benefits. Meanwhile, the corresponding private-sector numbers were only $17.21 and $7.03. That comes to a total compensation gap of $11.22 per hour, meaning governmental workers were making almost 50 percent more than their private-sector counterparts.[83]

Far more of today's new positions now fall into what has been called the "secondary labor market." Also referred to as "dead-end jobs," these positions offer little prospect of launching one into the more secure middle class. These tend to be lesser-skilled jobs in restaurants, retail stores, and private hospitals. They often pay little more than minimum wage; entail few, if any, benefits such as health insurance, paid vacation and holidays, or a retirement plan; involve little to no skill development or opportunities for significant advancement; and are often only part time, further reducing the likelihood that the job's compensation will include benefits beyond hourly wages. Forty percent of today's jobs can be learned in less than one month.[84]

Not surprisingly, then, real dollar wages for production and nonsupervisory personnel have become stagnate. Looking at the period between 1973 and 2004, for example, the median hourly pay of male workers remained virtually the same in real dollars, as did median household income.[85] Meanwhile average weekly pay seems to have been declining, most likely due to the downward skew created by an increase in part-time employment.[86] After generations of growth, men in their thirties now make less than their fathers did at that age.[87] In addition, many new jobs now pay a family head poverty-level wages.[88] One-quarter of the current U.S. workforce now earns wages that would still leave them below the federal poverty level even after a forty-hour workweek.[89]

Nearly forty million Americans find themselves living below the federal government's poverty level, including twelve million families and more than twelve million children. Another fifty-seven million Americans can be classified as "near poor," meaning their income is less than twice the national poverty rate. One in four of America's working families can now be classified as either poor or near poor.[90] Beyond the breadth of poverty in the United States, however, it is also important to consider its depth. The "very poor" are those whose income is less than half the federal government's poverty level. The number of "very poor" people has been growing of late and is now more than 40 percent of those in poverty, making it that much more difficult for them to escape.[91]

For all age groups under seventy years of age, the odds of experiencing at least temporary poverty doubled in 1990s, while the risk of spending a year or more in poverty increased as well. In the 1980s, 13 percent of Americans in their forties spent at least one year in poverty. By the 1990s, as income instability continued to increase nationwide, that figure had risen to 36 percent,[92] with Sheldon Danziger and Peter Gottschalk seeing "no prospects—given existing labor market conditions and public policies—for significant declines in poverty."[93]

Beyond sagging wages, more work has come to be expected "off the clock." In addition, the number of part-time workers has been growing at twice the rate of the workforce as a whole, and many of those part-timers would prefer to be working full time. An ever smaller percentage of the workforce is covered by cost-of-living adjustments, which guarantee wage increases to compensate for inflation. The proportion of jobs without health insurance has risen markedly, while roughly one-half of all U.S. workers no longer receive paid sick leave. Meanwhile, work-related stress has increased, while the proportion of jobs with unemployment compensation coverage also has declined.[94]

In 1968, General Motors was the corporate poster child, with many unionized lifetime employees and an average wage of $29,000 in present dollars, not to mention hefty health and retirement benefits. Today, Wal-Mart is the country's largest corporation. It has no unionized employees, and the average full-time wage leaves that worker earning below the federal government's poverty line.[95] As Paul Krugman put it, "the end of the era in which ordinary working Americans could be part of the middle class moves much closer. . . . Almost everywhere you look, corporations are squeezing wages and benefits, saying they have no choice in the face of global competition."[96] As a result, corporate profits are now the highest they have been since the 1960s, while wages and salaries make up a smaller share of the nation's gross domestic product than at any time since government began keeping those records in 1947.[97] As economist Jared Bernstein concluded, "it comes down to bargaining power and the lack of ability of many in the work force to claim their fair share of growth."[98]

Polarization. The postindustrial economy has tended to create jobs at the top and at the bottom of the employment ladder, with those in the top brackets requiring more skills than ever. Meanwhile, there are ever fewer established and stable bottom rungs upon which underskilled workers or even small-scale entrepreneurs can successfully begin their way up the ladder of economic success. This poses serious challenges for those trying to rise out of the inner cities of the twenty-first century.

According to Robert Reich, trends in automation and offshoring have enlarged "the widening gap between those who are getting a good education . . . and those who don't have a good education and who are almost inevitably kept in the local service economy, where pay and benefits are paltry."[99] As Douglas Massey put it, "In a globalized economy, two classes of people can be expected to fare well and one poorly. Owners of financial and human capital (the wealthy and the educated) will do well because the things they offer on the global market (money, knowledge, skills) are in short supply. Owners of labor (workers) will not do well because what they have to offer (physical work effort) is cheap, plentiful, and oversupplied on a global scale."[100]

The group at the top has been getting richer by both absolute and relative measures. From 1950 to 1970, for every dollar made by the bottom 90 percent of the nation's population, the top one-tenth of 1 percent made $162. Since 1990, that multiplier has grown to $18,000.[101] Not surprisingly, then, the richest 1 percent makes more income than the bottom 40 percent combined, and that gap has more than doubled since 1980.[102] At the very top of that group, the number of centimillionaires and billionaires more than tripled since 1980, leaving them even further removed from average household than the rest of the top 1 percent.[103] The combined income of the wealthiest 300,000 Americans is now roughly equal to what the bottom 150,000,000 Americans bring home.[104]

These trends also hold when looking at household income, where the respective households often have more than one wage earner. The income of the bottom quintile of households grew by 6.4 percent between 1980 and 2000, thanks in large part to robust economic growth in the 1990s. Meanwhile, the income of the top quintile grew by 184 percent, with that of the top one-tenth of one percent growing even faster. In 1980, the top 1 percent of households made 133 times the income of the bottom 20 percent combined, and that figure had grown to 189 times by 2000. In absolute terms, the average household in the top 1 percent of American households makes roughly $1 million per year.[105]

Beyond income, however, it is also important to consider trends in the distribution of wealth. Wealth is accumulated money invested in stocks, bonds, savings accounts, real estate, and the like. There is little personal security without the cushion of at least some accumulated wealth. Living paycheck to paycheck, one can become destitute virtually overnight due to a lay-off, extended illness, or large medical bills. Wealth also can generate income, and it can be handed down to one's offspring in the form of inheritance.[106]

The top 1 percent of American households in terms of wealth have consistently owned a clear majority of the nation's business assets;[107] and, their wealth holdings guarantee virtually all of them enough unearned income to keep them in the nation's top 5 percent of income earners even if they do not work at all.[108] The 400 highest paid taxpayers, those making average of $174 million per year, derived less than 17 percent of that income from wages. The rest came from investments.[109] Corporate wealth from capital gains, dividends, interest, and rent also has gravitated to the top. The share of capital gains acquired by the top 1 percent grew from 39 percent in 1991 to nearly 60 percent today. The share of every group beneath them declined.[110] The top 1 percent of U.S. households currently holds a larger share of the nation's income and wealth than at anytime since pre-Depression years.[111]

At the opposite end of the spectrum are the bottom 20 percent of American families in terms of wealth, where the average household owes more than it owns and rarely makes more than 125 percent of the federal poverty level.[112] They will usually remain rather hopelessly in debt, often to unscrupulous loan sharks. For several reasons, they are also exceptionally vulnerable to economic downturns these days. Their inflation-adjusted incomes have not risen. The welfare safety net has been reduced considerably, and workfare only helps if there are jobs to work. Unemployment insurance is harder to come by, with fewer than 30 percent of the unemployed receiving it. In addition, federal job training and low-income housing have been reduced, while states and localities have been too strapped to pick up the slack in such services.[113]

These aggregate measures also mask the fact that the distribution of income and wealth has become bimodal—meaning there are increasingly more people at the relatively higher and lower ends, with fewer in the middle.[114] Not only is the owning class getting richer, but a division is developing within the middle class. Skilled technicians and professionals, especially those who can process and analyze information, continue to do well in the more technological postindustrial era. This is the group Barbara Ehrenreich refers to as the "professional middle class,"[115] or Robert Reich calls the "symbolic analysts."[116] Meanwhile, much of the rest of the class has slipped into the secondary labor market.[117] The top quintile of Americans generally appear to have high skills, high wages, and job security. The other 80 percent of the working population seems to be forming the "new working class."[118]

According to financier Felix Rohatyn, "What is occurring is a huge transfer of wealth from lower-skilled middle-class American workers to the owners of capital assets and to the new technological aristocracy."[119] As Greg Duncan et al. summarize, "the rising tide of economic growth. . . . appears to have lifted the yachts, but neither the tugboats nor the rowboats."[120]

Beyond all that, however, the present does not appear as bad as it has become, and the future looks even less promising for many in the next generation of middle-class families. That is because:

1. The large baby boom generation has reached its peak earning years.

2. The number of multiple-income families has been growing markedly, with two incomes now required to maintain the family status that used to be manageable with one.[121]

3. Individuals are working longer hours and retiring later, in jobs that are increasingly less likely to provide health insurance and retirement benefits.[122]

4. Baby Boomers married later and had smaller families than their predecessors, allowing for more discretionary per-capita income, even when hourly wages have been declining.[123]

5. Savings has declined and short-term borrowing has increased in an attempt to maintain existing living standards.[124]

6. Welfare reform, immigration, and offshoring also have left more American workers chasing fewer jobs, while China is emerging as a major global competitor in several economic sectors.[125]

In an attempt to maintain existing living standards, savings has declined to the point that we now have a negative savings rate as a nation. Debt-to-income ratios have soared, with household debt at 132 percent of household income in 2005. Short-term borrowing has increased to more than $2 trillion, leaving the average American family spending nearly 20 percent of its income on debt payments. Meanwhile, home foreclosures have increased, and personal bankruptcies are at an all-time high. In addition, the nation's trade deficit is approaching a trillion dollars annually, while we are adding national debt at twice the rate of gross domestic product for the first time in the nation's history. In 1958, for instance, overall national indebtedness was 84 percent of gross domestic product. Today it is more than 160 percent.[126]

As Bob Herbert concluded, "The end result of all this is a portrait of American families struggling just to hang on, rather than to get ahead. The benefits of productivity gains and economic growth are flowing to profits, not worker compensation. The fat cats are getting fatter, while workers, at least for the time being, are watching the curtain come down on the heralded American dream."[127]

Postindustrial Cities. Amidst the postindustrial developments described above, America's urban economies have undergone a considerable metamorphosis. Most manufacturing went from the Snowbelt cities in the Northeast and Midwest to their suburbs and then to the Sunbelt states of the South and West. Today, they are increasingly likely to be relocating overseas to the Third World. Even service positions have now begun to follow that path. As a result, most of the nation's largest cities continue to lose jobs, despite urban empowerment zones or urban renewal efforts.[128]

Urban manufacturing and retail centers have been giving way to office complexes, specialty services, entertainment facilities, convention centers, and government buildings. In addition, although the cities may well get the corporate headquarters, the suburbs often get the divisional headquarters, regional sales offices, and the research and development laboratories. Grand hotels have been refurbished in the central business districts, and new shopping malls, sports facilities, and entertainment complexes also have been erected, often with the help of sizable governmental subsidies and tax breaks.[129]

One major result of all this has been what George Sternlieb calls "a mismatch between the people who live in cities and the new kinds of functions cities have taken on."[130] Many city residents lack the skills increasingly required for work in today's primary labor market, not to mention the lack of transportation necessary to reach the increasing number of such positions that have come to be located in outlying areas.[131] Consequently, an ever larger number of inner-city dwellers, even if fortunate enough to have found work, often toil in the less attractive secondary sector of the labor market. Here they are employed primarily by private service-producing businesses, where unionization is rare, wages are low, benefits are few, and their job futures are tenuous. Not surprisingly, urban social problems like poverty, crime, and homelessness have increased significantly, in the shadow of the renovated loft apartments and central-city entertainment complexes enjoyed largely by those fortunate enough to work in the primary labor market.[132]

Racial History

It is not a random sample of Americans who are concentrated in contemporary urban ghettos, grappling with these postindustrial dilemmas. These ghetto residents are disproportionately likely to be African American. In 1944, Swedish historian Gunnar Mydral described twentieth-century race relations in the United States as an "American Dilemma" because the American creed of equal opportunity did not seem to mesh with the lagging position of African Americans.[133] The next half century was highlighted by several governmental efforts to ease such racial disparities. These included federal civil and voting rights acts, sweeping U.S. Supreme Court decisions, school busing, and a variety of affirmative action programs. Despite those efforts, however, many of the racial disparities have persisted.

The United States of America is a nation of immigrants. The only truly "native Americans" were long ago conquered and shepherded onto reservations. Everyone else, at some point in their family histories, immigrated here from another established country. Millions of them, many of whom were poor peasants or unskilled laborers, left their native lands to make new lives for themselves in the United States. Many were seeking economic opportunities. Others fled from class barriers, religious persecution, military conscription, or economic downturns. In essence, these immigrants were being pushed by hardships, pulled by perceived opportunities, or both. Yet one group came under very different circumstances. Most African American immigrants were forcibly removed from their homelands and arrived enchained as slaves.

Following their legal emancipation from slavery in the 1860s, the large majority of African Americans stayed in the South, either migrating to the cities or remaining in the rural areas as tenant farmers and farm hands. Toward the end of the nineteenth century, however, the boll weevil, cotton gin, and overall mechanization of southern agriculture thrust many of them out of work. In addition, they continued to be plagued by blatant forms of discrimination as well as by night riders and lynch mobs. Then, the plummeting of cotton and tobacco prices during the Great Depression destroyed many of the remaining opportunities to sharecrop. The prospect of a better life in Northern cities became increasingly alluring. A more promising future appeared evident in advertisements run in Chicago's widely circulated black newspaper, *The Defender,* or in letters written by relatives who had already made the move. Coupled with the availability of transportation, many made the trek to the industrial cities of the North despite extensive efforts by southern political and economic elites to keep them where they were.[134] The combination of opportunities and escape was proving attractive in much the same way that this promise had attracted other immigrant groups before them.[135]

Postindustrial Cities. From an almost exclusively rural existence in the nineteenth century, more than one-quarter of all African Americans resided in urban areas by 1910. More than three-quarters do today, most of them in central cities and approximately one-fifth in suburbs. Roughly 12 percent of the United States population, African Americans came to make up more than one-quarter of the population in the nation's largest central cities, with one-third of them concentrated in fourteen such cities.[136]

African Americans, however, would face several unique circumstances by the time they began to immigrate to large U.S. cities. Cities in the industrializing era tended to serve as processing centers for wave after wave of poor, lesser-skilled immigrants beginning their way up the economic ladder of material success. The newest arrivals normally huddled together in ethnic ghettoes and were looked down upon by many of the longer-residing natives. Nevertheless, economic opportunities offered the newest immigrants a way out. In the postindustrial period, however, economic exit avenues began disappearing. Rather than staging areas for impending economic advancement, large cities often became veritable holding tanks for the economically marginal. And, the economically marginal have tended to be the most recently ghettoized poor—in this case, racial minorities.

It was not just the businesses that were moving and the economic climate that was changing. For those with the financial means to make the move, there was also a sizable shift of population from the older center cities to the outlying suburbs and beyond. In the process, neighborhoods became even more polarized by income and race, leaving many center cities predominantly poor and black and their surrounding suburbs predominantly white and better off.[137] Douglas Massey found the black-white segregation index to have doubled since 1950, and the economic disparity between white and black areas to have grown as well.[138] Massey and Nancy Denton found many of these metropolitan areas actually becoming "hyper-segregated," meaning blacks were not likely to see whites in their own neighborhoods, adjacent ones, or ones adjacent to those.[139] According to James Ryan, "no other group has historically experienced the same isolation as have blacks."[140]

This degree of socioeconomic isolation has come with its own set of problems. Among these are that prices tend to be proportionately higher for retail goods, and loans harder to attain. Cultural and linguistic isolation can make it even harder to enter the economic mainstream, and there are fewer established networks through which to make needed economic contacts. In addition, there are fewer visible role models, which can contribute to a contagion of hopelessness.[141] Marshall Kaplan, deputy assistant secretary for urban policy in the Department of Housing and Urban Development, found all of this to suggest a "permanent underclass" comprised disproportionately of African Americans trapped in America's inner cities.[142]

Socioeconomic Disparities. Not surprisingly, then, blacks and whites remain far apart economically. Blacks remain twice as likely as whites to be unemployed or among the working poor, and three times as likely to live below the poverty level and in overcrowded housing. Black income is roughly 40 percent less than that of whites, and the gap has been increasing of late. When blacks and Hispanics are combined, they comprise a clear majority of the urban poor, with central city blacks three times as likely to be poor as central city whites. In addition, more than 60 percent of black teenagers are out of work; and scarcely more than 50 percent of all black males have employment—with those who are employed overrepresented in lower-echelon blue-collar and domestic-service positions, in lower-paying industries, and in the governmental sector.[143] Lastly, the *New England Journal of Medicine* notes that a black man in Harlem has less chance of seeing his sixty-fifth birthday than does a man in Bangladesh, one of the poorest countries on earth.[144]

There is also the sociologically complex issue of family disintegration, a phenomenon with definite income implications. This is a nationwide dilemma that is even more problematic in the African American community. Whereas 28 percent of black families were headed by a female in 1969, for example, that figure exceeds 40 percent today.[145] A majority of black children are now growing up in fatherless households, a reality compounded by the close correlation between female-headed households and poverty. Some 60 percent of black households headed by a single woman live below the poverty level.[146] There is also mounting evidence that children growing up in fatherless households are more apt to be victims of child abuse or neglect, drop out of school, commit crimes, abuse drugs and alcohol, and commit suicide.[147]

Fatherless families are explained in part by the disproportionate number of black men either murdered or confined in American jails and prisons. Blacks, for example, are two to three times more likely than whites to be victims of rape, robbery, or assault, and they are seven times more likely to be murdered. One in ten African Americans are victims of a violent crime in any given year. One in twenty-one black males will fall victim to murder, with homicide the most common cause of death for black males between the ages of fifteen and twenty-four.[148] To make matters worse yet for the black community, most of this crime is committed by other black men, who then serve longer and harder time than their white counterparts. This results in roughly one in five adult black men having been incarcerated at some point, a fate likely to await one in three black males born today if current trends continue. More blacks are now in prison than in college, a reality that does not bode well for their future postindustrial employability.[149]

Analytical Framework

> Of all the civil rights for which the world has struggled and fought for 5,000 years, the right to learn is undoubtedly the most fundamental.
>
> —W. E. B. DuBois, "The Freedom to Learn," 1949

As indicated at the outset of this chapter, Horatio Alger (1834–1899) was a successful author who inspired generations of American youth with tales such as *Ragged Dick, Tattered Tom,* and *Luck and Pluck.* In these stories, penniless heroes gained wealth and fame through a combination of goodness and courage. The "Horatio Alger mythology," as it came to be known, read something like this: "It is possible to go from rags to riches in the United States if one displays the correct combination of abilities, hard work, thrift, and wise investment. Conversely, the existence of considerable economic inequality must be taken as a given, the necessary result of healthy competition between free, variably talented individuals."[150]

It remains debatable to what degree Horatio Alger's vision was a practical reality for very many people, even in the heady days of the nineteenth century's rapid industrialization and economic growth. Nonetheless, the myth took hold, for rich and poor, black and white. In a Gallup Poll taken almost a century later, nearly two-thirds of all adults under thirty years of age considered themselves at least somewhat likely to be rich someday.[151] In addition, even nine in ten black men said they would tell their sons they could become anything they wanted to in life.[152] Conversely, nearly half of "Middletown" youth agreed that "it is entirely the fault of the man himself if he cannot succeed," whether asked early or later in the twentieth century.[153]

One of the primary bulwarks of that faith is the belief that education provides a vehicle for anyone to rise almost limitlessly if the person is talented enough, has enough ambition, and works hard. Besides training the nation's workforce, universal public education was to level the playing field so that all children would have a reasonable opportunity to develop their talents and succeed in America's free-market system.[154] Indeed, the more education one has, the more likely one is to be employed and the more income one is likely to earn. Thus, on the face of it, publicly provided educational opportunities would seem to offer a springboard to economic prosperity. According to a once quite popular public-service advertisement, "To get a good job, you need a good education."

Complicating this equation is the fact that the employment status and income of a child's parents correlate with the number of school years completed, meaning that the children of better-off parents generally finish more school years. In addition, parental economic position often affects the quality of the school attended. Lower-income areas have less of a property tax base from which to fund their public schools, making those schools less attractive places to teach, and so on. In addition, elite private schools offer educational opportunities and prestige beyond the financial reach of most parents, not to mention the additional job contacts these schools and more affluent parents also can provide after graduation.

Overall, then, education can affect one's economic position in life, but the economic circumstances into which one is born appears to have a significant impact on one's education. One's ultimate socioeconomic position appears, at least in part, to be a function of the socioeconomic circumstances into which one was born. The socioeconomic circumstances into which most inner-city children are born today does not bode well for twenty-first century rags-to-riches metamorphoses.[155]

Horatio Alger's potential heroes are now low-income African Americans living in postindustrial urban ghettos, heavily reliant on troubled urban public schools for their socioeconomic salvation. A combination of court rulings and legislative actions have put an end to governmentally mandated racial segregation, as well as prompting a significant increase in urban public school spending. Nonetheless, glaring problems remain. It is the thesis of this book that postindustrial economic changes and a history of racial exclusion have combined to make it extremely difficult for these children to rise from rags to riches in today's postindustrial information age.

There has been a growing body of empirical literature on the advantages and disadvantages of various school reform regimens. These have included analyses of alternative funding formulas, curricula, administrative structures, promotion requirements, and so on. There also has been a proliferation of studies on the political reasons why many of these reform efforts have or have not been adopted by federal, state, and local governments.[156] Nevertheless, this particular study of the Memphis City Schools suggests that there are underlying education-related forces that essentially fall outside the reach of most contemporary educational reform efforts.

In their seminal 1972 book, Christopher Jencks and colleagues at Harvard University's Center for Educational Policy Research assessed education in the United States during the 1960s. Their book was entitled, *Inequality: A Reassessment of the Effect of Family and Schooling in America*. One of their most controversial findings was that "the characteristics of a school's output depends largely on a single input, namely the characteristics of the entering children. Everything else—the school budget, its policies, the characteristics of the teachers—is either secondary or completely irrelevant."[157] For all intents and purposes, then, they saw school reform efforts amounting to little more than shuffling the location of deck chairs on the sinking *Titanic*.

They concluded that "equalizing opportunity is almost impossible without greatly reducing the absolute level of inequality, and the same is true for eliminating deprivation."[158] As they saw it, government must first use its taxing and spending powers to redistribute wealth and thus alter the American class structure. Meanwhile, they concluded, the educational system provides only an illusion of equal opportunity. To expect it to lead the way toward more societal equality is little more than wishful thinking.[159]

Consider the analogy of a marathon race between two equally skilled and motivated contestants. One runner has had easy access to the best training facilities, coaches, and nourishment available. She trains full time, eats well, and arrives at the starting line in peak condition. The other runner, through no fault of her own, cannot gain access to comparable resources and is forced to train after a hard day's work and on weekends. The rules of the race may be the same for both runners once they arrive at the starting blocks, but in fact the race is anything but fair, and the result is all but preordained. The advantaged runner will win. There will be an occasional upset; but, in the last analysis, Jencks and his coauthors would argue that such exceptions will do little more than provide false hopes to the large majority and divert their attention from the real underlying problems.

Yet despite such serious impediments, there would seem to be a governmental responsibility to continue to work toward resolving this now even more complex "American Dilemma," where race and class have converged to make advancement a serious challenge in postindustrial urban America. One of the ways of accomplishing this is to provide as much equality of opportunity as possible for all runners in the foot race, doing the best that can be done to disconnect disadvantages of birth from a runner's opportunity to have a fair shot, even if this will not put an end to all poverty.

The Memphis City School System should provide a good case study of this American urban challenge. Located in a postindustrial city, it has a student body that is roughly 90 percent black, with nearly three quarters of its students living in poverty.[160] The city's economics, race relations, and school desegregation efforts will be chronicled, focusing on their relationship to the contemporary educational situation. What is the condition of the city's schools? How did they get to where they are? And which of the many education-related alternatives are more likely to improve the economic competitiveness of the students currently attending urban schools such as those in Memphis, Tennessee?

Chapter 2

Memphis

As will be obvious rather quickly, the Memphis City School system faces many serious educational problems. This study will attempt to determine to what degree such problems can be explained by the factors of race and class, as well as what approaches are more likely to be successful in addressing the city's school difficulties.

A variety of questions will be posed over the course of the chapters below. Is Memphis a postindustrial city? Have the city's race relations reflected the tensions found elsewhere in the nation? And, how have these trends been reflected in, and effected by, the city's public schools? In terms of economic class more specifically, do the poor simply have less money spent on their schools, resulting in inferior educational experiences? Do the poor bring extra education-related social problems to school with them? As for race, has white abandonment, indifference, or worse contributed to the troubled state of black education in a large city such as Memphis? And, do problems generated within the black community itself contribute to the racial differences that continue to mark the American educational system?

Memphis History

David Goldfield, an urban historian, has noted that southern urbanism developed relatively late, and its lifestyle and cultural values were transplanted from the rural South: "The worlds of the cotton field and of the skyscraper are essentially the same. They both sprang from the rural traditions. . . . The southerner carried the burden of his past into the present and left its legacy for the future. In no other region is the past so much a part of its present, and its cities so much a part of both."[1] Most importantly, like its rural counterpart, the southern city would begin with a biracial caste system. Whites were dominant, blacks were subordinate, and change was impeded by the peculiar nature of the southern economy.

Historical accounts of Memphis provide much support for Goldfield's contentions. For a variety of reasons, Memphis never really developed into a diverse industrialized city. As a result, it maintained a political culture that more closely reflected the values held in surrounding rural areas. In terms of race, whites controlled the city's primary political and economic institutions, and this biracial caste system survived wave after wave of black migration to the city. Yet, beginning in the 1970s, fundamental changes began to occur. To understand these most recent developments, however, requires tracing the city's evolution, beginning as far back as the Civil War.

Initial Growth

As of 1860, on the eve of the Civil War, Memphis had grown to a population of 22,623. That figure would double by the following census, making Memphis a large city by southern standards.[2]

The composition of the population during this stage was much different from any subsequent time in Memphis history. Being a trading center on the economically vibrant Mississippi River attracted a large number of foreign-born immigrants and provided a heterogeneity that was unusual for the South.[3] By 1860, foreign-born residents constituted more than 36 percent of the city's white population. The largest groups were the Irish, with 5,242 people, and the Germans, with 2,596. There were also 3,822 African Americans, more than 3,600 of whom were slaves.[4]

The Irish immigrants were initially lured to this bustling Mississippi River town by the promise of an array of manual jobs. They often settled in racially integrated neighborhoods and competed directly with blacks for these lesser-skilled positions. They also had a reputation for exhibiting unruly behavior. The mayor of Memphis, for example, actually called out the militia one time simply because a group of two hundred Irishmen had arrived to work on the Mississippi River levee.[5]

The smaller German population, by contrast, was more apt to comprise shop owners, tradesmen, and artisans. Viewed as a whole, they were seen as having a modernizing influence on the city. They brought with them their musical heritage, for instance; and Clayton Robinson describes the sounds of Hayden and Schubert emanating from the German households. They also brought with them ideas such as trade unionism that were alien to the native Memphis culture.[6]

Yellow Fever

Meanwhile, most of Memphis lacked even the most elementary sanitation facilities. In particular, an area just east of town known as Bayou Gayoso drained 5,000 acres of an open sewer, receiving deposits from thousands of private privies. This, combined with the often stagnant waters of Nonconnah Creek to the city's south, created a fertile breeding ground for mosquitoes carrying yellow fever.[7]

A series of yellow fever epidemics devastated the city from the latter 1870s into the 1880s, marking the second stage of city development. The 1878 epidemic alone produced the highest death rate from an epidemic that any city in the United States had ever seen. Between deaths and departures, Memphis recorded a huge loss of population in the 1880 census. From an estimated 80,000 people before the fever struck, the Memphis population shrunk to 34,000 residents.[8]

Among other things, the heterogeneity of the city changed dramatically. With the exception of many low-income Irish, virtually all of the white ethnics departed, and few of them returned. Most blacks also were too poor to leave, but a much higher proportion of them survived as they proved more resistant to the disease. Where whites contracted yellow fever, the death rate was 70 percent, while the death rate was only 7 percent for afflicted African Americans.[9]

Moderate Growth

The years between 1880 and 1920 marked the third stage, as the population increased by approximately 30,000 to 40,000 per decade. The nature of that moderate growth, however, had a lasting impact on the city's political culture. The better off and more cosmopolitan whites who had fled were replaced by poorer and more parochial whites from the surrounding rural areas of Tennessee, Mississippi, and Arkansas.[10] By 1900, the city's foreign-born population had declined to 15 percent; while 80 percent of its residents now hailed from the Tennessee and Mississippi countryside.[11]

Roger Biles indicates that "Memphis developed a personality determined in large measure by its southern location."[12] John Harkins observes that, among other things, "the newcomers' conservative rural values were at odds with the urban conception of the good life with its conspicuous consumption and conspicuous leisure. The resulting sense of disorientation and alienation may have contributed to high rates of crime and violence which troubled Memphis well into the 20th century."[13] In the early twentieth century, for instance, the Ku Klux Klan was active locally and even was openly involved in electoral politics.[14]

Urbanization

The period from 1920 to 1970 was marked by the largest population increases in the city's history. The Memphis population increased by approximately 100,000 per decade, except during the Depression years. Much of that growth continued to originate from the rural South, and a sizable share of it resulted from the annexation of surrounding areas.[15]

Among other things, this continuing immigration pattern produced a very conservative electorate. By the 1968 presidential election, as a case in point, Democrat Hubert Humphrey received 12 percent of the vote, Republican Richard Nixon received 46 percent, and American Independent George Wallace received 42 percent. The votes for Wallace, and to a somewhat lesser degree a number of the votes for Nixon, can be seen as quite conservative overall. In addition, Wallace's support cut across all income groups, although it came disproportionately from working-class whites.[16]

Besides the transplantation of rural culture into southern cities, Goldfield also notes how the nature of the southern economy limited both economic and social development.[17] In Memphis, historians have indeed found the political culture intertwined with the city's economic system, thus creating Goldfield's social and economic constraints.

In 1873, for instance, local merchants established a cotton exchange that became the largest "spot market" in the world.[18] An economic system developed that financed and marketed cotton from planting to production. It was a highly lucrative process since a variety of businesses were able to make commissions and profits even in years when the price of the commodity was low. Because of the stability of such profit, there was little reason for Memphis financiers to spend inordinate amounts of money industrializing the city.[19]

The types of employers coming to Memphis also reflected this adherence to traditionalism. Many were companies that manufactured machinery and chemicals for the agricultural base of Memphis, or processed the farm commodities that eventually included more than cotton.[20] Rather than harbingers for social change, however, most of them were drawn to Memphis, at least in part, because of low wages and the lack of labor unions.[21]

Studying a variety of U.S. cities in 1970, Daniel Elazar concluded that Memphis was one of the only large southern urban centers to retain what he termed a dominant "traditionalistic" political culture. He defined that as including domination by a small group of business elites, a weak white working class, exclusion of blacks whenever possible, and a penchant toward providing only a minimum of public services.[22]

The Racial Divide

Within that economic setting and its conservative political culture, Goldfield's third theme deals with the impact of race. He argues that a biracial society with its established segregation and hierarchical relationships moved from the rural South into the region's urban settings. Such a biracial system developed in Memphis, although it was to have its own unique history and characteristics. To understand the city's contemporary racial circumstances requires departing from our historical progression for a moment and going back to the beginning, tracing that racial evolution from the time of the Civil War.

To begin with, Memphis fell to the Union army early in the Civil War. Soon some ten thousand black Union troops were stationed locally at Fort Pickering. The city also became a magnet for escaping slaves and was the site of a large Freedmen's Bureau during postwar Reconstruction. The Freedman's Bureau assisted and protected former slaves as they made their transition to freedom.[23]

As a result of these developments, the city has had a large African American population since the 1860s. The black population proportion reached almost 40 percent in the 1860s, a proportion that blacks held or exceeded for most of the city's subsequent history.[24] The 1900 and 1980 census figures showed blacks to be approximately 50 percent of the city's overall population, while the 2000 figure of 61 percent was an all-time high.

The historical literature on Memphis does not paint a pretty picture of the white response to this formidable black community. It suggests that tenets of white supremacy affected the Memphis historical landscape, particularly after 1880. Yet, there were problems even before then.

Despite efforts by the Freedmen's Bureau, for example, interracial strife developed, particularly between the blacks and Irish who resided in many of the same neighborhoods and competed for many of the same job opportunities. In 1866, for instance, struggling Irish residents turned their frustrations on many of their more recently arriving black neighbors in a three-day riot that left forty-six blacks dead, nearly twice that many injured, five women raped, approximately one hundred blacks robbed, and ninety-one homes, four churches, and all twelve black schools destroyed.[25]

Then, beginning around 1900 and lasting for more than half a century, an elaborate Jim Crow system of legally mandated racial segregation developed. Public facilities such as streetcars, parks, libraries, theaters, shops, and restaurants all were formally segregated. Until 1923, LeMoyne High School was the only accredited four-year high school blacks were allowed to attend, and there were no college opportunities until LeMoyne added a college level in 1932. Not until legal pressure began to build in the 1950s and 1960s were Memphis facilities finally desegregated.[26] Nonetheless, the city has remained one of the most racially segregated cities in the nation. By 2000, for instance, Memphis ranked second only to the city of Detroit in terms of overall residential segregation.[27]

Violent intimidation occurred as well. There were, for example, well-publicized lynchings of blacks in 1892 and 1917. There were also a number of controversial killings of black suspects by white police officers. Some of the most prominent examples include the killings of Levon Carlook (1933) and Elton Hayes (1971), as well as the Shannon Street seven (1983), an incident remarkably similar to another such event in August of 1916.[28]

Other twentieth-century laws and public policies, regardless of intent, also reinforced white dominance. For example, repeated annexations of predominantly white suburban areas helped maintain a white majority, while at-large city elections and a runoff provision helped ensure that the white majority would be able to have its way electorally.[29]

Beneath such behavior stood a bedrock belief system that had been nurtured by continued rural white in-migration. As late as the 1940s, Gerald Capers described the dominant Memphis ideology as a combination of "Protestant

Fundamentalism, loyalty to a fantastic ideal called the Old South, and uncompromising insistence upon the preservation of white supremacy."[30] William Miller's study of Memphis during the Progressive Era argues that "the white supremacy ideal as it became defended in the Old South was an inevitable folk response to a difficult social problem produced by two racial groups living together in a master-servant relationship."[31]

In some quarters, an important component of the city's race relations was the paternalistic white view of noblesse oblige. Such southern whites felt they had an obligation to protect, uplift, and care for what they perceived as the less fortunate race. John Terreo reported a quotation from the *Daily Appeal* in 1889 suggesting that African Americans "must be educated and Christianized, and so fitted for the duties of life."[32]

Considerable documentation of a white supremacy viewpoint can be found in the pages of the local press. As late as 1918, a prominent white businessman called for repeal of the Fifteenth Amendment to the U.S. Constitution (the amendment guaranteeing blacks the right to vote) "in order that normal political life might be restored to the South."[33] More than a decade later, the *Commercial Appeal* declared that "the Anglo-Saxon will not be ruled no matter what the odds are against him. He possesses the imperious and unyielding despotism of conscious superiority."[34] Local white newspapers also regularly used terms like "darkey" and "nigger," called Booker T. Washington an "Alabama coon," and the *Commercial Appeal* ran a racially offensive "Hambone" cartoon strip from October 1915 until a week after the King assassination in 1968.[35]

Nonetheless, at least from the mid-1920s forward, neither the White Citizens Council nor the Ku Klux Klan were political forces in Memphis, and the city's white politicians did not participate in the worst of the overt race-baiting that was prevalent among vocal southern segregationists such as Lester Maddox and George Wallace. As a matter of fact, Harry Holloway concludes that Memphis "lacked the ardently conservative factions, whether racially or economically oriented, that were present in [cities like] Atlanta and Houston."[36] He even goes so far as to label Memphis of the 1960s a "prototype of a modern southern community," where "the white population tends to be chiefly concerned with progress and making money."[37]

But where were the white "liberals"? Studying Memphis between 1900 and 1930, Lester Lamon concludes that "Memphis was almost totally lacking in white liberalism."[38] In 1960, for instance, the Dedicated Citizens' Committee, as liberal a white group as had existed in the city, would not even allow an African American on its executive committee and supported the maintenance of an all-white school board.[39] In addition, Memphis business groups did not endorse a single black candidate for any office from 1950 through 1980.[40] As late as 1993, the Memphis City Council split precisely along racial lines when considering whether to bar members of discriminatory private clubs from being named to city boards and commissions.[41]

An Era of Change

As the 1960s wound to a close, population growth slowed to a trickle, and the city actually lost population over the course of the following decade. Part of this change may have been related to adverse publicity following Martin Luther King's assassination in Memphis. Even more directly, however, there was the continual movement of wealthier black and white citizens to the suburbs surrounding Memphis. This reflected a suburbanization that was occurring in metropolitan areas across the country, in no small part fed by anxieties created as a result of court-ordered school busing for the purpose of racial desegregation. Beneath all of this, however, there was significant economic, political, and social change beginning to occur.

Memphis Economics. The Memphis economy had long been based largely on commerce and services, as opposed to manufacturing. As one of the earliest regional transportation hubs, for instance, it prospered as a market for cotton and slave trading. Even after the Civil War, it remained a viable cotton market, as it had not been damaged nearly as much during the war as had a number of its southern counterparts.

The yellow fever epidemics of the 1870s posed a major setback, however. Conditions were so bleak and the city's finances so devastated, that a number of the remaining white elites convinced the state legislature to repeal the city's charter. Those town fathers, now with nearly complete political control, set out to construct a reliable city infrastructure. By the turn of the century, they had done so. Most impressively, the city had a developed both an artesian well for its drinking water and a sanitation system.

Meanwhile, although the boll weevil was wreaking havoc on the cotton crops, Memphis rebounded in the first two decades of the twentieth century by developing a more diversified local economy. It became the largest hardwood lumber market in the world; and, its invested industrial capital soared from a mere $10 million in 1899 to $467 million by 1920. Among the manufacturers locating in Memphis were giants such as Ford and Firestone. This industrialization reached its peak during World War II.

In the post–World War II period, however, the Memphis economy quickly returned to its commercial and service orientation, exhibiting early signs of what has come to be labeled "postindustrialism." Most all of the city's large manufacturers departed. Among the last to leave were RCA, with 4,000 employees; International Harvester with 3,300; and Firestone with 1,600. Birmingham Steel was one of the last to come to Memphis, arriving in 1997 and employing 250 workers. Yet, Birmingham Steel would be gone within three years. Manufacturing jobs, which paid roughly 25 percent more than the area average, had been reduced to just over 10 percent of the county's nonagricultural employment.[42]

By the 1990s, ten of the metropolitan area's fifteen largest employers were governmental entities. Only eight institutions employed more than 5,000 workers. Federal Express was the largest at 18,831; while five of the others were government agencies and two were regional hospitals. Of the top forty, employing more than 1,200 workers apiece, only five were manufacturers, with Cleo (gift wrapping and cards) the largest, at 2,200 employees. Meanwhile, Memphis had become the world's busiest cargo airport and the second largest port on the Mississippi River.[43]

The nature of the city's postindustrial economy has taken its toll on the Memphis workforce. Per capita income remains well behind that of its peer cities.[44] Circumstances are worse yet at the lower ends of the contemporary workforce. By 1990, despite the federal "War on Poverty," six census tracts had a median household income below $5,500, while three zip codes had median household incomes below $6,500.[45] As another indicator of the size and intensity of this poverty problem, the city also has the highest infant mortality rate of any of the nation's sixty largest cities.[46] After billions of governmental dollars were spent to reduce poverty across the United States, one in four Memphians were still impoverished, and that includes nearly 40 percent of its children. This has left Memphis among the nation's ten poorest cities.[47] The city's crime rate also has come to be 2.5 times greater than the national average.[48]

Memphis Politics. Meanwhile, the 1970s and 1980s brought a degree of political change. This change did not replace the dominant political culture, but it may have sensitized it some as Memphis moved toward becoming a more modernized city. To begin with, a group of black political leaders emerged who appeared to inspire more trust in the white community. A more moderate white leadership cadre also emerged, and the city hired a number of highly competent professional administrators. In addition, organizations like the Memphis Peace and Justice Center and the local branch of the National Council of Christians and Jews provided the black community with a small but reliable group of white liberal allies. They were not large enough, however, to provide the base for a significant electoral coalition.[49]

Memphis also gradually became somewhat more demographically diverse. Immigration from the countryside slowed. Meanwhile, its political landscape came to include Southeast Asians, Native Americans, Hispanics, gays, an artist colony, and professionals from across the United States. Memphis colleges and universities prospered and brought cultural diversity to their students. Beyond that, Memphians developed new political and social institutions such as a rich fabric of neighborhood organizations.[50]

The churches were important agents of political change, as well. Selma Lewis's study of the 1968 sanitation strike showed that white churches played no real interventive role in that tragic series of events.[51] The 1970s and 1980s brought a much greater commitment by those churches. The Memphis Inter-Faith Association (MIFA) formed and has been particularly effective at providing food for the indigent. Calvary Episcopal Church developed programs for the homeless, while the Catholic diocese focused much attention on Vietnamese and Hispanic immigrants. Churches founded Vollintine Evergreen Community Association (VECA), the city's largest integrated neighborhood organization. Meanwhile, Shelby County Interfaith brought together white and black churches to address community problems.[52]

Another major source of change was a new generation of businesses choosing to locate in Memphis. The 1920s and 1940s had brought many firms interested in little more than a city with low taxes, low wages, and fewer unions. The 1970s and 1980s found the companies that replaced them more interested in using and improving the city's amenities. Large companies such as Federal Express, International Paper, Holiday Inn, and Auto Zone played a significant role in supporting the arts, improving community institutions such as the zoo and Pink Palace museum, bringing professional sports teams to Memphis, and participating in a variety of neighborhood and social groups.[53]

The Chamber of Commerce contributed to this evolution as well. Because of the bad press the city received after the garbage strike and the King assassination, these business leaders attempted to alter the city's image by means of a one-million-dollar advertising campaign.[54] They hired an enlightened executive director, David Cooley, who spoke in a language not often heard in white Memphis: "The greatest barrier to a better Memphis is ignorance. What are some problems of urban growth? . . . a deteriorating central city . . . bad housing for a large percentage of our population . . . lack of skills training . . . poor worker mobility . . . undereducated and underemployed people in large numbers . . . token acceptance of blacks in decision making position."[55]

Nevertheless, on the eve of the 1991 mayoral election, most white political attitudes in the community at large were a product of a historically traditional political culture that had produced highly polarized voting behavior. Whites simply had been unwilling to relinquish political control to black elected officials. This could be seen in the minimal white crossover voting for black mayoral candidates and the fact that only one black at-large city councilperson was elected between 1967 and 1987. Thus, most whites were not ready to vote for Dr. W. W. Herenton as mayor in 1991.

Race Relations. Since 1870, Memphis has had at least a 37 percent African American population—despite black out-migration and repeated annexations of predominantly white suburbs.[56] Given the size and separation of the black community, there has long been a degree of social and economic independence, generating a number of black businesspersons, professionals, and ministers.[57] From this group emerged a number of pragmatic black leaders willing to seize whatever political opportunities arose.[58] As is not uncommon, however, these leaders often struggled amongst themselves, dividing the black community. In addition, unlike in most other cities, African Americans did not have a sizable group of white liberals with which they could align in a formidable long-term coalition. As Harry Holloway put it in 1969, "The lack of continuing coalition ties with a particular segment of the white community means that Negroes really are on their own [in Memphis]."[59]

Meanwhile, at the other end of the socioeconomic spectrum, Memphis was a magnet for many black sharecroppers or farm laborers who were either driven from the land by mechanization or were simply weary of their agricultural peonage. They were attracted to Memphis by the lure of economic opportunities, yet the city's economy generally offered them only low-wage positions. Consequently, black Memphians have ended up disproportionately poor, disillusioned, and militant, as well as suspicious of political leaders, including many of their own black leaders.[60]

Black Economy. The size and segregation of the city's black population has required the black community to develop its own economic institutions. For example, these circumstances created a need for black doctors, lawyers, and teachers, as well as black groceries, barber shops, hair salons, funeral parlors, and even banks.[61] Beale Street, the black commercial center in its Jim Crow heyday, was lined with real estate and banking offices, dry goods and clothing stores, theaters, saloons, and gambling joints.[62]

More recently, despite desegregation, a number of black businesses have continued to develop and prosper. By the 1980s, there were more than three thousand black-owned enterprises, with gross receipts of approximately $150 million. Fewer than 1 percent were manufacturers, however, leaving the overwhelming majority operating in the lower-paying commerce and service sectors.[63] Nevertheless, these businesses provided blacks with goods, services, and employment that were not always accessible in the city at large. They also generated a number of black leaders who have been quite active in the city's political arena. Black business success, however, has not "trickled down" to sizable portions of the African American community as a whole.

Even in the city's brief period of industrialization, discriminatory union and employer practices left black men "overwhelmingly concentrated in jobs that entailed hardly any responsibility, skill or prestige, (and) wages and salaries that were at best marginal."[64] Black menial labor was such a bargain that the Tennessee state legislature passed "emigrant agent codes" in 1917, making it illegal for outsiders to come into the state in order to recruit away black workers.[65]

Meanwhile, of the black women working outside the home, 82 percent were domestics or laundresses, while another 10 percent were either seamstresses or in semiskilled employment.[66]

As late as 1950, despite the job experiences that had been accumulated during World War II, black men once again found themselves largely in manual labor and service positions, while black women remained largely domestic servants. As a result, black family income was only 44 percent of comparable white family income. And, the figures might have been worse yet had it not been for job opportunities in local branches of federal government agencies.[67]

As desegregation efforts and antidiscrimination laws gradually began to dismantle the old Jim Crow system, the racial income gap narrowed. Where the median black family made 44 percent of median white family income in 1950, that figure grew to 48 percent by 1990 and 55 percent by 2000.[68] Nevertheless, that figure is still one of the very worst among the largest metropolitan areas in the United States, and little has improved for a sizable proportion of black Memphians. This problem has only been exacerbated by the fact that much of the city's job base has increasingly come to consist of low-wage, unskilled, or semiskilled positions.[69] In addition, desegregation eliminated the need for many black-owned businesses. By 1992, for instance, there were roughly eight hundred black-owned businesses that had paid employees, but they only had an average of three and one-half employees.[70] To make matters even worse, teen pregnancy is now 60 percent higher than the national average, which has contributed to the fact that nearly half of all black children are born to single mothers, a syndrome closely associated with poverty.[71]

The combined results have been devastating. Where blacks made up 58 percent of all Memphis families earning less than $1,000 in 1949, that figure grew to 71 percent by 1969.[72] Nearly a quarter of the inner-city workforce made less than two dollars per hour (as compared to 8.6 percent in Newark, for instance).[73] Not surprisingly, then, nearly 60 percent of the city's African Americans lived below the federal government's poverty level.[74] Beyond that, the *Metropolitan Area Fact Book* noted that Memphis had the second poorest black population in the nation.[75]

At the other end of the economic spectrum, civil rights laws and desegregation efforts did improve job opportunities for black "officials and managers." Yet, black numbers in those ranks still remained disproportionately low. In 1971, for instance, blacks held fewer than 4 percent of those positions countywide, despite being nearly 40 percent of the county's population. By the mid-1990s, that percentage grew to more than 16 percent of those better-paying jobs, although African Americans were now a near majority of the county's population.[76]

One of the results has been a tendency for the black working and lower classes to be suspicious of white and black leaders. These circumstances have generated a certain propensity to shun traditional electoral politics, even when viable black candidates are available, as well as a tendency to engage in more "direct political action."

As George Lee stated in the *Baltimore Afro-American* in 1929: "The type of leadership these dark times demand is the aggressive and two-fisted kind that will contend, contend, contend. . . . [We must] banish, ostracize and destroy the type of leadership and that kind of doctrine that stands against the Negro in his effort to find himself. . . . We are too far behind to seek the palm and the olive branch."[77]

Black Politics. A number of Memphis blacks resisted the day-to-day degradations of Jim Crow. In 1881, for example, prominent musician and school teacher Julia Hooks was arrested for her vociferous protest over not being seated in a theater's white section. In the late nineteenth century, educator Ida B. Wells led protests against segregation and lynchings, and even proceeded to air these grievances internationally. In particular, she aimed her message at British cotton buyers. Beyond protest, when Mary Morrison was arrested for resisting streetcar segregation in 1905, a huge rally followed in Church Park and several thousand dollars were raised for her legal defense.[78]

There were also forms of even more direct grassroots resistance. The following incidents occurred in 1915 and 1916 alone. Thomas Brooks, for example, killed two white attackers.[79] When white men tried to physically remove them from their trolley seats, Charley Parks stabbed one,[80] while John Knox ended up in a gun battle with another.[81] A white trolley conductor was stabbed when he tried to collect extra fare from a black rider.[82] Ambush shootings and arson took place on occasion.[83] And, at times, lower-class blacks resorted to "physical means" in order to resist the brutality of local white police officers.[84]

By 1960, a sizable number of student sit-ins appeared, and boycotts were launched against downtown retailers. Harry Holloway estimates that there were more of these in Memphis than in any other city in the nation.[85] Meanwhile, privately organized groups such as the Greater Race Relations Committee and the Committee on Community Relations helped usher in gradual desegregation even before the Civil Rights Act of 1964. Bus seating was desegregated in 1958, public libraries in 1960, and public parks, court house water fountains, and airport restaurants in 1962. In addition, the public protests against police brutality that began in the nineteenth century continued into the 1990s.[86]

A heavily black labor movement also began early in the twentieth century.[87] Prominent black union leaders included Clarence Coe at Firestone, Thomas Watkins of the dock workers, and George Holloway of the auto workers. As an example of their success, the CIO was able to organize Firestone in the 1940s; and, soon, carpenters, longshoremen, and laundry workers were unionizing as well. At the same time, waiters, busboys, and elevator operators were engaging in wildcat walkouts.[88] More recently, there was the major sanitation workers' strike in 1968, while the police, firefighters, and teachers walked the picket lines ten years later.

The 1968 strike by black sanitation workers is probably the best known. It began with a sewer worker's grievance over an incident of differential treatment by race. It then accelerated when two blacks were accidentally crushed to death in a garbage compactor. Mayor Loeb's hard-line reaction allowed black leaders to turn the incident into a major civil rights struggle. The full-blown strike, ultimately involving 1,100 workers and lasting sixty-five days, was led by AFSCME local #1733 and included support from the NAACP, prominent black ministers such as James Lawson and Martin Luther King Jr., and a group of young Black Power militants calling themselves "The Invaders."[89]

Mass violence also reared its head as the sanitation strike progressed. On March 28, for instance, one of the rallies became unruly when windows were smashed and rocks thrown. The police response left one dead and sixty-two injured; and soon four thousand national guardsmen were called in to restore order. Then, following the assassination of Reverend King, the city exploded into days of looting, burning, sniping, and other forms of mass unrest, leaving the city "traumatized and divided."[90]

At the elite level, black fraternal and benevolent associations arose after emancipation and played active political roles.[91] "Political leagues" and "civic welfare groups" lobbied on behalf of black interests.[92] In 1917, businessmen such as Robert Church Jr., Bert Roddy, and W. H. Bentley founded the first Memphis branch of the NAACP, following the lynching of Ell Persons. It was the first such branch in the state of Tennessee. Subsequently, led by individuals such as Jesse Turner and Maxine Smith, the NAACP would be at the forefront of much of the city's black resistance. Besides leading protests, the association filed federal lawsuits against numerous public segregation practices.[93] Beginning in the 1940s, organizations such as the Negro Chamber of Commerce, the Negro Junior Chamber of Commerce, and the Shelby County Democratic Club also were politically active.[94]

As an example of the cross pressures faced by black elite activists, however, consider the case of Benjamin Bell. In 1943, Bell was chosen as the chief executive officer of the Community Welfare League (CWL), which had recently become affiliated with the National Urban League (NUL). Attempting to move the local organization more into line with national NUL priorities, he pressed the call for black civil rights in Memphis. This led to a drop in CWL's private contributions, and soon Bell was replaced by the more accommodationist Rev. James McDaniel, whose political approach was then criticized by NUL.[95]

Such economic pressure did not deter subsequent assertions of black power, however. The 1960s, in particular, marked a time when "the politics of moderation was replaced by the politics of race."[96] By the 1970s, John and Harold Ford came to symbolize this militancy as they stood up to the city's white leadership. In 1974, for example, City Councilman John Ford was cheered by many in the black community when he publicly told a fellow white councilperson to "go to hell" in the course of a council debate.[97] Or, on election night 1991, Congressman Harold Ford also was applauded when he challenged the election board's tallying of absentee ballots in a fiery televised tirade. Responding to the incident, a prominent white leader referred to Ford as "the embodiment of evil."[98]

Historic changes took place in Memphis as a result of the 1991 election. An African American was elected mayor in a hotly contested race that ended more than a century of white conservative control of that office. In addition, blacks were elected to at-large positions on the city council, school board, and the city court.

Two developments provided critical context for the historic election of 1991. First, annexation had become more difficult because state law now allowed the target area more tools with which to fight. When challenged, the burden of proof would rest with the city to convince a jury that the annexation was necessary for the health and safety of both the city and the annexed area.[99] With whites continuing to move out of the city and with fewer legal opportunities to annex them back in, the 1990 census showed that blacks had come to comprise a majority of the Memphis voting age population.[100] Secondly, the U.S. Justice Department charged that runoff elections in the Memphis context were racially discriminatory, eliminating "the possibility that black candidates could win elections by a plurality vote." Federal District Judge Jerome Turner agreed and enjoined the city from using the runoff in the 1991 citywide elections.[101]

In the end, the final audited voting returns for mayor in 1991 indicated that W. W. Herenton had prevailed over Dick Hackett by a mere 142 votes out of the 248,000 votes cast—slightly more than one-half vote per precinct.[102] Not only was the 1991 mayoral election the closest in the city's history, but it was also the most racially polarized. Estimates indicate that 96 percent of the white voters cast their ballots for incumbent Dick Hackett, while 99 percent of the black voters cast theirs for Herenton. Conversely, 1 percent of the blacks cast their votes for Hackett, while 3 percent of the whites opted for Herenton (the other 1 percent voting for independent candidate "Prince Mongo" Hodges).[103]

The city's black majority also was reflected in the district results, with African Americans winning four of those seven district seats. The major change in the city council, however, would be in the six at-large positions. Only one black had ever been victorious in one of these citywide elections, and all six of those seats were held by whites. With blacks winning two of the at-large positions in 1991, the city council's racial balance changed from ten whites and three blacks to a much narrower seven-to-six white majority.

The Memphis City Schools were governed by a single school board of nine members. Although the precise size of the board had varied some over the years, all members had long been elected at-large, even after the electoral reforms of 1966. Following the racial unrest of 1968, however, the state legislature intervened and altered that arrangement. Since 1970, there had been seven district seats and two members selected at-large.[104] In 1991, blacks and whites split the two at-large elections for the board of education.

With impetus from a well-run Herenton campaign, which became a virtual racial crusade, black participation rates soared to an all-time high. That turnout proved essential to black success in all but two of their citywide victories. In the end, the Herenton and black at-large victories of 1991 were part of a black electoral tide that had been pressing at the dam of white conservative control for more than a century, a dam that finally began to spring visible leaks and break in 1991.[105]

The subsequent three city elections served to validate and extend what had transpired in the seminal election of 1991. This time, incumbent Mayor Herenton easily won reelection, garnering large majorities of the vote to defeat relatively token opposition, the highest white crossover voting any black mayoral candidate had ever attracted. Meanwhile, blacks developed and maintained majorities on the city council, school board, and city court.[106]

Memphis has come to exhibit many characteristics of a postindustrial city. Although it always has been more of a trading center than a manufacturing hub, the mechanization and mobility of industries have left most of the city's lesser-skilled city workers employed in the services rather than in the more promising unionized factory jobs. As a result, the city's racial and ethnic ghettos have become repositories for a sizable number of extremely poor residents with very limited job prospects. The city's cost of providing badly needed services for the disproportionately poor population that has remained has in fact become a significant drain on their tax base, with educational services being the most expensive.

Meanwhile, the city's race relations have only very recently begun to stabilize. After decades of black exclusion and turmoil, many whites have fled to the outlying areas, causing the city to remain one of the most racially segregated in the nation. This time, however, annexation has not been used to secure an ongoing white dominance. Memphis has evolved into a city with a clearly established African American majority and solid black control over all of its major governmental entities.[107] These developments have had a significant influence over the educational arrangement in the Memphis metropolitan area. They also have contributed to the city's educational challenges.

Chapter 3

Memphis City Schools

In 1647, colonial Massachusetts decreed that there should be an elementary school for every fifty families and a Latin school for every one hundred, to provide education within the Puritan's Calvinist faith. Meanwhile, most education in the United States would remain informal, normally conducted in the home. The schools that did exist tended to be private and were attended primarily by those wealthy enough to afford them.

Between 1820 and 1860, cities began emerging around manufacturing industries, drawing their workforces from rural migrants and foreign immigrants. Many people were driven to towns and cities when machines began doing farm tasks previously done by hand and family farms were subsumed by large agricultural businesses. At the same time, there was a huge influx of immigrants from Europe. More than three million immigrants arrived between 1846 to 1856 alone, a number equal to one-eighth of the United States' population. A more formal education process would help assimilate these new urban residents and better prepare them for industrial jobs.

Massachusetts again paved the way. A petition was presented at an 1817 Boston town meeting, calling for the establishment of a system of free public primary schools. Support for the idea came largely from local businessmen and wealthy artisans. Many wage earners, on the other hand, opposed the measure because of the taxes that would be required. Nevertheless, Boston English became the nation's first public high school in 1820, and the state made all grades of public school open to all pupils free of charge in 1827. In 1852, Massachusetts became the first state to adopt compulsory school attendance.[1]

The United States census has included information on school attendance and educational attainment since 1850. There is little historical record concerning the early days of African American education. Census information on slaves did not exist prior to the Civil War, and slaves accounted for more than 90 percent of all African Americans in the United States at the nation's founding. Best estimates are that only 5 to 10 percent of all slaves were literate, while the census found more than 80 percent of all blacks were still illiterate by 1870—ten times the comparable white rate. The 1870 census also revealed that roughly half of all southern white children were attending school, but fewer than 10 percent of southern blacks were in school.[2]

School attendance rates increased significantly in the subsequent decades, however, especially for African Americans. Some of the earliest formal education of former slaves began during the Civil War in cities occupied by the Union army. Classes often were conducted by former slaves, many of whom were only quasi-literate themselves. These efforts increased considerably after the war with the creation of the Freedmen's Bureau in 1865 and the assistance of teachers from the North. Nearly 90 percent of Freedmen's Bureau teachers were white. Soon, Reconstruction state legislatures began establishing public schools for blacks.[3]

The federal government's policy of Reconstruction ended in 1877, however, and blacks were rapidly disenfranchised by both legal and illegal methods.[4] In Louisiana, for example, half the state electorate was black in 1890, but that number shrunk to nearly zero by 1910.[5] Soon, school financing began to change, and differences in expenditures for black and white schools began to widen considerably. State monies previously earmarked for black schools began to be diverted to white schools, while localities began to create their own local assessments, which they directed largely to white schools.[6]

Meanwhile, the U.S. Supreme Court ruled that "separate but equal" Jim Crow schools did not violate the equal protection provision of the U.S. Constitution.[7] In addition, they said that states were not required to supply a black school in every school district, as it was not unreasonable to expect blacks to move to where one was available.[8] Most states continued to provide at least elementary schools for their black citizens, however, emphasizing basic skills necessary to allow them to be better field hands, cooks, and servants. Several of the states that had established separate facilities were clearly stretching the definition of "equal."[9]

The racial attendance gap increased in the immediate post-Reconstruction period; yet, that gap was cut by more than half by 1910 and all but disappeared by the 1940s.[10] Nevertheless, what passed for schooling varied considerably. Prior to World War I, for instance, many southern public schools were open fewer days each year than in much of the North, allowing students to harvest crops. The South also had many more ungraded schools, especially black schools and schools in rural areas with small populations. This was a practice that had been all but eliminated outside the South by the turn of the century.[11] Spending per student was lower in the South, and there were sizable differences in spending between their black and white schools. These gaps did not begin to significantly decrease until the latter 1930s as the South began to urbanize, private philanthropy increased, and desegregation pressures began to mount.[12]

Memphis Public Schools

The city of Memphis received its charter in 1826. According to the 1830 census, the city's population was a mere 663 people. Like most other cities, it took time before it was in a position to offer public education. The state of Tennessee established a public education system in 1836, but public schools did not emerge in Memphis until 1848, when the city's population was approaching nine thousand people. Prior to that time, as was true elsewhere in the nation, most early instruction was conducted at home or in private schools and academies. Even following the inception of public schools, many of the nation's wealthy families would continue to utilize private educational alternatives.[13]

The Memphis public school system developed in fits and starts, corresponding to the ebbs and flows of the city's own evolution. Like the encompassing city, the schools were significantly impacted at times by major events such as war, yellow fever epidemics, the emergence of a sizable African American population, a general population surge, and municipal bankruptcy.[14]

School Governance

The constitution of the state of Tennessee delegates to the state legislature all authority to establish and regulate public education. Yet, the legislature generally did not create schools and impose their creations on the state's localities. Either local legislatures or community committees normally would develop a school concept and petition the state for the authority to create their schools. The state legislature then had the option of delegating legislative authority to the county or municipality involved to create whatever academic administrative agencies they saw fit.[15]

The Tennessee legislature issued Memphis a new city charter in 1848, incorporating all provisions that had been added since its initial charter in 1826. Among other things, the legislature granted the city's petition and delegated to the mayor and city council (the latter also known as the "board of aldermen") the authority "to establish a system of free schools for the white children—to regulate the same—and to create an annual fund not exceeding one-eighth part of the annual revenue of the city to be appropriated in support of the same."[16]

In a matter of weeks after receiving the initial authority to do so, the City of Memphis passed an ordinance authorizing the formation of its own "ward schools." Each alderman was to choose a site, a building, and a teacher in his ward. Their choices, as well as subsequent funding, had to then be approved by the full city council. By June 1848, each of the city's four wards had an approved school,[17] but the city council battled over many of the school decisions.[18] As a matter of fact, only the mayor's tie-breaking vote saved the schools from dissolution in June of that first year.[19] Meanwhile, the mayor appointed a commission to investigate better ways of administering city schools.[20]

With the schools in place, ever so tentatively, the city council passed an ordinance that formally created the Memphis City Schools and their administrative structure. That founding ordinance had nine provisions.

> Be it ordained by the board of mayor and aldermen of the city of Memphis:
>
> 1. That the city be divided into territorial units and bounded into school districts in such manner as shall be most convenient having due regard to the present and future advantages and accommodations of each district.
>
> 2. That for the purpose of effectually supporting the common schools in the city of Memphis and securing the benefits and blessings of an education to all the white children therein, it shall be the duty of the council annually to levy and collect a tax amounting to one-eighth of the city revenues in conformity with the city charter to be exclusively appropriated to defray the expenses of the said schools and for no other purpose whatever, provided that the said schools in each scholastic district of the city shall at all times be equally free and accessible to all children between the ages of 6 and 16 years, who may reside therein, and subject only to such regulations for their government and instruction as the city council hereinafter may from time to time prescribe.
>
> 3. That all that part of Memphis lying north of Poplar Street, shall compose the first district and that part of the city south of Poplar Street, the second district.
>
> 4. That the board of managers shall be elected by the mayor and aldermen in the month of June in each year to consist of the mayor and two aldermen, and two citizens, one to reside in the first district and one to reside in the second district, a majority of whom to constitute a quorum.
>
> 5. That the board of managers shall provide schoolhouses of which there shall be two in each district, one to be used as a female school and one as a male school. That the board of managers shall employ school teachers and fix the rate of compensation and provide for the internal government of the schools.
>
> 6. That the only requisite for admission into the public schools be residence in the city and be between the ages of 6 and 16 years.
>
> 7. That the board of managers shall report to the board of mayor and aldermen at least every quarter.

8. That the teachers of instruction in the schools shall keep a record of the names and ages of all persons by them respectively instructed and the time each shall have attended the said school, and such record or copy thereof to the board of managers at the close of each current year they shall certify to the council the correctness, a full account of the expenses incurred to support of said schools as also their fiscal condition and all other information in relation to them that may be deemed necessary by the council, which report shall be published.

9. That it shall be the duty of the mayor and aldermen to purchase, lease or rent schoolhouses on such terms and conditions as they may think proper in the several school districts of the city for such time as they deem necessary.[21]

Over the course of the summer of 1848, the council added one more alderman and one more citizen to the schools' board of mangers. They also created the position of superintendent, detailing the position's powers and duties.[22] Colonel J. W. A. Pettit was appointed the first superintendent. Pettit was a prominent attorney, a member of the city council, and had been a vocal proponent of the schools' creation. Historian John Keating refers to Pettit as the "father of the Memphis free schools."[23]

The city's authorizing ordinance defined the superintendent's duties as follows:

1. See that each teacher opens and closes his school at the appointed hour.

2. See that the course of studies prescribed by the board of managers is pursued in each school.

3. See that all rules and regulations for the government of the schools are duly observed.

4. Visit the schools regularly and make himself acquainted with the courses pursued in each school by the respective teacher.

5. Give tickets of admission to the pupils before they can enter the schools.

6. Attend the meetings of the board of managers to make such suggestions . . . for . . . the schools.

7. Report the teachers to the board of managers in all cases of willful disregard or neglect by them of their duty.

8. Keep a correct record of the names of the pupils and their several studies.

9. Be able . . . to give to the city council or the board of managers all necessary information.

10. Report every quarter to the city council or board of managers and more often if required.

11. Suspend pupils for conduct requiring it, until the board of managers shall determine whether such pupils shall be expelled by rules prescribed by the board of managers.

12. Report teachers for misconduct or inefficiency.

13. Be responsible for the successful progress of the schools.

14. Assign each pupil to his school.

15. Distribute properly any books or stationery furnished the schools.[24]

On August 3, 1848, Superintendent Pettit posted a formal notice in the local newspaper. It notified city residents that the schools would open on the first Monday of September and would begin with English instruction taught by "eminently qualified" instructors. It also assured parents that the schools would be "placed on a footing of responsibility and utility inferior to none in this section of the country."[25] Male teachers were to receive a published salary of $800, while female instructors would receive $400.[26] In order to control who attended, the superintendent reminded parents that they had to seek him out to attain the necessary "tickets of admission," instituted to guard against "impositions" by ineligible students. The superintendent promised to be available at each schoolroom "in the forenoon of each day."[27]

Councilpersons who opposed one or more elements of this public education arrangement endeavored to tightly control school operations. Among other things, they continually altered the manner of school administration. Within weeks, for example, they eliminated the Board of Managers and returned full control to the council. They then altered such details as the school district boundaries and the age of students served.[28]

In 1852, they created a "Board of Visitors" as an advisory board to help the council's education committee oversee the day-to-day operations of the schools. Board members held one-year terms, elected their own president, chose a secretary, adopted by-laws, and were authorized to hire and fire teachers and staff. They were then required to report back to the full council at the end of each school session.[29]

As the Board of Visitors developed and gained council confidence, there came to be notably less council debate over the detail of school decisions.[30] This did not, however, end the bickering on city council. In regard to hours of instruction, for example, the council quickly threatened to withhold school funding so as to force the hand of the Board of Visitors. Such turmoil appeared to worry parents, as public school enrollment began to decline.[31]

After several such scuffles, the council finally agreed to petition the state legislature to incorporate this lay Board of Visitors and grant them their own independent administrative control of the schools. The first school charter was subsequently granted by the state in 1856.[32] Among other things, it authorized the newly created school board (Board of Visitors) to choose a president, create standing committees, fill their own vacancies during terms, hire and fire school employees, purchase school necessities, write school regulatory policies, design and implement a curriculum with competency examinations, establish a school calendar, provide an annual report to the council, and admit outside children on a strict tuition basis. It did not, however, grant the school board any independent taxing authority, and the council would still appoint their membership. Consequently, the school board would only be quasi-independent, as they would remain reliant on city council for their appointments and revenues.

A second school charter was issued two years later. Among other things, it moved school board appointment from the council to the voting populace. Members of the Board of Visitors would now be elected, one from each ward, and they could perpetually succeed themselves. They also would now be responsible for writing their own checks and otherwise expending the revenues provided by the council. To that end, they were authorized to choose and compensate a board treasurer.

The 1858 charter also outlined the relationship of the city of Memphis to Shelby County in this regard. The charter stated, "All monies accruing to those civil districts of Shelby County which embrace within their boundaries any portion of the city of Memphis shall be paid to the treasurer of the Board of Visitors in proportion to which those portions are entitled by their amount of scholastic population."[33] In other words, property taxes collected by jurisdictions that encompass any part of Memphis, must share those revenues with the Memphis city schools in proportion to the number of city students residing in the jurisdiction. Those revenues, then, would help the city educate those children.[34]

The Memphis school system operated under the 1858 school charter throughout the Civil War. Despite some very hard economic times, the system managed to survive and the charter remained intact. The Board of Visitors came to be comprised of eight members, one from each of the city's then existing eight wards. It was subdivided into four operating committees: Schoolhouses and Furniture, Teachers and Textbooks, Accounts, and Examinations.

Several problems developed, however, and these prompted the call for a new postwar charter. To begin with, most members lacked the time to meet the existing charter demand of regularly visiting the schools. In addition, the war had brought a doubling of the city's population and a gradual demand for more democratization of the school board.[35] To accommodate such increasing demands, the city's third school charter, established in 1866, required two school board members be elected from each ward, added disciplinary procedures for board members, loosened the limit on what could be borrowed for school construction, and explicitly disallowed any city or county official from also serving on the Board of Visitors. The schools also began to designate select teachers as school principals, for student numbers had compelled the one-room-school to give way to graded schools. Blatantly omitted, however, was any Reconstruction-era provision for educating African Americans.[36]

Meanwhile, the power of the board president and superintendent continued to grow. By 1868, the superintendent's job became a full-time position, with expanded curricular responsibilities.[37] At the same time, the duties of the school board president were summarized as follows:

1. To preside at all meetings of the board of education.
2. To appoint all standing committees.
3. To issue calls for special meetings of the board whenever he deems them necessary.
4. To act as the organ of communication between the school board and the city authorities.
5. To visit each school under the control of the board at least once each year.
6. To countersign all warrants on the treasury.
7. To be an ex-officio member of all standing and extra committees.
8. To be coordinate, ex-officio superintendent.
9. To exercise a general supervision over the interests of education . . .
10. To make an annual report to the board each year which should be published.
11. To be allowed a compensation whenever . . . his services [are] deserving of compensation.[38]

The board of visitors officially became the board of education in 1869 with the passage of the city's fourth charter. Quite significantly, however, this charter mandated that the city begin educating its African American students as well. "Separate schools shall be maintained for the white and colored, both systems of schools to be under the supervision of the Board of Education and its officers."[39] The 1869 charter provided the basic structure for Memphis school administration from this point forward. A century later, court-ordered racial desegregation put an end to legal separation of the races. What did not change is the fact that the Memphis city school system was a "special district" created by a "private act" of the state legislature. Among other things, this meant that it would exist within the boundaries of Shelby County, but it would not be part of the county school system. It would have governing authority separate from both the city and the county governments. However, it would be the only one of the fifteen special school districts in the state not to be granted its own taxing authority. Thus, the

Memphis city council would have to approve its operating and capital budgets, although the school district would have line-item authority over how its money was to be spent.[40]

A series of latter nineteenth-century events, particularly between 1869 and 1883, strained the city's ability to adequately fund its public schools. These events included many allegations of Reconstruction-era fiscal mismanagement, only made worse by an economic depression and a series of yellow fever epidemics. The city's population and tax base shrank to the point where the remaining town fathers convinced the state government to remove the city's charter and run the city from the state capital. These events created serious challenges for school administrators just to keep the schools viable.

The same town fathers who had convinced the state to remove the city's charter oversaw the reinstitution of local governmental control. Part of this reform involved the school board. In an attempt to limit political influences and thus create a more professional board, the Memphis Board of Education was reconstituted. Its twenty members were reduced to five paid members who were elected citywide instead of from the more parochial wards. The power and duties of the superintendent also were increased.[41]

A smaller board gradually ceded more and more power to an ever-increasing professional staff. By 1914, the superintendent routinely had one or more assistant superintendents and was an ex-officio member of all board committees.[42] In addition, school principals were charged with administering all extracurricular activities and making annual reports to the state Department of Education. Subject-area supervisors were added with the proliferation of more specialized instruction, initially in areas such as music and art. Beyond instruction, a school psychiatrist was added in 1916, and school counselors thereafter.[43]

The school charter was marginally amended several more times before the 1970s. The most notable of the charter amendments was a 1941 change that elevated the board president's position as a counter to the growing power the school superintendent. It made the president's status and salary equivalent to that of the superintendent, whose power also had grown at least in part by virtue of running an operation expanding in leaps and bounds. This change included making the board president a council appointee who would serve a four-year term.[44] In essence, the council-appointed board president assisted the council in monitoring council-provided school finances, while curricular-related matters remained the responsibility of the somewhat more independent board-appointed superintendent.

School Construction

Acquiring and maintaining adequate school facilities has been a point of constant challenge from the very beginning. The schools were initially housed in minimally adequate rented space. Continuing fiscal limitations required the earliest school construction to be inexpensive frame buildings. Only later was the city able to utilize brick designs.

Although it was years before the city chose to do so, the Tennessee legislature granted the city authority to raise capital revenues for the purpose of purchasing school land and buildings. The legislature did this shortly after granting the city its first school charter in 1848.[45] As the state statute spelled out, "Be it further enacted, that the mayor and aldermen of the city of Memphis are hereby authorized to assess and collect a special tax, upon such of the taxable property and privileges of the city as they may deem expedient and a poll tax upon all ratable polls in the city; to raise a fund which shall be deemed sufficient, in addition to such funds as may be donated for the purpose, to purchase grounds and erect buildings, for the establishment of a system of free education in the city."[46]

The initial ungraded ward schools were gender-specific, and each consisted of one rented room and one teacher. The first was opened at the northeast corner of Third and Overton Streets, in the house of its teacher, a Mrs. Moore.[47] As reported in the local press, "The schools are now open and . . . Mr. P. J. Carroll takes charge of the male school over the Market House, Mr. J. M. King opens in the second story of the engine house on Poplar Street, Mrs. Barnett and Miss Cochran have charge of the Female Academy on Poplar Street."[48]

Four years later, their number expanded to four girls' and four boys' schools: "Mr. B. Sawtell at the new brick building on Main Street near Market, Mr. J. Bell at the brick academy on Court Street, Mr. J. Lewis at the South Memphis Market House, Mr. G. K. Fisher at the schoolhouse on Hernando Street, Mrs. Irvin at the female academy on Poplar Street, Mrs. Sappington at the schoolhouse on Madison Street, Mrs. Creighton near the Second Presbyterian Church, and Miss Creighton at the brick apartment on Hernando Street."[49]

By the fall of 1852, the Memphis public schools had twelve rented school rooms scattered about the city's wards, and there was also the first attempt at gradation. There were three male and three female primary schools; two male and two female junior schools; as well as one male and one female high school. By 1865, the number of schools had doubled again, and school board members were complaining openly about the inadequacies of the rented facilities. Problems included poor ventilation and lighting, overcrowding, and the mounting costs of repair.[50]

As the city of Memphis developed, however, there were several public projects that seemed consistently to take precedence over the construction of school buildings. These projects included paving streets and developing the infrastructure necessary for shipping and rail commerce.[51] Then, just when public attention finally began to shift to the issue of school construction, the nation plunged into civil war, devastating southern trade and severely reducing available tax revenues.[52] Yet, the sheer number of school-age children simply overwhelmed the status quo. That number increased fivefold between 1855 and 1870, growing from 2,000 to 10,667.[53] This proliferation was fed in part by a significant growth in the number of African American students.

Memphis fell early in the Civil War and ultimately became the site of a large federal Freedmen's Bureau. It was the bureau's responsibility to process ex-slaves and their descendents from all across the general area. This also meant the importation of many federal bureaucrats and soldiers, a large share of whom were African American. After the war, many of these various black residents chose to remain in Memphis. Blacks were only 3,000 of the city's nearly 23,000 people in 1860, or 13 percent of the overall population. They were 15,000 of the city's 40,000 people by 1870, or nearly 38 percent. Obviously, this influx accelerated the growth of both the city and its school population.

The growth in Memphis population also strained the existing housing stock. Soon, it became difficult for the schools even to find rentable space. Then, the cost of repairing the spaces they had found began to soar. In 1866, for instance, the city schools were spending 18 percent of their revenues on rents and repair.[54] At this juncture, under charter authority granted in 1860, the council finally voted out a property tax measure for the purpose of building a limited number of public schools.[55]

One of the earliest construction plans had called for building three brick city schools: one north, one central, and one south.[56] Yet, what followed were years of planning and replanning, as well as repeated negotiations between the board's building committee and the city council. It was not until the 1872–73 school year that even part of the basic plan was actually built.[57] That year saw construction of the Market Street school, at the corner of Market and Third, as well as the completion of the Peabody school at the corner of Webster and Lea. The Peabody school had been made possible in part by a grant from the wealthy George Peabody family. In the fiscally strained interim, the city erected two frame buildings, one on Alabama Street and one on Linden Street. They were one-story buildings with eight rooms apiece, each room designed to accommodate thirty students.[58] As the student numbers above indicate, however, this combination of facilities did not begin to house anywhere near all the thousands of local students eligible for public education.

The political log jam was broken, in large part, by the intervention of the Reconstruction-era state legislature. That legislature would be responsible for the construction of a series of schools statewide. It was before this more sympathetic legislature that the Memphis Board of Visitors finally held sway. The city's postwar charter, granted in 1869, had two very significant educational provisions. Besides mandating that Memphis begin educating its African American students, it required the city council to raise $50,000 in each of the next ten years, exclusively for the purpose of finally building durable public schools.[59]

The aforementioned Market and Peabody schools were the first tangible results of the new state requisites. The Market Street school, serving the city's north end, was the system's first brick school building. It was described in the local press as follows:

> The building was rectangular including a basement and three floors above. In the basement were furnaces, coal bin, and water pump. The first floor, as the two above, contained four rooms, one at each corner of the building, measuring twenty-six by thirty- three feet, the ceiling being fourteen feet high. Attached to each room was a "wardrobe room," eight by twenty feet, containing pigeon holes for hats, rack for umbrellas, and a wash basin with running water. A large hallway ran through the middle of each floor from north to south, at the north end of which was a stairway to the next floor by means of one landing midway between floors. At the first ascending landing was the principal's office, with speaking tubes to each room, and at the landing between the second and third floors was a library room. Wash rooms were available for both men and women teachers. The building throughout was heated by furnaces and ventilated by air shafts. On the third floor a lecture room could be provided by opening large sliding doors which separated two classrooms.[60]

The Peabody school, completed the following year, was the south-side school and differed only in that it was two stories instead of three.[61] The Clay school became the third of these new brick buildings. Similar in design to Peabody, it was unique in that it was built at the corner of Clay and Desoto Streets for the purpose of educating African American students.[62] A "central school" was to be located east of the Gayoso Bayou and house both that area's white children and all the city's high school students. Hopes for building the "central school" fell victim, however, to the yellow fever epidemic, subsequent panic, and escalating city indebtedness.[63] As the yellow fever tragedy began laying waste to the city, Memphis had a total of nine school buildings (see table 1).

Upon careful analysis of table 1, one item stands out, especially in light of subsequent legal battles over the issue. The Board of Visitors emphasized that the all-black Clay school had "eight fine classrooms, with all needful conveniences constructed on the same plan as the Market Street and Peabody schoolhouses, and has been furnished throughout with new furniture of the latest and most approved kinds."[64] Even granting that purchasing a lot in the black area of town may well have cost somewhat less, that does not explain why the board only spent roughly half as much per classroom as they did for the all-white Peabody school. The city had neglected its African American students until its hand

Table 1

Cost of Lots Acquired and Buildings Erected, 1865–1873

	Cost of lot	Cost of building	Total outlay
Adams Street	$12,000	—	$12,000
Auction Street	20,000	—	20,000
Linden Street	20,000	$12,728	32,728
Alabama Street	leased	11,904	11,904
Adams Street	15,000	—	15,000
Peabody	3,650	30,450	34,100
Market Street	30,000	35,500	65,500
House on Adams	—	9,500	9,500
Clay Street	2,400	17,616	20,016

Source: David Moss Hilliard, "The Development of Public Education in Memphis, Tennessee, 1848–1945," Ph.D. diss., University of Chicago, 1946, 46.

had been forced by the state of Tennessee. Now, in its very first efforts at black education, it appears that the seeds of a legal challenge to the idea of "separate but equal" already were being sown.

Meanwhile, the overall progress Memphis had achieved in providing for the education of all its children would suffer a severe setback due to the events of the subsequent decade. From 1873 to 1883, there was nothing short of a panic surrounding the yellow fever epidemics. Nearly half the population had either died or fled the city by the end of the very first year.[65] Those remaining tended to be residents too poor to leave, disproportionately African Americans and Irish whites.[66] The city's mandate to spend $50,000 a year on school construction ended abruptly in 1874, and the city was in bankruptcy by 1880.

As could be expected, the impact on the schools was devastating. By the time the city went bankrupt, overall school budgets had been cut nearly in half. Building maintenance was neglected and classes were reduced to half-day schedules. Class sizes and teaching loads grew, while teacher salaries were reduced.[67] About the best that could be said is that the Memphis public schools somehow managed to remain open.

The state intervened in 1879, revoking the city's charter and assuming governance. Memphis was reduced to a "taxing district" of the state of Tennessee. Within only a few years, the city began to recover. Services began to return, and a health and sanitation system reduced the primary causes of the city's susceptibility to yellow fever. City debts were repaid. Population grew. And, with the renewal of the city's charter in 1893, a new governing structure had been put into place.[68]

In the interim, the school charter was amended, school budgets began to be replenished, and school construction began anew. Significant changes were in place, however, designed at least in part to reduce corruption and increase efficiency. Besides a smaller governing board elected citywide, all school construction funding was henceforth to be authorized by the state legislature as amendments to the school charter.[69]

Six new schools were constructed over the decade from 1889 to 1899, one for blacks and five for whites. Despite the racial imbalance of this effort in a city that was more than one-third black, this was still an impressive accomplishment, especially given the competition for public funds as the city fought to recover from the devastation of the previous two decades. As time passed, however, racial discrepancies became increasingly obvious. When audited in 1943, it was found that the five white schools had spent an average of $131,000 on land, buildings, additions, and equipment. Virginia Avenue, the black school, came in at $32,000.[70]

Meanwhile, as the twentieth century unfolded, annexations would proceed rapidly to encompass much of the outlying land and population. Corresponding student populations soared, actually doubling each decade for the following half century. This created many more school construction challenges.[71]

The areas of Shelby County annexed in 1899, for instance, had sixteen operant schoolhouses when annexation took place, nine for whites and seven for blacks. All were frame buildings and in various stages of disrepair. The black schools were the worst, generally containing only two or three rooms each. The board quickly proceeded to construct ten new school buildings to house these newly annexed students. The six white schools were made of brick. The four black schools were initially built with wood, although later they were subsequently replaced by brick structures.

What followed thereafter was considerable natural population growth as well as several annexations. As could be expected, this led to subsequent scrambling to house the additional student populations. Inadequate frame schools in the annexed areas of the county normally were replaced as quickly as funds could be accumulated. New schools were built, expanded, and then more were built. All of this was accelerated even further when the state adopted mandatory school attendance in 1913.

The evolution of the city's earliest high schools is instructive in this regard. High school students studied in rented quarters until 1893, when the city purchased what became the Leath school. Six years later, the Poplar Street school was the first school constructed exclusively for high school students. From the 1920s on, however, the high school population essentially doubled every decade. South Side, Central, and Humes high schools were quickly added for whites. The original Peabody school became the black high school, until Booker T. Washington and Manassas were built in 1926 and 1928 respectively.

This pattern repeated itself time and again for elementary, junior high, and high schools, until the population began to level off in the 1940s. It also is worth noting that the discrepancies in construction costs for white and black schools appear to have gradually diminished significantly over the course of this period.

Then came the baby boom. Like the nation as a whole, the Memphis area experienced a surge in students as the post–World War II baby boom generation reached school age in the 1950s. Shelby County not only had to deal with the baby boom, but it also had to accommodate those moving outward as part of the suburbanization trend beginning at the same time. Many schools were built during this period, beginning with elementary schools and later secondary ones, not even counting those schools that were renovated or enlarged to meet this demand.

School Finances

Although the Tennessee constitution allows local school boards to administer a school system, only local governments may be delegated taxing authority. Thus, all school funding has to come from state and local governments. This has led local school officials and interested citizens regularly to plead for more school funding from the state of Tennessee, the Shelby County Commission, and the Memphis City Council.

Since January of 1848, the state of Tennessee has delegated to the city of Memphis the authority to raise taxes for the purpose of funding its public schools. At the same time, however, the state has been careful to specify the maximum that could be raised. Initially, this was not to exceed "one-eighth part of the annual revenue of the city."[72] Of course, this did not mean the city was required to tax and spend for the purpose of education, and such funding was reduced significantly during various periods of fiscal difficulty.

Initially, however, the city took full advantage of its new taxing authority, adding a one-eighth additional tax on all property, licenses, privileges, and polls.[73] With only minor amendments, this remained the funding formula until 1856, when the school charter switched to allow a maximum funding of fifteen dollars for each white school-aged child.

In its first year of operation, the city school system spent $1,574.[74] Table 2 presents an itemized account of early school spending in the years prior to Union occupation during the Civil War. The student population tripled, while school expenditures more than doubled. One of the line items is of particular note in terms of subsequent analysis. From early on, education was a highly

Table 2

Annual Expenditures of the Board of Visitors, 1854–1860

Expense item	1853–54	1855–56	1856–57	1857–58	1859–60
Salaries	$8,365	$12,063	$13,430	$17,061	$17,399
Rents/repairs	1,128	2,746	2,361	2,199	4,171
Books/paper	—	—	202	271	160
Printing/ads	—	—	220	267	140
Furniture	711	400	458	418	998
Fuel	—	—	576	475	419
Misc./servants	949	1,030	1,035	795	609
Total	11,153	16,239	18,282	21,486	23,896

Source: Board of Visitors, Annual Reports, 1853–1860.

labor-intensive operation. Combined salaries for the teachers and the superintendent comprised roughly three-quarters of the schools' operating budgets. Consequently, it is very difficult to significantly reduce school expenditures without reducing the teaching staff.

Another pattern presented itself early on and continues to the present day. It is a familiar dance that has developed in the political arena. The school board normally crafts its annual budget request based exclusively on what it anticipates needing to spend to adequately educate all the children in the district. Thus, it will present its revenue requirements to the city council often constrained only by the maximums allowable under its charter. The city council, on the other hand, has been inclined to take existing school tax revenues as a given and expect the school board to be able to operate sufficiently within those limits. Raising taxes, for whatever purpose, is seldom a politically enviable chore for an elected official.[75]

During the federal occupation, which began in 1862, Confederate currency became obsolete, and much of the trade in Confederate states was forced underground. In the economic turmoil that followed, the city teetered on the verge of fiscal insolvency. Nevertheless, it did manage to extend enough credit to the schools so that they were able to survive. Then, just about the time the city and its schools were regaining their fiscal footing, along came yellow fever and more fiscal chaos.

Amidst the growing yellow fever epidemics and their economic repercussions, critical voices began to emerge challenging both the operation of the Memphis City Schools and the very concept of public education. Newspapers such as the *Memphis Daily Avalanche* and the *Memphis Public Ledger* were inundated with such articles and letters. The city schools were accused of such things as being run by carpetbaggers, constructing extravagant school buildings, employing unneeded administrators, and implementing a frivolous curriculum.[76]

The state legislature responded with an 1875 amendment to the city's charter. The city's total tax rate was not to exceed $1.60 per $100.00 of assessed property value. And, of that amount, no more than $0.10 per $100.00 could go to the schools.[77] In force until 1886, the city's contribution to its public schools dropped from a high of $66,954 in 1872 to a low point of $3,723 five years later. It would be 1889 before the city would return to its 1872 school funding levels.

Fortunately, at about the same time, the state and county began to step into the school funding breach. The state, in 1870, passed a state education tax of ten cents per one hundred dollars, which would be returned to its county governments according to their number of enrolled students. It also required the counties to initiate a school tax rate of at least ten cents per one hundred dollars. Table 3 reflects these developments.

Income from the state and county allowed the Memphis schools to compensate for lost city funding. Yet, as city funding sagged even further, state and county revenues were not enough. Serious cutbacks occurred. And given the labor-intensive nature of education, this included some relatively severe cuts in teaching staffs. Some of the city's very best teachers subsequently left the system.[78]

Beginning in the 1880s, things began to turn around. With Memphis reduced to a "taxing district" of the state, the city's finances finally stabilized and

Table 3

Memphis School Income and Sources, 1870–1889

Year	Memphis school tax rate per $100	Income from city school tax	Income from state and county taxes	Miscellaneous income	Total income
1870	$0.30	$64,942	—	$1,221	$66,163
1875	0.10	40,148	$22,759	2,178	65,085
1880	0.10	15,740	19,367	913	36,019
1885	0.10	22,513	25,174	1,012	48,699
1889	0.25	66,814	46,101	1,986	114,901

Source: David Moss Hilliard, "The Development of Public Education in Memphis, Tennessee, 1848–1945," Ph.D. diss., University of Chicago, 1946, 74.

its debts were gradually retired. Services began to be restored, and the yellow fever epidemics ultimately were contained. By decade's end, the city's education contribution had nearly returned to its 1870 level. Combined with state and county contributions, funding for the city's schools began to keep pace with a soaring growth in population. As the 1890s dawned, the city boasted 5,735 students and 143 teachers in twelve schools, with an annual operating budget of $126,185.[79] However, this was a forty-to-one student-teacher ratio, and only about one-third of the city's eligible students were enrolled in school. As the city's population continued to soar, there was much work left to be done.

School enrollment would reach nearly thirty thousand students by 1920. The state legislature had rather consistently granted charter amendments so the schools could borrow the money needed for new school construction. Yet, as population grew and service demands increased, the city's operating revenues were stretched thinly as well. This limited their ability to fund schools up to the full level allowed by the most recent charter amendment. Where the city schools had actually run budget surpluses throughout the 1890s, they were now facing annual operating deficits.

The city schools continued to face annual deficits despite two state supreme court rulings that weighed heavily in their favor. The court had ruled that school districts were chartered corporations separate from their encompassing city and county. They also ruled that school boards were free to determine their necessary appropriations, so long as they remained within the taxing limits spelled out in their latest charter.[80] The city was now being required by court order to spend to the maximum of the school system's state authorization if that was deemed necessary by the school board.[81]

The city administration then attempted to influence who sat on the school board. In 1912, for example, three board members were opposed and defeated in what were at least nominally nonpartisan elections. The end result was a school board in which all five members appeared to meet with the city government's favor.[82] Nonetheless, the deficits continued. There was a four-day teachers' strike in 1918. Thereafter, several local civic organizations did independent evaluations of the schools and found them severely wanting.[83] The real problem appeared to be one of growth, however, rather than extravagance. Finally the state intervened and authorized both a mandatory tax of fifty cents per one hundred dollars for the Memphis City Schools,[84] as well as five hundred thousand dollars in bonds for school construction and repair.[85]

The school board was back in business, and they were soon building schools at an unprecedented pace. Between 1920 and 1932, the schools' bonded indebtedness grew by roughly 260 percent. Meanwhile, school operating income grew by only 99 percent.[86] As a result, debt service kept taking a larger and larger proportion of the annual operating budget, leaving less of the operating budget for educational expenditures. Then, to make matters worse, the Great Depression both reduced city revenues and caused the banks to cease lending to a debt-laden school system.

Soon teachers were being paid in scrip, and something had to give. Large cuts were made across the board from 1932 to 1937. Among other things, this meant that teacher salaries were reduced by more than 16 percent, supervisory services were cut, several assistant principal positions were eliminated, and text-book purchases were all but suspended.

Yet, like the rest of the nation, the city of Memphis finally emerged from the Great Depression. As revenues began to grow, the school board was able once again to build schools and fund operations in a manner that began to match student demand. They also were able to do so without budget deficits. Following World War II, the state began to allow a portion of the sales tax to be used on public education; and, the federal government had even become a minor contributor. The city schools settled into a pattern of receiving roughly two-thirds of their revenues from the city, a quarter from the county, 10 percent from the state, and another 1 percent from a combination of the federal government and miscellaneous other sources.

As population growth finally began to level out, bonded indebtedness became less of a problem. New schools simply did not have to be built as rapidly. The tax revenues required to fund operating expenses, however, continued to rise. The Memphis tax rate for schools rose from fifty cents per one hundred dollars in 1919 to sixty-five cents by 1944 to eighty-six cents by 2002.[87] Over time, however, Shelby County and the State of Tennessee combined to assume three-quarters of the city schools' funding, besides the 12 percent received from local sales taxes, which has reduced the City of Memphis' responsibility to roughly 12 percent.[88]

Educating African Americans

Memphis had a relatively small African American population prior to the Civil War. When the city fell early in the war, however, many liberated slaves were drawn to Memphis for food, shelter, clothing, and protection provided by the Union troops, as well as educational opportunities available through missionary schools and later the Freedmen's Bureau. Blacks soon comprised roughly 40 percent of the city's population. After the Civil War, federally imposed Reconstruction included the added requisite of educating former slaves at public expense. Although the ground was broken by the Freedmen's Bureaus, this responsibility was passed to states such as Tennessee and subsequently to localities such as Memphis. At the state and local levels in Tennessee, like elsewhere in the former Confederacy, this meant the development of a separate black educational system.

Memphis was founded in 1826; and because of its strategic Mississippi River location, the city soon became an important trading center. It was a natural gateway for goods going to and from the North, South, and West. In particular, it was a critical cotton exchange center. Unskilled slave labor was little used in the city proper, in large part because poor Irish had flocked to the city, brought more skills, and were willing to work for very low wages.[89] Thus, the 1860 federal census shows the Memphis black population at 17 percent. When the rural areas of Shelby County are added, however, African Americans comprised a majority of the county's population, at 52 percent.

With civil war imminent, Memphis still placed its black residents under tight control. It was illegal to teach them to read; they were under a strict curfew; and they had to have special mayoral permission and police supervision if they were to meet at night or gather to hear a black preacher.[90] Yet, when the city fell to Union troops in 1862, volunteer efforts to educate African Americans began almost immediately.

Colonel John Eaton Jr. graduated from Dartmouth College and had actually been a school superintendent in Toledo, Ohio, before the war. He joined the Union troops as a chaplain; and he was hand selected by General Ulysses S. Grant "to look after the organization and care of colored labor in the Mississippi valley from Cairo to Natchez."[91] Eaton set up headquarters in Memphis. Soon, with the help of missionaries from the North and East, he began offering schools for black children. The schools were funded by northern church benevolent associations, local donations, and a small tuition charge for those students who could afford to pay.[92]

Opening in early 1863, within one year the schools had twenty teachers instructing 809 black children in nine separate "missionary schools."[93] The schools were organized very similarly to their existing white counterparts. They tended to be one-room structures with one or two teachers per school, took up operation in an existing frame building, and had a superintendent. The *Daily Post* describes the city's first black school as operating "in a barrack building in South Memphis" and taught "by a Miss Fannie Kiddo, from Illinois, a young lady of culture and high Christian character, sent here by the United Presbyterian Freedmen's Aid Society."[94] The black schools' first superintendent, Rev. L. H. Cobb, is described by the *Daily Bulletin* as a man "educated at Dartmouth College, and who has had considerable experience as a teacher in some of the best New England schools."[95]

The city's elected officials remained in their positions for the first two years of Union occupation. By 1864, however, the occupying soldiers decided that there had been too much "disloyalty" and replaced those officials with a military government headed by Maj. Gen. C. C. Washburn. In the fall of that year, Washburn issued Order #164. It read, "The control and discipline of the educational interests, schools, and teachers of the colored people of the city of Memphis are hereby entrusted to the municipal government of the city, and the committee on public schools is hereby constituted a school board with full powers for the efficient arrangement of the same."[96]

In the course of the next five years, although the number of schools and teachers remained essentially the same, the student population tripled,[97] and more than four thousand students had been taught to read.[98] Meanwhile, the Education Association of Memphis was formed to advance these "free schools." The *Daily Post* described their meetings as "large and enthusiastic" groups of colored people, well-meaning missionaries, and self-seeking carpetbag politicians.[99]

The publicly elected Memphis Board of Education continued to operate the city's white schools. Meanwhile, board minutes from 1863 to 1867 record virtually no mention of either black students or black schools. The board simply refused to recognize the responsibility of educating the area's African American children until it was compelled to do so by the state in 1867.[100]

In 1867, Gov. William G. Brownlow and the Tennessee Reconstruction legislature initiated an ambitious statewide educational program. Col. John Eaton of Memphis, by that time the state's superintendent of education, was to coordinate the effort. Among other things, state legislation required all school districts to adopt "one or more special schools for colored children," and it put these schools under the "control and management of the [local] board of education."[101] At this point, then, governance of the Memphis missionary schools formally passed from the control of the military government's school board to the long-standing and popularly elected Memphis Board of Education.

The board of education quickly redelegated the running of the black schools to the existing missionary structure. They even left them with their own superintendent, who by this time was a northern missionary by the name of J. H. Barnum. The board also expected them to continue to be financed largely by private sources, at least until state monies were forthcoming.[102] As the city's school superintendent W. Z. Mitchell summarized things for the board: "The means for [financing black schools] has not yet been placed at your disposal, nor by your charter are you empowered to assess a city tax for the education of colored children. The means of carrying on the colored schools must come from the state tax unless the board of mayor and aldermen will take steps to raise the funds. . . . The funds now raised are not sufficient to support the schools for white children."[103]

This whole process was expedited when the Reconstruction state government disenfranchised whites who had assisted the Confederacy and extended suffrage to the state's African American residents. Needless to say, the tenor of state politics began to change. Despite the war-torn condition of the state treasury, for example, state monies did start to arrive for the purpose of educating

African Americans, beginning in the summer of 1868.[104] Within a year, the state also mandated that the newly constituted local governments begin contributing tax revenues to this endeavor.[105]

Pursuant to the charter of 1869, school board elections were held that March. In an election marred by allegations of Ku Klux Klan intimidation, however, many newly enfranchised blacks stayed away from the polls.[106] The *Daily Avalanche* characterized the newly elected school board as being comprised of fourteen conservatives and six radicals.[107] Nonetheless, the new board initially left the missionary schools pretty much intact. The missionary system's twenty-three teachers averaged 5.3 years of teaching experience, with seven of them coming from Ohio, five from Michigan, five from Memphis, two from Illinois, and one each from Vermont, New York, New Hampshire, and Massachusetts. In addition, J. H. Barnum was retained, assuming the new position of assistant superintendent in charge of the colored schools.[108] The *Daily Post,* a longtime champion of black education, proclaimed that "The Board of Education today, notwithstanding a majority of them are Democrats, is providing impartiality for the education of all children of the city."[109]

Yet, Reconstruction was coming to a rapid end in Tennessee. Federal troops would soon be gone entirely; William Brownlow and John Eaton were in the process of moving on to higher federal offices; and the *Daily Post* ceased to exist. Superintendent J. T. Leath and the board of education quickly changed course. When school resumed in the fall of 1869, the board had slashed fourteen of the twenty-three teachers assigned to the black schools,[110] leaving Barnum little choice but to use older students to supplement the instructional staff.[111] In the spring of 1870, they eliminated Barnum's assistant superintendent position.[112] The board also ordered an end to religious instruction in the black schools, having become concerned that radical political ideas were being taught under the guise of religious education.[113] Of the African Americans who remained in Memphis, many former students were pressed into employment to support their families. By 1872, with no compulsory school attendance law, black school enrollment had fallen from 2,193 to 1,295.[114] It would be twenty years before it returned to its 1869 level.

Superintendent Leath was unceremoniously replaced in 1871, however, and the tide gradually began to turn once again.[115] Under the 1869 state mandate that $50,000 be raised and spent annually on school construction for blacks and whites, black school construction was renewed. The Clay Street school, the city's first brick school for African American students, opened to great fanfare in March of 1873. Principal J. H. Barnum oversaw a biracial staff of eight classroom teachers.[116] Once the city began to recover from the throes of the yellow fever epidemics, another black school was built as one of four constructed.

As an example of the black political activism of the time, a group of African American residents held a mass meeting in the summer of 1873. Out of that meeting came a petition that H. C. Slaughter be retained as superintendent of schools. Unhappy with the local white teachers who often appeared only to have reluctantly replaced their departing missionary predecessors, the assembled blacks asked that every effort be made to find African Americans to serve as principals and teachers at the system's black schools. Among other things, the petition stated,

> Resolved, that in view of the fact that white teachers in our schools have failed so utterly for the last two years, and as we believe that their educational training is calculated to render them unfit for positions in our schools, therefore, we would most respectfully ask that the service of those be dispensed with.
>
> Resolved, that in view of the fact that we are prescribed by law to separate schools for our children upon the presumption of "inferiority," we respectfully ask that we have the benefit in full, and that every teacher from principal down be elected from the prescribed class.[117]

Although Slaughter was replaced after an acrimonious debate, the number of black principals and teachers increased.[118] In 1875, for instance, Barnum himself was replaced by B. K. Sampson, an African American who had graduated from Oberlin College in Ohio.[119]

The two black and five white schools built between 1869 and 1890 were in relatively close proportion to the city's black/white student ratio.[120] That ratio would change, however, as an ever higher percentage of the black population gradually could afford the luxury of attending school and the state adopted a policy of compulsory attendance. By the turn of the century, blacks and whites were attending at essentially the same rates.[121] This increase in black attendance was added to the overall resurgence in population growth once yellow fever was in check. Among other things, this combination meant the demand for black education was about to soar.

Given funding limitations, the school board responded to the demand for more black and white schools by building brick schools for whites and frame ones for blacks. Nine such frame schools were in operation during the first two decades of the twentieth century, several with a series of portable classrooms attached. By the 1920s and 1930s, however, these frame buildings were gradually replaced with brick structures similar to those found in the white neighborhoods. The curriculum, administered by the system's white board and staff, appears to have been essentially the same in both black and white schools over time. As for teachers, like in the rest of the Jim Crow South, black teachers were paid at a lower wage rate than their white counterparts.[122] In addition, despite board concern about the teaching competence of many black candidates, there is no record of a white teacher working in a black school from the time the last northern missionaries left in 1876 until the desegregation period nearly a century later.[123]

Despite the Civil War, yellow fever epidemics, a general population surge, racial unrest, and municipal bankruptcy, Memphis City Schools took root. A combination of state pressure and the tireless efforts of local teachers and school administrators propelled this development. By the 1960s, the city schools were instructing more than 100,000 black and white students. It was the school system's racial divide, however, that would cause it to get caught in the winds of the desegregation movement sweeping the nation.

Chapter 4

School Desegregation

As the 1960s dawned, a clear racial division remained within the Memphis public schools. White students attended white schools taught by white teachers. Black students attended black schools taught by black teachers. For all practical purposes, this separation of students had been firmly in place for nearly a century, ever since the Reconstruction state government mandated black public education in 1867. As desegregation loomed in the late 1960s, the Memphis City Schools were the most racially segregated large-city school district in the United States.[1]

The practice of "separate but equal" schools, existing in Memphis and across the South, was approved by the U.S. Supreme Court in its famous *Plessy v. Ferguson* decision of 1896.[2] Yet, the Supreme Court sent shockwaves throughout the region when it reversed itself a half century later. In its equally famous 1954 *Brown v. Board of Education* decision, the Court declared that "separate but equal" was now "inherently unequal."[3] The Supreme Court's *Brown* decision, combined with Civil Rights Acts adopted by Congress, put an end to such "de jure" forms of forced separation. The practice of writing laws that mandated the segregation of students on the basis of their race, no matter how equal the facilities, was no longer to be tolerated.

The legal mandate was reasonably clear. School systems segregated by governmental action had to be desegregated. One of the biggest struggles in the quest for effective school desegregation, however, was distinguishing "de jure" from "de facto" segregation, the latter meaning segregation that resulted primarily from residential patterns as opposed to being required by law. In large cities across the nation, the NAACP was at the forefront of efforts to expedite desegregation. It was up to the federal courts to determine when enough effort had been made to dismantle the old legally mandated forms of segregation, leaving only those forms resulting as a by-product of individual housing choices.

The drawing of school boundaries, the location of new schools, and interschool transfer policies received close scrutiny in making those determinations.

The Legal Battle

School desegregation did not take place over night. For one thing, there was considerable opposition to this change in much of the white South. Thus, there was little incentive for local elected and appointed officials to accelerate this effort. Such dismantling progressed in fits and starts, requiring years of litigation over precisely when and how it was to be accomplished.

Memphis schools had been racially segregated by law for a full century. Combined with the city's high degree of residential segregation, it was not surprising that Memphis schools exhibited a high degree of racial division. The legal battle over school desegregation was joined in Memphis in the spring of 1960. But as in much of the rest of the region, the wheels of justice turned slowly in sorting out this politically volatile issue. Occurring six years after the landmark *Brown* decision, the case would not reach a settlement for another seventeen years.

A Unitary School System Standard

In response to the U.S. Supreme Court's decision in *Brown v. Board of Education*, the state of Tennessee passed the Tennessee Pupil Assignment Law of 1957. It required local school districts to develop administrative remedies that would begin to dismantle the century-old system of state-required school segregation. That very year, the Memphis City Schools implemented a voluntary transfer arrangement, designed to overcome segregation by allowing students more opportunity to attend the school of their choice. But in 1958, eight-year-old Gerald Young was refused admittance to the all-white Vollentine Elementary School. By 1960, only thirteen of the roughly one hundred transfer requests by black students had been approved.

On March 31, 1960, black plaintiffs, with the help of the National Association for the Advancement of Colored People (NAACP) Legal Defense Fund, sought "permanent equitable relief" from the Memphis Board of Education for the board's continued operation of what was alleged to be a racially dual school system. To that end, the plaintiffs filed a class-action suit in federal district court on behalf of eighteen school-aged children. The lawsuit was *Deborah A. Northcross, et al. v. Board of Education of the Memphis City Schools, et al.*[4] Deborah Northcross was eight years old and the daughter of Memphis dentist Dr. T. W. Northcross, who also served on the executive committee of the local NAACP. The eight plaintiff lawyers included Thurgood Marshall, Constance Baker Motley, and Benjamin Hooks.

The school board filed their answer in May, asking for dismissal of the complaint. They argued that the state-imposed dual system of education had been dismantled, and there was no illegal discrimination occurring anymore. The segregation that remained was instead the result of the city's residential patterns. Consequently, the plaintiffs were not due relief. For the next three decades, the school board would continue to deny that the schools were being operated in an illegal manner.

Meanwhile, the Memphis City Schools voluntarily began a gradual "grade-a-year" plan. A small number of black children were to enter previously all-white schools each academic year. In the fall of 1961, thirteen African American first graders became the first blacks in Memphis history to do so, crossing barriers that had been imposed by law nearly a century earlier.[5] Yet, these small steps did not spell the beginning of a steady march to Memphis school desegregation. Instead, the school board seriously reduced that likelihood by drawing school district lines that conformed to the city's residential segregation. In addition, white students were allowed to transfer out of schools that had become even minimally integrated.[6]

Nonetheless, Federal District Judge Marion S. Boyd ultimately sided with the school board one year after the initial *Northcross* lawsuit was filed, denying the existence of an unconstitutionally segregated school system. The system's voluntary transfer arrangement was deemed by Judge Boyd to be a sufficient mechanism for desegregating the schools. He declared that existing law had produced "a sound and complete plan, adequate to a fair deal to the colored pupils of this community." Thus, the plaintiffs were not entitled to relief.

The plaintiffs, frustrated that not a single Memphis school had yet to be fully integrated, appealed Judge Boyd's decision to the U.S. Court of Appeals. In March of 1962, the federal appellate court reversed Judge Boyd, finding that the school board's "good faith" plan simply did not go far enough. They specifically instructed the district judge "to restrain the defendants from operating a biracial school system in Memphis, or in the alternative to adopt a plan looking towards the organization of the schools in accordance with the Constitution of the United States."[7] The U.S. Supreme Court denied the school board's petition for review, which left standing the ruling of the court of appeals. After a rehearing, the district judge entered an order enjoining the defendants from operating a biracial school system and directing them to submit a new desegregation plan.[8]

The Memphis School Board presented a gradual "stair-step plan," so as to accomplish desegregation with the least amount of disruption. After hearing arguments in 1963, the district court approved the board's plan. School district lines would be redrawn to include a more reasonable mix of black and white neighborhoods. Students also would be allowed to transfer more easily between schools, so long as the end result improved the racial mix of the schools involved.

These plans allowed for both "majority-to-minority" transfers, as well as "minority-to-minority" ones. For example, if the overall school system was 40 percent black and a black student was in a school that was more than 40 percent black, that student could transfer to a school that had a black population of less than 40 percent. That would be a "majority-to-minority transfer." In the second instance, students could transfer out of situations in which they were tiny minorities, so that they could end up in a more comfortable circumstance where they would be part of a larger minority.

The plaintiffs argued that plan was too gradual and still did not go far enough. They appealed the district judge's decision, asking for additional relief. On June 12, 1964, the court of appeals returned the plan to the district court, calling it "too slow" and mandating that all junior high schools be integrated within a year and all high schools within two years. More specifically, they dismissed the transfer features and advised that close scrutiny be given to all zone lines in view of the court's finding of substantial evidence that the boundaries approved by the district judge had been "gerrymandered to preserve a maximum amount of segregation."[9] This action was followed by a considerable delay in the case. Meanwhile, the U.S. Department of Justice became more heavily involved.

In July of 1966, the school board submitted a "modified plan of desegregation," containing a revised student assignment and transfer plan. This was the same year that school faculties started to integrate, and all twelve grades were now at least very minimally integrated. The district court gave a tentative approval to the new plan but allowed the plaintiffs additional time to respond. Feeling it was still inadequate, the plaintiffs filed a "motion for preliminary injunction" in February of 1967,[10] seeking to prevent the board from carrying out their proposed student assignment plan. That motion was denied by District Judge Bailey Brown on March 3, but the court indicated that they might ultimately reject the board's assignment plan. No further action was taken on the case until the summer of 1968.

In May of 1968, the U.S. Supreme Court handed down its decision in *Green v. County School Board*.[11] The court noted that a "freedom-of-choice" plan could not be accepted as a sufficient step to effectuate the transition to a unitary system. On July 26, the Memphis plaintiffs filed a "motion for further relief," based in part upon on the Supreme Court's *Green* opinion. The motion sought to achieve several things. They called for complete faculty desegregation, as well as the cancellation of all transfers that reduced desegregation. They asked for a survey of local school facilities, with a complete report to be submitted to the district court. They also called for the adoption of a new plan of desegregation, prepared with the assistance of the Desegregation Center of the University of Tennessee.[12]

Judge Brown declined to order relief for the 1968–69 school year because of the imminent opening of school. At this point, the case was transferred to

Judge Robert M. McRae Jr. Judge McRae held November hearings with respect to plaintiffs' request for a facilities survey. On November 21, McRae ordered the defendants to conduct and file such a survey.

The district court held an evidentiary hearing in February of 1969 in order to evaluate the substance of the plaintiffs' larger motion for further relief. In its judgment, handed down on May 23, the court determined that "the existing and proposed plans [of the board] do not have real prospects for dismantling the state-imposed dual system at the earliest practicable date." Although the court did not void the free-transfer system or the proposed zoning alignment, it did find that "the zones are in need of revision for many purposes, including further desegregation where feasible."[13] The court asked that revisions to the zone boundary lines, as well as enrollment projections, be submitted on January 1, 1970. Also included in the opinion was the court's denial of the plaintiffs' request that all new school construction be halted pending the approval of new zoning lines. In regard to faculty desegregation, the court mandated a 20 percent systemwide desegregation of faculty for the upcoming school year, meaning some six hundred teachers would need to be transferred. Still dissatisfied, the plaintiffs responded with an unsuccessful "motion for summary reversal."[14]

Meanwhile, leaders of the local branch of the NAACP also were growing frustrated with such gradualism. On September 12, 1969, they made fifteen demands of the Memphis School Board.

1. The city school system be decentralized into 3 or 4 large racially mixed districts with Negroes actively involved in the preliminary planning for decentralization, and once decentralization has been accomplished, that at least half of the top positions be filled by blacks;

2. Schools be "paired" so that white children will be sent to formerly all-black schools and vice versa;

3. Two or more members of the Memphis School Board resign immediately, so that these vacancies can be filled by black citizens;

4. The personnel department be taken out of Administrative Services, and that a black man be made Assistant Superintendent;

5. The Director of Human Relations be made an Assistant Superintendent;

6. Black coordinators be appointed to the Departments of Administrative Services and Plant Management;

7. Black persons in substantial numbers be placed in administrative positions in Classified Personnel and in Plant Management;

8. Twice as many black recruiters be hired (since the Board maintains that black teachers are at a premium to recruit in all institutions across the state in other geographical areas);

9. At least 75% of new teachers hired in 1969–70 be black to offset the pattern of the past four years when 75% of teachers hired were white;

10. At least 80% of new administrative personnel hired this year (1969–70) be black, with a majority of these placed in predominantly white schools at the level of principal;

11. Courses in black culture—history, literature, music, art—be introduced into *all* high schools immediately;

12. Textbooks which do not reflect the racial composition of America or which minimize the Negro's contributions to American society must be eliminated;

13. Important books on black political life and culture should be placed on the shelves of all elementary and high school libraries;

14. The School Board provide money to finance a comprehensive program which will provide completely free lunches for every child of a poverty-level family. Private sources will not finance this program. The Board and other groups should not delude the public nor hungry children into false hope that an adequate program can be financed by that method;

15. All meetings of the School Board be open to the public and be televised.[15]

They also moved to bring political heat to bear on the elected school board. Led by Maxine Smith and LeRoy Clark, they initiated "Black Mondays." For six consecutive Mondays, black parents kept approximately sixty-seven thousand black students at home. Hundreds of black teachers also boycotted the city's schools, as did the Bethal Grove principal, Dr. W. W. Herenton. Besides dramatizing their demands, the boycotts confounded the school district's revenues, as those revenues were calculated on the basis of average daily attendance. In the end, the board agreed to hire more black teachers and to elect board members by districts instead of citywide.[16]

Back on the legal front, in its opinion in the case of *Alexander v. Holmes County Board of Education,* the U.S. Supreme Court declared that dual school systems based on race or color would no longer be tolerated. They directed such school districts to begin immediately to operate as a unitary desegregated school system. There were to be no more postponements, even if the beginning of school was imminent.[17]

Emboldened by the *Alexander* decision, the Memphis plaintiffs filed a motion with the court of appeals on November 3, 1969. It called for the "adoption of a unitary system now." They also filed a "motion to convene an emergency panel of the Sixth Circuit." The court of appeals denied the motion for an emergency panel, but they submitted the plaintiffs' *Alexander* motion to an assigned panel and scheduled arguments for December 17. Two days after oral arguments, the court of appeals remanded the case back to the district court for reconsideration of their previously approved plan in light of the *Alexander* ruling.

The plaintiffs then asked the court of appeals to implement a more clearly unitary system during the second semester of the 1969–70 school year. On January 12, 1970, the court of appeals entered an order denying this motion. The court stated, "We are satisfied that the respondent Board of Education of Memphis is not now operating a 'dual school system' and has, subject to complying with the present commands of the District Judge, converted its pre-Brown dual system into a unitary system 'within which no person is to be effectively excluded because of race or color.'"[18]

The federal courts appeared to be satisfied that the most recent combination of rezoning and transfer mechanisms promised sufficient desegregation to meet the U.S. Supreme Court's mandate in *Brown* and subsequent decisions. The case appeared to be reaching an end. Then, on March 9, 1970, the U.S. Supreme Court granted the plaintiffs' appeal and returned the case to the district court "with direction that the District Court proceed promptly to consider the issues before it and to decide the case consistently with *Alexander v. Holmes County Board.*"[19] Additionally, the Supreme Court reversed the court of appeal's finding that *Alexander* was inapplicable to the Memphis system and found "substantial evidence" to support a finding that the defendants were still operating a dual school system.[20]

The district court then set a hearing to determine the following:[21]

(1) Was the School Board operating a unitary system?

(2) If not, should the Court require defendants to adopt a new or modified plan utilizing any one or more of such methods as rezoning, pairing, contiguous zones or cross-transportation of pupils between zones?[22]

(3) And if so, should the Court eliminate the free-transfer policy; require a faculty desegregation ratio within a margin of 10 percent of the system-wide faculty racial ratio; enjoin further school construction by the defendants pending adoption of a plan; or request a new plan from an expert outside the system?

(4) When should any relief be put into effect?

The district court rendered its opinion on May 1, 1970, followed three days later by its implementation order. The judge rejected the board's proposed pairing and transportation techniques as inadequate desegregation measures. The free-transfer policy was altered so that only in two limited circumstances would transfers be permitted. In regard to faculty desegregation, the court held that the board had not complied in good faith with the court's May 1969 faculty desegregation order, therefore ordering the defendants to seek the assistance of the Educational Opportunities Planning Center at the University of Tennessee.

Following the submission of both the center's faculty desegregation plan and the board's counterproposal, the district court essentially approved the center's plan. Additionally, the court required that by the beginning of the 1971–72 school year, the white-black ratio of each school's faculty should be within 10 percent of the systemwide black-white ratio. The plaintiffs were not successful, however, in halting the board's acquisition and construction of two new sites in the predominantly white southwestern part of the system, moves they felt would have the effect of increasing segregation, even if only inadvertently. Before a verdict could be reached on the plaintiff's appeal, however, the U.S. Supreme Court sanctioned an additional and more radical mechanism for hastening school desegregation.

Court-Ordered Busing

In April of 1971, the U.S. Supreme Court decided *Swann v. Charlotte*[23] and *Davis v. Board of School Commissioners.*[24] In these decisions, the Supreme Court affirmed the right of both the district court and the court of appeals to implement more radical measures to ensure school desegregation. These more radical measures included the option of court-ordered school busing. The opinions in *Swann* and *Davis* would have a major impact upon the ongoing Memphis case. On June 7, the court of appeals remanded the case to the district court for reconsideration in light of *Swann* and *Davis.*

Judge McRae then offered to recuse himself from the case, citing his son's attendance at one of the defendant's schools. Despite the plaintiffs' request for the designation of a new judge, McRae's request was denied, and he was ordered to continue. In late July, he issued an "Order Pertaining to Assistance." It authorized the U.S. Department of Education's Division of Equal Education Opportunities to assign qualified personnel to assist the board in carrying out the court of appeal's mandate. The order also directed defendants to implement a majority-to-minority transfer plan with free transportation prior to the beginning of the 1971–72 school year, but no further desegregation would be required by the opening of school that fall.[25]

After conferring with counsel, board personnel and the Office of Education's team, McRae determined that the latter group would make a preliminary investigation of the existing system. A conference was held on September 9 in order for the team to inform the district court of its progress. At that point, the court began consideration of one of the team's initial questions—whether it mattered if the racial composition of any school was a result of de facto, as opposed to de jure, decisions. In other words, had the existing racial balance somehow been imposed as a dual system either directly or indirectly by government, or had it simply evolved as a result of residential patterns and thus should be left alone? At this time, the court also set a hearing for mid-November in order to determine certain factual and legal issues and provide guidance to the board and the team.[26]

In early November of 1971, Judge McRae issued a pretrial order enjoining defendants from entering into any new land purchases or construction contracts at this time. He also defined the term "virtual one-race school" as one in which the predominate race is 90 percent or more.[27] The mid-November hearing then lasted eight days and focused mostly on an in-depth analysis of both the historical and current causes of school segregation in Memphis.

The district court rendered an important judgment on December 10, concluding that the board had failed to prove that existing school segregation was unrelated to decisions the school system had made over time. It stated: "In regard to the overall issue of one-race schools, this Court concludes that the proof establishes that the defendant Board and its predecessors have played a significant role in establishment of the present large number of one-race schools which have resulted from discrimination by numerous persons and groups. Therefore, it is incumbent upon the Court to require the board to request that the team of the Division make recommendation to the defendant Board for ways that it should amend its present plan of desegregation to the end that the Memphis schools will be in compliance with the Constitution of the United States."[28]

The court then established criteria the team from the federal Office of Education was to use in their preparation of two alternative plans. This set the stage for what later would come to be known as "Plan A" and "Plan B." Within a month, after experiencing trouble with the cooperation of the federal team, Judge McRae entered an order relieving the team from further participation in the case. The task of complying with his December order then passed instead to the school board.

Meanwhile on the national scene, President Richard Nixon delivered a March message to Congress opposing the use of mandatory school busing for the purpose of school desegregation. He also indicated in later comments that he would not oppose a constitutional amendment banning busing as a means to solving school segregation problems.[29]

Just prior to President Nixon's remarks, three plans for school desegregation were filed in Memphis federal court. Given the overall level of residential segregation in the city of Memphis, each of the plans called for at least some court-ordered busing. Plan A and Plan B were filed by the school board, per the order of the court. The third plan was offered by the local branch of the NAACP, filed by Louis Lucas and William Caldwell. Of the three options presented to the court, Plan A required the least busing, involving only half the city's schools and calling for approximately 12,700 students to be bussed to schools outside their respective neighborhoods. Plan B would have required the busing of 37,982 students, and the NAACP's plan would have bussed 61,530 of the city's 146,000 students.[30]

The plans generated considerable public disagreement. Groups such as Citizens Against Busing (CAB) opposed any mandatory transportation between schools.[31] The organization sponsored a school lunch boycott, for example, to protest the plans' inclusion of busing. That protest eventually spread to forty-four schools and reduced meals purchased by 45 percent.[32] Meanwhile, African American board members George Brown, Maxine Smith, and Carl Johnson heavily criticized the inadequacies of both plans submitted by the board, claiming the board and Superintendent John Freeman were in contempt of the court order.[33] The board defended its two plans, even though they still left a considerable degree of racial separation. In doing so, they cited a Supreme Court opinion that stated, "any school necessary to the maintenance of the system which cannot be desegregated under those limitations (time and distance affecting health of child) must remain a one-race or virtual one-race school until housing patterns change or new schools are provided."[34]

There was even more intense opposition to the NAACP plan, due to the cost and magnitude of the proposed busing operation. The plan would have bussed 42 percent of the city's students; and, although no cost projections were included, they were assumed to be higher than those of the two board plans. The school board plans, estimated to cost $1,664,192 and $5,707,449, respectively, were already drawing concerns about the district's ability to finance them.[35] In response, the NAACP proposed that some junior and senior high school students pay for their own transportation on Memphis Transit Authority buses, with exceptions to be made for students from low-income families.

On April 20, 1972, the federal district court adopted Plan A and ordered that it be implemented by the beginning of the 1972–73 school year. The least disruptive of the plans submitted, it turned out to have been a plan prepared by the board's staff but to which many on the board had actually objected. Judge McRae's order stated, "The practicalities of the existing situation in the City of Memphis limit the change in the plan of desegregation to this extent at the present time."[36]

Although the decision was expected, few seemed pleased with the outcome. The school board had opposed the plan on several grounds, including budgetary concerns. Annual costs were estimated to be $629,192 on top of an estimated $1,664,192 in capital costs required to provide all the necessary buses. Forces from the plaintiffs' side continued their argument that it was simply not enough. Both the NAACP and CAB, two of the debate's most vocal opponents, called press conferences to immediately denounce the ruling. And with President Nixon's opposition to busing a matter of public record, local Representative Dan Kuykendall stated that he would ask Senators Howard Baker Jr. and William Brock to join him in requesting that the Justice Department "intervene to overturn or at least to mitigate as much as possible the effects of this decision."[37]

Racial tensions reached a feverish pitch across the City of Memphis. In some schools, most notably Westwood, meetings nearly erupted into violence. Police protection was offered to those who felt it necessary.[38] Among other things, people drew attention to the concern of white flight. Neal Small, board vice president, made what turned out to be a rather prophetic prediction. He asserted, "One of the big problems with any one of the three [plans] is that it would resegregate . . . the schools of . . . the entire city. If you count that [rising black enrollment in city schools] with the type of white flight that any one of these plans would cause, it would only be a matter of time until most of the areas of the city would be all black as the people move to adjoining communities and states to get out of what they would consider undesirable school situations."[39]

Legal appeals followed. Within weeks, a racially divided board filed a notice of appeal and a simultaneous motion to stay the court's order. They also requested certain modifications to the April judgment, particularly with regard to pupil transfers. Denied almost immediately by Judge McRae, the defendants applied to the court of appeals for a stay. Before the court complied and issued a temporary injunction, however, the board voted to delay entering into a pupil transportation contract with the low bidder, a private transportation company in Kansas City, Missouri. As late as July, they argued that an agreement could still be reached with the Memphis Transit Authority.[40]

The plaintiffs, believing this contract move to be a deliberate attempt to avoid compliance with the court's order, moved for a judgment of contempt against the defendants. Judge McRae denied their motion as well. They then filed in the court of appeals, requesting an expedited hearing and asking that the stay order be vacated. Over one dissent, the appeals court vacated the stay and directed the lower court to complete the desegregation process "in the minimum time required."[41]

The Sixth Circuit Court of Appeals affirmed Plan A on August 29 and ordered that it be implemented "forthwith." Nevertheless, the appellate court ruled that Plan A was only to be an interim measure, as it was still a constitutionally inadequate desegregation plan. Meanwhile, they mandated a "definite timetable" be established in order to accomplish a greater degree of desegregation.[42]

Shortly thereafter, the plaintiffs requested a conference with the district judge. That conference was held on September 5, 1972. On the following day, Judge McRae issued an order noting that the school year had already begun, yet directing the board to file a report by September 12 that would outline a proposed timetable for implementing Plan A. Additionally, the board was ordered to report any changes in the previous plan of operation which they had implemented without court approval.

The board complied and filed its September 12 report. In its report it requested that the implementation of Plan A be delayed pending a decision on its appeal. If the district court was to insist that the plan go forward, the board argued that it should be delayed until second semester for elementary grades and fall 1973 for secondary grades. Judge McRae ultimately ruled that implementation could be delayed until the second semester, with the exception of two senior high pairings. Nevertheless, the court disallowed certain modifications to Plan A that the board had implemented without the court's approval. A hearing was set for October 27 to determine how the board was succeeding in compliance with the court's mandate for a desegregation timeline. In a November 15 memorandum decision directing the board to prepare a pupil locator map, the district court noted that they envisioned a complete plan would be ready to implement at the start of the 1973–74 school year.

Meanwhile, a third-party complaint was filed against the City of Memphis when the board argued that the city's attempt to invoke an obscure 1935 transportation ordinance was primarily designed to obstruct the enforcement of Plan A. In a rare instance of agreement between the parties, both plaintiff and defendant joined in filing this request for relief. Judge McRae ruled that the 1935 ordinance was not applicable to school transportation, and that its attempted application was in fact an unconstitutional "antibusing" effort on the part of the city.[43]

Plan A, with only minor modifications, went into effect on January 24, 1973. Among other things, Plan A involved busing between 10,000 and 13,000 students, requiring forty-two buses. Bus purchase was estimated to cost roughly $1.5 million, as the Memphis City Schools did not even own a bus prior to Plan A.[44] On the first day of court-ordered busing, the *Commercial Appeal* noted that only about one-half of the designated students turned up to be bussed, and most of those who did were African American.[45] Nonetheless, city schools' transportation costs soon jumped from $51,000 to $524,000 per year.[46]

Judge McRae then gave the board a little more than a month to adopt a plan for further desegregation. On March 12, the board filed its additional plans—three for elementary education and two for secondary. At that time, they stated their preference for the approach that was the "least disruptive and least expensive means of accomplishing" a unitary system.[47]

In response to a joint complaint that spring by the board and the plaintiffs, the district court rendered a memorandum order holding that the City of Memphis had unconstitutionally withheld $250,000 from the board, the amount of the board's desegregation busing contract for the spring semester. The court ruled this to be a discriminatory and retaliatory action, based upon the unconstitutional application of two city antibusing ordinances.[48]

As the turbulent 1972–73 school year wore to a close, Judge McRae accepted a revised and more encompassing plan submitted by the board. The judge designated this as "Plan Z," and on May 3 he approved it, "in the hope that this will prove to be the terminal plan for this long-standing problem in the City of Memphis."[49] In doing so, the court rejected the plaintiffs' preference for another of the five board-proposed alternatives. The plaintiff's preferred plan would have resulted in greater desegregation, but with some increase in transportation times and distances.

Plan Z attempted to desegregate all but roughly two dozen of the city's westernmost schools, utilizing two-way busing. Elementary schools would continue to use pairing and clustering to determine which students would be bussed between which schools. Secondary schools would be desegregated by busing students within what came to be called "satellite zones."

This decision was met with many of the same concerns that had greeted the implementation of Plan A. From the antibusing side, there were serious concerns about white flight. Mayor Wyeth Chandler stated, "A sizable number of children will leave the system this year, and I think this new decision should be analyzed carefully by the city council with a view toward cutting the budget increases sought by the school board during the current budget hearings. I say this only in light of the fact that there will surely be a loss of students."[50]

To make things that much more complicated, a national oil crisis was sweeping the country in 1973. This meant gasoline needed for additional bus runs was in short supply. In an effort to force more collaboration between the board and the City of Memphis, Judge McRae issued a July 26 memorandum directing the city to share its gasoline with the board and directing both parties to cooperate in efforts to obtain additional gasoline from alternate sources. When the city again attempted to limit the board's gasoline supplies, another application to the district court was filed, resulting in additional orders from the court. On August 29, all parties entered into an agreement which finally resulted in the continued supply of gasoline to the board of education.

The lengthy stream of litigation surrounding the central elements of this case was winding to a close. In December, the court of appeals had affirmed a district court order enjoining the city from withholding funds in an attempt to interfere with the implementation of Plan Z. On April 22, the U.S. Supreme Court denied the plaintiffs' petition for certiorari seeking review of the court of appeals' decision affirming Plan Z. Plan Z then went into effect for the 1973–74 school year as planned.

Plan Z was to involve the busing nearly 40,000 Memphis students. This was a sizable number, but still short of the 57,000 the NAACP had originally requested. Some of the busing occurred between existing schools, while some resulted from redistricting. As for redistricting, a case in point was predominantly white East High School. Overwhelmingly black Lester High School was closed and those students were transferred to East, making the latter school much more evenly mixed by race.[51]

Judge McRae wavered some in 1976, however, quite possibly in light of the massive white flight that had already begun to limit the effectiveness of the busing orders. The judge decided that "newly annexed areas may legitimately be assigned to the nearest available desegregated school, and the court will not increase times and distances of transportation merely for the purpose of adjusting racial balance in some other schools." Several schools also came to be declustered when Judge McRae realized that more than two thousand students would have to be bussed just to bring in "a few dozen white students." For many involved, these decisions were seen as the beginning of the end for Plan Z.[52]

In the spring of 1977, the district court did determine that the plaintiffs were entitled to an award of costs, including attorneys' fees. Then in the last major decision in the *Northcross v. Board of Education* case, Judge McRae ruled for the plaintiffs in their opposition to the board's proposals to modify Plan Z. In a decision that included considerable criticism of the board, the court noted, "the defendant Board has consistently been reluctant to adopt the necessary means of effective desegregation," engaging in what the judge referred to as "deliberate acts favoring white students at the expense of the desegregation experience of black students." Judicial intervention in the form of Plan Z has been necessary "to correct the disparity which the defendants' ineffective plans had created." The judge concluded the nineteen-page decision by declaring that "there remains the affirmative duty to modify the plan in a manner that will eliminate the segregation which this Board caused by its action and inactions for many years before and after the *de jure* segregated schools were declared unconstitutional."[53]

After spending roughly $35 million on court-ordered school busing, these efforts were modified considerably and ultimately reduced, even though the schools remained more segregated than ever.[54] The desegregation order was in fact amended by consent decree on several occasions over the course of the two decades following adoption of Plan Z, often with little opposition. These generally involved incremental changes to student assignments, student transfer policies, transportation procedures, and optional school programs.

The most notable of these modifications occurred in 1982, with changes in policies and procedures significant enough that the court labeled them a

"Revised Plan of Desegregation." Reflecting more than three years of work by the biracial Plan Z Review Committee, most pairings and clusters were eliminated, leaving only a few satellite zones at the elementary level. In addition, the court imposed a five-year moratorium on contested proposals to change the plan. Judge McRae concluded that "because racial hostility in the community deprived Plan Z of some of its hoped-for effectiveness, steps had to be taken to modify Plan Z by removing the ineffective portions and thereby saving effort and expense."[55]

The history of Memphis school busing in many ways reflects why the system never did achieve racial integration. Many whites simply refused to be bussed. Interracial busing gradually disappeared not because the court lost its will to demand it, but far more because the system ran out of whites to bus and predominantly white schools to which to bus black students. When what remained was often black students being bussed across town to other black schools, both Memphis Mayor Wyeth Chandler and Dr. W. W. Herenton, school superintendent since 1978, concluded that continuing to bus was "asinine."[56] Gradually, the challenges came to an end. *Northcross v. Board of Education* faded away, even though Judge McRae never did officially declare the Memphis City Schools to have become a "unitary" system.[57]

In the end, only three types of busing continued. The Memphis City Schools continued to provide transportation for black students who at one time had been bussed to predominantly white schools for desegregation purposes, but now had no neighborhood schools to return to because their previous school had closed for lack of students. Douglass High School is an example. Transportation also was offered to students in "special education" categories, as required by state law, and to elementary students living in areas that required them to travel more than one and one-half miles in order to reach the school in their school zone—with a two mile radius for secondary students. As of 2004, fewer than 3 percent of the Memphis City School students were being bussed to school.[58]

The Educational Aftermath

Consistent evidence does exist in the Memphis City School System to support the contention that recent court-ordered desegregation decisions and the subsequent implementation of desegregation plans have contributed to rapidly increasing resegregation of the public school population—thus thwarting efforts to achieve the goal of meaningful integration.

—Dr. O. Z. Stephens, director, Division of Research and Planning, Memphis City Schools, 1976 [59]

Several important educational developments followed in the wake of court-ordered school busing for the purpose of desegregating the Memphis City Schools. These included a stunning degree of white flight, the emergence of a host of private school alternatives, and the evolution of the city's "optional school" attempt to stem at least some of the flight from the public school system. In the end, however, Memphis experienced a considerable amount of resegregation of its schools. Instead of being mandated by law, however, this time it came as the result of private decisions. The federal courts were not inclined to intervene. Like in much of the rest of the nation, school segregation returned to levels unseen since the 1960s.[60]

White Flight

The white flight phenomenon took several identifiable forms. Many whites chose to move from the city to the suburban areas outside the city limits, and whites new to the area often elected to live in the outlying suburbs instead of the city proper. Meanwhile, many of the whites who remained within the city's boundaries opted to attend one of the many private or parochial schools that began to spring up across the city.

Suburbanization. The twentieth century found Memphians moving from the central city to the outlying areas for many of the same reasons this phenomenon occurred throughout the United States. Pull factors included yards and trees, roomier housing, newer and more reputable schools, as well as the availability of governmental mortgage loans and individual methods of transportation. Beyond these incentives, there also were perceived push factors such as the city's deteriorating services, rising taxes, overall cost of living, accelerating blight, mounting crime rates, racial invasion of neighborhoods, and the fear of court-ordered school busing.[61]

The resulting numbers pretty much tell the story. To begin with, it should be noted that Shelby County encompasses the city of Memphis. Table 4 makes it clear that the entire area has been growing steadily in population over the past half century. Over that same period, the county's black population has drawn even in size with the area's white population. Then, with the rather sudden influx of Hispanics in the 1990s, Shelby County had a nonwhite majority by the year 2000. The eight-county Memphis metropolitan area has the highest black percentage of any of the nation's largest metropolitan areas, and it is poised to become the first to have a majority African American population.[62]

Thanks in large part to aggressive annexation, the city of Memphis actually has grown in population over the past half century. Table 5 suggests that this annexation has largely been a matter of the city drawing in predominantly white populations that chose to live outside the city limits. This is most evident in the

Table 4

Shelby County Measures, 1950–2000

	1950	1960	1970	1980	1990	2000
Total population	482,393	627,019	722,014	777,113	826,330	897,472
Square miles	NA	755	755	755	755	755
Black (%)	NA	36.3	36.8	41.7	43.6	48.6
Minority (%)	37.4	NA	37.1	42.5	44.9	52.7

fact that the city's minority population remained largely the same proportion of the overall city population as long as sizable annexations were occurring. When those annexations slowed in the 1980s, however, racial minorities quickly became a majority of the city's population.

The fact that Memphis successfully annexed outlying white enclaves in the 1950s, 1960s, and 1970s has not curbed white flight. Table 6 captures this phenomenon most clearly. Once annexation slowed in the 1980s, the outlying population grew and became more than 80 percent white. By 2000, Memphis ranked second to Detroit in terms of overall residential segregation.[63]

Just as the city's schools finally were forced to desegregate, more of the county's whites came to live outside the Memphis city limits. As Mayor Wyeth Chandler put it at the time, "busing has had an adverse effect on the city's population. There are a good number of people who are quite willing to move to Germantown or Bartlett and pay high taxes and pay the high price of homes in

Table 5

Memphis Measures, 1950–2000

	1950	1960	1970	1980	1990	2000
Total population	396,000	497,524	623,755	646,356	618,652	650,100
Square miles	104	129	217	264	256	279
Black (%)	37.2	37.0	38.9	47.6	54.8	61.4
Minority (%)	37.2	37.1	39.1	48.3	56.0	65.6

Table 6

Shelby County (outside Memphis) Measures, 1950–2000

	1950	1960	1970	1980	1990	2000
Population	NA	129,495	98,356	130,757	207,436	247,372
Square miles	NA	622	538	491	499	460
Black (%)	NA	33.6	23.5	12.5	10.2	15.0
Minority (%)	NA	33.7	24.6	13.3	11.8	18.8

order to save the money they would have spent to send their children to private schools."[64] Outside the city limits, their children could attend predominantly white Shelby County Schools without being subject to the possibility of a federal court busing order that might coerce their children back to the increasingly black Memphis City Schools. The U.S. Supreme Court cemented that barrier and spurred further out-migration, when it handed down its *Milliken v. Bradley* decision in 1974. *Milliken* prohibited federal district judges from ordering inter-district busing in order to achieve school desegregation.[65]

Not too surprisingly, these population shifts came to be reflected in the classrooms of the Memphis City Schools. Despite several major annexations, city school enrollment actually has declined since the early 1970s. From a peak "average daily attendance" of roughly 140,000 students in 1971, fewer than 110,000 remained as Plan Z got under way. The number hovered close to 100,000 from the latter 1970s until the sizable Hickory Hills area was annexed at the turn of the twenty-first century. With that annexation, the city schools added more than 15,000 students. Nonetheless, enrollment has been declining since then and has never begun to return to pre-busing levels.[66]

Now some of this student decline could well be a reflection of the baby boom phenomenon. Most of the baby boomers were born between 1945 and 1955, which meant they would be graduating from high school between 1963 and 1973. One then would expect school populations to decline thereafter, at least until the children of those same baby boomers began reaching school age. Table 4, however, reminds us that the overall population of Shelby County continued to grow throughout this period. It also should be noted that the school-age cohorts have been increasing faster than the population as a whole.[67]

An even more telling fact, however, is that despite all the annexation, the city school's share of the county's school population has declined considerably. Eighty-five percent of county residents attended Memphis City Schools at the outset of Plan A in 1973. That figure was down to 69 percent by 1999, just prior to the annexation of the Hickory Hills area. Yet, not only would city school enrollment decline, its racial composition also would change significantly.

City School Resegregation. Teacher desegregation began in 1966. To a large extent, it has been successful. By the 1990s, the teaching corps of the Memphis City Schools had come to be roughly half black and half white, relatively reflective of the city's population as a whole.

Far more striking is the reflection of the area's population shifts in the racial mix within the Memphis City Schools themselves. The city schools had a clear white majority until they gradually began to be desegregated in the early 1960s. Nevertheless, although the city's schools had a black majority from 1964 on, they still had roughly an equal number of black and white students as late as 1971. In April of that year, the U.S. Supreme Court sanctioned the use of court-ordered school busing in order to expedite the desegregation of the nation's public schools. Under court order, Memphis conformed. As discussed at length above, it began implementing "Plan A" in January of 1973, and Plan A was rather quickly succeeded by Plan Z.

Nearly ten thousand white students left the Memphis City Schools over the summer of 1972 alone. An additional group of more than seven thousand left between the end of the fall term that year and the actual court-required implementation of Plan A in January of 1973. Consequently, more than seventeen thousand white students had left the system in the seven months leading up to Judge McRae's first court-ordered school busing.[68] Nearly forty thousand would be gone by 1978, more than half the white students who had attended when the decade began.

These changes are equally dramatic when viewed from the perspective of the schools themselves. In the spring of 1973, just prior to the implementation of Plan Z the following fall, there were seventy-seven city schools with a white-student majority. The figure dropped from seventy-seven to thirty-two over the course of the next three years. Conversely, only twenty-six city schools had white populations of less than 20 percent at the onset of Plan Z, yet that figure jumped to sixty-four within three years.

Hillcrest High School provides a good case in point. Hillcrest had 695 white students and 374 black students as busing commenced in 1973. A portion of the school's white students were assigned to be bussed to a predominantly black school, while more black students were bussed into Hillcrest. By 1980, Hillcrest had 188 whites and 589 blacks. Conversely, predominantly black Hamilton High School was to receive 550 white students, most from the predominantly white Harding Academy area in east Memphis. By 1980, Hamilton had 22 white students. Melrose Junior High School, as another example, ended up with no

Fig. 1. Black students in Memphis City Schools, 1970–2005.

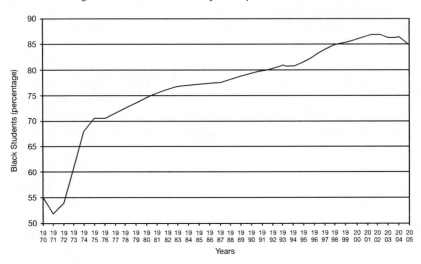

white students willing to ride the bus and was ultimately closed. Meanwhile, predominantly white Fox Meadows Elementary saw most of its white students leave, and it too was closed.[69]

In a four-year time period, the city school system lost nearly 40,000 white students, slowed only marginally by the annexations of predominantly white suburbs.[70] In addition, the city's black birth rate was nearly twice as high as the white birth rate.[71] By 1974, as indicated in figure 1, the city schools were more than 60 percent black. Two years later, they were more than 70 percent black. The number of white students dropped from 71,369 in 1973 to 27,173 by 1980.[72] By 1988, more than half of the Memphis City Schools had fewer than ten white students each.[73] Today the Memphis City Schools are roughly 90 percent minority, with black students comprising 85 percent and Hispanic students another 4 percent or more. Three-quarters of those schools have student populations that are at least 90 percent black, while approximately half the schools are at least 99 percent African American.

What this does not explain, however, is the whereabouts of all the white children still residing within the Memphis city limits. As Table 5 indicates, the city was more than 40 percent white in 1990, and still more than a third white in 2000. Whites, however, accounted for less than 20 percent of the student body in the Memphis City Schools. Where were the rest of those white students? Even accounting for the fact that many whites still living in the city may not have had school-aged children, it remains important to account for as many of the city's white students as possible.

School Options

> The white children of Memphis . . . have become a part of what
> has been termed the largest segregated "school system" in the
> South—the Memphis Private and Parochial School System.
>
> —O. Z. Stephens, "Induced Desegregation," 1976 [74]

Beginning in 1973, the federal courts ordered busing for the purposes of Memphis school desegregation. The ink had barely begun to dry on that order, however, when white students began leaving the city's public schools in droves.[75] There were soon roughly 100 private educational options within the Memphis city limits, in a city that had roughly 170 public schools. Private school enrollment nearly doubled, increasing by more than 14,000 students between 1972 and 1973. This was before Plan Z went into effect.[76]

Within a year, for example, groups such as CAB and Frayser Against Busing (FAB) had opened more than two dozen private schools, primarily in churches or at times in hastily rented buildings.[77] Often referred to simply as the "CAB schools," they quickly attracted as many as five thousand students. The schools were plagued almost immediately, however, with problems such as financial difficulties, few if any teacher standards, lack of accreditation, inadequate special education services, building safety issues, and little central administration.[78] Consequently, they provided only a temporary solution. Their attendance numbers shrank to 650 by the spring of 1974, and most did not reopen the following fall.[79]

In their place arose a host of more stable religious and secular private schools. Although labeled by many as the "white flight academies," it is impossible to determine precisely why each school was started.[80] Beyond the obvious impact of busing itself, the nation was experiencing a baby boom that inevitably led to some private school expansion. The 1960s also witnessed a growth of family affluence, which made private schools a more realistic option. In addition, the U.S. Supreme Court handed down its 1962 *Engel* decision outlawing teacher-led prayer in the nation's public schools. This provided additional stimulus for private school proliferation, especially in the Bible Belt, of which Memphis is a part.[81]

In an introductory letter entitled "Frayser Baptist Schools: A Dream in the Making," the impetus for those particular schools was described as "a deteriorating quality of education, a declining moral and spiritual atmosphere due to Supreme Court rulings banning prayer and Bible reading in the public schools, and the manipulation of children in sociological experimentation without the consent of parents." Auburndale's principal, Mrs. Stanley Smith, stated quite clearly that "this school is not soliciting people fleeing from busing. . . . Our students attend Auburndale because they feel it is the finest education in Memphis." Dr. Gary Roper, headmaster of the C. H. Spurgeon Academy, said his school was created not for escape from desegregation and busing, but because of a "difference in basic philosophy in the state school system and Christian education." Mrs. Shannon Glise of St. Agnes Academy found many of their parents wanting "a Christian environment, where there are religious studies and a religious atmosphere."[82]

Evan Jenkins of the *New York Times* described what had come to be called "segregation academies" in various cities across the country and "particularly notable in Memphis." As he described them, "The new schools appear to both backers and enemies to be capable of successful long-term competition with the public systems, urban-based, usually church-affiliated and tax exempt, willing to admit blacks in token numbers . . . promising to offer competent education."[83]

At one end of the spectrum, opposite the haphazardly assembled CAB schools, stood the ten members of the Memphis Association of Independent Schools. This organization had become formalized in 1956, and each of its members had been in existence prior to Plan A. These schools included St. Mary's Episcopal School (founded in 1847), St. Agnes Academy (1851), and the Hutchison School (1902), all women's academies. The others were Grace St. Luke's Episcopal (1919), Lausanne (1926), Presbyterian Day School (1949), Harding Academy (1952), Memphis University School (1954), St. Dominic School for Boys (1958), and Whitehaven Presbyterian (1969).

Several other private schools predated the beginning of desegregation in 1961 and the subsequent implementation of Plans A and Z. These included Christian Brothers High School (1871), Memphis Junior Academy (1910), Miss Lee's School (1924), Longview Heights Seventh Day Adventist School (1930), Mann Private School (1932), Memphis Hebrew Academy (1949), Trenor's Day School (1956), Holy Cross Lutheran (1957), Woodland Presbyterian (1957), Christ Methodist Day School (1958), and Christ the King Lutheran (1960).[84]

The Catholic Diocese of Memphis also had been operating schools well before the turmoil surrounding court-ordered public-school busing. The largest single source of private school options in the area, there were fifteen Catholic schools by the time Plans A and Z got under way. They were Bishop Byrne, Blessed Sacrament, Catholic, Deneuville Heights, Father Bertrand, Holy Rosary, Immaculate Conception, Little Flower, Our Lady of Sorrows, Saint Anne's, Saint John's, Saint Joseph's, Saint Louis, Saint Michael's, and Saint Paul's. Formally desegregated in the mid-1960s, the stated position of the diocese in 1973 was that "Catholic children are given first preference to the schools. The Catholic School System is integrated and will not be a haven for those who seek to escape integration."[85] As Superintendent Mary McDonald recently stated, "We were here long before there was ever such a thing as a bus."[86]

Lastly, a sizable group of private schools formed during desegregation and survived to the end of the 1980s or later, many still existing today. Thus, they lasted well beyond the demise of the ill-fated CAB schools and others like them. These included Bethel Baptist (1971), Calvary Temple (1975), Central Baptist (1975), Elliston Baptist (1972), Evangelical Christian School (1965), First Assembly Christian School (1972), The Frady School (1962), Frayser Academy of Christian Education (1972), Frayser Assembly Christian School (1973), Immanuel Lutheran (1974), Lamplighter Montessori (1967), Lutheran High (1975), Macon Road Baptist (1973), Memphis Preparatory School (1973), Oakhaven Baptist (1974), Randall Christian Academy (1972), Sky View Baptist (1973), Threshold Montessori (1973), and Southern Baptist Educational Center (1973).[87]

The Briarcrest Baptist Schools are arguably the most prominent of this latter group, quickly establishing a veritable private school system of their own. They opened in 1973, enrolling some 1,800 elementary and junior high students in eleven East Memphis church settings. By the following year, they had more than 2,200 students, a $6 million high school building, and one of the city schools' most reputable principals.[88]

Regardless of why any of the individual private schools chose to form, the timing of the white student exodus from the Memphis public schools to these private schools suggests at least part of the reasoning behind many of these families' decisions. Billy Stair, a research analyst for the Tennessee legislature's House Education Committee, noted that "when speaking privately, many parents confess that their decision to reject public education stems from a belief that the public schools no longer are providing adequate training, and apprehension over placing their children in an atmosphere of potential racial conflict. It is difficult not to believe that these two attitudes are primarily responsible for the resurgence of private education in Tennessee."[89]

The local newspaper noted that a "large number of church and private schools [have] started since the implementation of the busing plan."[90] Ray Jordan, writing for the Memphis *Commercial Appeal*, was even more direct as the events unfolded before his eyes. Jordan concluded, "The racial aspects of the public-vs.-private controversy are unavoidable. Most of Memphis private schools, whether they like to admit it or not, were set up to oppose busing."[91]

Around the time of Memphis desegregation, there also was a predictable proliferation of religious and private schools outside the Memphis city limits. Some of the more prominent and longer lasting of those schools were St. George's, the Auburndale School, and Rosemark Academy. Shorter lived were Eastdale Academy, Rossville Academy, Woodlawn Terrace Baptist, and Highway Baptist Academy. Although the exception and not the rule, Council Academy was opened by the Memphis Citizens Council, and Fayette Academy was openly discriminatory in its 1972 admissions policy, although prior to the U.S. Supreme Court's ruling concerning segregation at Bob Jones University.[92]

These suburban private schools enrolled roughly 3,000 students at the onset of desegregation. That number grew to some 3,600 students in the mid-1970s, before annexations began pulling a portion of those students back within the city's boundaries.[93] De Soto County, Mississippi, lies on the southern border of the city of Memphis, and it also added students during this upheaval. From the fall of 1972 to the fall of 1979, for instance, De Soto County's public school enrollment increased by some 3,700 students.[94]

Many of these private schools would not be long lived. To begin with there was the force of competition. There were more than one hundred private school options, many of which were well established and capable of expansion. There was concern about many of the new schools lacking accreditation and the impact that might have on their students' subsequent efforts to attend college. At the time of desegregation, new private schools did not have to be state accredited. They only had to submit their enrollment lists to the state and pass basic health and fire safety standards. Parents also rather quickly felt the cost of sending their children to private schools, especially when there was more than one school-aged child in the family.[95] Then, the city and state began to conduct safety inspections, which several private schools failed.[96] The state also began requiring competency examinations in all its schools.

In addition, tax code pressure was brought to bear in order to counter race discrimination in private schools. From the early 1970s, the position of the federal government was that an all-white private school could not continue to receive its federal tax exemption. By 1976, the IRS was reading this to mean that tax exemptions would be denied unless the private school had a clearly published nondiscriminatory admissions policy. Black plaintiffs challenged that interpretation as too lenient, however, and argued for some numerical goals or the showing of a good faith nondiscriminatory effort that went beyond a mere statement of policy. In Memphis, this battle was joined when black parents challenged the admissions efforts of the Briarcrest Baptist Schools.[97] Although the Briarcrest suit was ultimately dismissed on technical grounds, the subsequent U.S. Supreme Court opinion in the case of Bob Jones University did at least uphold the federal government's right to deny tax exemption to any school that refused to have a nondiscriminatory admissions policy, regardless of the religious views they claimed to justify such discrimination.[98] Coupled with the Supreme Court's 1976 opinion that allowed the federal government to outlaw racial discrimination in nonreligious private schools, this seemed to settle the primary legal questions surrounding government's right to attack overt racial discrimination in private schools.[99] The federal government did not always share this priority, however. In the 1980s, for instance, the Reagan administration returned to allowing tax exemption for private schools that discriminated on the basis of race.[100]

The majority of the private schools survived and continued to thrive, even after the last bus had rolled for the purpose of school desegregation. The number of Memphis children in private schools was just over 13,000 in 1970. It jumped to 33,000 during the tumultuous 1973–74 school year and reached its peak at 35,300 in 1974–75. There are still more than 100 private schools enrolling nearly 30,000 students today. The Catholic Diocese, for instance, currently enrolls more than 8,000 students, its highest enrollment since 1976.[101]

When all the county's private schools are combined, some 15 percent of the area's schoolchildren are currently enrolled in a private school at tuitions that can rise to more than $15,000 per year. That private-school enrollment figure is somewhat higher than the national average of 11 percent. When recently questioned, private school parents listed smaller classes, more discipline, and "academic atmosphere" as primary reasons they had opted for those schools.[102]

Countywide Resegregation. The overall result of white flight to the suburbs and to private schools has been a considerable resegregation of area schoolchildren. While the Memphis City Schools are nearly 90 percent black, at least 80 percent of local white students now attend either a Shelby County School or a private school.[103] The Shelby County Schools remained racially segregated until successfully sued by black parents in 1963. Initially more than one-third black, they have remained between 20 and 30 percent black despite the sizable infusion of white students following court-ordered busing in the early 1970s.[104] Meanwhile, the area's private schools have remained far more segregated yet, hovering between 95 and 97 percent white.[105] Thus, in the three decades since Plans A and Z took effect, most local black students now attend overwhelming black schools and most local white students attend overwhelmingly white schools.

It also should be noted that religious schools across the United States are often more racially segregated than the nation's public schools. Secular private schools, on the other hand, are actually less so.[106] In Memphis, most all the private schools are overwhelmingly white, even though the city now has a sizable black majority. The Catholic Diocese recently opened three Jubilee Schools in inner-city Memphis, but those predominantly black student bodies are clearly the exception in terms of Memphis private schools taken as a whole.

Optional Schools

> The teachers love it. The NAACP Defense Fund loves it. . . . The taxpayers like it in Memphis because it reduced by $2 million a year the amount of money they had to spend on cross-town busing. They spend that on academic things now.
>
> —Gov. Lamar Alexander, *Commercial Appeal,* 1989

One of the more enduring attempts to accomplish a semblance of racial integration in the Memphis City Schools has been the optional school program, although it was never explicitly proffered as an alternative to court-ordered busing. The basic idea was to create high caliber schools that would specialize in either academic, artistic, or vocational subject areas. These would be either freestanding schools or schools within existing schools. The program is tuition-free to all city students meeting the particular school's academic prerequisites. First priority goes to those living in the school zone and second to those transferring from other city schools. Students from outside the city are eligible to apply for any remaining slots on a tuition basis. Flexible racial quotas have been established within each program, although only a handful of the optional programs have been regularly oversubscribed.[107] In the summer of 2007, the U.S. Supreme Court barred virtually all uses of race in determining a student's school assignment. It remains to be seen what impact this will have on the Memphis optional program.[108]

The Memphis optional school experiment began in 1976 as one of the many consent agreements between the plaintiffs and the board. Initially it comprised four schools. One was a special program focusing on performing arts at Overton High School, while the others were accelerated academic programs at Bellevue and Snowden Junior High Schools and Central Senior High. Assisted with sizable grants from the federal government and the Ford Foundation, the program then grew to more than thirty such schools enrolling more than 12,000 Memphis-area students, including more than 6,000 transfer students. Enrollment peaked in the mid-1990s at just under 13,000 and hovers at slightly more than 11,000 today.[109]

These schools have provided attractive educational alternatives and have allowed the city's public schools to compete with area private schools for some of the most talented students available. Their popularity is evident by the long lines of parents who have assembled each year to vie for available openings.[110] The ability of the optional schools to lure large numbers of whites back into the Memphis City Schools, however, has been somewhat limited. From the program's outset, whites regularly comprised just over 40 percent of optional-school enrollment, providing less than a third of that enrollment today. Meanwhile, the bulk of those white students who transferred chose either Grahamwood or White Station, each of which was predominantly white to begin with and was located in a predominantly white neighborhood. Those two schools and the more recently added suburban Cordova School are the only optional programs with white majorities, or anywhere near white majorities. Combined, they enroll nearly three-quarters of all white students currently in the optional system.

The history of Grahamwood Elementary School is instructive. Located in a largely white residential neighborhood, it was originally paired with predominantly black East Elementary. Students were bussed between the two schools for desegregation purposes. Grades one through three were assigned to Grahamwood, and grades four through six to East. Both schools rather quickly became more than 80 percent black. When busing was all but eliminated, an optional school-within-a-school was added at Grahamwood. Most all the transfer applications, however, came from whites in other city school districts, leaving Grahamwood two-thirds white by the end of the 1980s. For whatever reason, black students chose not to transfer to that predominantly white school, while whites chose it over an array of predominantly black alternatives. Grahamwood remained predominantly white, its optional program almost entirely white. Meanwhile, the Memphis City Schools as a whole retained more white students then they might well have been able to retain, but this did not necessarily mean that many more white and black students were experiencing an integrated school day.

Economic Segregation

Before moving on to measures of school quality, there is one additional educational aftermath to explore. We have seen the impact of white flight on the racial composition of the Memphis City Schools. It is also important to explore whether it is a socioeconomic cross-section of students who have chosen to leave. Other than the social implications of remaining racially segregated, the fact that city's public schools may have gotten progressively blacker does not in and of itself portend negative educational consequences. Given the correlations between family income and school progress, however, there is grounds for concern if the Memphis City Schools contain a much more economically disadvantaged student body.

Existing indices do indeed suggest increasing impoverishment. Students currently are eligible for federally subsidized school meals if their family incomes do not exceed a fixed percentage of the federal government's "poverty level." This makes the percentage of children eligible for this subsidy a reasonable indicator of the overall poverty level of the student population.[111] Where fewer than 40 percent of Memphis public school students received that subsidy in 1971, roughly three in four qualify for subsidized meals today. Meanwhile, the comparable figure for Shelby County School students has not been exceeding 15 percent in any given year.[112] Therefore, the city school district has five times as many students eligible for this subsidy as does the surrounding county school district. In light of the empirical studies cited, such impoverishment does not bode well for Memphis City Schools.[113]

The limitations of the optional school program aside, it has helped Memphis City Schools retain talented white and black students they may have lost to private schools or to the suburban Shelby County Schools. The program has not, however, contributed to a major reversal of white flight from the system that has continued since the days of Plans A and Z. Court-ordered school busing failed to integrate the Memphis City Schools, and, like in many other cities across the country, it has left them even more segregated in terms of both race and class than before it was implemented.[114] Yet, Memphis busing advocate Maxine Smith notes at least one ray of hope resulting from the busing ordeal: "There was a great discrepancy in supplies, teachers and everything. . . . We wanted to receive the same benefits for our school system as did other children. . . . Our [main] point never was to have our children sit next to white children. . . . Funds followed white children, and we wanted to follow the funds. . . . We struggled for equity in education that should have come down without busing."[115]

Political scientist Dr. Peter Irons remains skeptical. In his book *Jim Crow's Children: The Broken Promise of the Brown Decision*, he studied educational developments in the five communities involved in the landmark 1954 *Brown* decision, as well as in the twenty-five largest school districts in the country. Not one of the largest twenty-five districts had a white majority, and one-third of them were more than 90 percent black. He also notes considerable differences in quality between the schools attended by black and white children. He concludes that there is a new wall of separation between black and white children, leaving black schools separate, unequal, and failing.[116]

In *The Price They Paid: Desegregation in an African-American Community*, Curtis and Vivian Morris note many of the same results in Tuscumbia, Alabama. They argue that black schools got worse following the desegregation battles, and black students ended up paying a huge price in terms of lower achievement and poorer subsequent job opportunities. They also contend that "the mere fact of closing down poorly equipped, segregated buildings and having Black kids sit next to White kids in desegregated buildings does not ensure that they are getting a good education."[117]

Chapter 5

Educational Results

I would submit that quality education can take place in all-black schools.

—Mayor W. W. Herenton

[Busing] has turned the Memphis educational system from a Grade A system to a Grade D, or possibly an F.

—Mayor Wyeth Chandler

Memphis exhibits symptoms of having become a postindustrial city. Although it always has been more of a trading center than a manufacturing hub, the mechanization and mobility of industries have left most of the city's lesser-skilled workers employed in the services rather than in the more promising unionized factory jobs. As a result, the city's racial and ethnic ghettos appear to have become repositories for a sizable number of extremely poor residents with very limited job prospects. In addition, the city has experienced a considerable degree of racial separation. Many whites have fled to the outlying areas, and annexation is no longer being used to maintain white dominance. As a result, Memphis has evolved into a city with a clearly established African American majority, with solid black control over all of its major governmental entities, including its school board. At the very least, this level of political incorporation should helping to ensure that the interests of the city's African American community are finally receiving equal consideration in the city's governmental decisions.[1]

Measures of Quality

There is little doubt that a widespread panic followed court-ordered school bus-ing designed to hasten the desegregation of the Memphis City Schools in the early 1970s. Thus, the early 1970s represent a key historical turning point and a logical place to begin when analyzing the evolution and current state of the city's schools.

Shelby County is composed of the city of Memphis as well as surround-ing suburbs and unincorporated areas. Consequently, county residents share the same basic geographical space, and their schools are bound by the same state curricular and achievement requirements. Within the county lie two dis-tinct school districts, existing under the watchful eye of the federal courts after years of racial segregation. One district is the Memphis City Schools, drawing its students from the city of Memphis itself. The other is the Shelby County Schools, drawing students from the various suburbs and unincorporated areas surrounding the center city.

On the face of it, the most glaring differences between the districts are their size and demography. The Memphis City Schools is the largest school sys-tem in the state of Tennessee, and one of the largest in the country. It seeks to educate some 120,000 students in more than 190 graded school buildings, spending roughly $1 billion per year doing so. Its county schools counterpart is scarcely more than a third that size. Demographically, the Memphis school dis-trict has become overwhelmingly African American and contains a far poorer student population than does its far whiter and less poverty-stricken suburban counterpart.

This study compares the poor and heavily black Memphis public schools to the far less poor and disproportionately white Shelby County public schools. It also attempts to isolate the impact of poverty by comparing a select group of very poor black city schools to a less poor group of black city schools. The pri-mary difference between the two sets of schools, then, are their degree of pov-erty. Measures for the city and county schools and the poor and less poor select city schools are drawn from the best available data that could be compiled from 1970 to 2005. Specifically, these comparisons are based on trends in educational input components such as spending per student, student-teacher ratios, aver-age teacher education, average teacher experience, and average teacher salaries. The measures also include trends in educational output components (results) such as achievement scores, student attendance, failure rates, and disciplinary actions.

There are numerous empirical challenges, however, when studying educa-tional trends over time. When the schools compile their data, definitions get changed and new compilation methods or formulas get implemented. Tests are administered to different grades, at different times of the year, and differing proportions of students may choose to take some of the optional exams.[2] Existing records are often compiled and maintained in separate offices and then warehoused in relatively inaccessible ways after a given number of years. In addition, if it was not required by the state or federal governments, the annual compilation of various records may or may not have occurred, or the records may or may not have been retained after a certain period of time. Beyond that, there is the possibility of underreporting and overreporting, as well as data manipulation such as data slanting, prompting during achievement tests, and encouraging weaker students to stay home at achievement test time.[3]

It is particularly tough to measure educational trends when there are so many underlying historical events, each with their own unique impacts on those trends. Populations shift. District lines change. The state's "zero tolerance" discipline policy effected school suspension rates by establishing mandatory penalties for various offenses beginning with the 1996–97 school year. The 1992 Better Education Program, established under the Tennessee Education Improvement Act, requires increased expenditures to reduce student teacher ratios, as well as a more systematic testing regimen that includes standardized Tennessee Comprehensive Assessment Program (TCAP) testing.[4] Then there are the array of new initiatives designed to help the state comply with the federal No Child Left Behind legislation. Such empirical difficulties definitely impede the ability to precisely gauge educational trends over the long term. Thus, the input and output measures used in this study are suggestive and not definitive of long-term trends.

Input Measures

The educational input measures in this study are spending per student, students-per-teacher ratios, average teacher education, average teacher experience, and average teacher salaries. All monetary amounts have been standardized by converting them to 2000 dollars using the federal cost-of-living index. Thus, they will be reported here as "constant (2000) dollars." Student enrollment is the year-end average daily attendance (ADA) number whenever available.[5] Spending per student is calculated by dividing school-reported current operating expenditures by the total number of enrolled students. The student-to-teacher ratio is the ADA enrollment figure divided by the number of teachers in the system. Average teacher education, experience, and salary use the compilations reported to the state.

Expenditures per Pupil. There has been a relatively steady increase in constant dollar-per-pupil expenditures for the Memphis City Schools. It has nearly tripled since 1970. As shown in figure 2, such spending edged upward in constant dollars, with exceptional increases in the early 1970s and late 1990s.[6]

Fig. 2. Expenditures per pupil, 1970–2005.

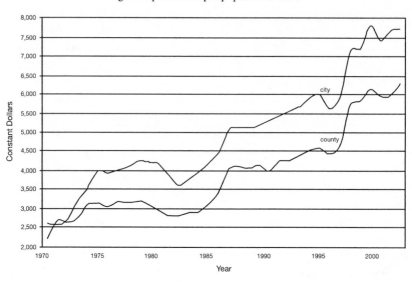

The earliest surge can be largely explained by the growth of transportation costs related to court-ordered school busing. The city schools, for example, spent only two-tenths of 1 percent of their operating expenditures on transportation in 1970. By 1975 they spent more than 2 percent, and it was more than 3 percent by 1980. Meanwhile, county school transportation spending increased from 4 to 5 percent of their total operational spending. These latter figures represent the more rural nature of the outlying areas served by the county school system, requiring a greater reliance on busing in order to get students to school. Transportation expenditures, then, explain some but not all of the city increases vis-à-vis their county counterparts.

The very latest jump can be explained in part by last-minute compliance with mandates of the state and federal governments, especially the need to meet externally imposed limits for student-to-teacher ratios. City school increases also reflect transitional costs related to adding the more than six thousand students in the annexed Hickory Hills area, including increased funding for textbooks, equipment, school nurses, and an employee assistance program.[7]

Meanwhile, most people in the area's more affluent suburban neighborhoods send their children to the Shelby County Schools. Although the county system actually spent slightly more per pupil in 1971, it has gradually come to spend roughly 20 percent less per pupil than its city schools counterpart, only a portion of which can be explained by expanded city spending on student transportation. At the very least, the greater Memphis area does not appear to have been underfunding its inner-city schools in relation to what it spends on its suburban schools.

Beyond a sizable operational budget, the city schools also have received millions of dollars in capital monies. Capital spending has allowed the city schools to have all its classrooms wired for Internet connections, as well as gaining facilities such as the nation's first public school "Teaching and Learning Academy" and the state's only public school "Telecommunications Center" for radio and television production. Such capital revenue has been available, in part, because Tennessee's average daily attendance funding formula requires counties to spend funds proportionately across the county. Thus, for every capital dollar raised and spent on the county schools, three dollars have to be raised and transferred to the city schools, where there are three times as many students. As the county has struggled to build schools fast enough to keep up with out-migration, the city schools have received a windfall of capital revenues from the county government, besides capital funds appropriated by the City of Memphis.[8]

What all of this does not take into consideration, however, is the particular educational needs of the two student bodies. The city of Memphis has a very indigent student population overall. This may well mean that those students come to school with greater academic needs because of less educationally enriched home environments. They also may suffer disproportionately from problems such as learning disabilities due to less prenatal care or poorer childhood nutrition. If that is true, then it is possible that the city schools need to spend even more than they are proportionate to the county just to maintain a level playing field.[9] Federal research has indicated that it costs roughly 40 percent more to educate a low-income student as opposed to a middle-income student.[10]

The special needs of the city school student body, however, are not borne out by the number of students with learning-related disabilities requiring special education. Those students number roughly nine thousand in Shelby County and fifteen thousand in the Memphis City Schools—or 21 percent of the county's overall student body and only 13 percent of the city's.[11] Unless the city school students are being seriously undertested, their higher level of poverty, and any prenatal and nutritional problems that implies, does not seem to have translated into noticeably greater special education needs.

Students per Teacher. As figure 3 indicates, there has been a small but steady decline in the student-to-teacher ratio in both the city and the county schools. Part of that decline can be explained by a combination of the state's Better Education Program and by federal mandates,[12] but the ratio had been trending downward prior to the full impact of those laws. This trend suggests a more manageable workload for the teacher and better quality of education.

As with expenditures per pupil, the Memphis City Schools have at least a slightly more desirable input measure. The city school student-to-teacher ratio stood at roughly twenty-one students per teacher just prior to desegregation. It has declined considerably since then, approaching roughly fourteen students

Fig. 3. Students per teacher, 1970–2005.

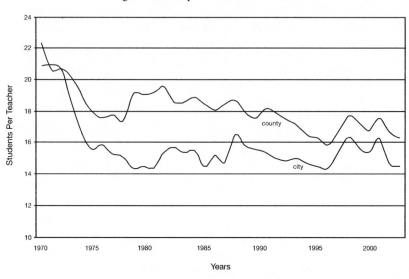

per teacher at present. The comparable numbers are twenty-one and sixteen for the county schools. However, this analysis does not take into consideration the particular educational needs of the far more indigent student body attending the Memphis City Schools.

Teacher Training. Using total years of college education as an indicator of teaching quality, there also have been improvements. Figure 4 indicates that the average years of college education have been increasing steadily for teachers in both school systems. The average teacher now has more than a year's worth of education beyond a bachelor's degree. This city school input measure also remains slightly higher than that found in the county schools. City school teachers have consistently had slightly more college training than their county counterparts. This measure, of course, provides no indication of the selectivity of the college attended or how well the instructor performed academically while in college.

As a cross-check, I considered the proportion of teachers who had no college work beyond a bachelor's degree, since the average years of education may not be as significant as the number of instructors teaching without having graduated from college. This measure serves only as an estimate of that latter figure, however, as the schools did not separately report the number of teachers without a degree. All teachers in both systems had at least a B.A. degree by 1987, although a few exceptions were made in subsequent years in the face of teacher shortages.[13] In 2000, for instance, roughly 17 percent of the active teachers were not fully certified to be teaching what they were teaching.[14]

In figure 5 there is improvement across the board. Teachers in both systems continued to become more likely to have postgraduate education. Where roughly

Fig. 4. Teachers' average years of college education, 1970–2000.

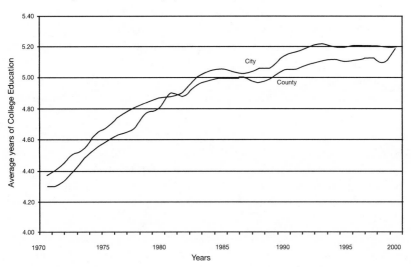

three-quarters of all city and county teachers had a B.A. degree or less in the early 1970s, that figure shrunk to fewer than one-half by the 1990s. Conversely, the majority of teachers in both systems now have taken coursework beyond the B.A. degree. And, although the city schools enjoyed a slight advantage until the late 1990s, there has essentially been parity since then. The city schools were actually beginning to lose ground early in the twenty-first century, but state and federal demands for certified teachers seem to have corrected that slippage.

Fig. 5. Percent of teachers with a B.A. degree or less, 1970–2005.

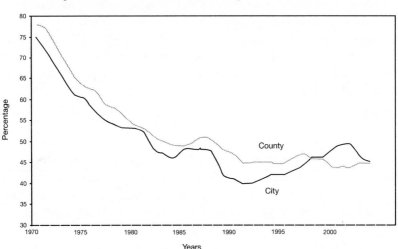

Teacher Experience. Although not reported as consistently over time, the measures that do exist are contradictory. Where city school teachers exhibited more college training than teachers in the county, as a group they also appear to be somewhat less experienced. More of the city's teachers have fewer than four years of teaching experience. In the one directly comparable year, 1992, 12 percent of the county teachers had fewer than four years of experience, while the comparable number was 16 percent for the city. The city's proportion doubled across the 1990s to one in three city teachers. Meanwhile, the number has actually been declining in the county. That means city teachers are now roughly three times more likely to be minimally experienced. At the other end of this experience continuum, however, only 5 percent of county teachers have taught for thirty years or more, while that figure is 11 percent for city teachers.

Overall, then, the limited data available suggest that the Memphis City Schools have a disproportionate number of new teachers, as well as teachers who have taught for thirty years or more. Nevertheless, the relatively high percentage of lesser experienced teachers in the city schools suggests a growing difficulty retaining new teachers. And given that tenure allows teachers more choice in where they teach, high turnover would seem more likely to occur in the city's least desirable schools.[15]

Teacher Salaries. Until recently, city teachers were paid less than their county counterparts.[16] When comparing teachers with the same levels of education and experience, the county pay scale was higher. Nonetheless, the two pay scales have gradually been brought into parity. The starting salary for a new teacher in the Memphis City Schools, for example, equals that of the Shelby County Schools. It was $36,107 in 2004–5, essentially identical to the county schools.

Meanwhile, as figure 6 indicates, the average salaries in the city and county schools have been similar. Both lost ground during the high inflation years between 1975 and 1985, but they have increased in real dollars over time.[17] The average city teacher has consistently been paid a bit more than his or her county counterpart, given that the city's teachers have more formal education and experience. The city schools are now having a harder time retaining experienced teachers, and larger salaries may be needed to hire and retain high quality new teachers.

Output Measures

The educational output measures to be reviewed are achievement scores, student attendance, graduation rates, failure rates, and disciplinary actions. The attendance rate is calculated by taking the average number of students attending on any given day and dividing it by the average number of students enrolled at that time. Suspensions are disciplinary actions where a student is not allowed to

Fig. 6. Average teacher salary (constant dollars), 1970–2002.

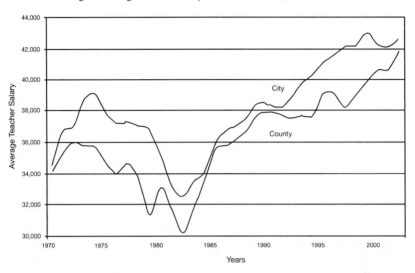

attend class for a specific amount of time, not to exceed ten days, but remains on the school rolls. Graduation rates reflect the percentage of students who graduate within four years of starting high school. Failure rates are the percentage of students not promoted in a given year. The measures of achievement are American College Test (ACT) test scores and the percentage of ninth grade students passing their Tennessee proficiency exams on the first try, as well as TCAP and Value-Added scores in reading, language arts, math, science, and social studies.[18]

Attendance. As can be seen in figure 7, county school attendance rates have been far more consistent than city school rates over time. And, with only a couple of exceptions, they have been consistently higher. The attendance rates for the city schools have varied considerably, with no obvious explanation. Major annexations appear to correspond to significant upturns. North Raleigh was annexed in 1976, just prior to that jump. Hickory Hills was annexed in 2000, but the upswing had already begun before that. Meanwhile, no annexations can explain the surge in the mid-1980s. Higher attendance mandates from the state under the 1992 Education Improvement Act would seem to explain the most recent surge.

One thing figure 7 masks is the fact that there is a considerable difference between the attendance rates of lower school and upper school students. This is less true for the county schools, where K–6 attendance rates generally run even or just slightly above those for the district as a whole. Far more noticeable is that the K–6 attendance rates for the city schools tend to run 2 to 3 percentage

Fig. 7. Attendance rates (K–12), 1970–2002.

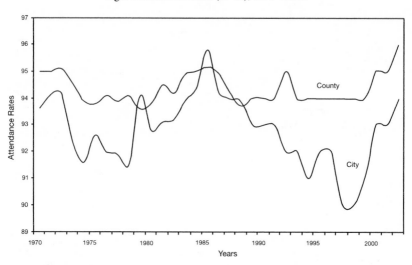

points higher than the district overall. That reality cuts the attendance difference between the city and county schools nearly in half for those grades. Thus,
there is an attendance differential, but it is one that increases considerably in the
upper grades.

Bob Archer, associate superintendent of Memphis City Schools, explained
the notably higher attendance rates in the lower grades. "Parents are more
involved in getting their kids to schools at that age, so we see higher attendance.
But the higher you go up into middle and high school, you see those attendance
rates drop."[19] Peer influence and other factors external to family and school
intervene to an increasing extent as the student gets older.

The federal government upped the ante by including relatively stringent
attendance requirements in the 2002 No Child Left Behind Act. Despite the
existence of these requirements in February of 2003, the Memphis City Schools
still had seventy schools that did not meet the attendance requisite, and at least
twenty schools with attendance rates that were less than 90 percent.[20] Figure 7
shows some improvement in city schools attendance of late, but that attendance
level continues to lag behind the comparable rate for the Shelby County Schools
and will obviously be monitored closely by the state and federal governments.

Disciplinary Action. Not lost on parents of school-age children are the incidents
of crime and disruptive behavior in the nation's public schools. Besides high
profile incidents like the one at Columbine High School in Colorado, a 2001
U.S. Department of Education study found "students in public schools nationwide were about twice as likely to be victims of rape, sexual assault, robbery, or

aggravated assault as students in private schools."[21] In response, Congress passed the 1994 Gun-Free Schools Act. It required states to adopt zero-tolerance laws with the goal of producing gun-free schools. Noncompliant states risked losing federal Elementary and Secondary Education Act (ESEA) funds. Most states, including Tennessee, went beyond this focus on guns and decided to apply zero tolerance to a wide variety of disciplinary infractions in an attempt to standardize discipline and reduce violence in general.[22] Students also have become more apt to be arrested for offenses that previously would have been handled by school officials. Tennessee appropriated $10 million in 1999 and another $5.6 million the following year to fund such things as security cameras, metal detectors, and more uniformed officers to patrol higher-risk schools.[23]

All of this was implemented, despite the fact that zero tolerance hindered administrators' ability to address marginal incidents, and school suspension has been found to be a moderate to strong predictor of a student's dropping out of school.[24] Nonetheless, with a combination of zero tolerance, metal detectors, more security officers in schools, and antibullying measures, school violence did appear to decline markedly nationwide over the course of the 1990s.[25] Yet, there also have been published incidents of underreporting in Gwinett County, Georgia, as well as in Houston, Roanoke, New York, and Memphis.[26]

Until fairly recently, the Memphis City Schools reported suspension incidents representing between 6 and 12 percent of their student body. The county numbers have normally been slightly lower, at least until very recently when the county rates caught and at times slightly exceeded those in the city. The state adoption of a zero-tolerance rule in the mid-1990s, however, makes it difficult to know if there are more instances of serious misbehavior now, or if there are simply more suspensions being meted out for behavior that has been occurring all along. Nevertheless, the overall number of disciplinary actions has risen noticeably over time. In 2005, for instance, the city schools either suspended or expelled nearly 22 percent of its student body, while the comparable figure for the county schools was only 7 percent.[27]

A point of controversy in recent years has been the fact that African American students have been suspended at a higher rate than their white counterparts. In the 1999–2000 school year, for instance, the Memphis City Schools suspended 6.6 percent of their black students, while that number was only 2.9 percent for whites. There also has been a difference in the types of offenses for which black students drew their suspensions. Blacks were far more likely to be suspended for violence or intimidation, while white suspensions tended to be more related to tardiness, cutting class, and tobacco use.[28]

It should be noted, however, that most of the administrators delivering these disciplinary measures in Memphis were African Americans. In addition, such racial discrepancies are not unique to Memphis. For example, those figures were 25 percent and 12 percent nationally; 10.7 and 5.3 statewide; 20.0 and 10.0 in Nashville; 20.0 and 8.4 in Knoxville; 12.7 and 6.2 in Chattanooga; and 8.8 and 3.5 in Shelby County.[29]

Sam Anderson, then the lone African American on Tennessee's Knox County school board, voiced concern. He stated, "It's not something new. . . . This is a major problem for my community and my district and for all African Americans in Knox County and their parents. . . . It's hard to improve test scores if you're suspending kids at that kind of rate."[30]

Citing the disproportionate number of African American students who have been expelled, the American Bar Association approved a resolution in February of 2001 that challenged the inflexibility of zero tolerance. The resolution opposed "policies that have a discriminatory effect, or mandate either expulsion or referral of students to juvenile or criminal court, without regard to the circumstances or nature of the offense or the student's history."[31]

Failure Rates. The graduation rate is typically almost 90 percent in the Shelby County Schools, but only around 65 percent in the Memphis City Schools. That means nearly four out of every ten city students will fail to attain a high school diploma at the end of four years, a figure that approaches 50 percent or more for black males. It is also a rate that is more than three times higher than in the county schools.

Beneath such failure-to-graduate figures often lie a string of academic failures, in this case meaning the student did not do well enough to advance to the next class. With only a few exceptions in the 1970s, failure rates have been consistently higher in the Memphis City Schools. Yet, as indicated in figure 8, both the city and county failure rates seem to have peaked in the latter 1980s, and both have come down steadily since.[32] We also see the absolute gap diminish, although the city school failure rate remains roughly twice that of the county schools.

When focusing on grades K–6, there were some additional variations. In both systems, the failure rate in the elementary grades tends to be considerably lower, at least until recently, when state and federal pressure seem to have driven up the elementary failure rate in the Memphis City Schools. Relatively speaking, however, the city's elementary school failure rate remains roughly five times higher than that found in the county. Nevertheless, as with attendance, the city schools seem to have been able to meet most of the higher state standards imposed by the 1992 Education Improvement Act.

Achievement. It is virtually impossible to track achievement score trends across a thirty-year time period. The schools continually choose new exams, test different classes, and report results in different ways. In addition, as with most school

Fig. 8. Failure rates (K–12), 1970–2002.

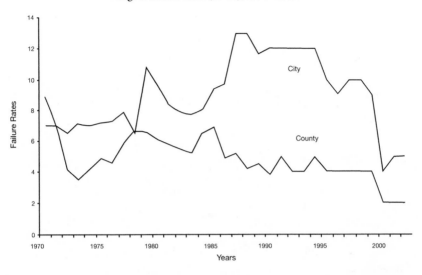

data, if it is required to be filed with the state or federal government, there will be a written record. If such filings are not required, maintenance of such records normally ends up spotty at best. The main challenge, then, is to find tests that actually have been administered consistently over a period of time and their results reported in a consistent manner. We are left, then, more with indicators then precise measures of this educational factor over time.

Although no attempt has been made to assess city and county achievement score trends over time, four recent measures have been chosen to analyze variations in achievement between the city and county schools, and later between select city schools, at select junctures. First, we will look at seven years worth of standardized (TCAP) test scores in reading, language arts, math, science, and social studies for students in the third, fourth, and fifth grades, which will provide a snapshot of how the city and county students compare at a specific period in time. Second, we will compare educational progress over the course of a school year, by analyzing value-added measures. This should better indicate how much each group of students gained from their collective education that year. Third, we will compare the percentage of city and county ninth grade students passing their Tennessee proficiency exams on the first try. Lastly, we will compare the ACT scores of senior high school students in each school system.

Table 7 examines average TCAP percentile scores for third, fourth, and fifth graders. The Memphis City Schools are compared to the Shelby County Schools from 1996 to 2002, the only directly comparable data available. County averages hover around the seventieth percentile, with little variation from subject to subject or from grade to grade. The very highest are the early language arts

Table 7

City vs. County TCAP Percentile Averages, 1996–2002

TCAP average	Shelby County	Memphis	Difference
Reading			
Grade 3	67	39	28
Grade 4	67	38	29
Grade 5	68	35	33
Language arts			
Grade 3	72	46	26
Grade 4	73	44	29
Grade 5	69	42	27
Math			
Grade 3	69	46	23
Grade 4	71	42	29
Grade 5	70	42	28
Science			
Grade 3	69	33	36
Grade 4	69	34	35
Grade 5	68	35	33
Social studies			
Grade 3	68	37	31
Grade 4	67	37	30
Grade 5	66	38	28

scores, with a very minimal drop-off from fourth to fifth grades in all but reading. City averages run roughly 30 percentile points lower. City students start furthest behind in science, and that turns out to be the one subject area where they narrow the gap a small bit each year they are in school. They actually lose ground to their county counterparts in reading, language, and math as they move from third to fifth grade, although the latter two are their highest scoring subjects overall and the ones in which they are slightly less far behind.

Value-Added Scores. There are two main value-added achievement measures reported each year for Tennessee's public schools. The first measure is the per-

Table 8
K–5 National Norm Gain (Percentages), 1999–2001

Average gain	Shelby County	Memphis	Difference
Reading	115.1	105.2	9.9
Language arts	86.9	76.5	10.4
Math	111.7	95.3	16.4
Science	108.7	114.9	6.2
Social studies	110.9	106.3	4.6

centage of national-norm gain in math, reading, language, social science, and science. This represents how much the students gained compared to what the average student gained nationally over the course of that academic year. A score of 100 percent would mean those students were gaining approximately as much as the average student gained nationwide.[33]

Table 8 presents the K–5 value-added averages for the 2000 and 2001 academic years, the only years when directly comparable elementary school scores were available. The county students almost always gained more than the national average, while the city students were less likely to do so. Nonetheless, city student progress in the elementary grades exceeded the national average in reading, social studies, and science, and it actually exceeded the county in science. In addition, there are no differences between city and county students as extreme as found in the TCAP scores. This suggests that the city students' annual progress rate is closer to that of the county students, while once again emphasizing how much further behind the city students are when they begin school. Taken together, the combination of TCAP and Value-Added scores tells us that city students start out at a lower place. They also tend to gradually fall further behind as the years go by, given that they do not progress as quickly as their county counterparts.

Table 9 presents the K–12 value-added averages for the 1994 through 1997 academic years, the only years when directly comparable K–12 scores were available. The differences suggest that city student progress falls further behind the national norm as students get into middle school and high school, and the progress gap between city and county students increases as well. Assuming the quality of facilities and instruction are essentially the same in the elementary and post-elementary schools, it would seem that the Memphis City Schools reflect a problem known to have existed in schools comprised disproportionately of

Table 9

K–12 National Norm Gain Percentages, 1993–1997

Average gain	Shelby County	Memphis	Difference
Reading	105.3	85.3	20.0
Language arts	112.6	82.3	30.3
Math	96.3	83.3	13.0
Science	102.0	96.9	5.1
Social studies	100.8	88.7	12.1

lower-income students. The problem is that those schools will have an increasingly difficult time countering negative environmental influences, which seem to impede learning as their students get older. The difference is greatest in reading and language, where more learning normally goes on outside of school.[34]

The other progress measure is what is called "high school subject value-added." This compares how the students performed in Pre-Algebra, Algebra I, Algebra II, Geometry, and Math for Tech I, compared to how they would have been expected to do based on their TCAP scores. It is reported here as the "average gain," taking the actual average and subtracting the predicted average. Most of these are elective courses, taken by a self-selected group of students. As a result, one would expect better absolute results than in required courses.

Table 10 again shows city students losing ground, scoring lower than would have been predicted by their TCAP scores. Meanwhile, county students nearly always exceed the predicted benchmark. In the process, then, city students seem to be slipping further behind their county counterparts with each math course taken.

Competency Exams. Since 1982, besides completing all mandatory coursework, both of the state's gateway competency exams in language and math have to be passed if a student is to receive a high school diploma. Students begin taking this exam in the ninth grade.[35] This study shows the percentage of students who passed this exam when first taking it in the ninth grade, before weaker students began dropping out of school and artificially inflating the results. There are glaring contrasts between the level of preparedness for the city and county ninth-grade students from 1995 to 2001. In math, an average of 80 percent of county ninth-graders passed on their first attempt, while that number was only 52 percent in the city schools. The numbers were 89 and 63 in language. When consid-

Table 10

High School Subject Value Added, 1995–1999

Average gain	Shelby County	Memphis	Difference
Pre-Algebra	+8	-10	18
Algebra I	+6	-11	17
Algebra II	-3	-8	5
Geometry	+6	-9	15
Math for Tech I (1996–99)	+2	-19	21

ered together, 77 percent of the county ninth graders passed both, as opposed to only 45 percent of the city students.[36] Both city and county students appeared to be slightly better prepared in language than in math.

There are comparably stark differences in the ACT scores of city and county students. This study begins with 1996, the year after it became a graduation requirement that all students take either the ACT, the Standardized Achievement Reasoning Test (SAT I), or the ACT Work Keys exam. From that point forward, at least 80 percent of all students took the ACT. ACT scores are recorded in English, math, reading and science, as well as an overall composite score. Although math scores were slightly lower than the others for both city and county students, the minimal amount of variation across the subtests made the composite a good representation.

Figure 9 shows the average ACT composite score of county students as consistently higher than the city averages. This is true even though only 60 percent of city school students were still around to graduate, while that graduation rate was 88 percent in the county schools. It seems safe to assume that those dropping out would have scored lower on the ACT than did those who stuck out high school to graduation. Thus, the real gap between city and county students may actually be greater yet.

Comparing such diverse achievement measures is of only limited analytical value. Nevertheless, if educational deficits were brought to school from lower-income homes, this should have been evident in city-county achievement gaps in the early grades. If such gaps then widened by the end of junior high school, this might well say more about the schools, peer influence, and the fact that

Fig. 9. ACT composite scores, 1996–2005.

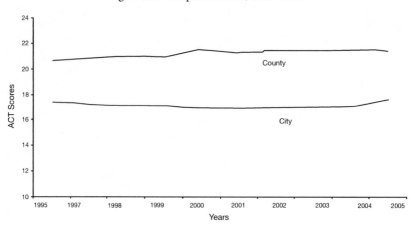

more independent work is required as one progresses through school. This was not uniformly borne out by the data. City school elementary students averaged roughly 30 percentage points behind their county counterparts, for example, and value-added data suggested that they were falling further behind with each passing year. Yet, the average percentage gap between the ACT scores of city and county students is only roughly 23 percent. What these numbers mask, however, is just how far behind those city students had fallen who dropped out or did not take the ACT exam. Consequently, it seems safe to assume that educational deficits were indeed brought to school from lower-income homes, and these deficits widened as the students got older.

Controlling for Race

The most obvious demographic difference between the city and county schools is race. Yet, following the desegregation efforts of the 1970s, the student body of the Memphis City Schools not only became noticeably blacker but rather quickly also became considerably poorer. In order to delineate the separate impact of poverty, this study compares relatively poor black schools to ones that are even poorer. The main difference between the two groups of schools, then, is their level of poverty.

Seven elementary schools have been selected because they were the only ones that fit two primary criteria. Each retained the same basic district lines; and, until very recently, their demography varied little across time. Because no middle-income black schools met these criteria, the schools under study will be referred to as "poor" and "poorer." Each has been 100 percent black from 1985 to the present. Calculations were made from 1992–2002 data, as it was the most comparable data available.[37]

The three "poor" schools selected were Alcy, Magnolia, and Hamilton. Their average enrollment remained steady at roughly 650–700 students. Just prior to desegregation, slightly more than a quarter of those students came from families whose incomes put them below the federal government's poverty level. An average of 86 percent were eligible for free or reduced-price school meals by the 1990s, exceeding the roughly 75 percent eligibility rate for the Memphis City Schools overall.

The four poorer schools were Georgia, Locke, Larose, and Lauderdale. Their enrollment continued to decline, with the average falling from 750 in 1985 to just over 450 by 2001. On average, 60 percent of these students lived below the federal poverty level in the early 1970s, while a full 97 percent were eligible for free or subsidized school meals by the 1990s.[38]

Input Measures. The student-to-teacher ratio in the poor schools averaged 19.5 students. Yet, that number was only 15.5 students per teacher in the poorer schools. As for the teachers, a slight majority of the district's teachers were African American. The average in the poor schools was 57 percent, while it was 68 percent in the poorer ones. An average of 32 percent of the teachers in the poor schools had taught for fewer than four years, while that number was only 27 percent in their poorer counterparts. And, where an average of 52 percent of the teachers in the poor schools had a B.A. degree or less, that number was only 50 percent in the poorer schools.

Overall, then, the poorer schools had smaller classes and were more likely to be taught by black teachers with more teaching experience and advanced educations. Such advantages would suggest the likelihood of better corresponding output measures. Yet, as was also true when comparing the city and county schools as a whole, that did not prove to be the case.

Output Measures. Attendance averaged 94 percent for the poor and 93 percent for the poorer schools. Meanwhile, suspension and failure rates were more than twice as high in the poorer select elementary schools. Where an average of 1.2 percent of the poor children were suspended in a given year, that figure was 2.6 percent for the poorer students. Similarly, where an average of 3 percent failed in the poor schools, that number was 7 percent in their even poorer counterparts. In summary, despite more attractive input measures, the poorer schools had lower attendance and rates and higher suspension and failure rates.

In terms of TCAP achievement, table 11 compares the poor to the poorer schools from 1995 to 2002.[39] These were the only directly comparable years that could be located. The poor schools improved in each subject each year, and, although they scored lower than the city schools as a whole in the third and fourth grades, they exceeded the citywide average by the fifth grade. Meanwhile,

Table 11

Poor vs. Poorer TCAP Percentile Averages, 1995–2002

TCAP average	Poor schools	Poorer schools	Difference
Reading			
Grade 3	36	36	0
Grade 4	33	33	0
Grade 5	39	32	-7
Language arts			
Grade 3	44	34	-10
Grade 4	42	40	-2
Grade 5	48	38	-10
Math			
Grade 3	45	43	-2
Grade 4	41	40	-1
Grade 5	48	39	-9
Science			
Grade 3	32	27	-5
Grade 4	33	33	0
Grade 5	40	33	-7
Social studies			
Grade 3	33	30	-3
Grade 4	35	34	-1
Grade 5	42	37	-5

the poorer schools actually declined each year in all but the language arts, leaving them either even with or more often behind their less poor counterparts and the city schools in general. This was true in each subject in each grade.

Similar results can be seen in these schools' value-added measures. The 2002 academic year presents a recent and a reasonably representative case in point. It also was the last year in which the actual numbers were reported.[40] In that year, table 12 demonstrates that the less poor students gained at the national average, or at least close to it, in all but language arts. Meanwhile, the poorer students progressed at well below the national average except in math.[41]

Table 12

Poor vs. Poorer National Norm Gain Percentages, 2002

Average gain	Poor schools	Poorer schools	Difference
Reading	95	83	-12
Language arts	76	50	-26
Math	100	91	-9
Science	93	66	-27
Social studies	92	86	-6
Writing	91	75	-16

Conclusions

In terms of input measures, a slight but consistent advantage goes to the Memphis City Schools over the Shelby County Schools. They have a slightly better student-to-teacher ratio, spend more per pupil, and have teachers with more college training. Such trend lines and differentials suggest a city system that ought to be functioning at least as well as the county system, if not better. Output, however, is a far different story. City school students lag well behind county school students in key performance measures at all grade levels. Although, as indicated above, these output gaps may have more to do with the level of preparation low-income students bring to school with them than with anything the city schools are or are not doing once they arrive.

The most obvious demographic differences between the city and county schools are race and class, although the above indicators suggest that output gaps may have more to do with the city schools getting poorer than with them getting blacker. The fact that court-ordered school busing altered the racial make up of the Memphis City Schools may be considerably less important than the departure of middle-income blacks and whites. Nevertheless, the end result is an increasingly impoverished student body, having poorer academic output measures than their wealthier suburban counterparts despite efforts to focus more educational resources on the schools in the poorer neighborhoods.[42]

To be fair, the Memphis City Schools have had some shining examples of educational success. In 2004, for instance, graduates were offered a total of more than $70 million in college scholarships. As a model optional school, White Station High School offers nineteen advanced placement courses and was ranked as one of the top high schools in the United States by *Newsweek* and in the nation's

Table 13

Characteristics of Sample School Systems, 1992–1993

System	Enrollment	Black (%)	Poverty (%)[a]	H.S. attendance	Dropout rate[b]
Memphis	105,736	80.9	63.0	80.8	10.0
United States	42,734,746	15.2	38.6	93.2	4.4
Baltimore	110,662	82.3	62.0	79.3	—
Boston	62,407	47.6	58.3	83.0	8.7
Chicago	411,582	56.2	68.1	79.7	14.8
Cleveland	70,532	69.6	78.0	—	11.2
Detroit	175,036	88.4	57.5	87.0	—
Milwaukee	100,163	57.8	64.0	80.0	17.4
Philadelphia	206,898	63.2	—	—	—
Pittsburgh	41,160	53.0	61.3	79.4	7.0
St. Louis	42,278	78.3	85.0	79.5	14.1
Nine-city average	135,635	66.3	66.8	81.1	12.2

[a]Percentage of students eligible to receive free or reduced-price meals.
[b]Average annual dropout rate for high schools.

Source: Council of the Great City Schools, National Urban Education Goals: 1992–1993 Indicators Report (Washington, D.C.: Council of the Great City Schools, 1994). As presented in John Portz et al., City Schools and City Politics (Lawrence: University of Kansas Press, 1999).

top twenty high schools by Forbes. Keystone Elementary, Delano Optional, and Mitchell High all have been named Blue Ribbon Schools by the U.S. Department of Education. Meanwhile, the John P. Freeman optional school was one of only twelve of the nation's schools to be honored by the American Board of Teacher Excellence. In addition, the Memphis City Schools finally achieved "adequate yearly progress" under No Child Left Behind, in part thanks to innovative programs like MCS Reads, Connect Mentoring, and the Blue Ribbon Behavior Initiative.[43] Unfortunately, such successes appear to be the exception rather than the rule.

As is evident from table 13, the Memphis City Schools is a pretty typical large city school system, similar to the larger postindustrial cities of the Northeast and Midwest. Memphis does, however, have a somewhat higher proportion of African American students and a slightly lower high school dropout rate.[44]

Severe problems remain, and improving public schools ranks high on the political priority list of residents across Shelby County. In a recent public opinion poll, for example, education topped the list when residents were asked to indicate the most important problem facing the area. Education was followed by county finances and then consolidation, both with educational dimensions. When asked which issues are "very important," school funding ran second only to crime, with 81 percent of the respondents listing crime and 80 percent listing school funding.[45]

Chapter 6

Educational Alternatives

> Demographically speaking, any child with a father willing to
> call on a teacher to discuss if it's best for that child to spend a
> third year at a $10,000-a-year preschool is going to be fine.
>
> —Elizabeth Weil, "When Should a Kid Start
> Kindergarten?" *New York Times*, 2007

School reform movements have appeared throughout U.S. history, at least in part because educational opportunity has been seen as essential to allowing everyone access to the American Dream.[1] Recently, several reform waves have followed the National Commission on Excellence in Education's 1983 publication of *A Nation at Risk: The Imperative of Educational Reform*.[2] Initially there were increased state standards for students and teachers.[3] These were followed by a change in classroom approach, moving beyond the basics to emphasize higher-order thinking skills and more leeway for teachers to innovate.[4] The end of the 1980s was marked by attempts to substantially restructure the organization of school systems. This began with a decentralization movement that emphasized site-based management. It was followed not long thereafter by considerable recentralization.[5] Most recently, reformers have pressed privatization and school choice models.[6]

Early Intervention

> We face a massive job of education and training—starting before kindergarten.
>
> —"Human Capital: The Decline of America's
> Work Force," *Business Week*, 1988

> We keep obsessing about the schools, but we're not doing
> what we need to do to get children ready for teachers to do
> anything with them.
> —Barbara Holden, executive director of the Community
> Institute for Early Childhood, *Commercial Appeal*, 2003

Blanche Bernstein, former commissioner of the New York City Human Resources Administration, notes that poverty has increased as the causes of poverty have evolved in the United States. It used to be that a household was more apt to fall into poverty as a result of a national unemployment surge or the death, ill health, or disability of its breadwinner. More recently, however, there are the added complications of family structure deterioration, teenage pregnancy, and dropping out of school. This has led to a growth of poverty since the late 1960s. Of the roughly one in four children growing up in poverty in the United States, more than 10 percent have teenage mothers and nearly half will live in a single-parent home by the time they reach eighteen years old.[7]

Poverty also appears to contribute to increased family stress, as well as poor nutrition and poor medical care, not to mention the fact that poor children are talked to less and end up with vocabularies that are about half that of middle-class children. And as Elizabeth Weil notes, "Reading experts know that it's easier for a child to learn the meaning of a new word if he knows the meaning of a related word and that a good vocabulary at age 3 predicts a child's reading well in third grade."[8] By the time poor children reach school, they will have lower verbal and intelligence scores and be more prone to behavioral problems. More than one-quarter of them will not graduate from high school.[9] According to John Berrueta-Clement et al., "The risk of educational failure falls heavily on children who live in poverty."[10]

More than a decade ago, an official at the Educational Testing Service warned that five variables explained nearly 90 percent of the achievement score differences between schools. All five appeared to be essential parts of the learning atmosphere found in the child's home. They were the number of days absent, the number of hours spent watching television each day, the number of pages students reported reading for homework, the extent and nature of the reading materials in the home, and the number of parents in the home.[11]

There is also an emerging body of scientific evidence suggesting just how critical the first years are in shaping a child's capacity to learn. It appears to be very essential to brain development that babies are spoken to, read to, cuddled, and allowed to engage in physical play. There are short critical periods when the those parts of the brain that control vision and language are open to be stimulated; and there are longer sensitive periods that shape a child's ability to learn math, music, and second languages.[12] There is also evidence that malnutrition causes irreversible damage in the first two years of life.[13]

Looking beyond the issue of brain development, David Weikart concluded for the Ford Foundation's Project on Social Welfare and the American Future that "many poor children are handicapped when they enter school because they have not had the chance to develop the skills, habits, and attitudes expected of children in kindergarten and first grade. This lack of development is manifested in low scores on tests of intellectual or scholastic ability. Poor children may be developmentally advanced in other respects, but their lack of preparedness for school can lead to unnecessary (that is, preventable) placement in special education classes, being kept back a grade, repeated scholastic failure, and eventually dropping out of high school."[14]

Journalist Aimee Edmondson chronicles real-world examples from three- and four-year-old preschools in the Memphis area. There is "Tweety," who came to preschool not even knowing his first or last name. There was Jasper, whose teachers took three months just to figure out what he was saying. There was Malika, whose standard response to greetings for the first month was pretty much limited to "Shut up, boy."[15] "It's heartbreaking," said Patricia Reeves, who had taught kindergarten for twenty-eight years in Maryville, Tennessee. "Some of the children can't even count to five. They don't know their colors. They can't concentrate. Often, they don't know how to interact with other children."[16]

The New Jersey Supreme Court found that "many poor children start school with an approximately two-year disadvantage compared to many suburban youngsters. This two-year disadvantage often increases when urban students move through the educational system without receiving special attention."[17] "Literacy school readiness skills" include recognizing letters, counting to twenty, writing one's name, and either reading or pretending to read. Fewer than one in five poor children between the ages of three and five possessed even three of those four skills. Nearly half of all other children in that age group had acquired those skills.[18]

Children entering the kindergartens of the Memphis City Schools in 2005 scored in the sixteenth percentile nationally in math and the nineteenth percentile in language. That means more than 80 percent of the nation's entering kindergartners were better prepared to begin their studies. Meanwhile, a third of the Memphis elementary schools reported scores below the tenth percentile in at least one of the two areas.[19]

Meredith Phillips and her colleagues concluded that "we could eliminate at least half, and probably more, of the black-white test score gap at the end of the twelfth grade by eliminating the differences that exist before children enter the first grade."[20] Meanwhile, Blanche Bernstein argues that children getting little help at home need more help from the school. As she put it, "The key to success is early humane intervention . . . to insure good nutrition and health for infants, early childhood education, mastery of the elementary school curriculum, and development of the values that will enable the youngsters to reject the trail that leads to failure—dropping out of school and associated problems of drug use, juvenile delinquency, early sexuality and teen pregnancy."[21]

The federal government's Title I program put its focus on providing remedial reading assistance, especially in the early elementary grades. David Sojourner, longtime director of Student Information of the Memphis City Schools, found the Title I Early Childhood Program to be one of the few governmental initiatives that seemed to show significant results. According to Sojourner, testing in the 1970s regularly showed inner-city children to be "18–24 months lower academically than their chronological age prior to entering Kindergarten." After a year of Title I remediation, "most of the kids had gained 12 or more months mental age." Then, the program was gradually phased out.[22]

Preschool programs also have been a mechanism for attacking such deficiencies. Although they existed in one form or another in various locations scattered across the United States, most remained privately operated.[23] Then, in 1965, President Lyndon Johnson led the fight to establish the Head Start program, a much more comprehensive governmental approach at providing these services. Besides education, it also provided school meals, vaccinations, and dental care to millions of qualifying children. Encouraged by its prospects, a host of presidents including Richard Nixon and Ronald Reagan spared Head Start from the budgetary chopping block.[24] Although never coming close to serving all eligible children, it currently serves roughly one million three- and four-year-olds at a cost of roughly $7 billion per year.[25]

Former U.S. Secretary of Education Richard Riley concluded that "an extraordinary amount of scientific research has been developed that tells us in very clear terms that all of our children, even in the earliest months of their lives, have an amazing ability to learn. . . . We know that it is absolutely imperative that we put new, powerful, and sustained focus on the early years—birth to 5—before children even enter first grade."[26]

There is empirical evidence to support the prospect that high quality, intensive early education helps students come to school better prepared intellectually and socially; and it appears to improve academic success, reduce dropout rates, and reduce the need for special education programs and grade repetition. In the long term, it also can have the effect of increasing the likelihood of subsequent education or training, as well as reducing delinquency, arrests, teen pregnancy, and welfare reliance.[27] Such gains have been particularly noticeable in students from disadvantaged backgrounds and where the children enter such programs by the age of two.[28]

The Perry Preschool Project studied children from their preschool experience until they turned nineteen. More of the preschool children ended up finishing high school, getting advanced education, being gainfully employed, and were less likely to become pregnant or get arrested. It should be noted, however, that those who turned out to be self-supporting and law-abiding tended to have family support for education, positive role models, a sense of responsibility beyond one's self, and active goal orientation. Preschool was seen as capable of reinforcing family support for education and a sense of personal responsibility, but not overcoming a negative orientation. Nonetheless, it was viewed as capable of helping students remain in school until nonfamily role models became more influential by adolescence and also building the kind of confidence that contributes to goal orientation.[29]

In a Mason-Dixon Polling and Research survey of eight hundred kindergarten teachers across the United States, 93 percent agreed that kindergarten would improve "if all families had access to quality pre-kindergarten programs." And, two-thirds agreed that graduates of such programs are "substantially better prepared to start school ready to succeed."[30]

The bipartisan New Commission on the Skills of the American Workforce has recommended, among other things, that public education begin at the age of three for most all American students.[31] According to Cynthia Brown and her colleagues, initial research suggests that the most successful programs are those "staffed by teachers with college degrees and early education certification; offer developmentally appropriate education, including a focus on language development and comprehensive services such as meals and health and developmental screenings; and encourage parental involvement."[32]

The large majority of states now offer at least some state-supported pre-K education, most often for low-income children and those with learning disabilities. Besides Head Start, billions in federal block grant monies have flowed into an array of state programs. A small handful of states have even established pre-kindergarten programs for all their four-year-olds. Georgia began theirs in 1995, New York followed in 1997, and Oklahoma was next in 1998. No state has yet to offer universal preschool education for three-year-olds, although it has been proposed in Illinois.[33] Meanwhile, the number of three-year-olds enrolled in pre-kindergarten education grew from 43 to 46 percent over the course of the 1990s, while the number of four-year-olds in school grew from 62 to 70 percent over that same period. More than $2 billion per year is now expended on these programs.[34]

Preliminary analysis of short-term benefits in Oklahoma have found increased cognitive/knowledge, language, and motor skill scores, although no apparent gains in social/emotional test scores. Gains were most pronounced for racial minorities and/or those from low-income backgrounds.[35] Similar gains were noted when comparing Memphis-area children with and without preschool training. TCAP scores for first graders with preschool training averaged seven points higher across the board and twelve points higher on the language exam.[36] A particularly strong connection was noted between such training and the students' reading ability in the third grade.[37]

Tennessee has been phasing in a statewide pre-kindergarten program since 1998, allowing school districts to opt in gradually. Designed for low-income children, the program is to involve at least five and one-half hours of instruction per day and be staffed by certified teachers, with caregiver involvement and training required. Memphis already has more than one hundred classes and employs an early childhood coordinator. The cost of making such education available just to the 38,000 low-income four-year-olds in the state is estimated to be roughly $190 million per year, or $100,000 for every twenty-pupil class.[38] According to Tennessee Gov. Phil Bredesen, "At the moment there is no higher priority for me than early childhood education. We need to work hard to help our youngest children arrive on the first day of kindergarten prepared to take advantage of what lies ahead."[39] Even the police chiefs of Memphis and Nashville urged increased spending on early education initiatives as a long-term crime reducing proposition.[40]

Nonetheless, enduring challenges remain. To begin with, society is being asked to tax and spend to create and maintain high quality pre-K programs, even when the results tend often to be indirect and difficult to measure. There is, for example, scant evidence of single-year programs boosting standardized test scores to any significant degree.[41] Language skills improve, but still do not equal those of children from more affluent families.[42] In addition, there is a growing body of empirical evidence that the value of early intervention begins to taper off as the child ages and other influences intervene, especially for African American children.[43]

As one possible explanation of the latter phenomenon, several authors have studied what they refer to as "anti-achievement" peer culture. Hugh Price and others note how some African Americans view educational achievement as "irrelevant, unimportant, 'uncool,' or 'acting white.'"[44] Meanwhile, Richard Milner extends this to a possible social or psychological predisposition within the African American community.[45] Scholars such as Ronald Ferguson, John Ogbu, and Astrid Davis even found this to be true for suburban middle-class blacks.[46] Ogbu emphasizes what he calls "academic self-doubt" born from the internalization of whites' prejudicial views.[47] Yet, this disparagement of academic achievement does not tend to be borne out as consistently in prominent national data sets.[48] Karolyn Tyson and others have noted this to be less true where there are sufficient concentrations of high achieving black students, particularly in the elementary grades.[49] In addition, it is not an exclusively black phenomenon, as high achieving whites are at times socially castigated as "nerds."[50] Nevertheless, Ronald Ferguson notes that it may be having a more significant negative effect on blacks, given their struggle to close the black-white achievement gap.[51]

At the very least, there is a need for far more transition planning to help students make the adjustment from these various preschool programs to elementary school.[52] Most poor children will continue to need the same extra comprehensive services that programs like Head Start provide, and it is very important to have continued assistance in vocabulary development.[53] These extra services also include support provided by nutritionists, social workers, psychologists, and people hired to encourage caregiver involvement. As educational budgets have shrunk, providing such additional services has become highly unlikely.[54] In addition, education is labor intensive and qualified teachers are already in short supply.

Edward Zigler, one of Head Start's first administrators, puts it this way: "The problems of poor people are not going to be solved by giving their children one year of preschool. The problem is jobs and housing. Let us not act as if one year of preschool will make these kids middle class."[55] Nonetheless, David Weikart concludes that "by helping children start on the road to achieving their potential, however, high quality early childhood programs can provide a means to ameliorate these problems and thereby serve all of society, however indirectly."[56]

Caregiver Involvement

> Until parents step up to the plate, we can pour a million dollars into this school and still not see the improvement we need to see.
>
> —Kriste Chaney, music teacher, Cherokee Elementary School

If much of a child's learning capacity is established in the first five years, some form of early intervention appears imperative for children from less privileged backgrounds. As mentioned, some states already have established publicly funded educational opportunities for their four-year-olds, and a few have even begun to extend this to three-year-olds. Yet some of the most crucial learning begins from birth to three years of age.

Research indicates that an infant's brain develops in response to stimulating experiences such as being talked to, read to, and cuddled. Brain scans verify these findings, and they are additionally supported by higher IQ scores that appear to last throughout the child's school years.[57] In one of the first longitudinal studies of its kind, the Ypsilanti-Carnegie Infant Education Project found children who became effective problem solvers and performed well academically tended to have mothers who interacted with them from infancy in ways that were verbally supportive and responsive.[58]

The human brain more than triples in size from a child's birth to age three, accounting for roughly 80 percent of brain development.[59] Dr. Jane Wiechel is the president of the National Association for the Education of Young Children. Dr. Wiechel concludes that "birth to age three is the critical period for social and emotional development. If you aren't exposed early in life to experiences that will enhance brain development, it is an unfortunate fact of life that your brain's plasticity declines throughout the rest of your life."[60]

Since 1999, researchers at the National Institute of Health have been using Magnetic Resonance Imaging (MRI) to study brain development in more than 1,300 children between ages six and eighteen. They also correlated this development with social background variables as well as numerous external measures of intellectual development. Among other things, they found that cognitive performance improves rapidly from ages six to ten, and then appears to level off. Brain capacity for higher learning is pretty much in place by the age of twelve. Income ends up as a strong predictor of both IQ and academic achievement, with reasoning and integration of cognitive skills most vulnerable to income differences.[61]

Teachers at schools that draw heavily from low-income neighborhoods resent being compared to schools in more affluent areas. Many of the lower-income children live in one-parent households or in households in which one or both parents work long hours and are simply not around very much. Others have bounced from one relative's home to another, often switching schools several times in a relatively short period of time. They arrive at kindergarten not knowing their own name, their mother's name, their colors, or even the difference between a letter and a number.[62]

At Cherokee Elementary School in Memphis, for example, one-fourth of the students will transfer in or out of the school over the course of the normal school year. Roughly 85 percent of the children live in poverty. There is no active PTA, and it is not unusual for only one or two parents out of twenty to turn up for parent-teacher conferences. Students often arrive unbathed, inadequately clothed, and without all their books.[63]

LeAndre's story is not all that unlike many of his classmates at Cherokee. His mother is serving time for voluntary manslaughter. His father was just released from prison but has yet to visit. LeAndre lives with his twenty-year-old aunt, Tarsha, who stays home with her one-year-old and is on public assistance. His teacher wonders aloud whether this well-mannered, soft-spoken honor student will be able to overcome the scars of abandonment. "He may decide nobody wants him, and his potential will turn to anger," she laments.[64]

No Excuses: Closing the Racial Gap in Learning is a highly controversial book written by Abigail and Stephan Thernstrom. Regardless of what one thinks of their conclusions, however, they do cite some telling research findings with obvious implications for urban education. They note, for example, that the average minority child was punished for grades when they fell below a C-, as opposed to a B- for whites and an A- for Asians. Nearly half of black fourth-graders watch five or more hours of television per day, while that figure is only 18 percent for whites. The average black five-year-old's home was found to have fewer than half the books of the average white five-year-old. Meanwhile, fewer than 37 percent of black children were growing up in two-parent households, placing additional strain on the single parent.[65] John Ogbu also found middle-class black parents to be spending no more time monitoring their child's homework and academic progress than did the poor white parents.[66]

Meredith Phillips et al. found that family background and practices explain as much as two-thirds of the black-white achievement score gap.[67] African American scholar and journalist Arthur Webb concludes that "the cold hard fact is that uneducated and/or irresponsible parents are in all likelihood going to reproduce uneducated and/or irresponsible children even to the second and third generation unless steps are taken to change the situation."[68]

From birth until age eighteen, the average child will spend less than 9 percent of his or her life in school.[69] Thus, it is obvious that much of the educational process will inevitably have to occur in the home. Short of removing disadvantaged children from their homes or offering public education from birth, clearly more of an effort must be made to better instruct and involve parents in the education of their children.

Anne Henderson, of the Center for Family and Community Connections with Schools, reviewed fifty-one studies undertaken between 1995 and 2002. She concluded that students having involved parents were more likely to possess more acceptable social skills, attend school regularly, make higher grades and test scores, enroll in higher-level courses of study, be promoted, graduate, and ultimately attend college.[70]

Hugh Price, president of the National Urban League, describes what he refers to as a "preparation gap" in the inner city. Recognizing that home is where most education occurs, he argues that parents or guardians need to set the tone for learning in their households, beginning with what he refers to as an "achievement culture." By this he means that parents need to strive to overcome negative peer pressure by conveying a faith in the power of learning and in their children's ability to learn. Beyond that, he also argues that parents need to become actively involved in their child's school, working to make the school experience as valuable as possible.[71] John Ogbu suggests utilizing the black churches to help cultivate parental trust in the system, as well to teach them about their children's academic options and how to assist in their children's learning process.[72]

Beverly Owens, president of the Kirby Middle School PTA, finds that "parents involvement decreases dramatically when their children reach sixth grade. . . . In a school with more than 700 students, a turnout of 20 at a parent organization meeting may be considered good." C. C. Warren, legislative chair of the Bolton High School PTSA, feels strongly that there needs to be a "meaningful two-way respect, trust, and most of all, communication" between the parent and the school. While Mary Murphy Guest, president of the Ford Road Elementary School PTA, notes that "it could be the time of the meeting, it could be the parent's working two jobs. . . . [W]e have to meet them where they are and show them how they can become involved."[73]

Commercial Appeal columnist David Waters concludes that "we've got to confront the educational crisis that begins and ends, for too many of our children, at home. . . . When it comes to educating children, parents aren't mere spectators in the stands. Parents are the head coaches. . . . Students don't need more and better tests. Above all, they need more and better parents."[74]

Increased caregiver involvement, as well as early intervention, have been significant components of many of the comprehensive reform models utilized in one form or another in school districts across the country. Some of the better known are Success for All, the Modern Red School House, Direct Instruction, the School Development Project, America's Choice, Baby Steps, Motherread/Fatherread, and the Knowledge Is Power Program (KIPP). Some have resulted in clear achievement score gains, especially among minority students, but it is difficult to determine just how much is attributable to any particular component of these models.[75] Nonetheless, Samuel Casey Carter notes that a common component of the twenty-one high performing inner-city schools he studied was a "parental contract" that required parents to read to their children, check homework, and monitor assignments.[76]

At the earlier stages, there are programs such as Early Head Start, which began in 1996 with 143 programs. Early Head Start works with parents of infants, from birth to three years of age. It teaches them how to become better early educators for their infants. "Early Head Start was a very important (response to) brain research," according to Helen Blank, director of child care for the Children's Defense Fund. Initial research results seem to bear this out, demonstrating that beneficiaries of the program had better language, cognitive, and social skills than other three-year-olds.[77]

Chicago's Cradle to Classroom program focuses on unwed teen mothers. Beginning prior to delivery, staff members arrange for access to prenatal care and make monthly home visits. After birth, the program sends trained mentors into the homes on a weekly basis. The mother is taught how to play cognitive learning games with her infant, beginning in the child's very first month. By age three, only 9 percent were found to be at risk for developmental delays in language and social skills. The figure was 59 percent for a control group of babies with teen mothers who did not have benefit of the program.[78]

The Memphis City Schools took a step in this direction in September of 2000. The school board mandated that every school produce a detailed plan for reaching out to their respective parents, as well as reporting their progress at the end of each school year. The schools were also to initiate parent assemblies to assist in this endeavor.[79] In addition, the local Mothers of the Nile engage in parental mentoring through their Parent Partner Program.[80]

Class Size

Once the child arrives at school, there is a clear obligation to provide both the child and the taxpayers the most efficiently effective educational process that can be purchased with available tax revenues. Even if the ultimate impact of schooling is limited by external circumstances such as the preschool home environment and peer group influence later on, there is still a need to reform schools themselves so that they deliver as much as they possibly can.

Ask most any educator, and the one factor that he or she will be virtually certain that matters is class size. If there are too many students in the classroom, there will not be sufficient time to spend with each child to be sure those children are learning. In such circumstances, some children are almost certain to fall through the educational cracks, especially problematic for those most in need.[81]

Lisa Goldstein was a second and third grade teacher in a New York City public school. She concluded that "smaller classes are so much more manageable. And they're especially important in these early grades because at that age the children really need a lot of individual attention."[82] In 1996, California began capping their elementary classes at twenty. Dolly Yee-Nishio, a first grade teacher in Sacramento, noted, "I could actually get through the whole room and check off everyone's work. I had a chance to hear every child read every day, to zoom in to help them, to give every child a chance to respond—not once—numerous times. . . . I know the kids, and I know the parents, too."[83]

It also appears to be the reform most favored by students. A Peter Hart survey of high school students across the nation found smaller class sizes to be the most popular reform, preferred by nearly two-thirds of the students polled.[84]

Meanwhile, study after study has shown positive results stemming from small class sizes, especially in the early elementary grades and especially for poor and minority students. Tennessee's Project STAR study is one of the most often cited, beginning in 1985 and following eleven thousand students. It found that grade school students who attended classes in the thirteen- to seventeen-student range had higher grades, especially in reading and math and particularly in the first grade. Ultimately, they were more likely to take advanced courses in high school, had higher graduation rates, and had an increased likelihood of college attendance. The black-white achievement gap shrank, and black students were significantly more likely to take a college entrance exam.[85]

New York City's Educational Priorities Panel found similar results when the city's early elementary grades reduced class sizes to twenty students. Besides many of the same things the STAR study found, New York also witnessed fewer disciplinary problems, more enthusiasm for reading, higher teacher morale, and increased parental involvement.[86]

The state of Wisconsin experimented with its Student Achievement Guarantee (SAGE) program. This was an effort to reduce elementary school class sizes to fifteen in high poverty areas. When comparing these students to their peers in larger classes, University of Wisconsin researchers concluded that students in these smaller classes witnessed "significantly greater improvements in test scores in reading, language arts, and math." The very largest gains were found among African American males.[87]

African American students in the early elementary grades seem to be particularly advantaged by small classes. This was evident in the achievement gains demonstrated by students in both Wisconsin and Tennessee. It was also important to note that black students gained without white students losing ground.[88]

Convinced of its various benefits, legislatures and school boards have been reducing class sizes, particularly in the nation's elementary schools. By 1999, the average elementary school class had been reduced to 18.6 children.[89] Then, in 1999, Congress passed and President Bill Clinton signed legislation allocating $12 billion over seven years for the purpose of helping localities further reduce class sizes.

One of the few studies to reach contrary conclusions was Caroline Hoxby's analysis of class size variations in the Connecticut public schools. Focusing on unplanned reductions due to population changes, she was unable to find statistically consistent correlations between smaller class sizes and higher achievement scores in math, reading, or writing. This proved just as true for schools with high concentrations of poor or minority students.[90]

Drawing heavily on the work of Abigail and Stephan Thernstrom, *National Journal*'s Stuart Taylor Jr. also notes that after adjusting for inflation, spending per pupil nearly doubled nationwide between 1970 and 2000, most of the same years we are reviewing in our analysis of the Memphis City Schools. During that time frame, class sizes shrank significantly, yet achievement scores were essentially unaffected.[91]

Additionally, it has been pointed up that class reduction policies have created unanticipated negative side effects. At least in the short term, funds get switched from other school programs to meet the mandates. In addition, many new teachers must be located, leading to schools making do with inexperienced and often inadequately certified teachers. Stanford economist Eric Hanushek adds that "suburban schools raided central city school districts. . . . It's a waste of money and harms the students who need it the most."[92]

Such findings have helped spawn a conservative backlash of sorts. In Florida, for instance, Gov. Jeb Bush and many of Florida's Republican representatives opposed the voter-approved state constitutional amendment that mandated smaller class sizes. As Governor Bush put it, "In light of the tremendous cost and minimal return on investment to students, the best solution is to allow voters a chance to repeal this obstacle to quality education in Florida."[93] George W. Bush, president of the United States, was quick to discontinue the Clinton efforts as well.

Meanwhile, consider these two contrasting situations in the Memphis City Schools. Danielle Paul is able to give considerable individual attention to her fourteen second-graders at Manor Lake Elementary School. Down the hall, however, Andre Turner has twenty-nine fifth-graders and finds himself staying after school to tutor students he could not get to during the rush of the school day. "I need more time to work with students at their own level," Turner stated. Manor Lake test scores seem to support smaller classes. State and federal monies allowed the school to reduce its lower elementary classes to between fourteen and eighteen students. Disciplinary problems have been reduced and achievement test scores have been improving.[94]

Teacher Development

There is empirical evidence that there is a correlation between high quality teachers and enhanced student performance, especially for minority students in elementary grades.[95] Consequently, for school reform to be successful, the schools need to be able to attract some of the nation's best and brightest individuals into the teaching profession. If our schools are indeed responsible for educating the future leaders and workforce of our nation, such a significant responsibility should be carried out by some of the very best our nation has to offer. To do this requires adequate incentives. Salaries need to be commensurate with other professions requiring advanced and specialized education, and there is a need for a school day and a school year that will allow sufficient time for planning, preparation, and continuing education.[96]

Compensation. Alan Campbell was director of the Office of Personnel Management under President Jimmy Carter. He also headed up an education task force organized by the Committee for Economic Development. As a result of the latter work, Campbell concluded more than two decades ago that we no longer had the luxury of a "captive audience" in the teaching profession, meaning the talented women and minorities who had few other options for a professional career. With many of those gender and racial barriers having been reduced, he argued that it was essential to upgrade the teaching profession so that it would attract the best and brightest. According to Campbell, we could no longer afford to allow "often unpleasant working conditions, poor pay and declining respect for their profession" to reduce teaching to a pursuit for the least qualified of our undergraduate students.[97]

To support his claim, Campbell cited some rather telling statistics. In the latter 1960s, for instance, 75 percent of parents said they would like to see their child pursue a career in education. By the mid-1980s, that number had shrunk to 45 percent. Meanwhile, college-bound students indicating teaching as a likely career path consistently had lower SAT scores than those who anticipated pursuing other professions. Beyond that, he noted that "the best and brightest who have chosen the teaching profession are among the first to abandon it." Citing a North Carolina study, Campbell noted that two-thirds of the teachers who scored in the top tenth percentile on the National Teacher Examination had abandoned the profession within seven years.[98]

Little has changed in the twenty years since Campbell wrote. Today, the average teacher is paid 27 percent less than those with comparable education in other professions. Only one in every ten teachers is "very satisfied" with his or her current salary, and three-quarters of all teachers consider themselves to be "seriously underpaid." *Education Week* notes that this is worst for early elementary teachers, where the average salary is "about as much as parking-lot attendants and dry-cleaning workers make."[99] Not too surprisingly, then, only 18 percent of college graduates say they would ever consider teaching as a profession. Some one in three practicing teachers will leave the profession within the first five years, while Business-Higher Education Forum is predicting a national shortage of a quarter million math and science teachers by the year 2015.[100]

To begin with, it would appear that base pay must increase if the teaching profession is to become competitive with those in business professions where comparable training is required. There also is mounting empirical evidence that high enough salaries, if effectively advertised, can lure teachers into pretty much any circumstance. Thus, it may be necessary to have pay scales vary by school, offering a combination of pay incentives, tax breaks, and school loan forgiveness, until the point at which each school becomes comparably attractive to prospective teachers. The state of Tennessee recently mandated that each school board develop an incentive pay plan for its hard-to-staff schools, something Memphis has been doing since 2005.[101] Matt Miller suggests that inner-city teachers should receive a starting salary of $60,000, an average of $90,000, and a maximum of $150,000.[102] Yet, as Alan Campbell points out, salaries only get the teachers in the school house door. From there, it will be incumbent on schools to develop attractive career advancement structures with step incentives over the entirety of one's teaching career.[103]

Besides salary issues, it also seems imperative to address working conditions in the public schools. Randi Weingarten, head of the New York City teachers' union, lamented that "every minute of the day and every inch of a classroom is dictated. The arrangement of desks, the format of the bulletin boards, the position in which teachers should stand. Teachers are demeaned, they are stripped of their professionalism and they are expected to behave like robots incapable of any independent thought."[104]

Beyond regimentation, these work condition issues include unruly classrooms, inadequate materials, a lack of preparation time, and unduly time-consuming clerical and housekeeping responsibilities. Too often teachers fear for their own personal safety both in the classroom and in the parking lot. Budget restrictions oftentimes compel conscientious teachers to spend their own money on lesson materials, and they devote evenings, weekends, and unpaid summer months preparing for class. They often end up cleaning and repairing their own classrooms. Then, on top of all that, bureaucratic red tape leaves them spending an inordinate amount of time filling out paper work.[105]

The position of public school teacher would surely become more attractive if adequate class preparation periods were built into the class day. In Mt. Vernon, New York, for example, student achievement increased noticeably following the district's doubling of professional development money for teachers and adjustment of teacher schedules to allow more planning time.[106] In addition, it seems inefficient for certified teachers to be spending their time doing attendance counts, recess duty, or collecting lunch money. Many such clerical duties could be performed by lesser trained aides, allowing certified teachers to spend their time teaching and preparing to teach.

If the United States is truly serious about professionalizing the job of primary and secondary school teachers, its public schools might well consider the model employed at the college level. Teachers would have their own office, computer, phone, access to clerical assistance, and sabbatical leave tract. They also would have virtually complete control over their school's curriculum, screen and recommend teaching candidates, and have a voice in the criteria by which meritorious teaching was to be determined.[107]

Accountability could be established by systematic peer review, as is common at the college level. Instead, states and school districts are increasingly tying teacher salaries to their students' test scores.[108] The main problem with this, however, is that it can create disincentives for teachers to work in schools with a disproportionate number of slow learners. At the Georgia Avenue elementary school in Memphis, for example, teachers came in forty minutes early to prepare, besides staying around to tutor students after school and on weekends. Yet the school still failed to meet state and federal achievement standards.[109] Rewarding or punishing teachers on the basis of their students' test performances is seen as analogous to paying doctors only if their patients get well.[110]

Preparation. If public school teachers are finally to be treated as bona fide professionals, it will be essential that they are qualified to hold such positions. Elected officials will have a far easier time justifying the sizable increases in expenditures required to provide these upgrades if they can verify that the increase in spending is in fact producing impressively qualified instructors. Yet, at present time, urban public school systems often are struggling just to find certified teachers, let alone the best and the brightest of that group. Many of those districts also lack the funds to provide even basic orientation for their new teachers.[111]

When a coalition of civil rights groups challenged disparities found in the California public schools, it was noted that at least one hundred such schools had teaching corps in which fewer than half the teachers were fully certified to teach.[112] Indicative of the problem locally, the Memphis City Schools had roughly 8,500 teachers in the 2003–4 school year. Of the 890 new teachers hired during that period, 58 percent were not fully licensed. Beyond that, one in four new teachers quit the city schools after their first year.[113]

In October of 2004, the U.S. Department of Education chose Memphis and Cleveland as test cities for their Urban Teacher Hiring Initiative. The goal was "to put a highly qualified teacher in every classroom." The thrust of this effort was to be an implementation of various recruitment techniques outlined in a three-year study entitled, "Missed Opportunities: How We Keep High-Quality Teachers Out of Urban Classrooms." Early indications are that Memphis has been able to utilize these techniques to attract more applicants and hire at least marginally better qualified teachers.[114]

Beyond finding a way to recruit more certified teachers, there is also a need to determine that the certification process is stringent enough to guarantee high quality. In 2001, for instance, the National Council for the Accreditation of Teacher Education strengthened its requirements for accrediting teacher education programs. Prospective teachers would have to meet higher grade requirements when tested in their subject areas and on teaching skills. In addition, they would have to demonstrate that they actually could teach. The latter could be accomplished, for example, by accumulating a teaching portfolio that included evidence of teaching lessons, diagnostic work with actual students, and more extensive evaluations by the teachers under which they did their practice teaching.[115]

Utilizing money provided by the Plough Foundation, the Memphis City Schools recently launched a mentoring program for new teachers. Highly rated veteran teachers were to be selected as mentors and trained over the summer months. They were then to be released from their teaching duties to provide weekly support to new teachers in their first two years. Each mentor was assigned fifteen new teachers and was to meet roughly two hours per week with each of them. In March of 2006, that mentoring program received the Tennessee Board of Regents' Academic Excellence Award for its contributions to increased teacher retention and instructional effectiveness.[116]

Time Utilization

We have been asking the impossible. The reform movement . . . is destined to founder unless it is harnessed to more time for learning.

—National Education Commission on Time
and Learning, *Prisoners of Time*, 1994

A common complaint among classroom teachers relates to the disproportionate amount of the school day spent on nonacademic matters. A two-year study, for example, was conducted by the National Education Commission on Time and Learning. They found that "the traditional school day must now fit in a whole set of requirements for what has been called the new work of the schools. . . . [This includes] education about personal safety, consumer affairs, AIDS, conservation and energy, family life, and driver's training." The average American high school student, for example, spends only about three hours of each class day on core academics.[117]

Similar developments can be found in the nation's elementary schools, especially those in the inner city. With the dismantling of much of the welfare safety net in the 1990s, schools have often become the "safety nets of last resort." Schools are now often asked to provide low-income children with such things as basic personal hygiene, immunizations, a school uniform, school supplies, and even a winter coat.[118]

The McKinney-Vento Law was passed by Congress in 1987 and reauthorized in 2002. It requires each school district in the United States to designate a "liaison for homeless children and youth." That person's duties involve "searching for children living in shelters, motels, campgrounds, and other irregular residences, helping them enroll in school, and insuring that they get immunizations and other medical and dental care."[119]

Then there are the disruptive students. It was noted in the previous chapter that the Memphis City Schools have reported suspension incidents representing between 6 and 12 percent of their student body. The state adoption of a zero-tolerance rule in the mid-1990s makes it difficult to know if there are more instances of serious misbehavior now, or if there are simply more suspensions being meted out for behavior that has been occurring all along. Nonetheless, it is clear that suspension rates are high, suggesting that the policing of unruly behavior is yet another responsibility falling on the shoulders of the public schools.[120]

If the schools' teachers and staff are to become the nation's new police officers and social welfare caseworkers, on top of the responsibilities of educating the children, at least two things need to occur. First, the school day needs to be lengthened and restructured, allowing more time for needy students to receive these additional services. In addition, more staff needs to be hired with appropriate training for such tasks. Teachers have plenty enough to do simply trying to educate their students.[121]

There is also the issue of total time spent in school. Given that slower learners appear particularly inclined to regress when outside the more formal educational structure, it may be time to seriously consider broadening the availability of year-round education.[122] The original purpose of suspending schools for the summer was to allow children to help out in the fields on their family farms, but those days are long gone for most students. Whether extending the school day or the school year, lengthening the amount of time children spend in school has been on the educational reform agenda since the U.S. Department of Education's landmark study, *A Nation at Risk*.[123]

A sizable number of states and individual school districts have taken the first tentative steps in this direction. Spurred by federal pressure to improve achievement scores, especially among the poor, states such as Massachusetts, New York, Connecticut, and New Mexico have been experimenting with the option of longer school days. Miami has targeted thirty-nine low-performing schools for an extra hour each day and five more days each year, while Fresno County has added an hour per day for students in the fourth through eighth grades of low-testing schools.[124]

The Children's Defense Fund helps sponsor Freedom Schools. Serving school age children from five to eight weeks each summer, Freedom Schools provide integrated work in "reading, conflict resolution, and social action in an activity-based curriculum that promotes social, cultural, and historical awareness." In 2006, there were Freedom Schools in forty-nine cities serving some seven thousand youngsters.[125]

A combination of charter schools across the country have been experimenting with the KIPP plan. It includes extended school days, weeks, and years. Students are in school from 7:30 A.M. until 5:00 P.M., with additional half-day classes on Saturdays. Students also attend a two- to four-week summer session. On average KIPP students spend roughly 60 percent more time in school than their average public school counterparts. Gaston College Preparatory School in Gaston, North Carolina, has adopted the KIPP plan. It has a student body that is 95 percent African American, with 85 percent of the children qualifying for reduced-price meals. Where fewer than half of the incoming fifth-graders were performing at grade level, that figure rose to 90 percent after one full year in KIPP.[126]

An even more comprehensive model would be to have the children attend their regular schools for all twelve months, interspersing the school year with two-week breaks. The breaks would allow for family vacations and school building maintenance, as well as allowing teachers time to plan and take additional courses. Athletic teams also could do more of their intensive practicing during these breaks, so that the school day could be dictated more by curricular priorities rather than football practice times. In addition, child care could be provided during those breaks, in order to accommodate the needs of working parents. This would have the additional advantage of creating employment opportunities.

Marisa Trevino cautions, however, that simply super-sizing troubled schools will not solve many of the underlying problems. And, she notes that several cash-strapped cities were forced to abandon much more modest hour-extending models as they proved just too expensive.[127] There clearly would be even more costs involved in the latter model, as teachers would move to twelve-month contracts, and some child-care workers might need to be hired on a part-time basis. Yet, the infrastructure is already in place. We have the school buildings and the administrators. We actually would be taking fuller advantage of both. And, as Samuel Casey Carter noted in his twenty-one high performing schools, "Extended days, extended years, after-school programs, weekend programs, and summer school are all features of outstanding schools."[128]

School District Consolidation

As populations have shifted, the number of schoolchildren has grown, and school operating costs have mounted, states and localities have looked to a combination of school closures and school system consolidations as a way of making ends meet. Since World War II, for example, the number of the nation's schoolchildren doubled amidst the baby boom. Yet, at the same time, the number of school districts in the United States declined from 117,000 to roughly 15,000, while the number of schools shrank from 185,000 to 85,000, often after significant resistance from affected parents.[129]

School system consolidation remains a controversial issue.[130] In the middle of the nineteenth century, Horace Mann was one of the first to advocate consolidating neighborhood schools under township control. The arguments then were similar to ones presented by James Conant a century later, and many echo them today. They included fiscal efficiency, professional leadership, more equally distributed resources, and updated educational practices in the smaller districts.[131]

By the turn of the century, professional school administrators were increasingly supportive of the large and bureaucratic district model of governance. Yet resistance to this model continued in many of the rural districts, where there was support for the existing smaller and more personally oriented schools as well as concern about losing local control.[132] Nevertheless, assisted by advances in transportation, the more urban bureaucratic model began to proliferate in the 1930s and 1940s, spawning consolidation waves in most states between 1940 and 1980. In Nevada, for instance, the number of school districts shrank from 177 to 17 (the number of counties) in a mere two-year period beginning in 1952.[133]

General findings across the nation have been mixed when studying the impact of consolidating school districts.[134] Often cited is the fact that such consolidation is seldom followed by a marked decline in overall costs, not immediately anyway. There are at least two major reasons for that. First, states may operate under the principle of equalization. Equalization means that no district should lose any services as a result of such a reorganization, while every student in the new consolidated district should receive equal services. Thus, each student in the new district will receive every service that any of the various students were previously receiving in their smaller districts. Secondly, education is a very labor-intensive operation, and most all the previously existing teaching and middle-range administrative jobs will still need to be done. In 2004–5, for example, the Memphis City Schools spent more than three-fourths of their operating budget on instructional salaries and benefits, and only 1 percent on administration.

Meanwhile, there have been several other conflicting findings. Among the potential benefits to such consolidation are flexibility as to how funds are spent across the larger district; specialization can allow a broader array of curricular options as courses and facilities can be shared; some central office administrators and some duplicate facilities can be eliminated; and more extracurricular opportunities may be offered. Nonetheless, larger districts tend to be less personal, involve more red tape, remove teachers and principals further from district-level decision making, require more time in transit, and have lower attendance rates and higher dropout rates, while the impersonal nature of the larger district may cause caregiver involvement and community support to wane some, too.[135]

Under Tennessee law, when a city opts to maintain its own separate school district, these special districts operate independently of county control, although they do receive state and county funds through the county government. Beyond that, the city school district normally elects its own school board and superintendent, makes its own financial decisions, develops its own curriculum, hires and fires its own teachers and administrators, and reports directly to the State Department of Education.[136]

The Memphis City Schools charter is somewhat unique in the state. The Memphis City Schools is a special district created by a private act of the state legislature. It is, however, the only special school district in the state that was not granted its own taxing authority. Thus, the Memphis City Council approves its operating and capital budgets, although the school district retains line-item authority over how its money is to be spent.[137] Meanwhile, the state government has steadfastly refused to allow the Shelby County Schools to convert to a separate special district of its own, a repeatedly proposed change that would lock in the existing boundaries between the Memphis City Schools and the Shelby County Schools.[138]

As for school district consolidation in Tennessee, the pace has been slower than in the nation as a whole. In 1960, for instance, there were 153 school districts in the state's 95 counties, and that number shrank by only 15 over the next four decades. Nevertheless, 138 remains below the national average number of school districts per state, even when controlling for population.[139]

Three of the state's four largest counties have implemented metropolitan-wide school consolidation. Only the Memphis area has not. Nashville consolidated its city and county schools in 1962. Knoxville followed in 1987. Then, Chattanooga consolidated in 1997. In each instance, consolidation was followed rather quickly by both a reduction in administrative duplication and evidence of a more efficient utilization of existing resources. In addition, student-to-teacher ratios declined; per-pupil expenditures increased; teacher qualifications and remuneration improved; students gained access to more course options and special services; and city school students got additional supplies, transportation, and building improvements.

Nevertheless, school consolidation in Nashville, Knoxville, and Chattanooga has not produced an educational nirvana. School expenditures actually increased some, in large part as a result of state equalization requirements. Overall attendance rates remained pretty much unchanged. Both suspensions and expulsions increased with the introduction of the state's zero-tolerance policy. Some long-settled desegregation agreements had to be reopened, and, although the latter led to some involuntary reassignment of teachers, it did not lead to a new wave of student busing for the purpose of desegregation. Some schools lost their Title I eligibility as they were consolidated with more needy schools. And, serious academic and behavioral problems continued to plague some of the systems' poorest schools long after the consolidation dust had settled.[140]

The Memphis area has grappled with the prospect of consolidation on several recent occasions. State legislation, defeated in 2001, called for the consolidation of all the state's school systems, leaving just one system per county.[141] Ten years earlier, a local proposal faded away as suburban mayors threatened to secede from Shelby County and form a new "Neshoba County" should city-county consolidation pass at that juncture.[142] Wholesale consolidation of the Memphis and Shelby County governments went to referendum in the 1960s and in the 1970s, losing both times. Memphis voters narrowly approved it in 1971, while suburban voters defeated it by more than a two-to-one margin, percentages of support and opposition which local polling indicated still seemed to hold more than three decades later.[143]

Memphis Mayor W. W. Herenton pressed the case for city-county school consolidation from the time he was first elected in 1991, including a comprehensive model that included five smaller subdistricts.[144] When prospects for full consolidation appeared untenable, however, he suggested a "single-funding source" proposal that would cement the current school district lines by making the Shelby County Schools its own special district. The plan would create separate taxing districts for capital funding, eliminating the need for the costly ADA formula, and Shelby County would assume full local responsibility for funding the operations of both school districts. County Mayor A. C. Wharton presented his own pared down alternative, with an attendance-zone agreement between the two systems, a joint board of control, and an end to the ADA formula for capital spending.[145] Subsequently, although neither the Herenton nor Wharton proposal achieved any real political traction, the two systems have worked together to jointly build, repair, and renovate area schools.[146]

Meanwhile, there is the possibility that such school consolidation could occur by default, without the approval of those living outside the city limits. Should the city school board vote to surrender its special district charter, the issue would then be placed before the Memphis voters in the form of a referendum. Were it to pass, it appears that Shelby County would be required to assume control of the city's schools.[147] The Memphis City Council finally voted seven to five to ask the city's school board to put the referendum to the city voters.[148] The school board, however, has demonstrated little interest in eliminating itself and the system it governs.

Opponents of city-county school consolidation stress that it would create a mammoth and unwieldy single district, one of the largest in the nation and equal to Tennessee's next three largest school districts combined. There is the concern that the more academically successful Shelby County Schools, with their 40,000 students, would have their interests subordinated to those of the less successful Memphis City Schools, with its 120,000 students.[149] In addition, county residents living outside the Memphis city limits would be responsible for their share of the city schools' operating budget. After equalization, it is estimated that would mean roughly an eighty-two-cent property tax rate increase for those households.[150] Whether the city can legally discontinue that payment, leaving it to the county by default, is less clear.[151]

Administrative Models

Whether metropolitan-area school districts are consolidated or not, a case can still be made for maximizing the efficiency of administrative decision making. One general approach has been to press for more decentralization of authority and responsibility, the presumption being that those closest to the children know best how to structure their educations. Decentralization can involve anything from a subdistrict model to varying degrees of site-based management, with the latter involving delegating more hiring and curricular authority to local school principals. The case also can be made for a more centralized interventionist approach, such as imposing more corporate-style administration in order to increase accountability.

Decentralization. School consolidation holds out the promise of a more efficient allocation of scarce educational resources. However, a city like Memphis already has a public school system with roughly 120,000 students. If it were to consolidate with the Shelby County Schools, that would create a single school system with more than 160,000 students and a significant risk of overcentralization.

In a system that size, there would almost certainly have to be several subdistricts in order to keep decision making from getting too far removed from the individual school and classroom. When he was superintendent of the Memphis City Schools, Memphis Mayor W. W. Herenton actually experimented with area superintendents as a small step in that general direction. Subsequently, the system employed several zone directors to oversee school principals.

The idea of less centralized school decision making has been advocated for some time.[152] It would appear to make intuitive sense that those closest to the day-to-day learning environment of the children would be in the best position to make the key education-related decisions affecting those children's educations. This concept was particularly popular during the experiments with community control in the latter 1960s and in the school choice movement today.[153] Decentralization can take many education-related forms. Among those are neighborhood input in hiring and curricular matters, or at least allowing principals more leeway to hire whom they feel will best be able to teach the children at that particular school. There is also a sense that individual classroom teachers should have more leeway in terms of curricular decisions.

Detroit and New York were two of the first large school systems to attempt significant decentralization, including relatively high levels of community control. Detroit implemented subdistricts in 1970, in part because black leaders wanted black control over the city's predominantly black schools. The eight subdistricts, or "regional school boards" as they were called, were granted authority to handle curricular and personnel matters, student policies, and spending decisions. At the time New York City decentralized in 1969, it had nearly one thousand schools and more than a million students. It subsequently subdivided into thirty-two community school districts, each with its own locally elected school board. These community boards possessed similar authority to that held by the regional boards in Detroit. In New York, however, a larger role was established for the chancellor and citywide school board, although they also tried some school-based management approaches and even replaced community school boards with elected parent councils.[154] More recently, New York has experimented with regional superintendents and increased principal autonomy.[155]

These experiments continued into the 1980s and beyond, including attempts in school districts such as Boston, Chicago, Cleveland, Dade County (Florida), Rochester (New York), and Hammond (Indiana).[156] Boston is a classic example of the forces that drove large city school districts to consider such a plan. Like many other large cities, Boston's public schools had suffered serious out-migration following the implementation of court-ordered school busing. Soon, the district's dropout rates grew, achievement averages fell, and school buildings were allowed to deteriorate. In an attempt to turn the tide, Boston's teachers and administrators agreed on a decentralization plan. Each school was to be run by a council that included the principal, teachers, and parents. Those councils would then set their school's educational goals and curriculum, as well as being responsible for budgeting and hiring. Evaluated annually by the central administration, failing schools could have their principal and teachers replaced if they did not improve after help from a union-management team.[157]

Beginning in 1989, Chicago—whose public schools were labeled the worst in the nation by Secretary of Education William Bennett—attempted the most decentralized effort of them all, transferring considerable authority from the city's central board of education to the parents and neighborhood residents of each of its 540 public schools. These locally elected, ten-member "school councils" assumed authority to hire and fire their principal, approve the school budget, and make curricular recommendations.[158]

When studied over time, however, there has not been much empirical evidence to support this overall approach. Decentralization efforts increase school expenditures by adding personnel, and they have been plagued by accusations of cronyism and waste. Fewer than 10 percent of residents took the time to vote in the subsequent school board elections.[159] In addition, decentralization efforts have not appeared to substantially broaden caregiver involvement, professionalize the teaching environment, consistently increase achievement, or lessen the public's sense of educational crisis.[160] There may well be a threshold at which a large city school district becomes so big that some form of subdistricting needs to occur both for school accountability and for responsiveness to the special needs of any given school. But, decentralization does not seem to be a quick fix for substantially improving student performance.

Centralized Intervention. In part as a response to the failures of decentralized experiments, various more centralized intervention models also have been tried. Mayors or states have assumed control of individual schools or entire school systems, school boards have been appointed by the mayor or abolished altogether, and administrators from outside the education field have been brought in and empowered. The goal is often to bring more corporate-type discipline to the school district's operations, cutting through impeding bureaucratic networks and pressing the districtwide reforms that are deemed necessary.

For the interventionist, the crisis in the public schools is seen largely to stem from the fact that education is a closed system far too wedded to inefficient modes of operation. More than 95 percent of all school boards are elected, and these boards often become mired in personality clashes and petty turf wars.[161] Teachers unions are seen as placing work rules and compensation matters ahead of the educational interests of the children. The school bureaucracy can be replete with competing fiefdoms, often inefficient, antiquated, inflexible, and even corrupt. Wilbur Rich refers to it as an education cartel, where "a coalition of professional school administrators, school activists, and union leaders maintains control of school policy to promote the interests of its members . . . [and] bureaucratic inertia is the rule."[162] In the end, too many of the district's children continue to graduate without the basic skills they need to be employable or further educable.

The state legislature of Ohio approved a mayor-appointed school board in 1997. Five years later, the Cleveland electorate overwhelmingly endorsed that move by referendum vote. Cities such as New York, Boston, Detroit, and Chicago also have experimented with appointed school boards. Michael Usdan, a senior fellow with the Institute of Educational Leadership, sees one of the primary strengths of this arrangement to be the direct line of accountability to the city's mayor.[163]

An outside entity is also often introduced to rein in or even replace the school board, challenge the unions, control the bureaucracy, and hopefully inspire students and their parents to commit to higher achievement. It has been tried in one form or another in numerous cities, including Baltimore, New York, Milwaukee, Detroit, Chicago, Los Angeles, and Philadelphia. When outside administrators are brought in, for example, they are normally drawn from a background in the military, business, government, or academia. New York City brought in a corporate lawyer; San Diego, a federal prosecutor; Chelsea chose Boston University; while Jacksonville, Seattle, and Washington, D.C., turned to former military officers. The outsider then usually hires an instructional administrator with training and experience in education who assumes responsibility for devising and administering the instructional and curricular programs.[164]

These external interventions are seen to have several advantages over the traditional administration by a career educator. For one thing, the outsiders are deemed to be freer of the dogmas of the education profession and organized school labor, hopefully making them more open to new approaches to teaching, teachers, and curriculum matters. For example, some have hired college graduates from fields other than education, eliminated seniority as the basis for teacher selection, prosecuted parents of chronic truants, linked teacher pay to student performance, and imposed longer school days and mandatory summer school. In addition, they have not been part of the local school bureaucracy or its culture, thus freeing them to focus on restructuring initiatives like cutting out layers of administration. They are generally more comfortable with achievement benchmarks by which teachers and schools can be held accountable, because the world outside academia is continually assessed using quantifiable indicators. They also may bring a business approach to everything from personnel assessment to purchasing, instituting quality control procedures and internal audits, as well as consolidating and privatizing functions.

This type of intervention has been most common in larger, blacker, and poorer central city school districts, where students generally perform more poorly on standardized tests and are less likely to graduate. According to Peter Eisinger and Richard Hula, such intervention suggests that many politicians have lost faith in the competence of the education profession as a profession. Interventionists seem more interested in the administrators ability to impose order, unity, discipline, and accountability that will hopefully work their way down through the system to the classroom and perhaps even galvanize disorganized families and communities to take education more seriously.[165]

Meanwhile, there is little empirical evidence that either achievement scores or graduation rates are much affected by these administrative changes either.[166] In Chicago, for example, the state legislature reversed itself in 1995 and recentralized school governance under the city mayor. A mayoral takeover meant firing teachers and principals, mandatory summer school, uniform lesson plans, an end to social promotions, alternative schools for the disruptive, and tying pay raises to student achievement scores. Achievement scores rose marginally thereafter but remain quite low.[167] Baltimore, as another example, fired its private management company after it was accused of misstating test results in order to demonstrate academic success.[168]

Promotion Standards

An additional challenge to efficient classroom instruction is the need to adapt class pace to accommodate slower learners. Narrowly tracking students by perceived ability levels has obvious problems, even if it does not appear to have any negative impact on achievement scores.[169] Slower learners, ghettoized into remedial classes, can become stigmatized as "dumb," besides the fact that they will attend class day after day without higher achieving students to observe and emulate.[170] There is also evidence that racial stereotypes can lead to blacks being disproportionately placed in nonacademic tracks.[171] Nonetheless, fully mixing classes requires teachers to slow class progress in order to avoid losing the slower students. The alternative of structuring classes by actual academic progress, regardless of age, generates obvious social problems when those age differences become too great. As a result, schools have gravitated toward what essentially amounts to social promotion, allowing students to advance from class to class by age, then attempting to compensate with remedial instruction.[172]

Not surprisingly, Diane Ravitch notes that "when American students arrive as [high school] freshmen, nearly 70 percent are reading below grade level. Equally large numbers are ill prepared in mathematics, science, and history."[173] High school reading and math scores have been declining, and just more than one-third are reading on grade level.[174] There also have been high profile examples of students graduating from high school, yet unable to either read or write to any significant degree. A recent federal study found one in four high school seniors unable to read at a "basic proficiency level."[175] The U.S. Department of Education found seven in ten high school graduates inadequately prepared for either college or the workplace.[176] Such results have caused concern, as has the perceived decline in American student abilities when compared to their counterparts in other areas of the world.[177]

As a consequence, there has been a backlash to the social promotion concept in recent years. A Heritage Foundation study notes the stringent testing and promotion standards at twenty-one high performing inner-city schools.[178] Meanwhile, governmental bodies have increasingly been requiring their school students to pass competency exams before being passed along to the next level, and they also have been raising those gateway standards. One assumption is that we often have been underchallenging our students, and a 2004 survey conducted by the National Governors Association suggests that a good many of the nation's high school students appear to agree.[179]

A 1981 state law required all Tennessee high school students to pass the Tennessee Proficiency Test (TPT) as a graduation requisite. Beginning in 1995, a new Competency Test was implemented in an attempt to require higher level math and language skills. It is given in the ninth grade and can be retaken as many times as necessary. Beginning in 2002, Gateway Tests were required upon completion of Algebra I, Biology I, and English II. These tests were to be administered three times annually.

In February of 2005, the governors of thirteen states announced that they would be collaborating to develop tougher courses and more stringent and focused graduation standards in their high schools. There also would be more of an effort to publish test results and dropout rates as a way to hold individual schools responsible. In part, they were taking advantage of $23 million in foundation money designed to upgrade the quality of American high schools. Bill and Melinda Gates contributed about two-thirds of that money.[180] For those unable to meet the new standards, New York City instituted transfer schools offering intensive remediation for students having fallen far behind, as well as special centers to provide educational opportunities for those students whose advanced age can leave them stigmatized in the traditional classroom.[181]

Governors from many of these same states joined with business leaders in the 1980s and began holding National Education Summits on High Schools. These were designed to increase standards and accountability. Their fifth such summit was held in 2005, at which Bill Gates called the nation's high schools "obsolete" and in need of more rigor and a "radical restructuring" of their curricula if the American workforce was to be competitive in today's global marketplace. The group's 1989 summit focused on elementary schools and ultimately helped spawn the federal No Child Left Behind Act.[182]

No Child Left Behind. The twelve-hundred-page "No Child Left Behind" (NCLB) law was adopted by overwhelming bipartisan majorities in January of 2002, and its operational guidelines were clarified by the U.S. Department of Education. The legislation established national improvement standards that individual schools must meet by 2014 if their states are to continue receiving federal education revenues. All teachers and teacher aides are to meet a standard of high quality, and parents are to be informed of those who do not meet those standards. Students are to be tested annually in grades three through eight, as well as once in high school. Disparities in achievement scores among racial groups are to be reduced. Increased tutoring is to be provided for those students not making the grade, and parents are to be offered alternative school options within the school district if their children are in schools needing improvement for two consecutive years or deemed to be persistently dangerous. States are to establish intervention plans if individual schools are not making adequate yearly progress. The latter could include replacing teachers and principals or reopening as charter schools.[183]

In its first year, more than 17,000 of the nation's 90,000 public schools were deemed to be failing.[184] That number continued to grow, as the achievement score gap between white and nonwhite students actually increased.[185] Sandy Kress, the Bush administration attorney who helped draft the law and then advised states on implementation, predicted that as many as 50 to 90 percent of the schools in some states would ultimately be found out of compliance.[186] In Memphis, 149 of its 185 schools initially failed at least one or more of their governing standards.[187] The National Conference of State Legislatures and the Council of Chief State School Officers estimated that 85 to 90 percent of all public schools might ultimately fail.[188] Eugene Hickok, undersecretary of education, referred to the existing educational establishment as the "guardians of mediocrity" and called for "change in the culture of education."[189]

In Memphis, these federal definitions and mandates have resulted in a considerable amount of money being expended on individual tutoring, as well as a "fresh start" for several local schools.[190] "Fresh start" is a political euphemism for firing all the faculty and staff at schools with persistently low achievement scores. This was done initially at Fairview Junior High, Georgian Hills Junior High, Vance Middle, Longview Middle, Winchester Elementary, Airways Middle, Geeter Middle, and Sherwood Middle. According to Superintendent Carol Johnson, it was done "in an attempt to jump start academic achievement" before the schools ended up in the state's "alternative governance" category. In other words, it was done before the schools were taken over by the state.[191]

Multiple problems lie beneath the achievement scores of the Memphis City Schools, many indicative of the disproportionately low socioeconomic status of their student bodies. The schools in need of corrective action, for instance, had some of the lowest attendance rates and some of the district's highest percentage of inexperienced teachers and administrators.[192] One of the most glaring problems was the level of "mobility," meaning the proportion of the school's students who transfer in or out over the course of the school year as they move from one location to another. Districtwide, one in four students change schools at least once during the school year. Half of all poor children do so. In the fresh start schools, that figure was nearly seven in ten. Not only does such mobility retard student learning, it also seems to reduce the comparative value of achievement measures in high mobility schools, where much of the student body changes during the school year.[193]

Nevertheless, the federal focus on achievement gaps related to race and income has at least raised public awareness of these problems and spurred state and local governments to increase their efforts to reduce those gaps.[194] Kentucky, for example, actually began related reforms in 1990. By standardizing curricula to conform to state benchmark exams, the state was able to lift 91 percent of its failing schools above the passing threshold in just three years.[195] Nationwide, the achievement gap between white and minority elementary school students finally narrowed some, although nationwide National Assessment of Educational Progress (NAEP) scores have yet to reflect consistent gains since the passage of No Child Left Behind.[196]

The largest share of federal monies supporting the NCLB Act are allocated under Title I of the continuing Elementary and Secondary Education Act. The U.S. Congress budgeted $12.6 billion for Title I programs in 2005–6. Additional federal funding has been promised to those states able to comply with the provisions of No Child Left Behind. The biggest single complaint, however, has been that the federal government demanded successful reform; yet, it did not provide sufficient bridge funding by which the states and localities can make the necessary changes. In a Public Agenda poll, some 90 percent of school superintendents found the new law amounted to an unfunded mandate in many ways.[197]

Unfunded governmental mandates can clearly create dilemmas for school systems already strapped for cash. But beyond that is the harsh reality of the student body itself. Students attending William D. Kelley Elementary School in Philadelphia represent the reality faced by inner-city public schools across the nation: "The 375 students at Kelley live in North Philadelphia, one of the poorest sections in the city. For some, just getting to school is an achievement. Many of their parents work long hours at low-paying jobs that leave them little time or energy for their children. Others are being raised by grandparents and even great-grandparents, and the older generations are getting worn out. Some live with foster parents and some have parents in jail."[198] Urban school districts clearly have an uphill battle on their hands. It is a battle they have been waging for generations, yet now they must fight it under the watchful eye of the federal No Child Left Behind program.

Countertrends. In 1988 and 1995, the Chicago Public Schools implemented policies that focused the school system on getting passing scores on the Iowa Test of Basic Skills (ITBS) and the Illinois State Achievement Test (ISAT). Pauline Lipman analyzed this experiment and concluded that this focus on testing does not affect the intellectual development of students in schools that are not on probation. Meanwhile, those students in schools on probation are affected negatively because their teachers and administrations change focus from intellectual development to passing the test, the so-called test drive.[199]

Examples of test-drive skewing educational priorities is not exclusive to Chicago. "In the current atmosphere, the reality is that if it isn't tested, it isn't taught," concluded Margaret Altoff, social studies supervisor of the Colorado Springs School District.[200] John Hughes, principal of PS 48 in New York City notes, "You live and die by the fourth grade test," the test used at that time to determine whether an elementary school was failing under the guidelines of No Child Left Behind. "So you put your best teachers in the fourth grade," besides hiring an extra fourth grade teacher to reduce class size. Meanwhile, test scores declined in the third grade, the weaker of those third grade students were held back, so as not to damage the school's fourth grade test average, and the student-to-teacher ratio in the third grade soared.[201]

Another such study was a three-year analysis funded by the National Science Foundation and carried out by Boston College's Center for the Study of Testing, Evaluation and Educational Policy. It concluded that widely utilized standardized tests may actually be harming efforts to improve achievement in math and science. In particular, they criticized how test drive tended to put emphasis on memorization drills rather than the type of reasoning that problem solving requires. This was seen as especially harmful to minority students in urban schools straining to meet externally imposed testing standards. Special programs for gifted students also can be shortchanged.[202] Researchers at Arizona State University also found that while students increasingly showed improvement on their standardized state exams, they actually fell further behind on other independent measures of academic achievement.[203] Significantly less time is being spent on subjects like science, art, history, and physical education, and the national dropout rate has increased.[204]

In Chicago, retaining elementary school students was found to be counterproductive. Achievement scores did not improve for early elementary students. Special education placements increased. And, there was a noticeably higher dropout rate for those forced to repeat the eighth grade. Donald Moore, executive director of Chicago's Designs for Change, concluded that "retained students have shown no academic benefits and have been harmed." He went on to challenge the ethics of sacrificing "the most vulnerable children in the system to scare other children into doing better."[205]

George Madaus, director of the Boston College Center, concluded that "we are not going to test our way out of the nation's education problems. We need to look at materials teachers are using, how teachers are trained, the support teachers have, the social support kids have, a whole series of complex, inter-related factors that have to be tackled."[206] When evaluating school progress, then, it would seem important to look at multiple measures, according to Steven Ross, the director of the Center for Research in Educational Policy at the University of Memphis. Ross argues that schools should be evaluated by achievement scores as well as a school's academic atmosphere and many other factors.[207]

Just prior to the Florida legislature mandating strict test score requirements before promoting a child, their own Department of Education found "research on the subject is clear. Grade level retention does not work. Further, it would be difficult to find another educational practice on which the research findings are so unequivocally negative." Literally hundreds of studies over the past two decades have rather consistently concluded that retained students will lag behind again within two years and are more likely to drop out of high school.[208]

Beyond that, serious concerns have been raised about the adequacy of the testing data itself.[209] As part of the compromise to get the initial NCLB legislation passed, states were allowed to set their own achievement standards, rather than holding them all to a national standard such as the NAEP exam. As a result, some of the highest performing schools in certain states are still failing by federal criteria.[210] The Government Accountability Office, the investigative arm of the U.S. Congress, concluded that there was so much variation in testing methods between the states that comparisons of one state to another was essentially meaningless. In addition, they noted that the majority of school officials interviewed expressed being "hampered by poor and unreliable student data."[211]

There is also the question of just what the state does if it is forced to take over an underperforming school.[212] Thomas Watkins, Michigan state superintendent of schools, analogized states taking over troubled schools to a dog chasing a bus. "What do you do with it once you get it?" Watkins asked rhetorically.[213] Delaware principal Jim Grant concludes that "this is what you get when you mix politics with education, when the people doing it aren't educated about how education really works."[214] As a result, states like Michigan have experimented with various remedial measures short of the type of school takeovers mandated by the federal law.[215]

Other states have engaged in various types of evasion as well. Texas, for instance, has unearthed some significant underreporting of noncompliant test scores.[216] States also have been exaggerating teacher qualifications, increasing the minimum age for children to start school so that they will be older and more mature for their respective grades, and categorizing weaker students in ways that minimize the impact of their low scores on state averages.[217] There is additional evidence that states have been lowering published educational goals in order better to meet them. As an example, only about one-quarter of Tennessee's elementary school students are performing at grade level in reading and math according to the national NAEP assessment; nevertheless, the state's TCAP tests suggest that nearly 90 percent of those students are proficient or better.[218] Former Education Secretary Rod Paige called state officials "enemies of equal justice and equal education . . . [and] apologists for failure."[219] He also called the National Education Association, the nation's largest teachers' union, a "terrorist organization."[220]

Meanwhile, the governor of Connecticut, as well as school districts like the one in Reading, Pennsylvania, filed lawsuits in an attempt to limit enforcement of the law.[221] The National Education Association joined a lawsuit filed by school districts in the states of Michigan, Texas, and Vermont. Common claims are that the gateway tests are racially biased or that the federal law essentially amounts to an unfunded mandate, contrary to its own assurances.[222] Other districts in states like Connecticut and Vermont declined federal money altogether in an attempt to remove themselves from the confines of the No Child Left Behind Act.[223]

The Republican-dominated Utah state legislature has been one of the most openly adamant. Among other things, they voted to withhold most state funding from compliance with No Child Left Behind, claiming a state's right to set their own education agenda.[224] Patti Harrington, Utah's superintendent of public instruction, stated publicly that "we don't have much regard for No Child Left Behind in Utah," as "this law just gets in our way." She referred to its accountability process as "convoluted," its method of determining highly qualified teachers as "faulty," and the requirement that disabled children be tested at grade level, rather than ability level, to be "ludicrous."[225]

A bipartisan panel of lawmakers drawn from several states held hearings in six cities and then issued a seventy-seven-page report concluding essentially the same things articulated by Ms. Harrington.[226] In addition, the state legislatures in more than a dozen states called for the law's repeal, or at least for substantial revisions.[227] The Department of Education finally responded by modifying some of its more burdensome implementation decisions. President Bush also replaced Rod Paige with Margaret Spellings, and she quickly presented a more conciliatory posture than her predecessor.[228]

When the NCLB Act came up for renewal, however, considerable opposition remained. Two-thirds of the nation's adults opposed renewal, with that number highest among those most familiar with the law. Meanwhile, states continued to call for more flexibility, while congressional Democrats demanded significant revisions before they would be willing to renew the act.[229]

Voices of concern also can be heard in Memphis. Lola Bolden, president of the Memphis Education Association, fears that students will get shortchanged in other important areas when teachers are forced to give disproportionate emphasis to passing reading and math TCAP exams. In addition, she stresses how difficult it will be for Memphis to find highly qualified teacher assistants when it is only part-time work, pays just a little over minimum wage, and includes no benefits.[230]

Double Tree Elementary became Tennessee's first public Montessori school in 1997. Montessori students are to follow their own interests and pace, guided by specially trained teachers. The school's ability to adhere to this unique type of learning approach, however, has been jeopardized by the test score requirements of No Child Left Behind.[231]

LaVerne Dickerson is a fifth grade teacher at Oakshire Elementary and a twenty-seven-year veteran of the Memphis City Schools. She notes that "to help children, many of whom come to school with limited learning experiences, teachers must have the flexibility to teach many things." Yet, she worries because "we feel restricted in developing teaching plans that truly meet students' needs because the standards we are given center on testing objectives."[232]

The city of Houston has recently joined cities like Chicago in easing, as opposed to toughening, its rules on promotion. The goal was to reduce dropout rates. In Chicago, promotion requirements were eased for both elementary and high school students when studies found that test scores were actually declining by the sixth grade.[233] In Houston, high school students who fail one or more core subjects may now continue to the next grade as long as they have enough total course credits to do so. According to Superintendent Kaye Stripling, "A student sitting in the ninth grade at age 17 is a kid who's going to say 'Forget this; I'm dropping out.' And Houston can't afford to lose its children that way."[234]

There also is the issue of space, in that students in failing schools must be offered alternative school options. In Chicago, for instance, 365 of the city's 600 schools fell into the failing category. The city then sent 270,000 letters, offering parents the choice of either an alternative school or additional tutoring where they were. Unfortunately, there were only 1,100 seats available in higher-performing schools for the 20,000 parents who requested a transfer.[235] Moi Mecks, spokesperson for the Chicago Public Schools, responded that "if this law was going to cause overcrowding, we are not going to do it. Everyone knows that 40 in a class is not sound educationally."[236]

As might well be predicted, then, there has been a fairly high degree of underutilization. Only about 6 percent of the parents eligible to have their children transferred have actually done so. And, even some of those who transferred have chosen to transfer back after "not fitting in" at their new school. Meanwhile, of those students remaining in the underperforming schools, fewer than half have elected to receive the additional tutoring for which they are supposedly eligible under the federal law.[237] Such tutoring, with the potential of becoming a $2 billion-per-year industry, has only been minimally regulated and appears ripe for waste and fraud.[238]

The Department of Education has argued that the law "does not permit [local school districts] to preclude options on the basis of capacity constraints," even in the face of local initiatives to reduce class sizes or under the pressure of federal desegregation orders.[239] Thus, there is the very real possibility, whether intentionally designed to do so or not, that the No Child Left Behind legislation could end up requiring localities to issue school vouchers if economical public school alternatives cannot be found for parents of children in noncomplying schools. President George W. Bush and some congressional Republicans have even broached the idea of federal school vouchers as an alternative.[240]

School Choice

> The lack of school choice is the Berlin Wall of domestic social policy.
>
> —Lamar Alexander, *Commercial Appeal*, 1996

At the beginning of the new millennium, there were roughly fifty-seven million school-aged children in the United States. Some six million of those attended private schools, and another million were being home schooled. That left nearly 90 percent of America's children in ninety thousand public schools where $500 billion was being spent on their educations.[241] In the face of highly publicized problems in the nation's traditional public schools, especially those located in the largest cities, there has been a hue and cry for educational alternatives that provide more educational bang for the taxpayer buck. Prominent alternatives have included charter schools, school vouchers, and a handful of other approaches.[242]

Home Schooling. Over the years, this practice has taken many forms and has been utilized for a variety of reasons. The reasons have ranged from religious to academic, and from safety to convenience. The education itself tends to be offered by some combination of parents, the Internet, and tutors, while it is sometimes supplemented by public or private school courses and activities. Legal now in every state, the practice seems to be growing, from 850,000 in 1999 to more than 1,000,000 today. It also appears to include families from virtually every racial and income group. Meanwhile, the level of governmental regulation remains quite varied, with only about half the states requiring home-schooled children to pass state examinations. The only common standard appears to be evidence of meeting state attendance requirements.[243]

Public School Options. The days are gone when essentially the only actual school choices were to send your children to a local parochial school or to the neighborhood public school. Today, many cities have liberalized their transfer options between existing public schools, if the transfer promotes a goal of the district.

The Memphis majority-to-minority transfer plan was designed to advance racial desegregation. Most cities also provide one or more of the following options. A magnet school is a specialty public school, or school within an existing school, which offers a specialized curriculum and is open to students across the district. School districts also have contracted with private educational corporations to run some of their public schools. Charter schools, on the other hand, are publicly financed schools that operate under their own approved educational plan. This has allowed them varying degrees of independence from their host school district, especially in terms of hiring and curricular matters.[244]

Magnet Schools. These are public schools with specialized curricula, open to children both within and outside the particular school's boundaries. Some have entrance requirements, while others are open on a first-come basis. They began to emerge when the federal government offered grants under the 1976 Emergency School Aid Act. This was largely an effort to try and induce middle-class white students to return to the central-city public schools their parents had abandoned during desegregation. By the mid-1990s, magnet schools had become a significant component of the school-choice movement, aimed at retaining high achieving black and white students. Today some 1,700 magnet schools educate roughly 3 percent of all U.S. students.[245]

Kansas City, Missouri, has one of the model magnet school programs. Under court order, it spent roughly $1.5 billion to place magnet options in every one of its public schools. The program in Central High School, for instance, ended up with a gymnastics room, wrestling facility, indoor swimming pool, robotics lab, full-time weight trainer, gymnastics and fencing coaches, and a diving instructor. Other schools had educational enhancements such as a planetarium, dust-free diesel mechanic's room, a working farm, and a Model United Nations room.[246]

Most urban school districts worked to maintain a half white/half black ratio in their magnet programs. Some were compelled to so in order to comply with court desegregation orders. Others adopted that formula so they would meet the grant requirements of the federal government. Still others chose this approach as a way of avoiding resegregation by choice in their public schools.[247] It does appear, however, that the U.S. Supreme Court's opinions handed down in the summer of 2007 will seriously limit a school district's ability to use race as an admissions criterion, regardless of the purpose for doing so.[248]

Privatization. Those responsible for public school education also have entered into contractual relationships with private educational corporations. The practice dates back to efforts of the federal Office of Economic Opportunity in the 1970–71 academic year. At that time, private firms were hired to teach twenty thousand underperforming students from twenty different public school districts. The price tag was $6 million.[249]

The current list of private contractors includes Florida's Chancellor Beacon Academies and New York City's Victory Schools. Edison Schools Inc. has been the largest of these private corporations. In 2002, for instance, Edison was running more than 130 schools across twenty-two states, providing education for some 75,000 students.[250] Some of these private education providers are nonprofit corporations. Others, like Edison, run for profit and actually banded together as a billion-dollar industry to form the National Council of Education Providers in order to lobby their cause on Capitol Hill.[251]

Hartford, Connecticut, contracted with Education Alternatives Inc. to run all thirty-two of its public schools. In doing so, it became one of the first major cities to utilize this approach in a sizable way. Nonetheless, Hartford's privatization experiment failed within two years.[252]

Pennsylvania Gov. Mark Schweiker seized control of the Philadelphia public schools in December of 2001, after a majority of its 200,000 students failed state reading and math proficiency exams. Although he abandoned the idea of privatizing the system's central administration, he did appoint the majority of a School Reform Commission, which proceeded to engage in the largest school privatization experiment to date. It contracted with seven different outside managers to run forty-two of Philadelphia's public schools. The largest of these contracts went to Edison, which was to operate twenty city schools.[253] Teachers, however, began to flee the privatized schools almost immediately. After only one year, the city canceled its contract with Chancellor Beacon Academies when it failed to see any indication of educational improvement. Meanwhile, the Edison corporation failed to turn a profit in its first ten years of operation and struggled to borrow needed venture capital.[254]

Charter Schools. In this volume, "charter schools" refer to public schools that receive a relatively high degree of independence if the state approves their educational plans.[255] In 1992, St. Paul, Minnesota, became the first city to utilize charter schools in an attempt to stimulate improvement in their struggling public education system. By 2005, there were more than 3,500 charter schools educating more than a million public school students nationwide. A large majority of states and the District of Columbia have joined the experiment, most allowing a fixed number of such schools statewide, although they have often funded them at a lower level than their traditional schools.[256]

Dayton, Ohio, became a national leader, enrolling more than a quarter of its public school students in charter schools.[257] Bronx Prep is an example of a charter school able to supplement its budget with a sizable amount of private fundraising.[258] The Newark Charter School for Innovative Education was designed to create an inner-city elementary school to be operated by parents, bolstered by $5 million with which to supply each student with a computer and a video camera.[259] Other sizable charter ventures include the KIPP schools, Achievement First, and the Green Dot schools. The latter has even contracted with a teacher's union.[260]

Proponents see charter schools as valuable incubators for developing innovative curricular and instructional approaches while still maintaining public accountability for their outcomes. Joe Nathan, one of the pioneers of the concept, states, "The idea is to have accountable public schools and to encourage fair and thoughtful competition." Sarah Tantillo, a New Jersey charter school consultant, argues, "The intensive effort of charter schools to try to create a safe, nurturing and educationally challenging environment with high expectations is much needed."[261]

Abigail and Stephan Thernstrom hold up Newark's North Star Academy as a model for inner-city education, with its uniforms, extensive homework, "covenant" with parents, a school day that lasts an extra hour, an eleven-month calendar, and an administration freed of union concerns or excessive bureaucratic red tape. Its low-income black student body was challenged with writing poems, letters, skits, and essays, giving speeches, and engaging in mock trials and debates. Soon it was passing state proficiency exams at twice the rate of other schools in the area.[262]

Nevertheless, the National Center for Education Statistics surveyed principals and teachers from 86 percent of all charter schools operating in the 1999–2000 academic year. They found teachers to be better paid than in the corresponding public schools, but they were less likely to be certified and had less teaching experience. Principals tended to be paid less than their public school counterparts. In addition, the student-teacher ratio was higher, and tighter budgets meant fewer educational resources available per pupil. In particular, instructional supplements for low-achieving students were limited by the small amount of Title I monies they received.[263]

Critics also worry that when the money for charter schools has to come out of school districts' existing budgets, this may well amount to spending disproportionately for a few privileged students. If a district's per-student allotment follows the student, for example, the reduction of a student or two in any given class will not allow that school to reduce its staff or most fixed costs. Thus, the school that loses those pupils loses funds without proportionately reducing its costs.[264] In addition, critics fear that such schools will siphon off the top students from across the district and too readily exclude children with learning or behavioral problems. Teacher unions also have resisted charter school personnel policies that often violate contract guidelines, especially as related to teacher certification and tenure.[265]

Sizable infusions of private money have at times raised additional problems of their own. For example, there can be questions of public accountability when charter schools become too beholden to their private patrons. In Brooklyn's Beginning with Children's Charter School, as a case in point, Joseph and Carol Reich contributed hundreds of thousands of dollars. Unhappy with the school's academic progress, they threatened to withdraw their support unless most of the school's trustees agreed to resign, including five parent and faculty representatives.[266]

California Charter Academy, the nation's largest chain of charter schools, went bankrupt shortly before the start of the 2004–5 school year. In doing so, it left six thousand California students without schools and scores of teachers without jobs. C. Steven Cox had been allocated $100 million in state monies to build his sixty charter schools, even though the former insurance executive's only academic credential was that he had once served on a local school board.[267]

Rising costs and meager results have caused states such as New York and Massachusetts to scale back their charter school experiment, while voters in Washington voted down the state's charter school referendum, and the Michigan legislature turned down $200 million in private money to start fifteen charter schools.[268] Susan Winkler, a Long Island parent opposed to charter schools in her community, stated, "I can understand people wanting an alternative. That's fine. They're known as private schools."[269]

Private School Vouchers. School vouchers are educational scrip distributed to parents by government. They are redeemable, at least theoretically, at the existing private school of one's choice. In practice, they can take such forms as actual monetary vouchers, tax rebates for tuition paid, or the public school allocation per child following that child to whichever school he or she chooses. The basic idea has been advanced by ideological conservatives since the 1950s, and support for it has recently grown out of the frustration of inner-city parents, given the well-publicized failings of their existing public schools. The central idea is to let market forces reshape American education by creating competition between schools as they attempt to attract students. Most private schools have been doing this since their inception. School vouchers are designed to give less wealthy families access to educational choices as well.[270]

Individual cities have tended to take the lead on this issue. Milwaukee, for example, began its school voucher program in 1990. Today more than ten thousand low-income parents use vouchers worth up to roughly five thousand dollars per year. Cleveland began their own program six years later, with vouchers worth a little less than half as much as those in Milwaukee. About 5 percent of Cleveland's children were poor enough to receive them. There also have been privately funded voucher programs that have served at least sixty-seven thousand students in thirty different cities.[271]

Meanwhile, Florida was the first state to approve a statewide voucher program. Its Opportunity Scholarship Program passed in 1999 and came to fund more than ten thousand poor or disabled students prior to running into constitutional snags at the state level. Utah followed with an even more sweeping plan that allowed vouchers ranging from five hundred to three thousand dollars for any student in the state. States such as Florida, Arizona, and Pennsylvania also have given tax breaks to corporations that contribute to private scholarship funds.[272] Florida, Ohio, Utah, and Georgia have pioneered vouchers for students with special learning needs. Minnesota and Arizona are among the states that have offered tax refunds to lower-income parents for monies spent on private schools, while the federal government added tax-deferred, private-school savings accounts.[273]

In 2003, despite the strong opposition from the District of Columbia's congressional representative, Eleanor Holmes Norton, the Republican majority in the U.S. Congress managed to pass a school voucher program for the district. Supported by the city's mayor and the head of the local school board, it was designed to allow thirteen hundred D.C. students to switch to private schools, using vouchers that could range up to $7,500 in value.[274]

Opposition has most often been voiced by teachers' unions, blacks and whites over fifty, middle-class suburbanites, and black politicians. Opponents see school vouchers as inherently flawed. To begin with, they doubt that these programs will ever provide enough money for lower-income children to be able to attend the better schools, including the transportation costs of getting there. The City of Cleveland adopted a school voucher program, for example, yet not a single city student ended up using his or her voucher to attend a school in suburban Cleveland.[275] At very least, tuition at the more elite schools will rise with the additional demand. For the large majority of inner-city children, without private money to supplement their vouchers, the schools they attend are likely to face many of the same problems as the current public schools, yet those schools will be less regulated and even more segregated by economic class.[276] Christopher Jencks and his colleagues concluded that the only way to avoid such class segregation was either to give proportionately larger vouchers to poorer children or to require all schools to accept vouchers as full payment of tuition.[277]

In addition, there is very little achievement data that allows us to compare the academic success of public school students and private school students. The data that does exist does not support a general advantage for private schools. One of the most extensive studies was done by the U.S. Department of Education, comparing the 2003 fourth- and eighth-grade reading and math scores from nearly 7,000 public schools and more than 530 private schools. What they found was that public schools generally performed as well or better in reading and mathematics. The one exception was in eighth grade reading, where the private school counterparts fared better.[278]

The campaign for vouchers is also seen as a Trojan horse for finally achieving publicly funded religious education. In Florida, nearly 60 percent of the voucher-eligible children used their vouchers to attend religious schools.[279] In Cleveland, that number was 96 percent. The U.S. Supreme Court did not find Cleveland's results to be a violation of the first amendment's prohibition against governmentally establishing religion.[280] Nonetheless, limiting any such choice to nonreligious schools could help determine what the real underlying motivations actually are in this regard. The state of Maine, for instance, presently does this in their rural areas in lieu of building additional public schools.

Meanwhile, there have been indirect ways of advancing the general cause of governmentally funding private school tuition. The Pennsylvania legislature, for instance, provided dollar-for-dollar tax credits for private scholarship donations as well as some tuition payments. New Jersey proposed a similar plan but limited it to low-income urban school districts.[281]

Academic Results of Choice. When looking at the choice models taken as a whole, little replicable research currently exists that isolates the independent impact of these various programs on student achievement.[282] Meanwhile, the empirical evidence that does exist has been mixed at best. Some weak public schools have been forced to innovate in order to survive. In addition, parental satisfaction and school involvement does seem to be higher than normal when a choice has been made, although there is also evidence that lower-income parents generally operate with less complete information when making those choices. Even in instances where achievement scores are higher at the chosen school than at the standard public schools in the area, there is little evidence that much of anything improves districtwide. This would seem to support the contention that schools of choice are often just skimming the better students from the public school population.[283] Minnesota school superintendent Lewis Finch called them "an elitist wolf wrapped in egalitarian sheepskin."[284]

Magnet schools, for instance, have improved racial integration and have been able to demonstrate relatively high achievement scores. On the other hand, many have been selective in their admissions, all but preordaining higher than normal achievement numbers. They have been accused of spending a disproportionate amount per student and using procedures that make it easier for better-off parents to navigate the maze necessary to attain the limited number of seats available. Where they have been selective, they also have been accused of skimming away the best students and teachers from their cities' remaining public schools, leaving those schools with an even weaker student body, fewer role models, a corps of less-involved parents, and less desirable places to teach. Kansas City's high powered system, for instance, could not show relative systemwide gains when compared to other school districts in the state.[285]

Charter schools have experienced some measurable success, as indicated by the studies of scholars such as Caroline Hoxby, Francis Shen, Kenneth Wong, and Brian Hassel.[286] Nevertheless, controlling for demographic variables like race and income, the U.S. Department of Education found charter students performing similarly or worse than comparable public school students on key achievement exams. Beyond mixed achievement results, some of these schools also have benefited from private monies not as available to the standard public schools. In addition, they have been plagued by financial mismanagement scandals, besides struggling to balance their budgets, retain teachers, and meet their promised achievement scores, graduation rates, and college matriculation goals. Many of the charter school problems have been blamed on their limited accountability and the fact that their teachers are less likely to be certified or experienced.[287]

Privatized schools have struggled as well. Despite some relatively impressive claims of success, it has been difficult to independently verify their assertions. The General Accounting Office reviewed the advertised claims of Edison, Chancellor Beacon, and Mosaica Education in 2002. Only one of the industry's own studies held up to scientific rigor, and it was inconclusive. Meanwhile, the Department of Education found them with no better achievement results than nonprofit charter schools, and some of their gains have been linked to their exclusion of low-performing students.[288] Meanwhile, the federal Office of Economic Opportunity concluded that its $6 million "experiment" in privatization "did not materially affect student achievement."[289]

When vouchers are used to attend private schools, parental satisfaction does seem to rise.[290] Meanwhile, voucher students in private schools appear to perform slightly better on academic achievement tests than do public school students as a whole, and this seems even more likely to be true of African American students.[291] Researchers studying the impact of vouchers on student achievement have been quick to note, however, that "it is difficult to conclude with any degree of confidence" either way at this stage.[292] There is also evidence that parents using vouchers are better educated than other low-income parents,[293] and they appear to "provide more intellectual stimulus at home."[294]

Other Choices. If the goal is to add an element of school choice in order to jolt underperforming public schools into competing, one alternative within the current structure would be a more liberal transfer program within the existing public schools. If this included transportation, it would seem to accomplish many of the aims of school choice without some of the more dangerous potential side effects. The demand numbers, even if they could not all be readily accommodated, would serve as a strong indicator for school administrators to consider when evaluating the various schools in their district.

Faced with significant literacy problems among their high school students, some states have begun to provide more alternatives to the standard high school approach. The National Governors Association, for instance, has launched a major new initiative. They want to see high schools provide more remedial services for those who cannot read, as well as partial tuition reimbursement for students who opt instead for community college programs that lead to technical or industrial job certificates.[295]

Memphis Experience. The City of Memphis has not adopted school vouchers, and it has only recently begun to experiment with charter schools as the state of Tennessee gradually expands its support for those options. Memphis received six of the state's first seven charter schools, including its first, the Memphis Academy of Sciences and Engineering, in 2003.[296] The Shelby County Schools have yet to adopt a charter school, at least in part because none of their forty-seven schools have failed under No Child Left Behind.[297]

Memphis also experimented with the KIPP approach in charter schools, engaging students, parents, and teachers in extended-hour instruction.[298] A separate experiment in year-round classes at two elementary schools was discontinued, however, after no real achievement gains could be determined.[299] Former Superintendent Gerry House had moved the district to a more uniform curriculum, in part to minimize the educational disruption caused by the city's relatively high mobility rate. She also required each school to adopt one of eighteen reform models percolating around the nation. Some of those models generated more identifiable success than others, but most have subsequently been abandoned.[300]

Magnet schools within larger public schools have provided attractive academic alternatives, allowing the city's public schools to compete with area private schools for some of the most talented students available. Their popularity is evident by the long lines of parents who have assembled each year to vie for available openings in the more than thirty optional schools available.[301] The overall program enrolls more than eleven thousand Memphis-area students, including more than six thousand transfer students. In addition, a community report card allows parents to monitor the strengths and weaknesses of local public schools by listing special programs, average class sizes, both achievement and disciplinary numbers, as well as survey information gathered from the school's students, parents, and teachers.[302]

Nonetheless, the optional schools have not been without their critics. They have been accused of being a resource drain, siphoning away many of the better teachers and a disproportionate share of the educational resources—often at the particular expense of the larger host schools within which each resided. They were accused of creaming the best students out of neighborhood schools, depriving those left of positive academic role models. No transportation was provided, thus making such transfers much tougher for lower-income students. In addition, the first-come transfer policy has been seen as favoring parents who can afford to camp overnight at the board of education for several nights in a row—or at least regularly check in to hold spots. Some have even paid others to stand in line for them. The whole admission process has turned out to be far more difficult for lower-income single parents.[303]

Chapter 7

Conclusions

Can parity at schools ever make up for the differences between children born to college-educated, middle class parents and those born in abject poverty?

—Wendi C. Thomas, editorialist, *Commercial Appeal*

The problems we have in the schools today can largely be predicated on our ability to change the social and economic conditions of families.

—Dr. W. W. Herenton, mayor, Memphis, Tennessee

We can no longer use poverty as an excuse, but I think we ought to be cognizant of poverty.

—Johnnie B. Watson, former superintendent, Memphis City Schools

Many educational challenges face the United States in the twenty-first century. This book, however, has focused on how postindustrial economic changes and a history of racial exclusion have combined to make it harder than ever for low-income African Americans living in postindustrial urban ghettos to rise from rags to riches in today's postindustrial information age. When a society relies heavily on its public education system to provide opportunities for economic success, it is imperative that the educational system function as effectively as possible.

However, this is not the case in Memphis. Despite having better student-to-teacher ratios, spending more per pupil, and having teachers with more college training, city school students lag well behind county school students in key performance measures at all grade levels. Thus, it appears that output gaps have more to do with the academic disadvantages low-income students bring to school with them than with the quality of the educational resources available once they arrive. In addition, when comparing the poor and poorer black schools, the fact that court-ordered school busing altered the racial make up of the Memphis City Schools appears to be far less important than the fact that a momentum developed that drove away middle-income blacks and whites.

The Problem

In truth, we already are entering a second period of reconstruction in which disadvantaged minorities are being forced back into their "place" as a separate underclass (that is, caste) in our society. . . . Located primarily in racial and ethnic central city ghettos, the members of this underclass tend to grow up in low-income, female-headed families in which poverty and social disorganization are being handed down from one generation to the next.

—Allan Ornstein et al., *Reforming Metropolitan Schools*, 1975

The troubled Memphis school system has evolved amid considerable racial turmoil and economic transformation. Slavery postponed the education of African Americans. Jim Crow laws left their subsequent educations separate and unequal. Then, court-ordered school busing to achieve school desegregation instead encouraged many more affluent people to leave the city limits altogether, with serious social and economic implications for the public schools that remained. The status quo, then, is a city school system with a student body that is poor, black, and underperforming. How we got to this point matters far less at this stage than where we go from here.

The No Child Left Behind legislation was designed to make educational opportunities more inclusive. To be sure, that is most definitely a desirable goal. Abandonment is not part of the American Dream. Yet urban sociologist William Julius Wilson warns us that in order to address the learning gaps found in today's metropolitan areas, "programs that will have the greatest effect are those that attack all aspects of the structure of inequality. Only then can we drastically reduce and eventually eliminate the environmental differences that create the present gap."[1]

If significant brain development, as well as most education, inevitably takes place outside the school setting, is the United States ready to face up to the harsh reality that every time a child fails it does not necessarily mean the child's school has failed? There is considerable evidence that students who are born into poverty bring many disadvantages with them when they come to school. Supplemental funding and remediation efforts can certainly help level the playing field, but the schools would be in a much better position to educate, rather than just provide education, if underlying disadvantages could be significantly reduced.[2]

As Greg Duncan and Jeanne Brooks-Gunn pointed out in their book, *Consequences of Growing Up Poor,* "programs that raise the incomes of poor families will enhance the cognitive development of children and may improve their chances of success in the labor market during adulthood. Most important appears to be the elimination of deep and persistent poverty during a child's early years."[3]

A Solution: The Five Rs

Based on the previous discussion of both the educational problems faced by the Memphis City Schools and the range of reform alternatives available, it appears to be time to seriously consider a "Five Rs" approach: reasonable income, reforms, resolve, responsibility, and respect. Together, they hold out the promise of a society that conforms much more closely to its own ideals, not to mention creating a more productive, peaceful, and secure single nation. Should all of these be pursued, however, the end result will be quite costly. Each step, however, can be beneficial in and of itself, thus the comprehensive price tag should not deter us from beginning the effort.

Reasonable Income

> Economic mobility in the United States—the extent to which individuals and families move from one social class to another—is no higher than in Britain or France, and lower than in some of the Scandinavian countries. Maybe we should be studying the Scandinavian Dream (instead of the American Dream).
>
> —Bob Herbert, *New York Times,* 2005

There appears to be a vicious cycle of poverty at work. Children from poor families arrive at school less ready to learn and often do not achieve. Those who have not done well in school are less likely to go to college, or even to graduate from high school. They face a life of less gainful employment and thus more poverty for themselves and the children they rear. All of which will be even truer yet in the postindustrial information age, where advanced formal education is becoming even more important for one's economic prosperity. Economist Harry Holzer recently testified before Congress that having poor children costs the American economy some $500 billion annually, because once they grow up they are less productive, earn less, are more apt to commit crimes and incur more mental-health expenses.[4]

The first *R*, then, is reasonable income. Any discussion of a reasonable income has to distinguish between those who are and are not employable. In most cases, this will be self-evident and can be confirmed by medical examination. Those who because of age or disability are truly unemployable need to be supported. The nobility of a society may well be best reflected in how it takes care of its young, old, and infirm members.

Of course, there will be ambiguities. For example, is a mother with preschool children in the home employable? That, it would seem, is a societal decision. Just how important is it for mothers of small children to be in the home nurturing their infants and toddlers? We do know from the scientific literature that such interactions are absolutely crucial to the brain development and social development of the children involved. So, if the mother is to be expected to work or chooses to work, day care will need to be readily available to substitute for that crucial nurturing role.

Meanwhile, for those deemed to be employable, it would seem important for them to be able to work themselves out of poverty, so as to break the cycle previously discussed. The nonpartisan Economic Policy Institute annually calculates the costs of basic needs for a family of four. These are the costs of housing, food, childcare, healthcare, transportation, taxes, and other necessities. A living wage, then, is what a breadwinner would have to earn, working forty hours a week, fifty-two weeks a year, in order to provide for those necessities. That amount is currently estimated to be $10.72 per hour.[5]

Unfortunately, many workers do not earn a living wage in today's economy. Wal-Mart, for instance, has surpassed General Motors as the nation's largest employer, and it pays its full-time workers an average of $9.68 per hour. Although that wage is well above the current minimum wage of $6.55 and is higher than what is paid by many other service-sector employers, this still amounts to poverty-level wages if the employee is the sole breadwinner for a family of four. It also leaves the family eligible for Medicaid and food stamps, essentially requiring the American taxpayer to subsidize Wal-Mart's wages. Meanwhile, fewer than one-half of Wal-Mart employees receive health insurance coverage, and the Wal-Mart benefits package is less than two-thirds of the national average.[6]

In his 1944 inaugural address, Franklin Roosevelt expressed his support for "a second Bill of Rights." He argued that these rights should include "the right to a useful and remunerative job, . . . the right to earn enough to provide adequate food and clothing and recreation, . . . the right of every family to a decent home, . . . the right to adequate protection from the economic fears of old age, sickness, accident and unemployment, . . . [and] the right to a good education."

States and localities are competing with each other for postindustrial investment and thus are unlikely to take the lead in enacting the kinds of regulation, taxing, and spending that would be required to bring Roosevelt's vision to fruition. If there remains commitment to the concept that working full time should provide a livable wage that lifts one out of poverty, such leadership almost certainly will have to come from the federal government, as it did in addressing the Great Depression.[7]

A New Deal. A New Deal is particularly needed for the dispossessed locked in postindustrial cities. The goal would be to guarantee a decent job with livable wages and benefits for all working Americans. Health insurance and housing also could be tied to employment, as it often is for company executives today. In addition, there needs to be such things as wage insurance and retraining for those who lose their jobs due to the rapidly changing information age economy. In the end, the focus of federal economic policy needs to be maximizing the number of middle-class jobs. One of the main challenges, however, is doing this in a manner that does not simply inflate the costs of goods and services, thus nullifying wage gains.[8]

The good news is that there are European models to study, such as the Danish "Flexicurity" program which attempts to maximize both security and flexibility. It amounts to a social compact where labor accepts change, business supports a generous safety net, and government provides retraining and other benefits. In 2003, for instance, half of all Danish workers were engaged in supplemental training and skill development. There are few national labor laws, leaving things like minimum wages, working hours, and family leave to be determined by collective bargaining at the shop level. Unemployment insurance, which can pay benefits for up to four years, pays as much as 90 percent of one's wages for the lowest paid workers, adjusted downward for those better off. Yet, despite such generosity, one-half of the unemployed are back to work within six months, 70 percent within one year. If laid off, they are required to work with a specialist in their field and to be retrained within a year. A graphic designer may get retrained as a nurse; but, if he or she does not cooperate, the person is dropped from the Flexicurity program and is on his or her own.

As a result, Denmark has the highest employment rate and the most equal income distribution of all the industrialized nations. Polling data also indicate that their workers are the most satisfied in Europe. As one might imagine, the costs are high, requiring high value-added tax rates. Nonetheless, net public spending, after deducting indirect taxes and special tax breaks, is only slightly higher than in the United States.[9] Bruce Stokes concludes that "the Danish experience demonstrates that a more adaptable labor force supported by ample unemployment benefits and mandatory retraining is a boon for workers, for companies, and for countries in an increasingly competitive international economy."[10]

Domestically, there have been some innovative approaches at times as well. The Davis-Bacon Act, for example, required federal contractors to pay "prevailing wages" as early as 1931.[11] Federal minimum wage requirements went into effect in 1938. More recently, the living wage movement, comprised largely of church congregations and labor unions, pressed cities to pay living wages and to require them of their contractors. The Memphis living wage campaign began in 2004, with a goal of ten dollars per hour with benefits, or twelve dollars per hour without them. More than 115 cities currently have adopted such ordinances.[12]

The state of Massachusetts now has a universal health care program where employers must either provide health insurance or pay a fee of up to $295 per employee each year. Exemptions are made for small employers. Uninsured individuals can purchase coverage through The Connector, a quasi-public corporation that leverages collective buying power in order to get reasonable group rates and coverage. Meanwhile, a variety of tax models have been used in order to provide such assistance.[13]

The Center for American Progress recently published its own three-pronged proposal for significantly reducing poverty in the United States. Their plan called for a sizable increase in the minimum wage, expanding the earned-income and child-care tax credits, and expanding child-care subsidies for low-income families. At a cost to government of roughly $90 billion per year, the center estimated that this could eliminate half of all American poverty within ten years.[14]

Reforms

The fact that educational opportunities alone may be necessary but not sufficient to overcome major achievement gaps means there is only so much we can expect schools to be able to accomplish. Nonetheless, as former Memphis City Schools' Superintendent Johnnie B. Watson argues, that cannot become an excuse for failing to do everything possible to improve existing schools. Striving to significantly help many students while reducing the waste of scarce resources is clearly a part of the comprehensive approach required. What we must not do is simply throw more money or demands at a troubled school system. To do so can be wasteful and only makes the public even less inclined to provide more assistance in the future.[15]

Professor George Madaus, director of the Boston College Center for the Study of Testing, Evaluation and Educational Policy, reached the following conclusion more than a decade ago. Well before the No Child Left Behind Act was even being mentioned, Madaus was convinced that "we are not going to test our way out of the nation's education problems. We need to look at materials teachers are using, how teachers are trained, the support teachers have, the social support kids have, a whole series of complex, inter-related factors that have to be tackled."[16] Consequently, the second *R* is reform, and these proposed reforms will be presented in an arguable priority order.

Early Intervention. First of all, many children arrive at school severely underprepared and may never acquire the academic aptitude to succeed in the standard classroom. If the United States truly believes in the concept of equal opportunity and wishes to fairly hold people responsible for their failures, the nation must find a way to better level the playing field before students arrive at school. It is also necessary to keep that field level while they are there, for as James Ryan reminds us, "To the extent that a student's peers and the culture of a school exert demonstrable influence on student achievement, simply increasing expenditures in schools populated by poor students will not necessarily affect achievement."[17]

Given the city's disproportionate amount of poverty, many Memphis students face considerable disadvantages before they ever walk through the schoolhouse doors. High quality preschools offer advantages, especially to underprivileged children. Ideally, there would be high quality public preschool available to all children beginning at age one, with a special emphasis on language skills. These classes would be taught by certified teachers and available on a full-day basis. If a child's caregivers felt unable to offer appropriate stimulation and nurturing from infancy, this option would be there. Not only would it help the children, but it also would allow their caregivers an opportunity to work or return to school without having to pay for high quality day care.[18] Many states are already moving toward a public K4 option. This proposal would simply expand that option to K1, K2, and K3.

On a smaller scale, programs such as Early Head Start and Cradle to Classroom would seem to hold out considerable promise in a poverty-plagued city such as Memphis, especially if they were extended to include all low-income parents. In addition, there is a need for campaigns through churches and other social organizations to raise parental awareness of their role in their child's education, both before and after their child first heads off to school. There is also a need to guarantee that there is age-appropriate reading material in each and every home and that parents realize the importance of it being used.

Yet even when underprivileged children have had the benefit of preschool programs like Head Start, there is empirical evidence of achievement slippage that tends to occur as those children age and their impoverished peers and environment begin competing even more for their attention. Consequently, there is also a need to help these students make the adjustment from elementary school to the middle and upper grades. Poor children will still need the same extra services that programs like Head Start provided them when they were younger. Besides supplemental education, these services include nutritionists, social workers, psychologists, and people hired to encourage caregiver involvement.

Caregiver Involvement. Given all that is known about just how essential the caregiver is in a child's overall education, especially early in life, it would also appear to be critically important to find ways to encourage caregiver involvement and prepare caregivers to be effectively involved. Samuel Casey Carter noted that a common component of high performing inner-city schools was a "parental contract" that required parents to read to their children, check homework, and monitor assignments.[19] Yet, in his 2005 budget proposal, President George W. Bush proposed more money for school testing but less for programs designed to increase parental involvement for low-income children. That prioritization needs to be reconsidered in light of all that has come to be known about the intellectual and social development of children, especially in their infancy.

Small Classes. The principle that often guides public policy in the United States is that those closest to a problem are most likely to best understand what needs to be done to address that problem. So, what is the one thing that teachers have been telling us for years will most help them educate children once they arrive in their classrooms? The one factor that virtually every educator agrees on is a manageable class size. Children in a poverty-stricken city such as Memphis will arrive with greater than average needs, and more learning than usual will inevitably have to occur at school rather than in the home. Thus, classes will need to be smaller yet. African American students in the early elementary grades seem to be particularly advantaged by smaller classes. This was evident in achievement data from both Wisconsin and Tennessee.[20]

Teacher Development. Empirical evidence demonstrates a correlation between high quality teachers and enhanced student performance, especially for minority students in the elementary grades.[21] Consequently, for school reform to be most successful, schools need to be able to attract the nation's best and brightest educators. Sir Michael Barber notes that the world's top school systems "select their teachers from the top third of their college graduates, whereas the U.S. selects its teachers from the bottom third of its graduates."[22]

If our schools are indeed responsible for educating the future leaders and workforce of our nation, such a significant responsibility should be carried out by some of the very best our nation has to offer. To do this will require adequate incentives. Salaries need to be commensurate with other professions requiring advanced and specialized education, and there is a need for a school day and a school year that will allow sufficient time for teacher planning, preparation, and continuing education. Also, if public school teachers are finally to be treated as bona fide professionals, it will be essential that they are qualified to hold such positions. This will require far more stringent certification standards and increased salary and benefits, until a sufficient crop of teachers can be attracted who can meet those higher standards.

Linking teacher salaries to student achievement, on the other hand, is a counterproductive notion. In a city like Memphis, student mobility renders the test results all but meaningless in many schools. The student body the teacher begins with is too often not the same group being tested at year's end. Beyond that, the array of learning disabilities also makes comparing achievement scores across schools problematic. Tying teacher salaries to such student achievement only demeans the profession of teaching and discourages talented individuals from seeking that career. In the end, it truly does amount to the same thing as linking a physician's fees to his or her patient's health.

Better Use of Time. Public schools in cities like Memphis are continually called upon to provide a host of social services, on top of the responsibilities of educating the children. If that is to continue, at least three things need to occur. First, the school day needs to be lengthened and restructured, allowing more time for needy students to receive additional services. Second, more staff needs to be hired with appropriate training for such tasks. Teachers have plenty enough to do simply trying to educate their students. Third, given that slower learners appear particularly inclined to regress when outside the more formal educational structure, it would seem to be time to seriously consider year-round education.[23] As Samuel Casey Carter noted, "Extended days, extended years, after-school programs, weekend programs, and summer school are all features of outstanding [urban] schools."[24]

One possible model for year-round education would have the children attend their regular schools for all twelve months, interspersing the school year with two-week breaks for family vacations, school building maintenance, and teacher planning. The breaks would not be so long as to invite academic regress, and child care could be provided to accommodate working parents. This model would also take better advantage of the existing infrastructure.

Harlem's Children's Zone provides a comprehensive model that incorporates many of the above principles. Serving roughly nine thousand Central Harlem children, the program includes small classes, longer school days and school years, better paid teachers, family health care, family counseling, a low-cost produce market, and emergency financial assistance for families. The price tag is roughly $50 million per year, currently coming from both the city and substantial private donations. According to the program's author, Geoffrey Canada, "We think you start this at birth. And you continue it until kids graduate from college."[25]

167

School District Consolidation. Three of Tennessee's four largest counties have implemented metropolitan-wide school consolidation. In each instance, consolidation was followed quickly by both a reduction in administrative duplication and evidence of a more efficient utilization of existing resources. In addition, student-to-teacher ratios declined, per-pupil expenditures increased, teacher qualifications and remuneration improved, students gained access to more course options and special services, and city school students got additional supplies, transportation, and building improvements. Nevertheless, this consolidation did not produce an educational nirvana. School expenditures actually increased some, in large part as a result of state equalization requirements. Overall attendance rates remained pretty much unchanged. Long-settled desegregation agreements were reopened, leading to some involuntary reassignment of teachers for the purpose of desegregation. Some suburban schools lost their Title I eligibility as they were consolidated with more needy city schools. In addition, serious academic and behavioral problems continued to plague some of the system's poorest schools long after the consolidation dust had settled.[26]

On balance, however, consolidating the Memphis City Schools with the Shelby County Schools seems to hold out the promise of increased educational opportunities for students in both systems. Most students would continue to attend their existing schools, although there would be a more efficient prioritization for the use of scarce funds, and equalization would guarantee that all students would end up with more services than they had before consolidation. Consolidation of the two districts, on the other hand, would create a single school district of more than 160,000 students, making it one of the largest in the United States. Given the potential risks of overcentralization, Memphis Mayor W. W. Herenton proposed a consolidation model that included five smaller subdistricts.[27]

The idea of more decentralized school decision making has been advocated for some time.[28] It would appear to make intuitive sense that those closest to the day-to-day learning environment of the children would be in the best position to make the key education-related decisions affecting those children's educations. Principals, for example, need more leeway to hire those whom they feel will best be able to teach the children at that particular school, while individual classroom teachers should have more leeway to tailor learning approaches to their specific student bodies. However, such a decentralized plan requires close monitoring to avoid cronyism and waste.[29]

Mayor Herenton's subdistricts were drawn in an east-west fashion to allow a healthy socioeconomic mix of students in each subdistrict, joining the city and its suburbs in a unified pursuit of quality education for all the students in a subdistrict. In addition, school district lines were drawn within each subdistrict to increase socioeconomic diversity in the individual schools.[30] Schools with heavy concentrations of low-income children do not have good track records as learning environs, and empirical evidence shows that the integration of economic classes can lift the achievement of the poor without harming those better off. Classroom diversity also can be a net plus for all involved, as it provides better preparation for the real world students will soon enter.[31]

Promotion Standards and School Choice. Scientific evidence indicates the need to focus on early and continuing intervention, while educators in the trenches tell us that they need smaller classes, more academic hours, and more classroom-level discretion. It is also clear that current compensation packages and teaching environments are not attracting enough of the nation's very best and brightest into the teaching field. As a society, however our most recent response to educational dilemmas has been to implement more testing requirements and call for more competition between the schools. Although simpler and far less expensive, the problems each of these approaches entail seem to far outweigh any empirical evidence of their academic success.[32]

In particular, it is important to consider the inner-city realities faced by many of the children who are in most need of educational reform in a city like Memphis. For example, it seems wasteful to expend scarce education resources testing and retesting individual schools and classrooms in a city with the mobility rate of Memphis. It also amounts to expending funds testing students who come to school intellectually damaged by neglect, when that money could be better spent reducing that neglect and remediating its results. Similarly, school vouchers are of little value to children who bounce from caregiver to caregiver, lack the transportation necessary to reach most private schools, or do not have enough money to supplement the vouchers for tuition.

Memphis Reforms. The Memphis City Schools have been studied and restudied over the years, generating numerous reform proposals. Many of those proposals have subsequently been adopted, including several of those discussed here. Nevertheless, as the city's output measures indicate, the city schools still have far to go.

In terms of administrative practices, Future Memphis Inc. analyzed the school system's business practices in 1980, while its staffing patterns were reviewed by Security Pacific Inc. in 1988. Organization Consultants Inc. studied personnel policies and practices in 1989, and Tallahassee's MGT Corporation performed a "Management and Performance Review" in 2003. Most of the recommendations of those taskforces were subsequently implemented.[33]

More recently, the city schools unveiled a five-year master plan entitled "Achieving the Vision: A Five-Year Master Plan for Memphis City Schools." Announced in January of 2006, the plan calls for redrawing attendance boundaries, closing some schools and building some new ones, reducing busing, standardizing grade configurations to a K–5, 6–8, 9–12 model, and further standardizing curricula to help counter the impact of student mobility. Priorities also entailed increasing early childhood programs, including an early childhood literacy initiative, and further encouraging partnerships with parents.[34]

Other useful innovations have included KIPP, MCS Reads, New Leaders for New Schools, and the New Teacher Project. There also have been attempts to create parent academies to help parents learn ways to assist children's learning.[35] Teachers and principals have been retrained and intensive tutoring applied.[36] Retired teachers have been brought in to work as substitutes, tutors, and mentors.[37] In addition, the Shelby County Schools have experimented with a Start Smart program in Millington, adding 3K and 4K, as well as utilizing adult education and home-based education programs for parents of infants and toddlers.[38]

Resolve

Memphis Mayor W. W. Herenton set off a small firestorm of protest when he stated that serious school reform will not begin until "the education of white students in the suburbs begins to suffer."[39] Regardless of what it will take to get our collective attention, as a society we have long claimed to believe in equal opportunity. If that is still the case, we must come to grips with a very fundamental question. Do we see our responsibility to our children simply to provide them with educational opportunities, or are we truly committed to educating each and every one of them?

If we are serious about finding a way to educate all children so that they truly can rise or fall on their own merits, the proposals discussed above suggest a price tag that will be formidable. Effective education-related reforms will require significant sacrifice across society if we are to reduce poverty, provide quality education options beginning at age one, reach out to indigent caregivers, reduce class sizes, extend school days and school years, attract more of the nation's best and brightest into the teaching profession, and effectively consolidate and decentralize educational administration. As a nation, we are already spending roughly $1 trillion per year on education.[40] We can spend that amount more wisely, but we also will have to spend much more if anything resembling comprehensive reform is to be implemented.

David Grissmer and colleagues conducted a comprehensive state-by-state analysis of schools for the Rand Corporation that spanned a seven-year period of time. What they ended up concluding was that "we see gains in some states from reform efforts, and we see that resources, if they're properly targeted can be very effective at raising achievement."[41] They found that successful states were more likely to have higher per-pupil expenditures, lower student-teacher ratios, more publicly provided pre-K education, more teacher satisfaction, and less teacher turnover.[42]

Millington's Start Smart program combines several of these elements. There are also other models that could be refined and implemented across the poorer areas of Shelby County. Geoffrey Canada's Harlem Children's Zone, for example, monitors low-income children in a sixty-block area from birth to college, providing educational, social, and medical services. According to Marian Wright Edelman, no community based program is as comprehensive or holds as much promise.[43]

Meanwhile, the Center for American Progress and the Institute for America's Future sponsored a taskforce that scoured the United States looking for successful programs. Their efforts culminated in a 2005 report that called for lengthening the school year and extending the school day, all-day kindergartens as well as 3K and 4K programs, voluntary national standards, strengthening high school curricula, improving assessment devices, providing aid to lagging schools, upgrading teacher training and rewards for good teaching, mobilizing families to help students learn, and more community schools with social services for parents in the same building. The estimated cost was roughly $325 billion over ten years, although it would actually only require raising federal education spending from 3.0 to 4.5 percent of the federal budget.[44] The advantage of pursuing such funding at the national level is that state and local-level initiatives run the risk of driving businesses and individual taxpayers to lower-taxing locales.

School finance reform, as mandated by a near majority of state supreme courts, is a significant step, requiring states and localities to more equally fund the schools in the poorest school districts.[45] If we are serious about equal opportunity, however, schools will need to be funded in an even more equitable fashion. Ideally, the quality of the weakest public school would rise to the level of the best, or at least the average, elite private school. At one point, former Minnesota Senator Walter Mondale proposed that per-pupil funding in the public schools should be pegged at 90 percent of what is spent in the wealthiest private schools. Even if we do not go that far, such elite school spending still provides a reasonable benchmark by which to assess the quality of education being offered by the public schools to the overwhelming majority of our nation's students.

Yet even a formula that radical may not be enough for today's inner-city children. That is because it currently requires considerably more funds to educate a low-income child, as they often come to school with higher incidences of malnutrition, poor health, less parental involvement, less nurturing and stimulating home environments, frequent changes of residence, and more exposure to violence. Several recent studies peg the additional costs at roughly 40 percent more per child.[46] Maine's Essential Programs and Services system provides a school-funding subsidy model that compensates districts with low property values and provides subsidies for special needs students, students with limited English proficiency, and those from impoverished backgrounds.[47]

A recent Gallup Poll indicated that roughly two-thirds of all Americans see inadequate funding as the number one problem faced by schools today.[48] Nevertheless, it is also important to cultivate and maintain popular consensus for such spending. Charles Shaddow, a New Jersey school superintendent, reminds us that getting voters to sign onto education spending increases requires you "to show your citizens that this is what is needed and that it's not too much and not too little."[49]

Some of these costs actually can be recouped in the long run by ultimately decreasing the need for remediation and grade repetition, not to mention the health, welfare, and prison costs that accompany the release of undereducated citizens into society. In addition, one way to increase education revenues would be to set up a progressive school-funding arrangement nationwide. Federal legislation could require employers and employees to contribute a percentage of their incomes in proportion to what they are making. These federal revenues would then be set aside exclusively for equalizing school funding. This would not only help guarantee more equal educational opportunities; it would tax most heavily those who have gained the most from the American educational system as a whole.

Volunteerism also can help defray some of the expenses involved in this level of comprehensive educational reform. Programs can be created, for example, to encourage retired people to volunteer their services. There are established programs such of AmeriCorps and Teach for America whose contributions could be blended into this larger effort.[50] In addition, as a nation we might seriously weigh the benefits of a one- or two-year national service requirement, whereby all young people would be compelled to render some form of national service in fields such as the military, public works, or education.

Responsibility

It is time to expect responsible behavior on the part of all parties involved here, whether they be taxpayers, educators, students, or those rearing students. If the United States is to act responsibly and provide these far more equal opportunities at considerable taxpayer expense, it has a legitimate right to expect a reasonable degree of responsibility on the part of its students, their caregivers, and those who will administer costly education-related reform.[51]

There are external and internal impediments to student advancement. Children have a responsibility to do their homework, stay in school, master standard English, and stop having babies. Bill Gates, for instance, notes that half of all black children fail to graduate from high school, while nearly two-thirds of black teenage girls will become pregnant even though that will make them five times more likely to be poor. "Are white racists forcing black teens to drop out of school and to have babies?" he asks. He concludes, "We can't talk about the choices people have without talking about the choices people make." As well, Barack Obama emphasizes "diligent effort and deferred gratification."[52]

The adults in these students' lives have responsibilities as well. Fathers, for example, need to raise the children they help produce. Meanwhile, caregivers need to talk to their children, read to them, and monitor their academic work. Those caregivers also need to extol the virtues of diligence and academic success.

Educators also have a responsibility, especially if education is finally to become a profession with pay and benefits commensurate with its level of training and societal importance. Teacher certification will need to become far more rigorous.[53] In addition, teachers are already beginning to recognize the need for a reasonable evaluation and merit-pay system, especially when designed with teacher input and not overly tied to student achievement scores.[54] Once wages and benefits are high enough, it is reasonable for society to expect a high quality performance every year. It also may be possible to relax teacher tenure. Tenure should not have to be included as part of the benefit package in order to attract strong teachers. Unionization will remain as a method for redressing grievances, including those related to academic freedom.

Respect

If all of this is to be accomplished, it is time for the various parties involved to stop the finger-pointing and join together in a mutually respectful manner as they collectively pursue the goal of equalizing educational opportunities. Educators need to respect the fact that elected officials are normally attempting to be responsible guardians of the public purse as they make their decisions regarding education-related expenditures and methods for ensuring accountability. Elected officials also must respect the educators. They need to listen to them, as they are closest to the problems. They also need to quit using educators as scapegoats for an educational problem that is much more complex than anything the teachers do or do not do. Educators and students, engaged together on a daily basis, must treat each other with mutual respect at all times. Lastly, caregivers and educators must respect and support each other's decisions as both strive to educate the children in their care.

In the same 1944 inaugural address cited earlier, Franklin Roosevelt stated that his goal was "to make a country in which no one is left out." That same general principle would appear to lie beneath the notion of "No Child Left Behind." It is society's duty to educate every child, not just provide education. It is hard to argue that this is not an amiable egalitarian goal. A sad truth, however, is that some children come to school in such a state of academic disrepair that there may be little the public schools can do for them by that point.

It is also important to remember our comparison of the Memphis City Schools and the Shelby County Schools. The more attractive schools have better attendance, achievement scores, discipline, and graduation rates. The key difference between those and their less attractive counterparts does not seem to be spending per student, students-per-teacher ratios, average teacher education, average teacher experience, or average teacher salaries. Instead, it would seem to have more to do with the children the attractive schools do not have to take or keep. Poor parents who want school choice, for instance, are unlikely to accept simply transferring their entire school to a new building with new teachers. Why? Most want their children out of the atmosphere created by those other poor students, including crime, gangs, violence, chaotic classrooms, underachievement, and lack of positive role models.

We can, however, begin to address those conditions that contribute to severe educational disadvantage, many of which appear to be poverty related. For disadvantaged students to have equal opportunity in twenty-first-century Memphis, there needs to be a multifaceted approach that focuses on early intervention while directly and indirectly reducing intergenerational poverty. Such conclusions are not new. The Memphis branch of the National Association for the Advancement of Colored People recommended many of these reforms in a 1988 report to Judge Robert McCrae. Their recommendations included early childhood programs, smaller classes, year-round schooling, enhanced teacher preparation, school consolidation, and using school buildings for child care, social services, and adult education.[55] Such an approach will come with a considerable national, state, and local price tag. Nonetheless, each element adopted, however small, will move us in the direction supported by the best available research.

Postindustrial economic changes and a history of racial exclusion have made it very difficult for the low-income black residents of America's inner cities to rise from rags to riches. That has become even truer as the information age now requires ever more and better academic training as a prerequisite to success. These trends are increasingly evident in a city like Memphis, Tennessee. The current state of the Memphis City Schools appears to be closely tied to the city's considerable level of poverty. It would seem that such trends can only be reversed by significantly reducing poverty and by a multifaceted educational overhaul that will allow schools to better counter its enduring effects.

Notes

Preface

1. Christopher Jencks et al., *Inequality: A Reassessment of the Effect of Family and Schooling in America* (New York: Basic Books, 1972).

2. James Coleman et al., *Equality of Educational Opportunity* (Washington, D.C.: GPO, 1966). Known as the "Coleman Report," it was commissioned by the U.S. Dept. of Education pursuant to Section 402 of the 1964 Civil Rights Act. Later studies confirmed these findings. For example, see Janet Ward Scholfield, "Review of Research on School Desegregation's Impact on Elementary and Secondary School Students," in James Banks, ed., *Handbook of Research on Multicultural Education* (New York: Macmillan, 1995), 597–616.

Chapter 1
Memphis Schools in Context

1. See Sheryll Cashin, *The Failures of Integration: How Race and Class Are Undermining the American Dream* (New York: Public Affairs Books, 2005).

2. For example, see Clive Belfield and Henry Levin, eds., *The Price We Pay: Economic and Social Consequences of Inadequate Education* (Baltimore: Brookings Institute Press, 2007); Dept. of Commerce, *Educational Attainment in the U.S.: 2004* (Washington, D.C.: GPO, 2005), table 9; U.S. Dept. of Commerce, Bureau of the Census, *Statistical Abstracts of the United States* (Washington, D.C.: GPO, annual); Organization for Economic Cooperation and Development, *Education at a Glance* (Paris: Organization for Economic Cooperation and Development, annual); Wendi Thomas, "Math Tests Miss Point; Kids Need Career Spin," *Commercial Appeal*, Aug. 2, 2005; Greg Duncan and Jeanne Brooks-Gunn, eds., *Consequences of Growing Up Poor* (New York: Russell Sage, 1997); Gates Foundation data cited in Bob Herbert, "Education's Collateral Damage," *New York Times*, July 21, 2005; David Broder, "It's Not Just 'Their' Problem; It's All of Ours," *Commercial Appeal*, Feb. 27, 2006; Bob

Herbert, "Dropouts Dim Prospects for Better Days," *New York Times,* Jan. 31, 2006;
Anna Bernasek, "What's the Return on Education?" *New York Times,* Dec. 11, 2005;
Shelton Danziger and Peter Gottschalk, *Diverging Fortunes: Trends in Poverty and
Inequality* (Washington, D.C.: Russell Sage Foundation and the Population Reference Bureau, The American People Series, 2004); Pauline Lipman, *High Stakes Education: Inequality, Globalization, and Urban School Reform* (New York: Routledge,
2003); David Leonhardt, "The College Dropout Boom," *New York Times,* May 24,
2005; Lisa Barrow and Cecilia Elena Rouse, "Does College Still Play?" *Economists'
Voice* 2.4, article #3, 2005.

3. For example, see Jeanne Brooks-Gunn et al., "Ethnic Differences in Children's
   Intelligence Test Scores: Role of Economic Deprivation, Home Environment, and
   Maternal Characteristics," *Child Development* 65.2 (1996): 346–60; Jesse Rothstein,
   "College Performance Predictions and the SAT," Princeton University, Woodrow
   Wilson School *Policy Brief* (Apr. 2004); Guinier, "Admissions Rituals as Political
   Acts; Lani Guinier and Susan Strum, "The Future of Affirmative Action: Reclaim-
   ing the Innovative Ideal," *84 California Law Review* 953 (July 1996); Lani Guinier
   et al., *Becoming Gentlemen: Women, Law Schools and Institutional Change* (Boston:
   Beacon Press, 1997);Oliver and Shapiro, *Black Wealth/White Wealth,* 152–53; U.S.
   Dept. of Commerce, Bureau of the Census, "School Enrollment—Social and Economic Characteristics: Oct. 1993," *Current Population Reports* P20–479 (Washington, D.C.: GPO, 1994), 69.

4. *The Nation's Report Card: National Subgroup Results* (Washington, D.C.: National
   Center for Educational Statistics, Nov. 2003); Carnegie Corporation of New York,
   Years of Promise: A Comprehensive Learning Strategy for America's Children (New
   York Carnegie Corporation, 1996); Eric Hanushek, "The Economics of School-
   ing: Production and Efficiency in Public Schools," *Journal of Economic Literature*
   24 (1986): 1141–77; James Ryan, "Schools, Race, and Money," *Yale Law Review*
   109 (1999): 249–311; Clarence Stone, "Introduction: Urban Education in Political
   Context," in Clarence Stone, ed., *Changing Urban Education* (Lawrence: University
   Press of Kansas, 1998); Judith Smith et al., "Consequences of Living in Poverty for
   Young Children's Cognitive and Verbal Ability and Early School Achievement," in
   Greg Duncan and Jeanne Brooks-Gunn, eds., *Consequences of Growing Up Poor*
   (New York: Russell Sage, 1997), 132–67.

5. Harry Miller, *Social Foundations of Education: An Urban Focus* (New York: Holt
   Rinehart Winston, 1978), 199.

6. See Thomas Mortenson, "The Crisis of Access in Higher Education," *Academe*
   (Nov.–Dec. 2000): 41; James Ryan, "Schools, Race, and Money," *Yale Law Review*
   109 (1999): 249–311; Jesse Rothstein, "College Performance Predictions and the
   SAT," Princeton University's Woodrow Wilson School, Apr. 2004; David Kirp, "And
   the Rich Get Smarter," *New York Times,* Apr. 30, 2004; Sara McLanahan, "Parent
   Absence or Poverty: Which Matters More?" in Duncan and Brooks-Gunn, *Consequences of Growing Up Poor,* 35–48; Greg Duncan and Jeanne Brooks-Gunn,
   "Income Effects across the Life Span: Integration and Interpretation," in Duncan
   and Brooks-Gunn, *Consequences of Growing Up Poor,* 596–610; Jay Teachman et

al., "Poverty during Adolescence and Subsequent Educational Attainment," in Duncan and Brooks-Gunn, *Consequences of Growing Up Poor,* 383–415; William Axinn et al., "The Effects of Parents' Income, Wealth and Attitudes on Children's Completed Schooling and Self-Esteem," in Duncan and Brooks-Gunn, eds., *Consequences of Growing Up Poor,* 518–40; David Leonhardt, "The College Dropout Boom," *New York Times,* May 24, 2005. Also see Oliver and Shapiro, *Black Wealth/ White Wealth,* 152–53; U.S. Dept. of Commerce, Bureau of the Census, "School Enrollment—Social and Economic Characteristics: Oct. 1993," *Current Population Reports* P20-479 (Washington, D.C.: GPO, 1994), 69; National Center for Education Statistics, *Digest of Education Statistics* (Washington, D.C.: GPO, 1979), 93; U.S. Dept. of Commerce, Bureau of the Census, "Characteristics of American Children and Youth," *Current Population Reports* (Washington, D.C.: GPO, 1982).

7. Annie Casey Foundation, *City Kids Count: Data on the Well-Being of Children in Large Cities* (Baltimore: Annie Casey Foundation, 1997), 5.

8. See Karen Arenson, "Cuts in Tuition Assistance Put College Beyond Reach of Poorest Students," *New York Times,* Jan. 27, 1997; David Leonhardt, "The College Dropout Boom," *New York Times,* May 24, 2005; David Herszenhorn, "Scores on State Math Tests Dip with District's Income," *New York Times,* Oct. 12, 2006.

9. See Dept. of Commerce, "School Enrollment."

10. For example, see DeMott, *The Imperial Middle,* 139–40.

11. Jencks, *Inequality,* 109.

12. Jencks, *Inequality,* 255. More recently, see Elijah Anderson, "The Code of the Streets," *Atlantic Monthly* 273.5 (May 1994): 80–94.

13. Jencks, *Inequality,* 78.

14. James Coleman et al., *Equality of Educational Opportunity* (Washington, D.C.: GPO, 1966).

15. Eric Hanushek et al., "Does Peer Ability Affect Student Achievement?" *Journal of Applied Econometrics* 18.5 (Oct. 2003): 527–44.

16. Sklar, *Chaos or Community?* 107. More recently, see "School District Tries to Force Overhaul," *New York Times,* Jan. 4, 2004. For more examples of earlier spending disparities, see Thaddeus Spratlen, "Financing Inner City Schools," *Journal of Negro Education* 42 (1973): 283–307.

17. Sklar, *Chaos or Community?* 106–9. Specifically for racial implications, see, for example, Douglas Reed, *On Equal Terms: The Constitutional Politics of Educational Opportunity* (Princeton: Princeton University Press, 2001); Hacker, *Two Nations,* 173; E. D. Hirsch Jr., "Good Genes, Bad Schools," *New York Times,* Oct. 29, 1994. For discussion of a more recent Texas case, see Ralph Blumenthal, "No Easy Solution as Texas Must Revisit School Financing," *New York Times,* Mar. 28, 2006.

18. The U.S. Supreme Court decision was *San Antonio Independent School District v. Rodriquez,* 411 U.S. 1, 93 (1973). The first major state case was *Serrano v. Priest,* 487 P.2d 1241 (Calif., 1971). See James Ryan, "Schools, Race, and Money," *Yale Law Review* 109 (1999): 249–311.

19. *Serrano v. Priest* II, 557 P.2d 929 (1977).

20. See Gary Orfield and Susan Eaton, *Dismantling Desegregation: The Quiet Reversal of Brown v. Board of Education* (New York: Norton, 1996), 54.

21. Alison Cowan, "Schools' Deep-Pocketed Partners," *New York Times,* June 3, 2007; "Budget Arithmetic," *New York Times,* Jan. 11, 2001; John Levy, *Urban America: Processes and Problems* (Upper Saddle River, N.J.: Prentice Hall, 2000), 278; Diana Jean Schemo, "Neediest Schools Receive Less Aid, Report Shows," *New York Times,* Sept. 9, 2002; Richard Rothstein, "Money's Role in Making Schools Better, *New York Times,* Nov. 14, 2001; Hugh B. Price, *Achievement Matters: Getting Your Child the Best Education Possible* (New York: Kensington Publishing Corp., 2002); Ramon Flecha, "New Educational Inequalities," in Manuel Castells et al., *Critical Education in the New Information Age* (Lanham, Md.: Rowman and Littlefield, 1999); Michael Kelley, "Keeping Our Promise to the Kids," *Commercial Appeal,* June 22, 2003; Greg Winter, "Wider Gap Found between Wealthy and Poor Schools," *New York Times,* Oct. 6, 2004; Michael Winerip, "At Poor Schools, Time Stops on the Library's Shelves," *New York Times,* Mar. 10, 2004; Elissa Gootman, "Preschoolers Grow Older as Parents Seek an Edge," *New York Times,* Oct. 19, 2006; James Comer, *Waiting for a Miracle* (New York: Penguin Putnam, 1997); David Berliner and Bruce Biddle, *The Manufactured Crisis: Myths, Fraud, and the Attack on America's Public Schools* (Reading, Mass.: Addison-Wesley, 1995); Jennifer Lee, "Crucial Unpaid Internships Increasingly Separate the Haves from the Have-Nots," *New York Times,* Aug. 10, 2004; Tamar Lewin, "Children's Computer Use Grows, but Gaps Persist," *New York Times,* Jan. 22, 2001; U.S. Dept. of Education, National Center for Educational Statistics, *Computer and Internet Use by Students* (Washington, D.C.: GPO, 2003).

22. See Lani Guinier, "Admissions Rituals as Political Acts: Guardians at the Gates of Our Democratic Ideals," *Harvard Law Review* 113 (Nov. 2003): 117; David Leonhardt, "As Wealthy Fill Top Colleges, New Efforts to Level the Field," *New York Times,* Apr. 22, 2004; Robert Perrucci and Earl Wysong, *The New Class Society: Goodbye American Dream?* (New York: Rowman and Littlefield, 2002; Carnoy, *Faded Dreams,* 107; Phillips, *Boiling Point,* 12; Schor, *The Overworked American,* 39–40; Alexander Astin, *The Myth of Equal Access to Higher Education* (Atlanta, Ga.: Southern Education Foundation, 1975).

23. W. E. B. DuBois, *Black Reconstruction in America, 1860–1880* (New York: Athenaeum, 1971), 638. Also see Carter Woodson, *The Education of the Negro prior to 1861* (Washington, D.C.: Associated Publishers, 1919).

24. John Hope Franklin, *From Slavery to Freedom: A History of Negro Americans* (New York: Knopf, 1980), 237.

25. *Brown v. Board of Education of Topeka, Kansas* 347 U.S. 483 (1954).

26. For example, see James Cowmen and Norris Haynes, "Meeting the Needs of Black Children in Public Schools," in Charles Willie, Antoine Garibaldi, and Wormier Reed, eds., *The Education of African-Americans* (New York: Auburn House, 1991), chap. 5. And as for evidence of school succeeding in the political indoctrination of black children, see *New York Times,* July 4, 1990.

27. See Reed, *On Equal Terms;* John Portz et al., *City Schools and City Politics* (Lawrence: University of Kansas Press, 1999), chap. 1; William Evans et al., "School Houses,

Court House, and State Houses after Serrano," *Journal of Policy Analysis and Management* 16 (Jan. 1997): 10–31; Franklin, *From Slavery to Freedom*, 403. For a more detailed discussion of black educational opportunities, see Horace Mann Bond, *The Education of the Negro in the American Social Order* (Englewood Cliffs, N.J.: Prentice-Hall, 1934); Meyer Weinberg, *A Chance to Learn: A History of Race and Education in the United States* (New York: Cambridge University Press, 1977), chaps. 1–3, 7. And as for remaining discrepancies in school funding by race, see Andrew Hacker, *Two Nations: Black and White, Separate, Hostile, Unequal* (New York: Scribner's, 1992), 173; Cool, *Savage Inequalities;* E. D. Hirsch Jr., "Good Genes, Bad Schools," *New York Times,* Oct. 29, 1994; *New York Times,* June 4, 1997.

28. See Gary Orfield et al., *Status of School Desegregation: The Next Generation* (Alexandria, Va.: National School Boards Association, 1992); James Ryan, "Schools, Race, and Money," *Yale Law Review* 109 (1999): 249–311; George Curry, "Schools Are Re-segregating as U.S. Celebrates 'Brown' Decision," *Tri-State Defender,* Feb. 21–25, 2004; Dept. of Education data cited in *Journal of Blacks in Higher Education* 47 (Spring 2005); Janny Scott, "Cities Shed Middle Class, and Are Richer and Poorer for It," *New York Times,* July 23, 2006; Charles Clotfelter, *The Rise and Retreat of School Desegregation* (Princeton, N.J.: Princeton University Press, 2006).

29. Anna Quindlen quoted in the *New York Times,* Sept. 7, 1991.

30. Dept. of Commerce, Bureau of the Census, *Statistical Abstracts of the United States* (Washington, D.C.: GPO, various years); Dept. of Commerce, Bureau of the Census, Current Population Reports, P-23, No. 80, *The Social and Economic Status of the Black Population in the United States: A Historical Overview, 1790–1978* (Washington, D.C.: GPO, 1978); Dept. of Education, Office of Civil Rights, periodic reports (Washington, D.C.: GPO, various years); American Council of Education Reports (Washington, D.C.: American Council of Education, various years).

31. For example, see Jay Greene and Marcus Winters, *Public High-School Graduation and College Readiness Rates: 1991–2002* (New York: Manhattan Institute for Policy Research, 2005); Judge Greg Mathis, "2004 Showed Mixed Results in the Area of Education," *Tri-State Defender,* Jan. 8–12, 2005; Dept. of Commerce, *Educational Attainment;* Dept. of Commerce, *The Black Population in the United States;* Lee Sigelman and Susan Welch, *Black Americans' Views of Racial Inequality: The Dream Deferred* (New York: Cambridge University Press, 1991), 23; Morton Kendrick, "The Two Black Americas," *New Republic,* Feb. 6, 1989, 18.

32. 2004 U.S. Census Bureau data cited in "Income Gaps Found among the College-Educated," *New York Times,* Mar. 28, 2005.

33. Dept. of Commerce, *Statistical Abstracts;* Dept. of Commerce, *The Social and Economic Status;* Dept. of Education, Office of Civil Rights, periodic reports; American Council of Education Reports; Jennings, *Race, Politics, and Economic Development,* 87.

34. Gary Orfield, *Dropouts in America* (Boston: Harvard University Press, 2004).

35. John Bridgeland et al., *The Silent Epidemic: Perspectives of High School Dropouts* (Seattle: Bill and Melinda Gates Foundation Report, Mar. 2006); Bartholomew Sullivan, "Memphis Graduation Rate Lags Nation, Area," *Commercial Appeal,* June 21, 2006; Greg Toppo, "Big-City Schools Struggle," *USA Today,* June 21, 2006;

Thomas Mortenson, "The Crisis of Access in Higher Education," *Academe* (Nov.–Dec. 2000): 38–43; James Ryan, "Schools, Race, and Money," *Yale Law Review* 109 (1999): 249–311; David Halbfinger, "Kerry Calls for More Money to Cut School Dropout Rate," *New York Times,* May 5, 2004; Brian Friel, "High Schools Next on the Federal Agenda," *National Journal,* Mar. 13, 2004, 821.

36. See Bridgeland et al., *The Silent Epidemic;* Toppo, "Big-City Schools Struggle"; Council of Great City Schools, *Closing the Achievement Gaps in Urban Schools: A Survey of Academic Progress and Promising Practices in the Great City Schools* (Washington, D.C.: Council of Great City Schools, 1999); Oakland Unified School District, Third-Year Report (Oakland, Calif.: Oakland School District, 1999); P. R. Brown and K. Haycock, *Excellence for Whom?* (Oakland, Calif.: Achievement Council, 1984); M. Fine, *Framing Dropouts: Notes on the Politics of an Urban Public High School* (Albany: State University of New York Press, 1991); Oakland Unified School District, *Average 1995–1996 Language NCE by Language Category* (Oakland, Calif.: Oakland School District, 1996); G. G. Wehlage, "Dropping Out: Can Schools Be Expected to Prevent It?" in L. Weis et al., eds., *Dropouts from School: Issues, Dilemmas, and Solutions* (Albany: State University of New York Press, 1989).

37. 2004 U.S. Census Bureau data cited in "Income Gaps Found among the College-Educated," *New York Times,* Mar. 28, 2005.

38. Christopher Jencks and Meredith Phillips, *The Black-White Test Score Gap* (Washington, D.C.: Brookings, 1998); Harvey Kantor and Barbara Brengel, *Urban Education and the "Truly Disadvantaged": The Historical Roots of the Contemporary Crisis* (Princeton, N.J.: Princeton University Press, 1993), 367; A. J. Artilles and G. Zamora-Duran, "Disproportionate Representation: A Contentious and Unresolved Predicament," in A. J. Artilles and G. Zamora-Duran, eds., *Reducing Disproportionate Representation of Culturally Diverse Students in Special and Gifted Education* (Reston, Va.: Council for Exceptional Children, 1997); B. Harry and M. G. Anderson, "The Disproportionate Placement of African-American Males in Special Education Programs: A Critique of the Process," *Journal of Negro Education* 63.4 (1994): 602–19; J. M. Patton, "The Disproportionate Representation of African Americans in Special Education: Looking Behind the Curtain for Understanding and Solutions," *Journal of Special Education* 32 (1998): 25–31; C. J. Russo and C. Talbert-Johnson, "The Over-Representation of African American Children in Special Education: The Re-Segregation of Educational Programming," *Education and Urban Society* 29.2 (1997): 136–48; National Center for Education Statistics, *Trends in Academic Progress: Three Decades of Student Performance,* Report 2000469 (Washington D.C.: GPO, 2001); National Center for Education Statistics, *The Condition of Education 2001,* Report 2001072. Washington, D.C.: GPO, 2002); Diana Jean Schemo, "Most Students in Big Cities Lag Behind in Basic Sciences," *New York Times,* Nov. 16, 2006.

39. See Christopher Jencks and Meredith Phillips, eds., *The Black-White Test Score Gap* (Washington, D.C.: Brookings Institution, 1998), 1–2. There are indicators of a performance gap from kindergarten to graduate school, including middle-class suburbs. See the report of the National Task Force on Minority High Achievement, 1999, cited in Jodi Wilgorenn, "Minority students' grades lower on all economic

levels, study finds," *Commercial Appeal*, October 17, 1999. Also see the *Journal of Blacks in Higher Education*, Mar. 5, 2003. The latter article notes, for example, that "blacks from families with incomes of more than $100,000 had a mean SAT score that was 142 points below the mean score for whites from families of the same income level."

40. See Meredith Phillips, James Crouse, and John Ralph, "Does the Black-White Test Score Gap Widen after Children Enter School?" in Christopher Jencks and Meredith Phillips, eds., *The Black-White Test Score Gap* (Washington, D.C.: Brookings Institution, 1998); Michael Petrilli, "School Reform Moves to the Suburbs," *New York Times,* July 11, 2005; U.S. Dept. of Education, National Center for Educational Statistics, *The Condition of Education* (Washington, D.C.: GPO, 1994); Berkeley Unified School District, *An Equal Education for All: The Challenge Ahead* (Berkeley, Calif.: Berkeley Unified School District, 1985).

41. *Journal of Blacks in Higher Education* 46 (Winter 2004-5); 47 (Spring 2005); 50, (Winter 2005-6).

42. The College Board, *Reaching the Top: A Report of the National Task Force on Minority High Achievement* (New York: College Board, 1999); Ronald Ferguson, "A Diagnostic Analysis of Black-White GPA Disparities in Shaker Heights, Ohio," in Diane Ravitch, ed., *Brookings Papers on Education Policy* (Washington, D.C.: Brookings, 2001), 347–414; College Board, *College Bound Seniors Profile of SAT and Achievement Test-Takers: California Report* (New York: College Board, 1993); L. S. Miller, *An American Imperative: Accelerating Minority Educational Advancement* (New Haven, Conn.: Yale University Press, 1995); Patterson Research Institute, *The African-American Education Data Book: Higher Education,* vol. 1 (Fairfax, Va.: United Negro College Fund, 1997).

43. Dept. of Commerce, *Educational Attainment; The Chronicle of Higher Education,* Aug. 28, 1991; Dept. of Commerce, *Statistical Abstracts;* Dept. of Commerce, *The Social and Economic Status;* Dept. of Education, Office of Civil Rights, periodic reports; American Council of Education Reports; *New York Times,* June 8, 1990, Jan. 18, 1994, Apr. 26, 1996; *Crisis,* May–June 1995, 24. It also should be noted that black females comprise 60 percent of those blacks attending college.

44. Dept. of Commerce, *Educational Attainment;* Dept. of Commerce, *The Black Population in the United States; Journal of Blacks in Higher Education* 50 (Winter 2005–6); Judge Greg Mathis, "An Important Message to Black Men—College Is Calling," *Tri-State Defender,* Aug. 6–10, 2005; Jodi Wilgorenn, "Minority Students' Grades Lower on All Economic Levels, Study Finds," *Commercial Appeal,* October 17,1999; Richard Chait and Cathy Trower, "Professors at the Color Line," *New York Times,* Sept. 11, 2001; Lee Sigelman and Susan Welch, *Black Americans' Views of Racial Inequality: The Dream Deferred* (New York: Cambridge University Press, 1991), 23; Morton Kondracke, "The Two Black Americas," *New Republic,* Feb. 6, 1989, 18.

45. See Bob Herbert, "An Emerging Catastrophe," *New York Times,* July 29, 2004.

46. See Erik Eckholm, "Plight Deepens for Black Men, Studies Warn," *New York Times,* Mar. 20, 2006.

47. See Eckholm, "Plight Deepens for Black Men"; Ronald Mincy, *Black Males Left Behind* (New York: Urban Institute, 2006); Harry Holzer et al., *Reconnecting Disadvantaged Young Men* (New York: Urban Institute, 2006).

48. For example, see Brent Staples, "Why Slave-Era Barriers to Black Literacy Still Matter," *New York Times,* Jan. 1, 2006; Sam Roberts, "College Dwellers Outnumber the Imprisoned," *New York Times,* Sept. 27, 2007.

49. Jencks and Phillips, *The Black-White Test Score Gap,* 17; Meredith Phillips et al., "Family Background, Parenting Practices, and the Black-White Test Score Gap," in Jencks and Phillips, *The Black-White Test Score Gap,* 103–48; Also see, for example, David Sanger, "Big Racial Disparity Persist among Users of the Internet," *New York Times,* July 9, 1999.

50. For example, see Robert Blauner, "Internal Colonialism and Ghetto Revolt," *Social Problems,* 16.4 (Spring 1969): 393–408; Nathan Glazer, Blacks and Ethnic Groups: The Difference, and the Political Difference It Makes," *Social Problems,* 18.4 (Spring 1971): 444–61; Ray Rist, *The Urban School: A Factory for Failure* (Edison, N.J.: Transaction Publications, 2002).

51. See William J. Wilson, "Commentary," in Jencks and Phillips, *The Black-White Test Score Gap,* 501–10.

52. National Center for Education Statistics, "Computer and Internet Use by Students in 2003," (Washington, D.C.: GPO, Sept. 2006.

53. See Orlando Patterson, "A Poverty of the Mind," *New York Times,* Mar. 26, 2006; Anderson, "The Code of the Streets."

54. For example, see Signithia Fordham and John Ogbu, "Black Students' School Success: Coping with the Burden of Acting White," *Urban Review* 18 (1986): 176, 181, 187–98; John Ogbu, "Minority Education in Comparative Perspective," *Journal of Negro Education* 59.1 (1990): 45–57; John Ogbu, "Minority Coping Responses and School Experience," *Journal of Psychohistory* 18.4 (1991): 433–53; John Ogbu, "Voluntary and Involuntary Minorities: A Cultural-Ecological Theory of School Performance with Some Implications for Education," *Anthropology and Education Quarterly* 29.2 (1998): 155–88; John McWhorter, *Losing the Race: Self-Sabotage in Black America* (New York: Free Press, 2000).

55. For example, see Claude Steele, "Race and Schooling of African Americans," *Atlantic Monthly,* Apr. 1992, 68–78; Claude Steele, "A Threat in the Air: How Stereotype Shapes Intellectual Identity and Performance," *American Psychologist* 62 (June 1997): 613–29. Also see Richard Majors and Janet Mancini Billson, *Cool Pose: The Dilemmas of Black Manhood in America* (New York: Lexington, 1992).

56. James Coleman et al., *Equality of Educational Opportunity* (Washington, D.C.: GPO, 1966). Known as the "Coleman Report," it was commissioned by the U.S. Dept. of Education pursuant to Section 402 of the 1964 Civil Rights Act. Later studies confirmed these findings. For example, see Janet Ward Schofield, "Review of Research on School Desegregation's Impact on Elementary and Secondary School Students," in James Banks, ed., *Handbook of Research on Multicultural Education* (New York: Macmillan, 1995), 597–616; David Grissmer et al., "Why Did the Black-

White Score Gap Narrow in the 1970s and 1980s?" in Christopher Jencks and Meredith Phillips eds., *The Black-White Test Score Gap* (Washington, D.C.: Brookings Press, 1998), 182–228; Meredith Phillips, "Does School Segregation Explain Why African Americans and Latinos Score Lower than Whites on Academic Achievement Tests?" (unpublished paper prepared for the annual meeting of the American Sociological Association 1997).

57. For example, see Arthur Hu, "Education and Race," *National Review* 49 (Sept. 15, 1997): 52.

58. For example, see Jerome Morris, "What Is the Future of Predominantly Black Urban Schools? The Politics of Race in Urban Education Policy," *Phi Delta Kappa* 81.4 (Dec. 1999): 316–19.

59. For example, see Gerald Tirozzi, "Report on Three Perspectives on the Educational Achievement of Connecticut Students" (unpublished report submitted to Connecticut State Board of Education, 1988), 7.

60. For example, see John Portz et al., *City Schools and City Politics* (Lawrence: University Press of Kansas, 1999); David Berliner and Bruce Biddle, *The Manufactured Crisis: Myths, Fraud, and the Attack on America's Public Schools* (Reading, Mass.: Addison-Wesley, 1995); Jeffrey Mirel, *The Rise and Fall of an Urban Schools System: Detroit, 1907–1981* (Ann Arbor, Mich.: University of Michigan Press, 1993).

61. Ernest Boyer, "Quality of Urban Schools Must Be National Priority," *Commercial Appeal*, Sept. 14, 1986.

62. For example, see Katie Hafner, "Still a Long Way from Checkmate," *New York Times*, Dec. 28, 2000; John Markoff, "Behind Artificial Intelligence, a Squadron of Bright Real People," *New York Times*, Oct. 17, 2005; Neil Munro, "Minds of Their Own," *National Journal*, Mar. 24, 2007, 38–43.

63. See Daniel Bell, *The Coming of the Post-Industrial Society* (New York: Basic Books, 1975); Louis Uchitelle, *The Disposable American: Layoffs and Their Consequences* (New York: Knopf, 2006); Barry C. Lynn, *End of the Line: The Rise and Coming Fall of the Global Corporation* (New York: Doubleday, 2005), chap. 1; Joseph Stiglitz, *Globalization and Its Discontents* (London: Allen Lane, 2002); Manuel Castells, *The Information Age: Economy, Society, and Culture* (New York: Oxford University Press, 2000); Saskia Sassen, *The Global City* (Princeton, N.J.: Princeton, 1999); Beth Shulman, *The Betrayal of Work: How Low-Wage Jobs Fail 30 Million Americans and Their Families* (New York: New Press, 2003); Robert E. Scott, *The High Price of "Free" Trade: NAFTA's Failure Has Cost the United States Jobs across the Nation* (Washington, D.C.: Economic Policy Institute, 2003); Nelson Lichtenstein, ed., *Wal-Mart: The Face of Twenty-First-Century Capitalism* (New York: New Press, 2005); Judith Stein, *Running Steel, Running America* (Chapel Hill: University of North Carolina Press, 1998); Louis Uchitelle, "Renewed Corporate Wanderlust Puts a Quiet Brake on Salaries," *New York Times*, July 24, 2000; Thomas Friedman, "Small and Smaller," *New York Times*, Mar. 4, 2004; David Firestone, " A Chief Exporter, and Not at All Pleased About It," *New York Times*, Feb. 23, 2001; John Jacobsen, *Technical Fouls: Democratic Dilemma and Technological Change* (Boulder, Colo.: Westview Press, 1999); Robert

Hershey, "The Rise of the Working Class," *New York Times*, Sept. 3, 1997; William Julius Wilson, *When Work Disappears* (New York: Knopf, 1996); Sheila McConnell, "The Role of Computes in Reshaping the Work Force," *Monthly Labor Review* 119 (Aug. 1996): 3–5; Jeremy Rifkin, *The End of Work: The Decline of the Global Labor Force and the Dawn of the Post-Market Era* (New York: G. P. Putnam's Sons, 1995); David Bloom and Adi Brender, *Labor and the Emerging World Economy* (Washington, D.C.: Population Reference Bureau, 1993); Barry Bluestone and Bennett Peterson, *The Deindustrialization of America* (New York: Basic Books, 1982).

64. For example, see Somini Sengupta, "India Attracts Universities from the United States," *New York Times*, Mar. 26, 2007.

65. See U.S. Dept. of Labor, *Report on the American Workforce* (Washington, D.C.: GPO, 2001); Sheldon Danziger and Peter Gottschalk, *Diverging Fortunes: Trends in Poverty and Inequality* (Washington, D.C.: Russell Sage Foundation and the Population Reference Bureau, American People Series, 2004); Katherine Newman, *Declining Fortunes: The Withering of the American Dream* (New York: Basic Books, 1993); Leigh Strope, "Manufacturing Job Losses Getting Political Scrutiny," *Commercial Appeal*, Sept. 7, 2003; Paul Krugman, "Always Low Wages. Always," *New York Times*, May 13, 2005; Martha Mendoza, "High-Tech Economy Leaves New Underclass in Its Wake," *Commercial Appeal*, Sept. 20, 1999; Neil Munro, "For Richer and Poorer," *National Journal*, July 18, 1998; 1676–1681; Katherine Newman, *Falling from Grace: The Experience of Downward Mobility in the American Middle Class* (New York: Vintage Books, 1988).

66. See Steve Lohr, "Outsourcing Is Climbing Skills Ladder," *New York Times*, Feb. 16, 2006; Bruce Stokes, "And Away They Go," *National Journal*, Mar. 27, 2004, 940–45; Juliana Gruenwald," Outsourcing Dims High Tech's Luster," *National Journal*, Mar. 13, 2004, 822–23; Charles Schumer and Paul Craig Roberts, "Second Thoughts on Free Trade," *New York Times*, Jan. 6, 2004; Louis Uchitelle, "A Missing Statistic: U.S. Jobs That Went Overseas," *New York Times*, Oct. 5, 2003.

67. Stokes, "And Away They Go"; Steve Lohr, "Cutting Here, but Hiring There," *New York Times*, June 24, 2005; John Tagliabue, "Eastern Europe Becomes a Center for Outsourcing," *New York Times*, Apr. 19, 2007. In addition, there is now evidence that Indian companies have been outsourcing their outsourced work to even lower-paying locales. For example, see Avand Giridharadas, "Outsourcing Works, So India Is Exporting Jobs," *New York Times*, Sept. 25, 2007.

68. Quoted in Bob Herbert, "The White-Collar Blues," *New York Times*, Dec. 29, 2003.

69. Bob Herbert, "Bracing for the Blow," *New York Times*, Dec. 26, 2003. Also see Peter Gosselin, "That Good Education Might Not Be Enough," *Los Angeles Times*, Mar. 6, 2006.

70. Thomas Friedman, "What Goes Around . . ." *New York Times*, Feb. 26, 2004; Thomas Friedman, *The World Is Flat: A Brief History of the Twenty-First Century* (New York: Farrar, Straus, and Giroux, 2005).

71. Bradbury quoted in Paul Krugman, "The Dropout Puzzle," *New York Times*, July 18, 2005; "The Non-Working Man's Burden," *New York Times*, Aug. 8, 2006; Edmund

Andrews, "It's Not Just the Jobs Lost, But the Pay in the New Ones," *New York Times,* Aug. 9, 2004; Austan Goolsbee, "The Unemployment Myth," *New York Times,* Nov. 30, 2003; Louis Uchitelle and N. R. Kleinfield, "On the Battlefields of Business, Millions of Casualties," *New York Times,* Mar. 3, 1996.

72. Alan Blinder, "Offshoring: The Next Industrial Revolution?" *Foreign Affairs* 85.2 (Mar.–Apr. 2006): 113–28. Also see Robert E. Scott, *The High Price of "Free" Trade* (Washington, D.C.: Economic Policy Institute, 2003).

73. Kenney quoted in Stokes, "And Away They Go," 941. Also see Martin Kenney and Rafiq Dossani, *Went for Cost, Stayed for Quality: Moving the Back Office to India* (Stanford University, Asia-Pacific Research Center, Research Report, Nov. 2003); Mark Kesselman, ed., *The Politics of Globalization* (New York: Houghton Mifflin, 2007). In addition, David Ricardo's "comparative advantage" justification for free trade is challenged in an article by Paul Craig Roberts and Charles Schumer in the *New York Times,* Jan. 6, 2004; Jared Bernstein et al., *Pulling Apart: A State-by-State Analysis of Income Trends,"* Economic Policy Institute, Center on Budget and Policy Priorities, Jan. 2006.

74. See Erika Kinetz, "Who Wins and Who Loses as Jobs Move Overseas," *New York Times,* Dec. 7, 2003; Louis Uchitelle, "Is There (Middle Class) Life After Maytag?" *New York Times,* Aug. 26, 2007.

75. See Kinetz, "Who Wins and Who Loses"; Diana Farrell, "U.S. Offshoring: Small Steps To Make It Win-Win," *Economists' Voice* (Mar. 2006): 1–3; Rick Bragg, "More Than Money: They Miss the Pride a Good Job Brought," *New York Times,* Mar. 5, 1996; Rick Bragg, "Big Holes Where the Dignity Used to Be," *New York Times,* Mar. 5, 1996.

76. Steve Lohr, "Many New Causes for Old Problem of Jobs Lost Abroad," *New York Times,* Feb. 15, 2004.

77. Bob Herbert, "Jobs Don't Just Vanish; They Move Abroad," *New York Times,* Jan. 26, 2004.

78. For example, see Robert Perrucci et al., *The New Class Society: Goodbye, American Dream?* (New York: Rowman & Littlefield, 2002).

79. See Eduardo Porter, "Unions Pay Dearly for Success," *New York Times,* Jan. 29, 2006.

80. See Ruth Milkman, "A More Perfect Union," *New York Times,* June 30, 2005; Barry Hirsch and David Macpherson, *Union Membership and Earnings Data Book: Compilations from the Current Population Survey, 2005 Edition* (Washington, D.C.: Bureau of National Affairs, 2006); Dept. of Commerce, Bureau of the Census, *Statistical Abstracts of the United States, 2006* (Washington, D.C.: GPO, 2006), table 649.

81. Barbara Ehrenreich, *Fear of Falling: The Inner Life of the Middle Class* (New York: Harper Perennial, 1989).

82. For example, see Louis Uchitelle, "Two Tiers, Slipping into One," *New York Times,* Feb. 26, 2006; Lawrence Mishel et al., *The State of Working America* (Ithaca, N.Y.:

Cornell University Press, 2003); Richard Freeman and Lawrence Katz, "Rising Wage Inequality: The United States vs. Other Advanced Countries," in Richard Freeman, ed., *Working Under Different Rules* (New York: Russell Sage Foundation, 1994), 29–62; John Judis, "Why Your Wages Keep Falling," *New Republic* (Feb. 14, 1994): 26–29.

83. See Mary Williams Walsh, "The Flush Are Working for the Public," *New York Times,* Sept. 3, 2006.

84. For example, see U.S. Dept. of Commerce, Bureau of the Census, "All Workers and Poor Workers with Their Own Employment-Based Health Insurance Policy, By Employer Contribution and Selected Characteristics: 2001 (Washington, D.C.: GPO, 2001); U.S. Dept. of Commerce, Bureau of the Census, *Statistical Abstracts of the United States, 2006* (Washington, D.C.: GPO, 2006), table 638; U.S. Dept. of Commerce, Bureau of Labor Statistics, "Employee Benefits in Private Industry in the United States: March 2004, Summary 04–04 (Washington, D.C.: GPO, Nov. 2004); U.S. Dept. of Commerce, Bureau of the Census, *Statistical Abstracts of the United States, 2006* (Washington, D.C.: GPO, 2006), table 639; Barbara Ehrenreich, *Nickel and Dimed: On (Not) Getting By in America* (New York: Henry Holt, 2001); Eileen Applebaum et al., *Low-Wage America: How Employers Are Reshaping Opportunity in the Workplace* (Russell Sage, 2006); Sheldon Danziger and Peter Gottschalk, *Diverging Fortunes: Trends in Poverty and Inequality* (Washington, D.C.: Russell Sage Foundation and the Population Bureau, The American People Series, 2004); Steven Greenhouse, "Many Entry-Level Workers Find a Rough Market," *New York Times,* Sept. 4, 2006; Thomas Friedman, "Hippies, Yuppies, Meet the Zippie—He's Taking Your Job," *New York Times,* Feb. 23, 2004; Uchitelle, "Two Tiers, Slipping into One"; Louis Uchitelle, "The End of the Line as They Know It," *New York Times,* Apr. 1, 2007; Louis Uchitelle, "A Way to Break the Cycle of Servitude," *New York Times,* Aug. 31, 2003; Paul Osterman et al., *Working in America* (Cambridge, Mass.: MIT Press, 2001); Neal Rosenthal, U.S. Bureau of Labor Statistics, quoted in *Los Angeles Times,* Mar. 16, 1996; Sklar, *Chaos or Community? Seeking Solutions, Not Scapegoats for Bad Economics* (Boston: South End, 1995), 23–27; Peter Passell, "Earning Plight of Baby Boomers," *New York Times,* Sept. 21, 1988; Louis Uchitelle, "Service Sector Wage Issues," *New York Times,* Dec. 19, 1986. For a good case study, see David Shipler, "A Poor Cousin of the Middle Class," *New York Times,* Jan. 18, 2004.

85. For example, see Bruce Stokes, "The Lost Wages of Immigration," *National Journal,* Jan. 7, 2006, 58; "Life in the Bottom 80 Percent," *New York Times,* Sept. 1, 2005.

86. Pauline Lipman, *High Stakes Education: Inequality, Globalization, and Urban School Reform* (New York: Routledge, 2004), 11; Marc Miringoff and Marque-Luisa Miringoff, *The Social Health of the Nation* (New York: Oxford University Press, 2001); "Downward Mobility," *New York Times,* Aug. 30, 2006; Steven Greenhouse and Michael Barbaro, "Wal-mart to Add Wage Caps and Part-timers," *New York Times,* Oct. 2, 2006; David Cay Johnston, "2005 Incomes, on Average, Still Below 2000 Peak," *New York Times,* Aug. 21, 2007.

87. Isabel Sawhill and John Morton, *Economic Mobility: Is the American Dream Alive and Well?* (Washington, D.C.: Economic Mobility Project, 2007), 5.

88. Barry Bluestone and Bennett Harrison, "The Grim Truth About the Job 'Miracle,'" *New York Times*, Feb. 1, 1987; *New York Times*, May 26, 1991, May 12, 1992.

89. See Judge Greg Mathis, "The Working Poor in America Are in Need of a Safety Net," *Tri-State Defender*, May 20–24, 2006.

90. Erik Eckholm, "America's 'Near Poor' Are Increasingly at Economic Risk, Experts Say," *New York Times*, May 8, 2006; Daniel Altman, "The Disaster Behind the Disaster: Poverty," *New York Times*, Sept. 18, 2005; Bob Herbert, "Working for a Pittance," *New York Times*, Oct. 8, 2004; Bob Herbert, "Shhh, Don't Say 'Poverty,'" *New York Times*, Nov. 22, 2004; Jeff Madrick, "There Have Been Significant Changes in the Welfare System, yet a Rise in Child Poverty Rates Is Now a Real Risk in the U.S.," *New York Times*, June 13, 2002. The 2004 federal "poverty level" was $19,157 per year for a family of four.

91. See "Downward Mobility," *New York Times*, Aug. 30, 2006; Tony Pugh, "U.S. Economy Leaving Record Numbers in Severe Poverty," *McClatchy Newspapers*, Feb. 23, 2007.

92. See Daniel Sandoval and Thomas Hirschl, "The Increase of Poverty Risk and Income Insecurity in the U.S. since the 1970s" (paper presented to the annual meeting of the American Sociological Association, Spring 2004); Jacob Hacker, "Call It the Family Risk Factor," *New York Times*, Jan. 11, 2004; Daniel Gross, "Social Security as Dramamine," *New York Times*, Mar. 20, 2005; Mark Rank, *One Nation, Underprivileged: Why American Poverty Affects Us All* (New York: Oxford University Press, 2004); "Barely Staying Afloat," *New York Times*, May 10, 2006; Frances Clines, "In 'Boom' More Lint Lines Pockets of Poor," *New York Times*, Oct. 2, 1999; Nina Bernstein, "Poverty Snaring Families Once Thought Immune," *New York Times*, Apr. 20, 2000.

93. Sheldon Danziger and Peter Gottschalk, *Diverging Fortunes: Trends in Poverty and Inequality* (Washington, D.C.: Russell Sage Foundation and the Population Reference Bureau, The American People Series, 2004), 24. Also see Sheldon Danziger and Robert Haveman, *Understanding Poverty* (Cambridge, Mass.: Harvard University Press, 2002); Bob Herbert, "The Right to Paid Sick Days," *New York Times*, May 15, 2007.

94. For example, see U.S. Dept. of Commerce, Bureau of the Census, "All Workers and Poor Workers with Their Own Employment-Based Health Insurance Policy, By Employer Contribution and Selected Characteristics: 2001 (Washington, D.C.: GPO, 2001); U.S. Dept. of Commerce, Bureau of the Census, *Statistical Abstracts of the United States, 2006* (Washington, D.C.: GPO, 2006), tables 638, 639; U.S. Dept. of Commerce, Bureau of Labor Statistics, "Employee Benefits in Private Industry in the United States: Mar. 2004, Summary 04–04 (Washington, D.C.: GPO, Nov. 2004); David Leonhardt, "The Choice: A Longer Life or More Stuff," *New York Times*, Sept. 27, 2006; Steven Greenhouse, "Three Polls find Workers Sensing Deep Pessimism," *New York Times*, Aug. 31, 2006; Abby Goodnough, "Census Shows a Modest Rise in U.S. Income," *New York Times*, Aug. 29, 2007; Eckholm, "America's 'Near Poor'"; Ellen Goodman, "Sick Leave Draws Bewildering Debate," *Boston Globe*, Feb. 9, 2005; Steven Greenhouse, "Forced to Work Off the Clock, Some Fight Back," *New York Times*, Nov. 19, 2004; John Schwartz, "Always on the Job, Employees Pay with

Health," *New York Times,* Sept. 5, 2004; Julie Kosterlitz, "Taking Its Toll," *National Journal,* Mar. 27, 2004, 946–49; Marilyn Werber Serafini, "Katrina's Spotlight on the Uninsured," *National Journal,* Oct. 8, 2003, 3114–15; Robert Pear, "Without Health Benefits, A Good Life Turns Fragile," *New York Times,* Mar. 5, 2007; George Sternlieb and James Hughes, *Income and Jobs; New York Times,* June 18, 1991.

95. Krugman, "Always Low Wages. Always; Steven Greenhouse, "Wal-Mart, a Nation unto Itself," *New York Times,* Apr. 17, 2004; Steven Greenhouse and Michael Barbaro, "Wal-Mart to Add Wage Caps and Part-timers," *New York Times,* Oct. 2, 2006; Steven Greenhouse, "Report Assails Wal-Mart Over Unions," *New York Times,* May 1, 2007.

96. See Paul Krugman, "The Big Squeeze," *New York Times,* Oct. 17, 2005. Also see Paul Krugman, "Losing Our Country," *New York Times,* June 10, 2005; Michelle Maynard and Jeremy Peters, "Decision Time in Detroit," *New York Times,* June 9, 2006; Louis Uchitelle, "Renewed Corporate Wanderlust Puts a Quiet Brake on Salaries," *New York Times,* July 24, 2000; Louis Uchitelle, *The Disposable American: Layoffs and Their Consequences* (New York: Knopf, 2006); Sheldon Danziger and Peter Gottschalk, *Diverging Fortunes: Trends in Poverty and Inequality* (Washington, D.C.: Russell Sage Foundation and the Population Reference Bureau, The American People Series, 2004); Saskia Sassen, *Globalization and Its Discontents* (New York: New Press, 1999).

97. See Steven Greenhouse and David Leonhardt, "Real Wages Fail to Match a Rise in Productivity," *New York Times,* Aug. 28, 2006.

98. Quoted in Greenhouse and Leonhardt, "Real Wages."

99. Reich quoted in Neil Munro, "Stay-At-Home Jobs," *National Journal,* Mar. 27, 2004, 951. For some of the earliest analysis of this phenomenon, see Greg Duncan et al., "W(h)ither the Middle Class? A Dynamic View," in Papadimitriou and Wolff, *Poverty and Prosperity,* chap 7. Also see Sheldon Danziger and Peter Gottschalk, *America Unequal* (Cambridge, Mass.: Harvard University Press, 1995).

100. Massey, "The New Geography," 180.

101. Bob Herbert, "Who's Really Making It?" *New York Times,* June 6, 2005; David Cay Johnston, "Richest Are leaving Even the Rich Far Behind," *New York Times,* June 5, 2005.

102. Congressional Budget Office data analyzed by Isaac Shapiro of the Center for Budget and Policy Priorities, cited in Lynnley Browning, "U.S. Income Gap Widening," *New York Times,* Sept. 25, 2003. Also see Sebastian Mallaby, "Protecting the Hereditary Elite," *Commercial Appeal,* June 6, 2006; David Cay Johnston, "Very Richest's Share of Income Grew Bigger, Data Show," *New York Times,* June 26, 2003.

103. Phillips, *The Politics of Rich and Poor,* 157–72; Johnston, "Very Richest's Share." The number of billionaires had grown to more than 400 by 2007. See *Forbes,* Mar. 7, 2007.

104. For example, see David Cay Johnston, "Income Gap Is Widening, Data Shows," *New York Times,* Mar. 29, 2007.

105. David Cay Johnston, "Report Says That the Rich Are Getting Richer Faster, Much Faster," *New York Times*, Dec. 15, 2007; Eric Konigsberg, "A New Class War: The Haves and the Have Mores," *New York Times*, Nov. 19, 2006; "Ever Higher Society, Ever Harder to Ascend," *Economist*, Dec. 29, 2004; David Cay Johnston, "Richest Are Leaving Even the Rich Far Behind," *New York Times*, June 5, 2005; Eric Schmitt, "Census Data Show a Sharp Increase in Living Standard," *New York Times*, Aug. 6, 2001. Although somewhat less extreme, "families" also indicate these same trends. See Bernstein et al., *Pulling Apart*.

106. For example, see John Leland, "For Unemployed, Wait for New Work Grows Longer," *New York Times*, Jan. 9, 2005. For a more complete discussion of the value of holding "wealth" (bank accounts, stock, bonds, real estate, etc.), see David Swinton, "The Economic Status of African Americans: Limited Ownership and Persistent Inequality," in National Urban League, *The State of Black America 1992* (New York: National Urban League, 1992), 62-63.

107. For example, see Federal Reserve Board and Internal Revenue Service, *1992 Survey of Consumer Finances* (Washington, D.C.: GPO, 1992). For trend data, see works such as Edward N. Wolff, "Trends in Household Wealth in the United States, 1962–83 and 1983–89," *Review of Income and Wealth* (June 1994): 143-74; Edward N. Wolff, "The Rich Get Increasingly Richer," Economic Policy Institute, Briefing Paper, 1992; or the work of Edward N. Wolff, Claudia Goldin, and Bradford De Long, cited in Sylvia Nasar, "The Rich Get Richer, But Never the Same Way Twice," *New York Times*, Aug. 16, 1992.

108. For example, see John Harrigan, *Empty Dreams, Empty Pockets: Class and Bias in American Politics* (New York: Macmillan, 1993), 10. Also note that this presumes exceptionally safe investments. For those wealthy individuals willing to assume even a little more risk, there are investment vehicles such as hedge funds that provide substantially larger returns for those with a million or more dollars to invest. For example, see Saul Hansell, "Hush-Hush and for the Rich: Hedge Funds Under Scrutiny," *New York Times*, Apr. 13, 1994.

109. Internal Revenue Service (IRS) analysis cited in Johnston, "Very Richest's Share."

110. Congressional Budget Office figures cited in David Cay Johnston, "Corporate Wealth Share Rises for Top-Income Americans," *New York Times*, Jan. 19, 2006; Bernstein et al., *Pulling Apart*.

111. "Ever Higher Society"; Congressional Budget Office, *Effective Federal Tax Rats: 1979-2003* (Washington, D.C.: GPO, 2005); Thomas Pickety and Emmanuel Saez, "Income Inequality in the United States, 1913-1998," *Quarterly Journal of Economics* 118 (2003): 1-39.

112. Wolff, "Trends in Household Wealth"; Mary Jo Bane and David Ellwood, *Welfare Realities: From Rhetoric to Reform* (Cambridge, Mass.: Harvard University, 1994); *New York Times*, Nov. 27, 1985, June 22, 1996; Chicago Tribune Staff, *American Millstone* (New York: McGraw Hill, 1986), 83.

113. Bernstein et al., *Pulling Apart*; Robert Reich, "Lost Jobs, Ragged Safety Net," *New York Times*, Nov. 12, 2001.

114. For a good empirical depiction of this bimodality, see Greg Duncan et al., "W(h)ither the Middle Class?" Also see Sheldon Danziger and Peter Gottschalk, *America Unequal* (Cambridge, Mass.: Harvard University Press, 1995); *New York Times,* Feb. 22, 1992; *Washington Post,* Dec. 1, 1991.

115. Barbara Ehrenreich, *Fear of Falling: The Inner Life of the Middle Class* (New York: Harper Perennial, 1989).

116. Robert Reich, *The World of Nations: Preparing Ourselves for 21st Century Capitalism* (New York: Vintage, 1992), 178. Also see him quoted in *Newsweek,* Feb. 9, 1998, 32.

117. For example, see Bernstein et al., *Pulling Apart;* Pohlmann, *Political Power in the Postindustrial City,* chaps. 1, 3, 6; Reich, *The Work of Nations;* Starobin, "Unequal Shares"; Sylvia Nasar, "Puzzling Poverty of the 80s Boom," *New York Times,* Feb. 14, 1992; George Sternleib and James Hughes, *Income and Jobs: USA* (New Brunswick, N.J.: Center for Urban Policy Research, 1984), chap. 5; Jonathan Rauch, "Downsizing the Dream," *National Journal,* Aug. 12, 1989, 2038–43; Congressional Research Service, *Measures of Racial Earnings since 1970* (Washington, D.C.: GPO, 1988); Frank Levy, "The Vanishing Middle Class and Related Issues," *PS* (Summer 1987): 650–55; Frank Levy, *Dollars and Dreams: The Changing American Income Distribution* (New York: Norton, 1988); *New York Times,* Apr. 16, 1992; Phillips, *Boiling Point,* 195–97; Martin Carnoy, *Faded Dreams: The Politics and Economics of Race in America* (New York: Cambridge University Press, 1994), 99–103. Also see Robert Reich, "The Fracturing of the Middle Class," *New York Times,* Aug. 31, 1994; Peter Kilborn, "Even in Good Times, It's Hard Times for Workers," *New York Times,* July 3, 1995; Keith Bradsher, "Technology and Income Gap Are Linked, Greenspan Says," *New York Times,* Aug. 27, 1994; Guy Gugliotta, "The Minimum Wage Culture," *Washington Post National Weekly Edition,* Oct. 3–9, 1994, 6–7; *National Journal,* Sept. 10, 1994, 2109.

118. Robert Perrucci and Earl Wysong, *The New Class Society: Goodbye American Dream?* (New York: Rowman and Littlefield, 2002).

119. Quoted in A. M. Rosenthal, "American Class Struggle," *New York Times,* Mar. 22, 1995.

120. Duncan, "Whither the Middle Class?" 248.

121. For example, see Elizabeth Warren and Amelia Warren Tyagi, *The Two-Income Trap: Why Middle Class Mothers and Fathers Are Going Broke* (New York: Basic Books, 2003); "Ever Higher Society"; Bernstein et al., *Pulling Apart;* Katherine Newman, *Declining Fortunes: The Withering of the American Dream* (New York: Basic Books, 1993); Juliet Schor, *The Overworked American: The Unexpected Decline of Leisure* (New York: Basic Books, 1991); Sternleib and Hughes, *Income and Jobs,* chap. 5; Congressional Research Service, *Measures of Racial Earnings;* Levy, "Vanishing Middle Class"; Robert Reich, "An Economy Raised on Pork," *New York Times,* Sept. 3, 2005; Peter Beinart, "The Rehabilitation of the Cold-War Liberal," *New York Times,* Apr. 30, 2006; Lester Thurow, "The Boom That Wasn't," *New York Times,* Jan. 15, 1999; Tamar Lewin, "Now a Majority: Families with 2 Parents Who Work," *New*

York Times, Oct. 24, 2000; Louis Uchitelle, "Moonlighting Plus: 3-Job Families on the Rise," New York Times, Aug. 16, 1994. And as for the special position of African Americans, see, for example, Melvin Oliver and Thomas Shapiro, Black Wealth/ White Wealth (New York: Routledge, 1995), chap. 5.

122. For example, see Eckholm, "America's 'Near Poor'"; David Leonhardt, "The Choice: A Longer Life or More Stuff," New York Times, Sept. 27, 2006; Shankar Vedantam, "In Today's Rat Race, the Most Overworked Win," Washington Post, Sept. 4, 2006; Floyd Norris, "She Works, Her Grandson Doesn't," New York Times, Sept. 3, 2006; Ellen Goodman, "Sick Leave Draws Bewildering Debate," Boston Globe, Feb. 9, 2005; Steven Greenhouse, "Forced to Work off the Clock, Some Fight Back," New York Times, Nov. 19, 2004; John Schwartz, "Always on the Job, Employees Pay with Health," New York Times, Sept. 5, 2004; Julie Kosterlitz, "Taking Its Toll," National Journal, Mar. 27, 2004, 946–49; Timothy Egan, "The Rise of Shrinking-Vacation Syndrome," New York Times, Aug. 20, 2006; Jane Goss, "The Middle Class Struggles in the Medicaid Maze," New York Times, July 9, 2005; John Broder et al., "Problem of Lost Health Benefits Is Reaching into the Middle Class," New York Times, Nov. 25, 2002; Robert Pear, "60 Million Uninsured during a Year," New York Times, May 13, 2003; "More in Middle Class Lack Health Insurance," Commercial Appeal, Nov. 25, 2002; "Many on Job Lack Retirement Plan," Commercial Appeal, Dec. 15, 2002; Teresa Sullivan et al., America's Fragile Middle Class: Americans in Debt (New Haven, Conn.: Westbrook, 2000); Schor, The Overworked American; Phillips, Boiling Point, 161–62; Sternlieb and Hughes, Income and Jobs.

123. Duncan, "Whither the Middle Class?"; Levy, "Vanishing Middle Class."

124. See John Maggs, "Draining the Punch Bowl," National Journal, Mar. 4, 2006, 45–46; Bruce Stokes, "Micro-Confident; Macro-World," National Journal, Jan. 28, 2006, 64; Ellen Alt Powell, "What If Bills Come Due and We Can't Pay?" Commercial Appeal, Sept. 1, 2005; Niall Ferguson, "Reasons to Worry," New York Times, June 11, 2006; Rachel Konrad and Bob Porterfield, "Credit Card Debt Troubles Stacking Up," Commercial Appeal, Dec. 24, 2007.

125. Besides the postindustrialism discussion above, see Bernstein et al., Pulling Apart; Bob Herbert, "Bogeyman Economics," New York Times, Apr. 4, 1997. For more on the impact of immigration, see Marger, Social Inequality, 106; Laura Meckler, "Well-off Families Report Trouble with Bills," Commercial Appeal, July 9, 1999; Bruce Stokes, "The Lost Wages of Immigration," National Journal, Jan. 7, 2006, 58–59; Herold Bauder, Labor Movement: How Immigration Regulates Labor Markets (New York: Oxford University Press, 2006); Anthony DePalma, "15 years on the Bottom Rung," New York Times, May 26, 2005; Tim Johnson, "U.S. Faces Global Competitor," Commercial Appeal, July 17, 2005; Steven Greenhouse, "Middlemen in the Low-Wage Economy," New York Times, Dec. 28, 2003.

126. See Steven Greenhouse, "Borrowers We Be," New York Times, Sept. 3, 2006; John Maggs, "Draining the Punch Bowl," National Journal, Mar. 4, 2006, 45–46; Bruce Stokes, "Micro-Confident; Macro-World," National Journal, Jan. 28, 2006, 64; Jennifer Steinhauer, "Statistics Aside, Many Feel Pinch of Daily Costs," New York Times, May 6,

2006; Edmund Andrews, "Global Trends May Hinder Effort to Curb U.S. Inflation," *New York Times,* Aug. 28, 2006; "Curing the Debt Addiction," *New York Times,* Oct. 2, 2006; Ellen Alt Powell, "What If Bills Come Due and We Can't Pay?" *Commercial Appeal,* Sept. 1, 2005; Niall Ferguson, "Reasons to Worry," *New York Times,* June 11, 2006; "When a Stranger Calls," *New York Times,* July 9, 2006; Steven Weisman, "U.S. Trade Deficit Is Called a Threat to Global Growth," *New York Times,* Sept. 6, 2006; Jeannine Aversa, "U.S. in Record Debt, and Foreigners Hold Notes," *Commercial Appeal,* Nov. 11, 2005; John Maggs, "Gilded Age, Newly Minted," *National Journal,* Jan. 29, 2000, 306; Bob Herbert, "Admit We Have a Problem," *New York Times,* Aug. 9, 2004; James Grant, "Low Rates, High Expectations," *New York Times,* May 16, 2004; Brian Bucks, Arthur Kennickell, and Kevin Moore, "Recent Changes in U.S. Family Finances: Evidence from the 2001 and 2004 Survey of Consumer Finances," *Federal Reserve Bulletin* (Washington, D.C.: GPO, March 2006), A1–A38. Lawrence Mishel et al., *The State of Working America* (Ithaca, N.Y.: Cornell University Press, 2003); John Maggs, "Always a Borrower Be," *National Journal,* July 8, 2001, 2732–37; Lester Thurow, "The Boom That Wasn't," *New York Times,* Jan. 15, 1999.

127. Bob Herbert, "An Economy that Turns American Values Upside Down, *New York Times,* Sept. 6, 2004. Also see Roger Lowenstein, "The Inequality Conundrum," *New York Times,* June 10, 2007; Isabell Sawhill and John Morton, *Economic Mobility: Is the American Dream Alive and Well?* (Washington, D.C.: Pew Charitable Trusts, Economic Mobility Project, Feb. 2007); Economic Mobility Project, *Economic Mobility of Families Across Generations* (Washington, D.C.: Pew Charitable Trusts, Nov. 2007).

128. For example, see David Firestone, " A Chief Exporter, and Not at All Pleased About It," *New York Times,* Feb. 23, 2001; Stephen Ohlemacher, "Inner Cities Continue to Hemorrhage Jobs," *Yahoo! News,* Nov. 29, 2005; http:/news.yahoo.com/; Julie Kosterlitz, "Taking Its Toll," *National Journal,* Mar. 27, 2004, 946–49; Louis Uchitelle, "Renewed Corporate Wanderlust Puts a Quiet Brake on Salaries," *New York Times,* July 24, 2000; Louis Uchitelle, *The Disposable American: Layoffs and Their Consequences* (New York: Knopf, 2006); Wilbur Rich, *Black Mayors and School Politics* (New York: Garland, 1996), chap 7.

129. Bollens and Schmandt, *The Metropolis,* 82–83.

130. Sternleib, quoted in the *New York Times,* Oct. 8, 1979.

131. Robert Kweit and Mary Grisez Kweit, *People and Politics in Urban America* (Pacific Grove, Calif.: Brooks-Cole, 1990), chap. 3; Jon Kasarda, "Urban Change"; *New York Times,* Aug. 10, 1986.

132. For example, see Federal Bureau of Investigation, *Uniform Crime Reports* (Washington, D.C.: GPO, annual); Trymaine Lee, "Homeless Families in City Shelters Hit Record, Despite Mayor's Efforts," *New York Times,* Mar. 8, 2007.

133. Gunnar Mydral, *An American Dilemma* (New York: Harper, 1944).

134. See Dennis Judd, *The Politics of American Cities* (Boston: Little Brown, 1988), chap. 8.

135. For further reference on black migration north, see Robert E. Grant, *The Black Man Comes to the City* (Chicago: Nelson Hall, 1972); C. Horace Hamilton, "The Negro

Leaves the South," *Demography* 1 (Jan. 1964): 273–95; Meier and Elliot Rudwick, *From Plantation to Ghetto* (New York: Hill and Wang, 1969); Lehman, *The Promised Land*; Karl and Alma Taueber, *Negroes in the Cities* (Chicago: Aldine, 1965).

136. Bollens and Schmandt, *The Metropolis*, 44–49.

137. For example, see Kenneth Jackson, *Crabgrass Frontier: The Suburbanization of the United States* (New York: Oxford University Press, 1985); John Portz et al., *City Schools and City Politics* (Lawrence: University Press of Kansas, 1999), chap. 1; Douglas Massey, "The New Geography of Inequality in Urban America," in Michael C. Henry, *Race, Poverty, and Domestic Policy* (New Haven, Conn.: Yale University Press, 2004), 173–87; George Galster et al., "The Disparate Racial Neighborhood Impacts of Metropolitan Economic Restructuring," in Michael C. Henry, *Race, Poverty, and Domestic Policy* (New Haven, Conn.: Yale University Press, 2004), 188–218; John Pomfert, "Where Did All the Children Go?" *Washington Post*, Mar. 19, 2006; Rick Lyman, "Surge of Population in the Exurbs Continues," *New York Times*, June 21, 2006.

138. Douglas Massey, "The New Geography of Inequality in Urban America," in Michael C. Henry, *Race, Poverty, and Domestic Policy* (New Haven, Conn.: Yale University Press, 2004), 173–87.

139. Douglas Massey and Nancy Denton, *American Apartheid: Segregation and the Making of the Underclass* (Cambridge: Harvard University Press, 1993), 74–78.

140. James Ryan, "Schools, Race, and Money," *Yale Law Review* 109 (1999): 260.

141. See Massey and Denton, American Apartheid; Alex Kotlowitz, The Other Side of the River: A Story of Two Towns, a Death, and America's Dilemma (New York: Doubleday, 1999); Wilson, *The Truly Disadvantaged*; William Julius Wilson, *When Work Disappears: The World of the New Urban Poor* (New York: Knopf, 1996), Kenneth Clark's studies of Harlem youths; Erik Eckholm, "Study Documents 'Ghetto Tax' Being Paid by the Urban Poor," *New York Times*, July 19, 2006.

142. Kaplan quoted in the *New York Times*, Sept. 29, 1980. Also see Rosemary Batt et al., "How and When Does Management Matter? : Job Quality and Career Opportunities for Call Center Workers," in Eileen Applebaum et al., *Low-Wage America: How Employers Are Reshaping Opportunity in the Workplace* (New York: Russell Sage, 2006); Economic Mobility Project, *Economic Mobility of Black and White Families* (Washington, D.C.: Pew Charitable Trusts, Nov. 2007); Mark Allen Hughes, *Poverty in Cities* (New York: National League of Cities, 1989); Paul Peterson, "The Urban Underclass and the Poverty Paradox," in Christopher Jencks and Paul Peterson, eds., *The Urban Underclass* (Washington, D.C.: Brookings, 1991); Harvey Hilaski, "Unutilized Manpower in Poverty Areas of Six Major Cities," *Monthly Labor Review* 94 (Dec. 1971): 45–52; Paul Ryscavage and Hazel Willacy, "Employment of the Nation's Poor," *Monthly Labor Review* 91 (Aug. 1968): 15–21.

143. National Urban League, *State of Black America* (New York: National Urban League, annual); Dept. of Commerce, *Statistical Abstracts*; Dept. of Commerce, *Money Income of Families*; Bob Herbert, "An Emerging Catastrophe," *New York Times*, July 29, 2004; Bob Herbert, "The Unrecognizable Recovery," *New York Times*, Mar. 8, 2004;

Judge Mathis, "Why Black People Don't Feel the Economic Recovery," *Tri-State Defender*, July 3–7, 2004; Ronald Mincy, ed., *Black Males Left Behind* (Washington, D.C.: Urban Institute Press, 2006).

144. *New England Journal of Medicine* article quoted in the *New York Times*, Dec. 24, 1990.

145. For example, see National Urban League, *The State of Black America* (New York: NUL, 2006), 232; U.S. Census data cited in Genaro Armas, "Married Households Rise Again among Blacks, Census Finds," *New York Times*, Apr. 26, 2003.

146. Dept. of Commerce, *Statistical Abstracts;* Dept. of Commerce, *Social and Economic Status;* Jonathan Rauch, "The Widening Marriage Gap: America's New Class Divide," *National Journal*, May 19, 2001, 1471–72; Jason Fields, *The Living Arrangements of Children: 1996* (Washington, D.C.: Census Bureau, 2001); *Just the Facts: A Summary of Recent Information on America's Children and Their Families* (Washington, D.C.: National Commission on Children, 1993); Wilson, *The Truly Disadvantaged;* Stephen Baskerville, "The Politics of Fatherhood," *PS* (Dec. 2002): 695–98; Sybil Mitchell, "Babies at Risk," *Tri-State Defender*, May 20–24, 2006. Also see Robert Hill, *The Strengths of African American Families: Twenty-Five Years Later* (Lanham, Md.: University Press of America, 1999).

147. Wade Horn and Andrew Bush, *Fathers, Marriage, and Welfare Reform* (New York: Hudson Institute, 1997); Larry Reeves, "The Essence of Black Fatherhood," *Tri-State Defender*, June 12–16, 1999; Suet-Ling and Dong-Beom Ju, "The Effects of Change in Family Structure and Income on Dropping Out of Middle and High School," *Journal of Family Issues* 21 (1998): 147–69; Debra Dawson, "Family Structure and Children's Well-Being: Data from the 1988 National Health Survey," *Journal of Marriage and Family* 53 (1991): 573–84; *Survey of Child Welfare* (Washington, D.C.: National Center for Health Statistics, 1993); Andrew Cherlin et al., "Effects of Parental Divorce on Mental Health throughout the Life Course," *American Sociological Review* 63 (1998): 239–49; Taru Maekikyroe et al., "Hospital-Treated Psychiatric Disorders in Adults with a Single-Parent and Two-Parent Family Background," *Family Process* 37 (1998): 335–44; *National Health Interview Survey* (Hyattsville, Md.: National Center for Health Statistics, 1988); Christina Lammers et al., "Influences on Adolescents' Decision to Postpone Onset of Sexual Intercourse: A Survival Analysis of Virginity among Youths Aged Thirteen to Eighteen Years," *Journal of Adolescent Health* 26 (2000): 42–48; Dawn Upchurch et al., "Neighborhood and Family Contexts of Adolescent Sexual Activity," *Journal of Marriage and the Family* 61 (1999): 920–33; John Hoffmann and Robert Johnson, "A National Portrait of Family Structure and Adolescent Drug Use," *Journal of Marriage and the Family* 60 (1998): 633–45; *The Relationship between Family Structure and Adolescent Substance Abuse* (Washington, D.C.: Substance Abuse and Mental Health Services Administration, 1996); *Survey on Child Health* (Washington, D.C.: National Center for Health Statistics, 1993); D. Wayne Osgood and Jeff Chambers, "Social Disorganization Outside the Metropolis: An Analysis of Rural Youth Violence," *Criminology* 38 (2000): 81–115; Nicholas Davidson, "Life without Father," *Policy Review* 51 (1990): 40–44; Dewey Cornell et al., "Characteristics of Adolescents Charged with Homicide," *Behavioral Sciences and the Law* 5 (1987): 11–23; Anne-Marie Ambert, "The Effect of Male

Delinquency on Mothers and Fathers: A Heuristic Study," *Sociological Inquiry* 69 (1999): 621–40; M. Eileen Matlock, "Family Correlates of Social Skills Deficits in Incarcerated Adolescents," *Adolescence* 29 (1994): 119–30; Judith Rubinstein et al., "Suicidal Behavior in Adolescents: Stress and Protection in Different Family Contexts," *American Journal of Orthopsychiatry* 68 (1998): 274–84; Patricia McCall and Kenneth Land, "Trends in White Male Adolescent Young Adults and Elderly Suicide: Are There Common Underlying Structural Factors?" *Social Science Research* 23 (1994): 57–81; *Survey of Child Health; Third National Incidence Study of Child Abuse and Neglect* (Washington, D.C.: National Center for Child Abuse and Neglect, 1996), xviii; Catherine Malkin and Michael Lamb, "Child Mistreatment: A Test of Sociobiological Theory," *Journal of Comparative Family Studies* 25 (1994): 121–30; Sara McLanahan and Gary Sandefur, *Growing Up with a Single Parent* (Boston: Harvard University Press, 1994).

148. Dept. of Justice, Bureau of Justice Statistics, *Crime Victimization in the United States* (Washington, D.C.: GPO, various years); Hacker, *Two Nations,* 183; National Center for Health Statistics, *Vital Statistics of the United States: Volume II-Mortality,* table 1–22 and *Final Mortality Monthly Vital Statistics: 1992* (Advance Report), table 1–25 (Washington, D.C.: GPO, 1994); Dept. of Justice, Bureau of Justice Statistics, *Crime Victimization in the United States* (Washington, D.C.: GPO, annual); Jennifer Hochschild, *Facing Up to the American Dream* (Princeton, N.J.: Princeton University, 1995), 202; National Association for the Advancement of Colored People (NAACP), *Crisis* (Mar. 1986): 26.

149. National Urban League, *State of Black America* (New York: National Urban League, annual); Judge Greg Mathis, "Black Students Getting More Diplomas, Less Degrees," *Tri-State Defender,* July 10–14, 2004); Elizabeth White, "Number of U.S. Inmates Rises 2 Percent," Associated Press, May 22, 2006); Erin Sullivan, "Commission Listens to Inmates in an Effort to Provide Solutions," *Commercial Appeal,* Feb. 26, 2005; Fox Butterfield, "Prison Rates among Blacks Reach a Peak, Report Finds," *New York Times,* Apr. 7, 2003; Stephanie Gadlin, "Blacks Kicked out of Schools in Preparation for Jails," *Tri-State Defender,* Feb. 12–16, 2000; Becky Petit and Bruce Western, "Mass Imprisonment and the Life Course: Race and Class Inequality in U.S. Incarceration," *American Sociological Review* 69 (Apr. 2004): 151–69; Dionne Jones, ed., *African American Males: A Critical Link in the African American Family* (Edison, N.J.: Transaction Publications, 1994).

150. Horatio Alger, *Ragged Dick: Or, Street Life in New York with the Boot Blacks* (New York, 1867); Horatio Alger, *Tattered Tom: Or, the Story of a Street Arab* (New York, 1871); Horatio Alger, *Luck and Pluck: Or, the Progress of Walter Conrad* (New York, 1869).

151. Gallup Poll (July 1990), cited in Harrigan, *Empty Dreams,* 22. Also see Jennifer Hochschild, *Facing Up to the American Dream: Race, Class, and the Soul of a Nation* (Princeton: Princeton University, 1995); Harrington, *New American Poverty,* 148.

152. A 2006 survey conducted by the *Washington Post,* Kaiser Foundation, and Harvard University, cited in Steven Holmes and Richard Morin, "Poll Reveals a Contradictory Portrait Shaded with Promise and Doubt," *Washington Post,* June 4, 2006.

153. See Theodore Caplow and Howard M. Bahr, "Half a Century of Change in Adolescent Attitudes," *Public Opinion Quarterly* 43 (Spring 1979): 1–17.

154. Samuel Bowles, "Unequal Education and the Reproduction of the Hierarchical Division of Labor," in Richard Edwards, ed., *The Capitalist System* (Englewood Cliffs, N.J.: Prentice-Hall, 1972), 219; Portz et al., *City Schools and City Politics*, 11–19.

155. See Sheryll Cashin, *The Failures of Integration: How Race and Class Are Undermining the American Dream* (New York: Public Affairs Books, 2005).

156. For example, see Dorothy Shipps, *School Reform, Corporate Style: Chicago, 1880–2000* (Lawrence: University of Kansas Press, 2006); Carl Kaestle and Alyssa Lodewick, *To Educate a Nation: Federal and National Strategies of School Reform* (Lawrence: University of Kansas Press, 2007); Michael Barber and Ruth Dann, eds., *Raising Educational Standards in the Inner Cities: Practical Initiatives in Action* (New York: Cassell, 1996); Samuel Carter, *No Excuses: Lessons from 21 High Performing, High Poverty Schools* (Washington, D.C.: Heritage Foundation, 2001); Paul Hill and Mary Beth Celio, *Fixing Urban Schools* (Washington, D.C.: Brookings Institution Press, 1998); John Chubb and Tom Loveless, eds., *Bridging the Achievement Gap* (Washington, D.C.: Brookings Institution Press, 2002); Diane Ravitch and Joseph Viteritti, *New Schools for a New Century: The Redesign of Urban Education* (New Haven, Conn.: Yale University Press, 1997); Clarence Stone, ed., *Changing Urban Education* (Lawrence: University Press of Kansas, 1998); Jeffrey Henig et al., *The Color of School Reform: Race, Politics and the Challenge of Urban Education* (Princeton, N.J.: Princeton University Press, 2001); Clarence Stone et al., *Building Civic Capacity: The Politics of Reforming Urban Schools* (Lawrence: University Press of Kansas, 2001); Portz et al., *City Schools and City Politics*; Jean Anyon, *Ghetto Schooling: A Political Economy of Urban Educational Reform* (New York: Teachers College Press, 1997); Frederick Hess, *Spinning Wheels: The Politics of Urban School Reform* (Washington, D.C.: Brookings Institution Press, 1998); Larry Cuban and Michael Usdan, eds., *Powerful Reforms and Shallow Roots: Improving America's Urban Schools* (New York: Teachers College Press, 2003); Paul Hill, Christine Campbell, and James Harvey, *It Takes a City: Getting Serious About Urban School Reform* (Washington, D.C.: Brookings Institution Press, 1999); Charles Payne and John Furlong, *Education, Reform and the State: Twenty-Five Years of Politics, Policy and Practice* (New York: Taylor and Francis Publishing, 2001); Wilbur Rich, *Black Mayors and School Politics: The Failure of Reform in Detroit, Gary, and Newark* (New York: Garland Press, 1996); Shirley Dennis, *Community Organizing for Urban School Reform* (Austin: University of Texas Press, 1997).

157. Jencks, *Inequality*, 256.

158. Ibid., 4; Also see Nancy St. John, *School Desegregation: Outcomes for Children* (New York: John Wiley, 1975).

159. Jencks, *Inequality*. Also see, for example, Richard Kahlenberg, *A Notion at Risk: Preserving Public Education as an Engine for Social Mobility Reform* (Washington, D.C.: Brookings Institution Press, 2000).

160. Annual Reports, Memphis City Schools, 1970–2005. For recent examples, see http://state.tn.us/education/reportcard/. The "poverty" figure is estimated from the percentage of students eligible for free or reduced-price school meals.

Chapter 2
Memphis

1. David Goldfield, *Cotton Fields and Skyscrapers* (Baltimore: Johns Hopkins University Press, 1989), 2. We use Goldfield's thematic construct to frame our historical review of the white political culture in Memphis.

2. Goldfield, *Cotton Fields and Skyscrapers*, 64. This was a period in which southern urbanism lagged behind northern urbanism more than any time in history.

3. Denoral Davis, "Against the Odds," Ph.D. diss., State University of New York at Binghamton, 1987, 48.

4. Kathleen Berkeley, *"Like a Plague of Locusts": Immigration and Social Change in Memphis, Tennessee* (Los Angeles: UCLA Press, 1980), 4.

5. Clayton Robinson, "Impact of the City on Rural Immigration to Memphis," Ph.D. diss., University of Minnesota, 1967, 5. Also see Noel Ignatiev, *How the Irish Became White* (New York: Routledge Press, 1996). The Irish later played a significant role in government and would have substantial representation in fire and police departments.

6. Ibid.

7. John Ellis, "Disease and the Destiny of a City: The 1878 Yellow Fever Epidemic in Memphis," *West Tennessee Historical Papers* 28 (1974): 76.

8. Ibid., 82.

9. Ibid., 82, 87.

10. For example, see Ellis, "Disease and the Destiny of a City," 75–89. And for a more general account of rural influence on urban politics in the South, see Goldfield, *Cotton Fields and Skyscrapers;* Earl Black and Merle Black, *Politics and Society in the South* (Cambridge, Mass.: Harvard University Press, 1987).

11. Goldfield, *Cotton Fields and Skyscrapers*, 94.

12. Roger Biles, *Memphis in the Great Depression* (Knoxville: University of Tennessee Press, 1986), 6. Also see Rayford Logan, *The Betrayal of the Negro* (London: Collier and McMillan, 1965), 300.

13. John Harkins, *Metropolis of the American Nile* (Oxford, Miss.: Guild Bindery Press, 1982), 104. Also see William Miller, *Mr. Crump of Memphis* (Baton Rouge: Louisiana State University Press, 1964), 8.

14. Gerald Capers, *The Biography of a River Town* (New York: Vanguard Press, 1966), 216.

15. For example, see presentation in the *Commercial Appeal,* Feb. 17, 1991; Memphis and Shelby County Planning Commission, *Annexation: A Must for a Growing Memphis* (internal study, Sept. 1967), 16. Yung Wei and H. R. Mahood, "Racial Attitudes and the Wallace Vote," *Polity* 3 (Summer 1971): 532–49.

17. Goldfield, *Cotton Fields to Skyscrapers*, 8.

18. A "spot market" is a cash market where a commodity is sold for immediate delivery.

19. Harkins, *Metropolis of the American Nile*, 95–96.

20. Robert Sigafoos, *Cotton Row to Beale Street* (Memphis: Memphis State University Press, 1979), 86.

21. Gerald Capers, "Memphis: Satrapy of a Benevolent Despot," in Robert Allen, *Our Fair City* (New York: Vanguard, 1947), 226.

22. Daniel Elazar, *American Federalism* (New York: Crowell, 1972), 106-7.

23. For example, see Paul S. Pierce, *The Freedmen's Bureau* (Iowa City, 1904); *Report of the Joint Committee on Reconstruction* (Washington, D.C., 1866); *Documents Relating to Reconstruction* (Cleveland, 1906); Laura J. Webster, *The Operation of the Freedmen's Bureau in South Carolina* (Northhampton, Mass., 1916); George R. Bentley, *A History of the Freedmen's Bureau* (Philadelphia: University of Pennsylvania Press, 1955).

24. For example, see Arthur Webb, "Memphis during the Civil War: The Real Story," *Tri-State Defender*, Aug. 20-24, 2005.

25. See Jack Holmes, "The Underlying Causes of the Memphis Riot of 1866," *Tennessee Historical Quarterly* 17 (1958): 292-96; Altina Walker, "Class and Race in the Memphis Riot of 1866," *Journal of Social History* 18 (Winter 1984): 233-46; James Gilbert Ryan, "The Memphis Riots of 1866," *Journal of Negro History* 62 (1977): 243-57; James Hathaway, "A Social History of the Negro in Memphis," Ph.D. diss., Yale University, 1934, 77-80; A. A. Taylor, *The Negro in Tennessee, 1865-1880* (New York: Associated Publishers, 1941), 86.

26. See Harry Holloway, *The Politics of the Southern Negro* (New York: Random House, 1969), 281, 286-87; David Tucker, *Memphis since Crump* (Knoxville: University of Tennessee Press, 1980), 118-21, 133-36.

27. Lewis Mumford Center for Comparative Urban and Regional Research, *Ethnic Diversity Grows, Neighborhood Integration Lags Behind* (Albany: State University of New York, 2001). Report cited in James Brosnan et al., "Races Staying 'Isolated' in Memphis, Study Says," *Commercial Appeal*, Apr. 5, 2001.

28. For example, see Michael Honey, *Southern Labor and Black Civil Rights* (Champaign: University of Illinois Press, 1993), 61-63; *Memphis World*, June 29 and July 9, 1948; *Press-Scimitar*, Oct. 18-21, 1971, Oct. 28, 1971, Dec. 6, 1971, Dec. 10, 1971, Oct. 1, 1973, Oct. 9, 1973, Apr. 8, 1975; *Commercial Appeal*, Aug. 6, 1916, Jan. 12-15, 1983, Jan. 25, 1983, Feb. 23, 1983, Nov. 10, 1984; Tony Jones, "How Police Board Evolved," *Tri-State Defender*, Nov. 12-16, 1994; Arthur Webb, "The Lynching at the Curve," *Tri-State Defender*, Feb. 12-16, 2005; Michael Kelly, "Shannon Siege Backfire," *Commercial Appeal*, Jan. 13, 2008.

29. For example, see Sandra Vaughn, "Memphis: Heart of the Mid-South," in Robert Bullard, ed., *In Search of the New South: The Black Urban Experience in the 1970s and 1980s* (Tuscaloosa: University of Alabama Press, 1989), 105.

30. Capers, "Memphis: Satrapy of a Benevolent Despot," 216. Also see Elazar, *American Federalism*, 106-7; Logan, *The Betrayal of the Negro*, 300. For a more general discussion of the racial divide in southern politics, see Joel Williamson, *The Crucible of Race* (New York: Oxford, 1984); Paul Lewinsohn, *Race, Class and Party: A History of Negro Suffrage and White Politics in the South* (New York: Russell and Russell, 1963); V. O. Key, *Southern Politics in State and Nation* (New York: Knopf, 1949), chaps. 1, 24, 25, 30; Holloway, *The Politics of the Southern Negro*, 26; Blaine Brownell

and David Goldfield, *The City in Southern History* (Port Washington, N.Y.: Kennikat Press, 1977), 17; James Geschwender, "Social Structure and the Negro Revolt," *Social Forces* 43 (1964–65): 248–56.

31. William Miller, *Memphis during the Progressive Era* (Memphis: Memphis State University Press, 1957), 23.

32. John Terreo, "Reporting by Memphis Newspapers Prior to the 1866 Race Riot and during the 1968 Sanitation Strike: A Historical Study" (master's thesis, Memphis State University, 1987), 47–48.

33. Gloria Brown Melton, "Blacks in Memphis, Tennessee, 1920–1955," Ph.D. diss., Washington State University, 1982, 49.

34. Biles, *Memphis in the Great Depression,* 14.

35. See T. O. Fuller, *The Inter-Racial Blue Book* (Memphis: Inter-Racial League, 1925).

36. Holloway, *The Politics of the Southern Negro,* 297.

37. Ibid., 27–28.

38. Lester Lamon, *Black Tennesseans, 1900–1930* (Knoxville: University of Tennessee Press, 1977), 223.

39. James Jalenak, "Beale Street Politics" (honors thesis, Yale University, 1961), 92.

40. Laura Stein and Arnold Fleischman, "Newspaper and Business Endorsements in Municipal Elections," *Journal of Urban Affairs* 9 (Fall 1987): 325–36.

41. See discussion in *Commercial Appeal,* Oct. 6, 1993.

42. See Christopher Barton, "Memphis Economy Thriving Overall," *Commercial Appeal,* Aug. 6, 2000.

43. For example, see Cindy Wolff, "Distribution Jobs Are a Boon to Area: Experts Also Want Manufacturing," *Commercial Appeal,* July 3, 1994; *Commercial Appeal,* July 18, 1993; Joy Clay and the Division of Finance, Budget Office, *Strategic Financial Plan,* Apr. 2000, 1.

44. See Mark Watson, "Proponents Claim Success, Some Suggest Too Much So," *Commercial Appeal,* June 3, 2001; Stephanie Myers, "Memphis Economics Loses Ground to Like-sized Cities," *Commercial Appeal,* May 25, 2003.

45. Census Tracts: 20, 22, 41, 45, 46, 48. Zip Codes: 38103, 38105, 38126. U.S. Dept. of Commerce, Bureau of the Census, *Census of the Population, 1990* (Washington, D.C.: GPO, 1991). Reported in Jimmie Covington, "Census Tract Figures Show Wide Income Disparity," *Commercial Appeal,* Jan. 3, 1993. Also see "Memphis MSA Zip Codes, Household Income Distribution," compiled by Claritas Rezide and supplied by the Marketing Services Dept., *Commercial Appeal,* Apr. 17, 1986.

46. Sixteenth annual "Kids Count Report," discussed in Aimee Edmondson, "Tennessee Kids Faring Better," *Commercial Appeal,* July 27, 2005. Also see seventeenth annual report discussed in Richard Locker, "Tennessee Failing Its Children," *Commercial Appeal,* June 27, 2006; Sybil Mitchell, "Babies at Risk," *Tri-State Defender,* May 20–24, 2006; Associated Press, "Memphis Fights Its Infant Mortality Rate," *New York Times,* Nov. 10, 2007.

47. *Commercial Appeal,* Sept. 9, 2005; Michael Kelly, "We're Back," *Commercial Appeal,* Oct. 2, 2005; "Growing Poorer," *Commercial Appeal,* Oct. 2, 2005; Urban Child Institute, *The State of Children in Memphis and Shelby County* (Memphis: Urban Child Institute, 2006).

48. See Laura Moore, "Crime: A Community Problem," *Tri-State Defender,* June 10–14, 2006.

49. For more discussion of whether the "New South" is more myth or reality, see Bullard, *In Search of the New South;* Chet Fuller, "I Hear Them Call It the New South," *Black Enterprise* 12 (Nov. 1981): 41–43.

50. Nicholas Lehman, *The Promised Land* (New York: Alfred Knopf, 1991), chap. 1.

51. Selma Lewis, "Social Religion and the Memphis Sanitation Strike," Ph.D. diss., Memphis State University, 1976, 154.

52. Reference is to community organizer Saul Alinsky. For example, see Saul Alinsky, *Rules for Radicals* (New York: Random House, 1971).

53. Terreo, "Reporting by Memphis Newspapers," 58.

54. For more on this tactic, see Ronan Paddison, "City Marketing, Image Reconstruction and Urban Regeneration," *Urban Studies* 30 (2): 339–50.

55. Sigafoos, *Cotton Row to Beale Street,* 337.

56. As for out-migration, see Sandra Vaughn, "Memphis: Heart of the Mid-South," in Bullard, *In Search of the New South,* 102; Jimmie Covington, "Jobs in '80s Revamped Population of County: Young Blacks Left and Whites Arrived," *Commercial Appeal,* May 26, 1992.

57. For example, see Vaughn, "Memphis: Heart of the Mid-South," 99–115; Ira Berlin, *Slaves without Masters* (New York: Pantheon, 1974).

58. Holloway, *The Politics of the Southern Negro,* 272; Jalenak, "Beale Street Politics," chaps. 7 and 9. For a more general discussion of antebellum southern cities as incubators for black leaders, see Berlin, *Slaves without Masters;* Daniel Thompson, *Negro Leadership Class* (Englewood Cliffs, N.J.: Prentice-Hall, 1963).

59. Holloway, *The Politics of the Southern Negro,* 302.

60. See F. Ray Marshall and Arvil Van Adams, "Negro Employment in Memphis," *Industrial Relations* 9 (May 1970): 308–23; Katherine McFate, ed., *The Metropolitan Area Fact Book* (Washington, D.C.: Joint Center for Political Studies, 1989); Denoral Davis, "Against the Odds"; Vaughn, "Memphis: Heart of the Mid-South"; Gloria Brown Melton, "Blacks in Memphis, Tennessee, 1920–1955"; Jalenak, "Beale Street Politics," 163–66; Goldfield, *Cotton Fields and Skyscrapers.* As for black community fissures and mass suspicion of black leaders, see Charles Williams Jr., "Two Black Communities in Memphis, Tennessee: A Study in Urban Socio-Political Structure," Ph.D. diss., University of Illinois, 1982.

61. For example, see Lewinsohn, *Race, Class and Party,* 139; Davis, "Against the Odds," 211.

62. See George Lee, *Beale Street* (New York: R. O. Ballou, 1934), 13.

63. See Vaughn, "Memphis: Heart of the Mid-South," 113–15.

64. Davis, "Against the Odds," 223. Also, see Kenneth Wald, "The Electoral Base of Political Machines," *Urban Affairs Quarterly* 16 (Sept. 1980): 6.

65. See William Cohen, "Negro Involuntary Servitude in the South, 1865-1940," *Journal of Southern History* 42 (Feb. 1976): 39.

66. Davis, "Against the Odds," 50-55.

67. Ibid., 292-96. Also see Jalenak, "Beale Street Politics," 32, 163-66.

68. See Jimmie Covington, "Race Income Gap Narrowed in '90s," *Commercial Appeal,* Dec. 1, 2002.

69. See Vaughn, "Memphis: Heart of the Mid-South," 112.

70. U.S. Dept. of Commerce, Bureau of the Census, Economic Census Survey of Minority-Owned Business Enterprises (Washington, D.C.: GPO, 1992). Dee discussion in Kevin McKenzie, "Room at the Table," *Commercial Appeal,* Nov. 5, 1998.

71. Urban Child Institute, *The State of Children in Memphis and Shelby County* (Memphis: Urban Child Institute, 2006), 3, 11; *Commercial Appeal,* May 30, 1989.

72. Goldfield, *Cotton Fields and Skyscrapers,* 166.

73. Ibid., 191.

74. Marshall and Van Adams, "Negro Employment in Memphis," 308-23. Also see *Commercial Appeal,* June 20, 1986.

75. Joint Center for Political Studies, *The Metropolitan Area Fact Book* (Washington, D.C.: Joint Center for Political Studies, 1988 and various subsequent years). Also see *Crisis in Education: Investing in the Children of Memphis and Shelby County,* report of the Memphis NAACP, submitted to Federal District Judge Robert McCrae, Memphis, Oct. 10, 1988, 2; U.S. Dept. of Commerce, Bureau of the Census, *Statistical Abstracts of the United States, 2004* (Washington, D.C.: GPO, 2005); Peter Kilborn, "Memphis Blacks Find Cycle of Poverty Difficult to Break," *New York Times,* Oct. 5, 1999; Urban Child Institute, *The State of Children in Memphis and Shelby County* (Memphis: Urban Child Institute, 2006), 4; Chris Peck, "When Race Is an Asset, We All Win," *Commercial Appeal,* May 20, 2007.

76. See Kevin McKenzie, "Black Middle Class Grows, but So Do Income Disparities," *Commercial Appeal,* Apr. 6, 1998.

77. George Lee letter appearing in the *Baltimore Afro-American,* June 8, 1929. Also see his comments in *Messenger* (July 1925): 252-53.

78. Lamon, *Black Tennesseans.* Also see Herman Morris, "Memphis Case Presaged Historic Bus Protest," *Commercial Appeal,* Feb. 26, 2006.

79. *Chicago Defender,* Apr. 24, 1915.

80. *Commercial Appeal,* Aug. 14, 1916.

81. Ibid., Oct. 22, 1916. And similarly, see *Chicago Defender,* May 28, 1918.

82. *Commercial Appeal,* Dec. 4, 1916.

83. See John Dollard, *Caste and Class in a Southern Town* (New Haven: Yale University Press, 1938), 290.

84. Howard Rabinowitz, *Race Relations in the South, 1865–1890* (New York: Oxford University Press, 1978), 336. Specifically, see *Memphis Appeal-Avalanche,* Mar. 3, 1892, Mar. 6, 1892, *Commercial Appeal,* Nov. 11, 1916; Oct. 29, 1916; Aug. 6, 1916; *Chicago Defender,* Mar. 2, 1918. Also see Melton, "Blacks in Memphis, Tennessee," 202.

85. Holloway, *The Politics of the Southern Negro,* 287.

86. For example, see Melton, "Blacks in Memphis, Tennessee," 363–64; Vaughn, "Memphis: Heart of the Mid-South," 107; Holloway, *The Politics of the Southern Negro,* 287. As for the 1968 sanitation strike, see Joan Beifuss, *At The River I Stand;* Tucker, *Memphis since Crump,* chaps. 3 and 9; Robert Bailey, "The 1968 Memphis Sanitation Strike" (master's thesis, Memphis State University, 1974).

87. For example, see Honey, *Southern Labor and Black Civil Rights; Memphis World,* Aug. 8 and Aug. 25, 1944; *Chicago Defender,* Sept. 22, 1917, May 1, 1920; Tucker, *Memphis since Crump,* chap. 3.

88. *Memphis World,* Aug. 8, 25, 1944.

89. See Beifuss, *By the River We Stand;* Bailey, "The 1968 Memphis Sanitation Strike"; Tucker, *Memphis since Crump,* chap. 9.

90. Tucker, *Memphis since Crump,* 161.

91. See Melton, "Blacks in Memphis, Tennessee," 14.

92. See Margaret Price, *The Negro Vote in the South* (Atlanta: Southern Regional Council, 1957), 68.

93. For example, see Melton, "Blacks in Memphis, Tennessee," 363–64; Vaughn, "Memphis: Heart of the Mid-South," 107.

94. For example, see Arthur Webb, "The Civil Rights Movement Is Not Limited to a Single Era," *Tri-State Defender,* Feb. 11–15, 2006.

95. See Melton, "Blacks in Memphis, Tennessee," 253.

96. Tucker, *Memphis since Crump,* 142.

97. *Commercial Appeal,* Sept. 20, 1982.

98. Attorney John Ryder, former Republican County Chairman, quoted in Jackson Baker, "Election Aftermath as Simple as Black and White?" *Memphis Flyer,* Aug. 13–19, 1992.

99. When asked to interpret the act, the Tennessee Supreme Court handed down two important rulings. First, they decided that the test of reasonableness would be that the "overall well being" of both areas would have to improve. *Tennessee v. Pigeon Force,* Tenn. 599 SW 2nd 545 (1980s). Secondly, the court recognized the city's burden of proof and the fact that the "fairly debatable" precedent had been supplanted. However, they also noted that cities have a right to "orderly growth and development," especially to avoid being hemmed in by unsafe, unsanitary and substandard rural housing. *Pirtle v. Jackson,* Tenn. 560 SW 2nd 400 (1977).

100. The census indicated that Memphis had approximately 1 percent "others," which were primarily Asians. These are not the same "others" reflected in the registration statistics where some citizens do not want to provide their race. The election commission classifies these latter registrants as "others."

101. *United States v. City of Memphis*, Western District of Tennessee, case number 91–2139. And as for the significance of form on electoral participation and results, see John Kessel, "Governmental Structure and Political Environment," *American Political Science Review* 61 (Sept. 1963): 615–20; Robert Salisbury, "St. Louis Politics," *Western Political Quarterly* 13 (June 1960): 498–507; Robert Duggar, "The Relation of Local Government Structure to Urban Renewal," *Law and Contemporary Problems* 26 (Jan. 1961): 49–69; Donald Rosenthal and Robert Crain, "Structure and Values in Local Political Systems," *Journal of Politics* 28 (Feb. 1966): 169–96; Charles Adrian and Oliver Williams, *Four Cities* (Philadelphia: University of Pennsylvania Press, 1961).

102. The final audit by Watkins, Watkins, and Keegan showed 609 "over votes," meaning instances in which more votes were cast than the number of people who signed in at the polls. According to their report, "the differences are unreconciled and the causes undetermined." The Hackett camp seriously weighed a legal challenge based on these discrepancies, but in the end decided that "a challenge . . . would not be appropriate given the nature of the irregularities which have occurred, the limitations of the state law and the information available to us under state law and election commission procedures." Robert "Prince Mongo" Hodges had not received enough of the total vote to pose a challenge under existing election law. For discussion of this matter, see Terry Keeter, "Election Gets Official Seal," *Commercial Appeal*, Oct. 15, 1991; Charles Bernsen, "Advisers Concluded Challenge Too Difficult," *Commercial Appeal*, Oct. 15, 1991; John Branston, "The Election After Math," *Memphis Flyer*, Oct. 17–23, 1991.

103. Marcus Pohlmann and Michael Kirby, *Racial Politics at the Crossroads: Memphis Elects Dr. W.W. Herenton* (Knoxville: University of Tennessee Press, 1996), chaps. 6–9.

104. For example, see Tucker, *Memphis since Crump*, 152–61.

105. Pohlmann and Kirby, *Racial Politics at the Crossroads*, chap. 9.

106. Ibid., chap. 11.

107. See Jacinthia Jones, "Opening Hearts and Minds to Progress," *Commercial Appeal*, Jan. 27, 2008.

Chapter 3
Memphis City Schools

1. For example, see Edward Krug, *Salient Dates in American Education, 1635–1964* (New York: Harper & Row, 1966), 77. Also see material provided by the Applied Research Center's Race and Public Policy Program of Oakland, California. See http://www.arc.org/erase/j_history.html.

2. Much of this historical overview has been drawn from William Collins and Robert Margo, *Historical Perspectives on Racial Differences in Schooling in the United States*, Working Paper No. 03-W13, Dept. of Economics, Vanderbilt University, June 2003. For the data on African American education, see Marcus Pohlmann, *Black Politics in*

Conservative America (New York: Longman, 1999), 42–44; Janet Duitsman Cornelius, *"When I Can Read My Title Clear": Literacy, Slavery, and Religion in the Antebellum South* (Columbia, S.C.: University of South Carolina Press, 1991), 9.

3. See Ronald Butchart, *Northern Schools, Southern Blacks, and Reconstruction: Freedmen's Education, 1862–1875* (Westport, Conn.: Greenwood Press, 1980); Robert Morris, *Reading, 'Riting, and Reconstruction: The Education of Freedmen in the South, 1861–1870* (Chicago: University of Chicago Press, 1981); James Anderson, *The Education of Blacks in the South, 1860–1935* (Chapel Hill: University of North Carolina Press, 1988); Ronald Butchart, "We Can Best Instruct Our Own People: New York African Americans in Freemen's Schools, 1861–1875," *Afro-Americans in New York Life and History* 12 (1988): 27–49; Anderson, *The Education of Blacks in the South,* chap. 1.

4. See Morgan Kousser, *The Shaping of Southern Politics: Suffrage Restriction and the Establishment of the One Party South, 1880–1910* (New Haven: Yale University Press, 1974).

5. See Robert Margo, "Race Differences in Public School Expenditures: Disenfranchisement and School Finance in Louisiana, 1890–1910," *Social Science History* 6 (1982): 9–33.

6. Horace Mann Bond, *The Education of the Negro in the American Social Order* (New York: Prentice-Hall, 1934); Horace Mann Bond, *Negro Education in Alabama: A Study in Cotton and Steel* (New York: Associate Publishers, 1939); Louis Harlan, *Separate and Unequal: School Campaigns and Racism in the Southern Seaboard States, 1901–1915* (Chapel Hill: University of North Carolina Press, 1958); Richard Smith, "The Economics of Educational Discrimination in the United States South, 1870–1910," Ph.D. diss., University of Wisconsin, 1973; Morgan Kousser, "Progressivism—For Middle Class Whites Only," *Journal of Southern History* 46 (1980): 169–94; Margo, "Race Differences in Public School Expenditures"; Jonathan Pritchett, "North Carolina's Public Schools: Growth and Local Taxation," *Social Science History* 9 (1985): 277–91; Jonathan Pritchett, "The Burden of Negro Schooling: Tax Incidence and Racial Redistribution in Post-Bellum North Carolina," *Journal of Economic History* 49 (1989): 966–73; Pamela Walters et al., "Citizenship and Public Schools: Accounting for Racial Inequality in Education in the Pre- and Post-Disenfranchisement South," *American Sociological Review* 62 (1997): 34–52.

7. *Plessy v. Ferguson* 163 U.S. 537 (1896).

8. *Cummings v. Richmond County Board of Education,* 175 U.S. 528 (1899).

9. For example, see Smith, *The Economics of Educational Discrimination in the United States South;* Carl Harris, "Stability and Change in Discrimination Against Black Schools: Birmingham, Alabama, 1871–1931," *Journal of Southern History* 51 (1985): 375–416.

10. For example, see Collins and Margo, *Historical Perspectives on Racial Differences in Schooling in the United States,* 10–11.

11. See Joel Perlman and Robert Margo, *Women's Work? Schoolteachers, 1670–1920* (Chicago: University of Chicago Press, 2001); Robert Margo, "Race and Human Capital: Comment," *American Economic Review* 76 (1986): 1221–24.

12. See Collins and Margo, *Historical Perspectives on Racial Differences in Schooling in the United States*, 17–19, 31–32; David Strong et al., "Leveraging the State: Private Money and the Development of Public Education for Blacks," *American Sociological Review* 65 (2000): 658–81. For an overview of American educational history in general, see William Reese, *America's Public Schools: From the Common School to "No Child Left Behind"* (Baltimore: Johns Hopkins Press, 2005)

13. This review of the history of the Memphis city schools is drawn primarily from David Moss Hilliard, "The Development of Public Education in Memphis, Tennessee, 1848–1945," Ph.D. diss., University of Chicago, 1946. Dr. Hilliard drew on source materials from the Cossitt Library, municipal archives, the Shelby County Law Library, and files of the city's board of education. Also see secondary historical sources such as Gerald M. Capers Jr., *The Biography of a River Town; Memphis: Its Historic Age* (Chapel Hill: University of North Carolina Press, 1939); J. M. Keating, *History of Memphis*, vol. 1 (Syracuse, N.Y., 1886); O. F. Vedder, *History of Memphis*, vol. 2 (Syracuse, N.Y., 1886); J. P. Young, *Standard History of Memphis* (Knoxville, 1912).

14. On the issue of fiscal mismanagement, for example, see Capers, *The Biography of a River Town*, 128–29; Keating, *History of Memphis*, 412–13.

15. See Tennessee Constitution, Art. XI, sec. 12.

16. Acts of the State of Tennessee, 1847–1848, chap. 64, sec. 7, 114–19.

17. Vedder, *History of Memphis*, 143.

18. For example, see *Minutes of the City Council*, May 13, 1848, and June 3, 1848.

19. *Minutes of the City Council*, June 3, 1848.

20. Ibid., May 20, 1848.

21. Ibid., June 19, 1848.

22. Ibid., July 18, 1848.

23. Hilliard, *The Development of Public Education*, 9.

24. *Minutes of the School Board*, July 18, 1848.

25. *Daily Enquirer*, Aug. 3, 1848.

26. Ibid., Aug. 23, 1848.

27. Ibid., Sept. 6, 1848.

28. For example, see *Minutes of the City Council*, Oct. 21, 1848. Also see Goodspeed's *History of Shelby County, Tennessee* (1887; reprint, Nashville: Elder Booksellers, 1974), 840–41.

29. Minutes of the City Council, Sept. 11, 1852, and Dec. 21, 1852.

30. Hilliard, *The Development of Public Education*, 13.

31. *Memphis City Directory, 1856–1857*, 11–17.

32. *Public Acts of Tennessee, 1856–1857*, chap. 170, 400–402. Also see Goodspeed's *History of Shelby County, Tennessee*, 842.

33. *Public Acts of Tennessee, 1857–1858*, chap. 170, 400–402.

34. *Board of Education of Memphis City Schools v. Shelby County et al.* (1960) upheld the requirement that all such funds be shared proportionately by population. Further codified in the 1977 Tennessee Education Finance Act.

35. Capers, *The Biography of a River Town,* 160.

36. *Public Acts of Tennessee, 1866–1867,* chap. 8, 15.

37. *Sixteenth Annual Report of the Board of School Visitors,* 1867–68, 27–31.

38. *Minutes of the School Board,* July 6, 1868.

39. *Public Acts of Tennessee, 1868–1869,* chap. 30, 137–42.

40. For example, see Bill Dries, "Line-Item Budget Control Resides with City Schools," *Commercial Appeal,* Jan. 30, 2000.

41. *Minutes of the Board of Education,* Dec. 28, 1882; *Acts of the State of Tennessee,* chap. 17, 20–22; *Annual Report of the Board of Education,* 1882–83, 54–55. Nearly a century later, in 1992, the state legislature mandated that all the state's school boards be popularly elected and that those boards appoint their schools' superintendents.

42. *Rules and Regulations of the Public Schools of Memphis, Tenn., 1913–14,* 16–18, 29–33.

43. Hilliard, *The Development of Public Education,* 124–31.

44. *Private Acts of Tennessee, 1941,* chap. 42, 164–66.

45. *Public Acts of Tennessee, 1851–1852,* chap. 346, sec. 8, 633.

46. Due to an omission in the second charter, a subsequent amendment was passed reaffirming this authority. See *Public Acts of Tennessee, 1859–1860,* chap. 142, sec. 1 and 2, 450–51.

47. Goodspeed, *History of Shelby County, Tennessee,* 840.

48. *Daily Enquirer,* Aug. 23, 1848.

49. Ibid., Aug. 23, 1851.

50. See *Second Annual Report of the Board of School Visitors, Memphis City Schools, 1853–1854,* 4–8; *Fourth Annual Report,* 10; *Fifth Annual Report,* 8; *Fourteenth Annual Report,* 8, 10.

51. Hilliard, *The Development of Public Education,* 32–34.

52. See *Daily Appeal,* Mar. 28, 1860, Feb. 8, 1861, July 6, 1861; *Annual Report of the Board of Education, Memphis City Schools, 1883–1884,* 20.

53. *Annual Report of the Board of Education, Memphis City Schools, 1883–1884.* Also see compilations in Goodspeed's *History of Shelby County, Tennessee,* 843.

54. *Fourteenth Annual Report of the Board of School Visitors, Memphis City Schools, 1865–1866,* 8.

55. *Minutes of City Council,* Feb. 8, 1866.

56. See *Minutes of the City Council,* Oct. 21, 1848; *Fifth Annual Report of the Board of School Visitors, Memphis City Schools, 1856–1857,* 8.

57. Hilliard, *The Development of Public Education,* 30–31.

58. *Daily Post,* Mar. 25, 1867.

59. *Public Acts of Tennessee, 1868–1869.*

60. *Daily Appeal,* Jan. 7, 1872.

61. *Twenty-First Annual Report of the Board of Education of the City of Memphis, 1871–1872,* 21.

62. *Twenty-Third Annual Report of the Board of Education of the City of Memphis, 1873–1874,* 34.

63. Capers, *The Biography of a River Town,* 194.

64. *Twenty-Third Annual Report of the Board of Education of the City of Memphis, 1873–1874,* 6.

65. Keating, *History of Memphis,* 619.

66. Capers, *The Biography of a River Town,* 195.

67. Hilliard, *The Development of Public Education,* 49.

68. Young, *Standard History of Memphis,* 196–211.

69. *Acts of Tennessee, 1879,* chap. 17, sec. 1, 20.

70. *Audit of the Board of Education,* June 1943.

71. Hilliard, *The Development of Public Education,* 53–62. For a listing of the major annexations during this period, see the timeline presented by the Memphis City Schools, in "A Brief History of Memphis City Schools," http://www.memphis-schools.k12.tn.us/admin/communicaitons/MCS-History.html.

72. *Acts of Tennessee, 1847–1948,* chap. 14, 114.

73. *Minutes of the City Council,* May 22, 1848.

74. *Memphis City Directory, 1856–1857,* 11.

75. See Hilliard, *The Development of Public Education,* 66–71.

76. See *Public Ledger,* June 14, 1875, June 21, 1875, June 28, 1875, Oct. 18, 1875, Dec. 26, 1875.

77. *Daily Appeal,* Nov. 18, 1874, Jan. 12, 1875.

78. Hilliard, *The Development of Public Education,* 76.

79. *Daily Appeal,* July 10, 1889.

80. *Commercial Appeal,* Nov. 16, 1909.

81. For example, see *Annual Report of the Board of Education, Memphis City Schools, 1910–1911,* 13.

82. Hilliard, *The Development of Public Education,* 86.

83. *Commercial Appeal,* Jan. 28, 1919, Feb. 12, 1919, Feb. 28, 1919.

84. *Private Acts of Tennessee, 1919,* chap. 186, sec. 1, 441–42.

85. *Commercial Appeal,* Mar. 19, 1919.

86. Unpublished Financial Record of the Board of Education, cited in Hilliard, *The Development of Public Education,* 92.

87. Memphis tax payers, also being residents of Shelby County, pay property taxes to support both the city and county school systems. The combined school tax burden on city residents was $2.89 per $100 valuation in 2002. See Michael Kelly, "School Budget Fairness Is in the Eye of the Beholder," *Commercial Appeal,* Mar. 3, 2002.

88. For example, see city school funding numbers in the *Commercial Appeal,* Jan. 13, 2005.

89. Capers, *The Biography of a River Town,* 79.

90. Ibid., 114.

91. *Daily Post,* Apr. 25, 1867.

92. Hilliard, *The Development of Public Education,* 135.

93. *Daily Bulletin,* Jan. 7, 1865.

94. *Daily Post,* July 24, 1869.

95. *Daily Bulletin,* Oct. 29, 1864.

96. *Minutes of the City Council,* Sept. 5, 1864.

97. *Daily Post,* July 24, 1869.

98. Superintendent Barnum, reporting in the *Daily Post,* July 21, 1869.

99. *Daily Post,* Feb. 4, 1867, Feb. 20, 1867.

100. Hilliard, *The Development of Public Education,* 136.

101. *Acts of Tennessee,* Mar. 5, 1867, sec.17.

102. *School Board Minutes,* Dec. 2, 1867.

103. *Fifteenth Annual Report of the Board of Education of the City of Memphis,* 1866–67, 62.

104. *Daily Post,* Aug. 18, 1868.

105. *Acts of Tennessee, 1868–69,* chap. 30, 130–142.

106. Capers, *The Biography of a River Town,* 174.

107. *Daily Avalanche,* Mar. 7, 1869.

108. *Daily Post,* July 24, 1869.

109. Ibid., July 30, 1869.

110. Ibid., Aug. 23, 1869.

111. *Daily Avalanche,* Feb. 15, 1870.

112. *Daily Appeal,* Mar. 1, 1870.

113. *Daily Avalanche,* Mar. 15, 1870.

114. *Daily Appeal,* May 15, 1872.

115. Ibid., July 16, 1871.

116. Ibid., Mar. 14, 1874.

117. Ibid., July 5, 1873.

118. Hilliard, *The Development of Public Education,* 143–44.

119. *Public Ledger,* July 13, 1875.

120. Hilliard, *The Development of Public Education,* 143.

121. For a detailed 1885 comparison, see the table presented in Goodspeed's *History of Shelby County, Tennessee,* 844.

122. Hilliard, *The Development of Public Education,* 147–51.

123. See *School Board Minutes,* May 13, 1872.

Chapter 4
School Desegregation

1. James Coleman and Sara Kelly, "Education," in William Gorham and Nathan Glazer, eds., *The Urban Predicament* (Washington, D.C.: Urban Institute, 1976), 243.

2. *Plessy v. Ferguson,* 163 U.S. 537 (1896).

3. *Brown v. Board of Education of Topeka, Kansas,* 349 U.S. 294 (1954).

4. *Northcross v. Board of Education of the Memphis City Schools,* No. 3931. The parallel county case was *Robinson v. Shelby County Board of Education,* no. 4916.

5. Those students were Joyce Bell, Alvin Freeman, E. C. Marcel Freeman, Dwania Kyles, Sharon Malone, Sheila Malone, Pam Mayes, Jacqueline Moore, Leandrew Wiggins, Clarence Williams, Harry Williams, and Michael Willis. A few of them were children of prominent local civil rights activists.

6. For example, see John Branston, "Integration and Innocence," *Memphis Flyer,* May 20–26, 2004, 14–16; David Dawson, "Charade on Wheels," *Memphis Magazine,* 1981, 41.

7. Ernest Kelly et al., "History of the Case," prepared for Division of Research and Planning, Memphis City Schools (Memphis, 1981), 3a. Although Kelly's work will be cited as the primary source for much of this information, another excellent primary source consulted was Bruce Speck and Sherry Hoppe, *Maxine Smith's Unwilling Pupils: Lessons Learned in Memphis' Civil Rights Classroom* (Knoxville: University of Tennessee Press, 2007).

8. Kelly et al., "History of the Case," 3a.

9. Ibid., 4a.

10. Ibid., 5a.

11. *Green v. New Kent County Board of Education,* 391 U.S. 430 (1968).

12. Kelly et al., "History of the Case," 6a.

13. Ibid., 7a.

14. Ibid.

15. Speck and Hoppe, *Maxine Smith's Unwilling Pupils,* 76–78.

16. Anita Houk, "Maxine," *Commercial Appeal,* Mid-South section, Dec. 2, 1984, 8–9.

17. *Alexander v. Holmes County Board,* 396 U.S. 19 (1969).

18. *Northcross v. Board of Education of the Memphis City Schools,* 420 F.2d 548 (1970).

19. *Northcross v. Board of Education of the Memphis City Schools,* 397 U.S. 323 (1970).

20. Kelly et al., "History of the Case," 9a.

21. Ibid., 9a–10a.

22. "Pairing" and "contiguous zones" were methods of reassigning students between schools for the purpose of increasing racial integration in each of the affected schools.

23. *Swann v. Charlotte-Mecklenburg Board of Education,* 402 U.S. 1 (1971).

24. *Davis v. Board of School Commissioners*, 402 U.S. 33 (1971).

25. Kelly et al., "History of the Case," 13a–14a.

26. Ibid., 15a.

27. Ibid., 16a.

28. Ibid.

29. Press Services, "Nixon Keeps Door Open to Seek Ban on Busing," *Commercial Appeal*, September 18, 1972.

30. Jimmie Covington, "Judge Orders Busing for 13,789, Says 'Practicalities' Limit Change," *Commercial Appeal*, April 21, 1972.

31. Founded in 1971, the nine founding members of the legally chartered Citizens Against Busing Inc. were Ron and Peggy Weston, John and Wanda Harrelson, William and Juanita Duncan, Mary Lou Lane, Bobby K. Bush, and Claude Rollins.

32. "Lunch Boycott Hits 44 Schools," *Commercial Appeal* (1972).

33. Kay Pittman Black and Gerald W. Dupy, "3 Plans for City Schools Are Filed in U.S. Court—All Call for Busing," *Press-Scimitar*, no. 105 (1972): 1–2.

34. Black and Dupy, "3 Plans," 1–2.

35. "Cost of Busing Set in Millions," *Commercial Appeal* (March 16, 1972).

36. Jimmie Covington, "Judge Orders Busing for 13,789, Says 'Practicalities' Limit Change," *Commercial Appeal*, April 21, 1972.

37. Covington, "Judge Orders Busing."

38. Wayne Chastain, "School Official Defends His Disciplinary Actions." *Press-Scimitar* no. 105 (1972): 1–2.

39. Jimmie Covington, "Two School Board Plans Would Require Busing 12,686 to 37,982 Pupils," *Commercial Appeal*, March 4, 1972.

40. Kelly et al., "History of the Case," 20a.

41. Ibid., 21a.

42. Ibid., 22a.

43. Ibid., 27a.

44. Interview with David Sojourner, Division of Research, Memphis City Schools. Also see Speck and Hoppe, *Maxine Smith's Unwilling Pupils*, 216.

45. See summary of coverage presented in *Commercial Appeal*, May 16, 2004.

46. That number jumped to $1.9 million in 1974, $2.7 in 1975, $3.5 in 1976, more than $4 million in 1977, more than $4.6 million in 1978, and more than $6 million in 1979, before finally beginning to level off.

47. Kelly et al., "History of the Case," 27a.

48. Ibid., 28a–29a.

49. Jimmie Covington, "Board-Supported Busing Plan Is Ordered for 39,904 in Fall: Appeal Pledged by NAACP," *Commercial Appeal*, May 4, 1973.

50. Michael Lollar, "NAACP Plans Busing Order Appeal; Chandler Says Ruling Goes Too Far," *Commercial Appeal*, May 4, 1973.

51. Interview with David Sojourner, Division of Research, Memphis City Schools.

52. Johnnie B. Watson, "Information for Analyzing the Resolution on One Way Busing," prepared for the Memphis Board of Education, Apr. 2, 1984, 6.

53. Kelly et al., "History of the Case," 42a; Watson, "Information for Analyzing the Resolution on One Way Busing," 6.

54. Dawson, "Charade on Wheels," 44.

55. David Sojourner, "A Brief History of Desegregation and Transportation in the Memphis City Schools," submitted to the Dept. of School Administration and Student Support, Apr. 23, 2001, 2. For a detailed discussion of the efforts of the Plan Z Review Committee, see Watson, "Information for Analyzing the Resolution on One Way Busing," 7–11.

56. Quoted in Dawson, "Charade on Wheels," 39. Also see "School-Busing Did Not Achieve Its Purposes and Should Stop," *Tri-State Defender*, editorial, Dec. 6–10, 2003.

57. Judge McRae officially put the *Northcross* case on "inactive" status in November of 1992; it was finally dismissed by Judge Julia Gibbons in April of 1999, with the consent of both parties. The county's *Robinson* case also remains in limbo. For example, see Lindsay Melvin, "Desegregation Won't Go Quietly," *Commercial Appeal*, Jan. 27, 2007. Also see Lindsay Melvin, "Rezoning Will Add Bus Time for Some," *Commercial Appeal*, Feb. 26, 2007.

58. *Commercial Appeal*, May 16, 2004, p. A20.

59. O. Z. Stephens, "Induced Desegregation: Its Effects on White Pupil Population and Resegregation in the Memphis City School System," Division of Research and Planning, Memphis City Schools, March 19, 1976, p.6.

60. Michael Dobbs, "School Segregation at Levels Last Seen in '60s," *Commercial Appeal*, Jan. 18, 2004. Also see James Coleman, "Racial Segregation in the Schools: New Research with New Policy Implications," *Phi Delta Kappa*, Oct. 1975, 75–78.

61. For example, see David Waters, "A Better Quality of Life," *Commercial Appeal*, Aug. 24, 1997; Clay Bailey, "For Peggs, It Was About the Municipal Principle," *Commercial Appeal*, Mar. 10, 2003. For a fuller discussion of the suburbanization phenomenon in general, see Marcus Pohlmann, *Governing the Postindustrial City* (New York: Longman Press, 1993), 81–86.

62. See Jimmie Covington, "Metro Going Majority Black," *Commercial Appeal*, Dec. 31, 2006.

63. Lewis Mumford Center for Comparative Urban and Regional Research, *Ethnic Diversity Grows, Neighborhood Integration Lags Behind* (Albany, N.Y.: State University of New York, 2001). Report cited in James Brosnan et al., "Races Staying 'Isolated' in Memphis, Study Says," *Commercial Appeal*, Apr. 5, 2001.

64. Quoted in Dawson, "Charade on Wheels," 44.

65. *Milliken v. Bradley*, 418 U.S. 717 (1974).

66. Based on "average daily attendance" figures, Memphis City Schools, yearly reports. For a discussion of this and other repercussions of this flight, see Tom Charlier, "Suburb Flight Blights City Core," *Commercial Appeal*, Mar. 10, 2003.

67. See Jay Yuan and Yi Liu, *An Analysis of Population Changes by Age Groups in Shelby County, City of Memphis, and Non-Memphis Shelby Area,* report presented by the NBM Associates at the Memphis Regional Chamber of Commerce Research Council Meeting, Dec. 15, 2004, 2.

68. Stephens, "Induced Desegregation."

69. Dawson, "Charade on Wheels," 40–41, 46.

70. See Stephens, "Induced Desegregation."

71. The black birth rate was reported to be 23.2 births per 1,000 residents, while the corresponding white rate was 12.2 per 1,000. See "Student Sin City Now 59% Black," *Commercial Appeal,* Apr. 27, 1975. Also see Jimmie Covington, "White Enrollment Dip in Schools Is Linked in Part to Birth Rate," *Commercial Appeal,* Jan. 24, 1979.

72. Dawson, "Charade on Wheels," 40.

73. See Speck and Hoppe, *Maxine Smith's Unwilling Pupils, 307.*

74. Stephens, "Induced Desegregation."

75. Jimmie Covington, "Private Schools Grow with Busing Threats," *Commercial Appeal,* Oct. 22, 1972; Jimmie Covington, "New Private Schools Expect 3,025 Students in Fall," *Commercial Appeal,* Aug. 3, 1973.

76. Jimmie Covington, "Private Schools' Enrollment Nearly Doubles within Year," *Commercial Appeal,* Nov. 14, 1973.

77. The initial 26 "CAB Schools" were located in the following churches: Cottonwood Heights Baptist, Faith Temple, Frayser Baptist, Frayser Pentecostal, Georgian Hills Baptist, Georgian Hills Methodist, Grace Gospel, Graceland Baptist, Hollywood Baptist, Longcrest Baptist, Maranthan Baptist, Northview Baptist, Oakhaven Baptist, Orchi Baptist, Peabody Baptist, Raleigh Pentecostal, Rugby Hills Baptist, Sherwood Baptist, Westhaven Baptist, Bethal United Pentecostal, Eastland Presbyterian, Frayser New Testament Christian, Macon Road Baptist, Trinity Pentecostal, West Frayser Baptist; Whitney and Leawood Baptist. See "CAB School Checks to Start," *Commercial Appeal,* Feb. 13, 1973.

78. Jimmie Covington, "CAB Schools Elicit Varied Ratings," *Commercial Appeal,* Mar. 20, 1973; Shirley Downing, "Tuition Woes Reported for Frayser CAB Schools," *Commercial Appeal,* Apr. 5, 1973, 24; Evan Jenkins, "School Conflict in South Is Intensifying As Academies Challenge Public System," *New York Times,* Aug. 19, 1973; Jerry Robbins, "Many New Private Schools Are Not Accredited," *Press-Scimitar,* Apr. 23, 1973; interview with Maxine Smith, Nov. 2001.

79. "CAB to Have No Schools," *Commercial Appeal,* July 24, 1974.

80. For example, see Gregg Gordon, "Still Fighting the School Tax Flap," *Commercial Appeal,* Apr. 8, 1984.

81. *Engel v. Vitale,* 370 U.S. 421 (1962).

82. Smith and Roper quoted in Jimmie Covington, "The Private School Boom: Despite Disclaimers, White Flight from Desegregation and Possible Busing Has Spurred Growth," *Commercial Appeal,* Aug. 20, 1972; Glise quoted in Jimmie Covington, "Private Schools Show Effects of Competition, Slowing Flight," *Commercial Appeal,*

Nov. 18, 1974. Frayser Baptist quote from the original letter, copy held by Jimmie Covington.

83. Jenkins, "School Conflict in South Is Intensifying As Academies Challenge Public System."

84. For an early history of several of the oldest of these private schools, see Goodspeed's *History of Shelby County, Tennessee*, 845–48.

85. Elizabeth Lassiter Baker and Linda Brown Porter, *A Parent's Guide to Memphis Area Private Schools: 1973 Edition* (Memphis: Barton Press, 1973), 39.

86. Quoted in *Commercial Appeal*, May 16, 2004.

87. For a reasonably complete listing of the private school options that existed in 1973, see Baker and Porter, *A Parent's Guide to Memphis Area Private Schools.*

88. For example, see Gordon, "Still Fighting the School Tax Flap."

89. Billy Stair, "The Renewed Struggle between Public and Private Education," *Tennessee Teacher*, Sept. 1978, 10.

90. "CAB to Have No Schools," *Commercial Appeal*, July 24, 1974.

91. Ray Jordan, "Public Schools Face New Threat," *Commercial Appeal*, Mar. 21, 1974.

92. Jimmie Covington, "Private, Church Schools Gain Popularity," *Commercial Appeal*, Oct. 29, 1971; *Commercial Appeal*, Nov. 7, 1972.

93. Jimmie Covington and Bill Sonenburg records. Roughly 90 percent of these students lived outside Memphis.

94. Jimmie Covington calculations, Dec. 11, 1979.

95. Jimmie Covington, "Some Students Return to City Schools," *Commercial Appeal*, Aug. 14, 1973; Covington, "Private Schools Show Effects of Competition, Slowing Flight."

96. "CAB School Checks to Start," *Commercial Appeal*, Feb. 13, 1973; "CAB Schools Get Code Extensions," *Commercial Appeal*, Mar. 23, 1973.

97. *W. Wayne Allen v. Inez Wright, et al.*, 468 U.S. 737 (1984). The challenge initially was brought by Richard Fields, program associate, of the NAACP Legal Defense Fund. The named litigants were black parents of school-aged children. The case was dismissed by the U.S. Supreme Court eight years after filing on the grounds that the plaintiff parents could not demonstrate adequate real injury to justify their standing to sue in federal court. See Morris Cunningham, "Suit Charging Bias Challenges Private Academies' Tax Break," *Commercial Appeal*, Aug. 27, 1976; Gordon, "Still Fighting the School Tax Flap."

98. *Bob Jones University and Goldsboro Christian School v. U.S.*, 461 U.S. 574 (1983).

99. *Runyan v. McCrary*, 427 U.S. 160 (1976).

100. For example, see Linda Hilbun, "Tax Break for Biased Private Schools Rapped," *Press Scimitar*, Jan. 9, 1982; "Hart Challenges School Decision," *New York Times*, Oct. 10, 1982.

101. Numbers derived from compilations by Bill Sonenburg for the Memphis City Schools, as well as from the figures reported to the Tennessee Department of

Education. Also see Jimmie Covington, "Private Schools Show Decline in Enrollment; 3 Causes Cited," *Commercial Appeal,* Sept. 8, 1979; Whitney Smith, "Enrollment Losses in Private Schools Parallel Economy," *Commercial Appeal,* Jan. 17, 1983; Tom Charlier, "Opting for Tuition," *Commercial Appeal,* Apr. 10, 2005.

102. Charlier, "Opting for Tuition."

103. The 80 percent figure is a conservative number derived from the fact that the Memphis City Schools have roughly 15,000 white students, the Shelby County Schools have 44,000, and Memphis private schools alone have more than 14,000. All of which does not count the growing number of home-schooled white children.

104. From yearly reports filed with the Tennessee Department of Education. It should be noted that the percentage of blacks in the Shelby County Schools has remained roughly similar to the black share of that population. From 23 percent in the mid-1970s, it declined to less than 15 percent in the late 1980s as whites migrated to those suburban areas faster than annexation could recapture them. The black percentage now has rebounded back to mid-1970s levels, as more blacks have moved outside the city limits. In July of 2007, Federal District Judge Bernice Donald refused to dismiss the desegregation lawsuit against the Shelby County Schools. Judge Donald found that the county had achieved a unitary system in terms of staff, transportation, and facilities; but, it still had a ways to go regarding extracurricular activities, student assignments, and faculty integration. See the *Commercial Appeal,* July 27, 2007.

105. For example, the figures for all the private schools in Shelby County combined were 5.1 percent black in 1971; 3.1 percent in 1978; 5 percent in 2004. First two numbers from data compiled by *Commercial Appeal* journalist Jimmie Covington (private collection). Latest number comes from Wendi Thomas, "Decision Didn't Get Us There, It Was Only a Start, *Commercial Appeal,* May 16, 2004.

106. Sean Reardon and John Yun, *Private School Racial Enrollments and Segregation* (Cambridge Mass.: Civil Rights Project of Harvard University, June 26, 2002). Cited in Diana Jean Schemo, "Study Finds Parochial Schools Segregated along Racial Lines," *New York Times,* June 27, 2002.

107. For a discussion of the role of magnet schools in effective desegregation efforts, see Willis Hawley et al., Assessment of Current Knowledge About the Effectiveness of School Desegregation Strategies, Center for Education and Human Development Policy, Institute for Public Policy Studies, Vanderbilt University, Apr. 1981, 30–34.

108. *Parents Involved in Community Schools v. Seattle School District No. 1,* 127 S.Ct. 2738 (2007); *Meredith v. Jefferson County Board of Education,* 126 S.Ct. 2351 (2007); for an analysis of the decision's potential impact in another school district, see Joseph Berger, "A Successful Plan for Racial Balance Now Finds Its Future Unknown," *New York Times,* Aug. 22, 2007.

109. For example, see Aimee Edmondson, "Do Optional Schools Siphon from the Neediest?" *Commercial Appeal,* Oct. 28, 2002.

110. For example, see Jimmie Covington, "Memphis Magnet Strong Attraction to Children, Parents," *Commercial Appeal,* Apr. 23, 1978; Jimmie Covington, "Parents Begin 'Camping in' for Space in Optional Schools," *Commercial Appeal,* Feb. 1, 1989.

111. In recent years, that figure has been 185 percent to receive meal subsidies, and 130 percent for free meals.

112. Memphis Board of Education, "The Memphis Plan," submitted to the Federal District Court, Nov. 10, 1971, 15. The number of students eligible for meal subsidies had grown to 57 percent in 1992 and to 73 percent by 2002.

113. Also, see David Waters, "We're Paying the Price for Fleeing from Our Schools," *Commercial Appeal,* May 9, 2004.

114. Erica Frankenberg et al., *A Multiracial Society with Segregated Schools: Are We Losing the Dream?* (Cambridge Mass.: Civil Rights Project of Harvard University, 2003). Cited in Greg Winter, "Schools Resegregate, Study Finds," *New York Times,* Jan. 21, 2003.

115. Interview with Maxine Smith, Nov. 2001; Allan Ornstein, Daniel Levine, and Doxey Wilkerson, *Reforming Metropolitan Schools* (Pacific Palisades, Calif.: Goodyear Publishing Co., 1975), 180.

116. Peter Irons, *Jim Crow's Children: The Broken Promise of the Brown Decision* (New York: Viking Press, 2002). For a description of Dr. Irons's 2003 talk at the University of Memphis, see Kimberly Alleyne, "Fifty Years after Brown: The Black and White Issue Is Gray," *Tri-State Defender,* Oct. 4–8, 2003. The five school districts involved in the original *Brown* decision were Topeka, Kansas; New Castle, Delaware; Washington, D.C.; Prince Edward Co., Virginia; and Clarendon County, South Carolina. Also see Orfield and Eaton, *Dismantling Desegregation.* Also see Gary Orfield et al., *Schools More Separate: Consequences of a Decade of Resegregation,* Harvard University, Civil Rights Project Report, July 18, 2001; Charles Clotfelter, *After Brown: The Rise and retreat of School Desegregation* (Princeton: Princeton University Press, 2004).

117. Quoted in Kimberly Alleyne, "Unmet Promises: Educators' Book Reveals the Effects of Desegregation," *Tri-State Defender,* Mar. 1–5, 2003.

Chapter 5
Educational Results

1. For a discussion of the advantages of black political incorporation in such settings, see Rufus Browning, Dale Rogers Marshall, and David Tabb, *Racial Politics in American Cities* (New York: Longman Publishers, 2002).

2. For example, see Richard Rothstein, "The SAT Scores Aren't Bad. Not Bad at All," *New York Times,* Aug. 29, 2001.

3. For examples of data discrepancies, see "False Data on Student Performance," *New York Times,* June 27, 2005; Michael Dobbs, "States Fudging Grad Rate," *Commercial Appeal,* June 24, 2005; Diana Jean Schemo and Ford Fessenden, "Gains in Houston Schools: How Real Are They?" *New York Times,* Dec. 3, 2003; Sam Dillon, "School Violence Data under a Cloud in Houston," *New York Times,* Nov. 7, 2003; Diana Jean Schemo, "For Houston Schools, College Claims Exceed Reality," *New York Times,* Aug. 28, 2003; Diana Jean Schemo, "Questions on Data Cloud Luster of Houston Schools," *New York Times,* July 11, 2003; Diana Jean Schemo, "School

Achievement Reports Often Exclude the Disabled," *New York Times,* Aug. 30, 2004; Gregory Cizek, "High-Stakes Testing Must Pass the Integrity Test," *Commercial Appeal,* Sept. 21, 2003. For local examples, see Aimee Edmondson, "Exams Test Educator Integrity: Emphasis on Scores Can Lead to Cheating, Teacher Survey Finds," *Commercial Appeal,* Sept. 21, 2003; Aimee Edmondson, "Policing Cheating Teachers: Discipline by Districts Varies," *Commercial Appeal,* Sept. 22, 2003.

4. Educational Improvement Act (Public Acts of 1992, chapter 535).

5. The most recent report cards tend to use average daily membership (ADM).

6. Figure 2 reports constant dollar operating expenditures per student, using $2000. The number of students is based on each system's average daily attendance number, as compiled by the district and reported to the State Department of Education.

7. Information source on the anomaly was Nancy Richie, director of the Division of Fiscal Operations, Memphis City Schools, Nov. 19, 2003.

8. *Board of Education of Memphis City Schools v. Shelby County et al.* (1960) upheld the requirement that all such county funds be shared proportionately by population within its boundaries. This principle was further codified in the 1977 Tennessee Education Finance Act, which established the ADA formula.

9. For example, see Christopher Jencks and Meredith Phillips, "America's Next Achievement Test: Closing the Black-White Test-Score Gap," in *American Prospect* 9.40 (Sept.–Oct. 1998), http://www.prospect.org/print/V9/40/jencks-c.html.

10. See The Urban Child Institute, *The State of Children in Memphis and Shelby County* (Memphis: The Urban Child Institute, 2006), 3.

11. These numbers include those students with disabilities and exclude the high achievers who receive accelerated educational opportunities under the special-education umbrella.

12. For example, see Aimee Edmondson, "Efforts to cut class sizes may have hit the wall," *Commercial Appeal,* Mar. 17, 2002. Under the laws, the state of Tennessee can assess local school districts up to $50,000 to $75,000 per class if class size targets are not met.

13. In 1991, for instance, there were eighteen nondegree teachers in the county and seventy-nine in the city.

14. Aimee Edmondson, "Uncertified Teachers Filling Widening Gaps," *Commercial Appeal,* Aug. 20, 2000.

15. Conclusion arose from discussion with David Sojourner, former Director of Student Information, Memphis Public Schools, although the MCS Research Division never did come to its own definitive explanation. Also see Ruma Banerji Kumar, "Retired Teachers Bring an Expert's Touch to Classroom," *Commercial Appeal,* Mar. 13, 2006, indicating that one-third to one-half of all new urban teachers leave within five years.

16. See J. C. Williams, "An Option for Memphis: Merger of the Memphis City Schools with the Shelby County Schools" (paper prepared for the Memphis City Schools, May 29, 1989), p. 2 and figs. 1–4.

17. It should be noted that for most of the 1980s, these numbers were reported for "instructional personnel" and not just "teachers," although the addition of librarians and other instructional support staff should not have unduly skewed the numbers overall. Since then, they have returned to being reported for "classroom teachers."

18. Passing the proficiency exams in both math and language is required for a regular high school diploma. A score of 70 percent is considered passing. A student may be exempt from taking the proficiency exam by scoring sufficiently high on the TCAP exam in the eighth grade. All other regular high school students begin taking the proficiency exam in the ninth grade. The score reported here is the percentage of students who either exempted out or passed the test when first taken at the outset of the ninth grade.

19. Quoted in Ruma Banerji, "95% Attendance Rule Raises City's Testing Stakes," *Commercial Appeal*, Feb. 24, 2003.

20. See ibid.

21. Findings cited in Sam Dillon, "Enrollments Drop at Catholic Schools," *New York Times*, Jan. 22, 2003. Also see Siobhan McDonough, "Schools Beset by Unruly Kids, Bad Morale, Polls Say," *Commercial Appeal*, Apr. 23, 2003.

22. Tennessee Code: Title 49 Education/Chapter 6 Elementary and Secondary Education/Part 42 School Security Act/49–6-4216.

23. For example, see Sara Rimer, "Unruly Students Facing Arrest, Not Detention," *New York Times*, Jan. 4, 2004; Halimah Abdullah and Ruma Bannerji Kumar, "Schools' Discipline Program Posts Gains," *Commercial Appeal*, Nov. 14, 2005.

24. See Tobin McAndrews, "Zero-Tolerance Policies," *ERIC Digest* 146 (Mar. 2001): 1–7.

25. Federal reports indicate a 50 percent drop in school violence from 1992 to 2002. For example, see Fox Butterfield, "Crime in Schools Fell Sharply Over Decade, Survey Shows," *New York Times*, Nov. 30, 2004; Curt Anderson, "Violence at U.S. Schools Shows Drop," *Commercial Appeal*, Nov. 30, 2004.

26. See Dillon, "School Violence Data under a Cloud in Houston"; Ruma Bannerji Kumar, "School Board Gives Johnson Shining Review," *Commercial Appeal*, Jan. 4, 2005; Blake Fontenay, "Shades of Blue," *Commercial Appeal*, Jan. 22, 2006; Elissa Gootman, "Undercount of Violence in Schools," *New York Times*, Sept. 20, 2007; Marc Perrusquia, "Education in Crossfire," *Commercial Appeal*, April 27, 2008, p. A1.

27. "Discipline Better, but Unacceptable," *Commercial Appeal*, Dec. 4, 2005. The results appear to be mixed in terms of the "Blue Ribbon" disciplinary plan adopted by the Memphis City Schools in the fall of 2005. See Dakarai Aarons, "Black Eye for Blue Ribbon," *Commercial Appeal*, June 10, 2007; Kenneth Whalum Jr., "Lack of Discipline Is Schools' Biggest Failing," *Commercial Appeal*, June 10, 2007.

28. *Knoxville News-Sentinel*, Apr. 29, 2001; Richard Locker, "Zero-Tolerance Offenses Rise," *Commercial Appeal*, Sept. 3, 2003.

29. *Knoxville News-Sentinel*, Apr. 29, 2001; Tennessee State Board of Education, *Annual Report Card of the Knox County Schools* (Nashville: GPO, various years).

30. *Knoxville News-Sentinel*, Apr. 29, 2001.

31. Juvenile Law Center, Philadelphia, 2000. Cited in McAndrews, "Zero-Tolerance Policies." For text of American Bar Association resolution, go to http://www.jlc.org/home/updates/updates_links/aba_zerotol.htm.

32. There is a slight counter trend following city school efforts to reduce social promotions, beginning in 2000. For example, see Ruma Banerji Kumar, "20% fail middle school," *Commercial Appeal,* Aug. 11, 2003.

33. For more on this measure, see Siobhan Gorman, ""How Should Teachers Be Evaluated?" *National Journal,* Dec. 4, 1999, 3479–80.

34. For an earlier analysis of these income-related problems, see Ornstein et al., *Reforming Metropolitan Schools,* chap. 5.

35. A 1981 state law required all Tennessee high school students to pass the Tennessee Proficiency Test (TPT) as a graduation requisite. Beginning in 1995, a new competency test was implemented in an attempt to require higher level math and language skills. It would first be given in the ninth grade, and it could be retaken as many times as necessary. Beginning in 2002, gateway tests were required upon completion of Algebra I, Biology I, and English II. These tests were to be administered three times annually.

36. Half of the MCS high school juniors still had not passed a gateway proficiency test when this phenomenon was studied in January of 2004. See Richard Locker, "Half of city's 11th Graders Lack Ticket to Diploma," *Commercial Appeal,* Jan. 30, 2004.

37. These schools were selected with the assistance of David Sojourner, former director of student information, Memphis Public Schools.

38. Student poverty levels for the 1971–72 school year are provided in the Memphis City School Board's 1971 brief presented during legal consideration of the "Memphis Plan" for desegregation.

39. The actual years reviewed were 1995, 1996, 1997, 1999, 2001, and 2002. Comparable numerical data could not be located for 1998 and 2000.

40. Thereafter, the annual report card reported only letter grades in each area, less accurate to compare because of the range existing within each letter grade designation.

41. The correlation between income and achievement also was apparent in 2005. See the Urban Child Institute, *The State of Children in Memphis and Shelby County* (Memphis: Urban Child Institute, 2006), 8.

42. Also see Halimah Abdullah, "Scores Improve; Some Left Behind: Minority, Poor Kids Do Worse Than Others," *Commercial Appeal,* Nov. 2, 2005.

43. See Wendi Thomas, "AP Classes Are Key to Open Door of Success," *Commercial Appeal,* May 17, 2005; "Mitchell High Captures 'Blue Ribbon' Spotlight," *Tri-State Defender,* Mar. 4–8, 2006; Wiley Henry, "Making the Grade," *Tri-State Defender,* Jan. 21–25, 2006. In terms of the latter successes, see Superintendent Carol Johnson, "Raising the Bar for MCS in 2005–6," *Tri-State Defender,* Aug. 6–10, 2005.

44. Comparing attendance and dropout rates across states should be approached with caution, however, given the different ways states measure these indices. See Michael Janofsky, "Governors Endorse a Standard Formula for Graduation Rates," *New York Times,* July 18, 2005.

45. Results of *Commercial Appeal*/TV Channel 3 poll, cited in Jody Callahan, "Education Top Concern but Solution Is Elusive," *Commercial Appeal*, Mar. 25, 2002.

Chapter 6
Educational Alternatives

1. For example, see Portz et al., *City Schools and City Politics*, 11–19. For discussion of those various movements, see David Tyack and Larry Cuban, *Tinkering toward Utopia: A Century of Public School Reform* (Cambridge, Mass.: Harvard University Press, 1995); Maurice Berube, *American School Reform: Progressive, Equity, and Excellence Movements, 1883–1993* (Westport, Conn.: Praeger, 1994); Diane Ravitch, *The Troubled Crusade: American Education, 1945–1980* (New York: Basic Books, 1983); Ronald Goodenow and Diane Ravitch, eds., *Schools in Cities: Consensus and Conflict in American Educational History* (New York: Holmes and Meire, 1983); Larry Cuban, "Reforming Again, Again, and Again," *Education Researcher* (Jan. 1990): 3–13; Susan Semel and Alan Sadovnik, eds., *Schools of Tomorrow, Schools of Today: What Happened to Progressive Education?* (New York: Peter Lang, 1999).

2. National Commission on Excellence in Education's publication of, *A Nation at Risk: The Imperative of Educational Reform* (Washington, D.C.: GPO, 1983). This discussion draws heavily from Portz et al., *City Schools and City Politics*, 12–13.

3. For example, see Michael Fullan and Suzanne Stiegelbauer, *The New Meaning of Educational Change* (New York: Teacher's College Press, 1991); Douglass Archibald and F. M. Newman, *Beyond Standardized Testing: Assessing Authentic Achievement in the Secondary School* (Reston, Va.: National Association of Secondary School Principals, undated); more recently, see ACT, *Rigor at Risk: Reaffirming Quality in the High School Core Curriculum* (Iowa City: ACT, 2007).

4. For example, see William Firestone et al., *Education Reform from 1983 to 1990: State Action and District Response* (New Brunswick, N.J.: Consortium for Policy Research in Education, 1991); Andrew Porter, Douglas Archbald, and A. Tyree, "Reforming the Curriculum," in Susan Fuhrman and Betty Malen, eds., *The Politics of Curriculum and Testing* (New York: Falmer Press, 1991), 11–16.

5. For example, see Joseph Murphy and Phillip Hallinger, *Restructuring Schooling: Learning from On-Going Efforts* (Newbury Park, Calif.: Corwin Press, 1993); Jane Hannaway and Martin Carnoy, eds. *Decentralization and School Improvement: Can We Fulfill the Promise?* (San Francisco: Josey-Bass, 1993).

6. For example, see John Chubb and Terry Moe, *Politics, Markets, and American Schools* (Washington, D.C.: Brookings, 1990).

7. Blanche Bernstein, "A Way to Break the Welfare Cycle," *New York Times*, Oct. 31, 1986.

8. Weil, "When Should a Kid Start Kindergarten."

9. See Corine Hegland, "Starting Smart," *National Journal*, Sept. 13, 2003, 2771; Leah Wells, "Little Income Making Big Differences in Schools," *Commercial Appeal*, May 9, 2007; Greg Duncan and Jeanne Brooks-Gunn, eds., *Consequences of Growing Up Poor* (New York: Russell Sage, 1997); "America's Changing Outlook for Schools and Society," *Education Week*, May 14, 1986.

10. John Berrueta-Clement ed., *Changed Lives: The Effects of the Perry Preschool Program on Youths Through Age 19 (Monographs of the High/Scope Educational Research Foundation #8)* (Ypsilanti, Mich.: High/Scope Press, 1984); Fred Hechinger, "Preschool Found to Benefit Blacks," *New York Times,* Sept. 11, 1984.

11. Cited in George Will, "Shaming Power Has Its Limits," *Commercial Appeal,* Mar. 4, 2003. More recently, see Paul Barton and Richard Coley, *The Family: America's Smallest School* (Princeton, N.J.: Educational Testing Service, 2007). Also see articles such as Randolph Schmid, "Study: TV Makes Learning Less Efficient," *Yahoo! News,* July 24, 2006, http://News.yahoo.com/.

12. For example, see David Sousa, *How the Brain Learns* (Thousand Oaks, Calif.: Corwin Press, 2000); Rima Shore, *Rethinking the Brain: New Insights into Early Development* (New York: Families and Work Institute, 1997); Deborah Waber et al., *MRI Study of Normal Brain Development, U.S. Department of Health and Human Service, National Institute of Health, (Washington, D.C.: GPO, 1999 to present);* Betty Hart and Todd Risley, *Meaningful Differences in the Everyday Experiences of Young American Children* (Baltimore, Md.: Brookes Publishing, 1995); Tamara Koehler, "For Learning, First Five Years Is Peak Period," *Commercial Appeal,* May 11, 2003; David Waters, "A New Learning Curve: First Years Are Key to Brain Science," *Commercial Appeal,* May 11, 2003; Barbara Holden, "Developing Brain Gets Earlier Focus," *Commercial Appeal,* May 29, 2007; Barbara Holden, "Reading Boosts Kids' Brain Function," *Commercial Appeal,* Sept. 18, 2007. For early path-breaking studies, see Benjamin Bloom, *Stability and Change in Human Characteristics* (New York: John Wiley, 1964); J. McVicker Hunt, *Intelligence and Experience* (New York: Ronald Press, 1961).

13. World Bank report cited in Celia Dugger, "Report Warns Malnutrition Begins in Cradle," *New York Times,* Mar. 3, 2006.

14. David P. Weikart, *Quality Preschool Programs: A Long-Term Social Investment,* Occasional Paper #5, Ford Foundation Project on Social Welfare and the American Future, New York, 1989, 3–4.

15. Aimee Edmondson, "Good Preschools for All Could Help Needy Catch Up," *Commercial Appeal,* Mar. 18, 2001.

16. Quoted in Andrew Mollison, "Teachers Say Many Kids Not Prepared," *New York Times,* Aug. 15, 2004.

17. *Abbott* IV 693 A. 2d at 434.

18. Cynthia Brown et al., *Getting Smarter, Becoming Fairer* (Washington, D.C.: Center for American Progress, Aug. 2005).

19. See Urban Child Institute, *The State of Children in Memphis and Shelby County,* 3. For more on the Urban Child Institute and its projects, see Barbara Holden, "Developing Brain Gets Earlier Focus," *Commercial Appeal,* May 29, 2007.

20. Phillips, Crouse, and Ralph, "Does the Black-White Test 'Score Gap Widen after Children Enter School?" 257.

21. Blanche Bernstein, "A Way to Break the Welfare Cycle," *New York Times,* Oct. 31, 1986.

22. Interview with David Sojourner, former director of Student Information, Memphis City Schools, June 13, 2005.

23. For example, see Richard Heidenreich, ed., *Urban Education* (Arlington, Va.: College Readings, 1972), 24–46.

24. For example, see Edward Zigler, "Head Start's 'Perils of Pauline,'" *New York Times,* Jan. 29, 1982.

25. Hegland, "Starting Smart," 2771. For a case study, see Catherine Wilson, *Telling a Different Story: Teaching and Literacy in an Urban Preschool* (New York: Teachers College Press, 2000).

26. Riley quoted in *Doing What Works: Improving Big City School Districts,* AFT Educational Issues Dept., Educational Issues Policy Brief, no. 12, Oct. 2000, p. 8.

27. For example, see *The Impact of Head Start: An Evaluation of the Effect of Head Start on Children's Cognitive and Affective Development* (Athens, Ohio: Westinghouse Learning Corporation, 1969); Joseph Michalak, "Head Start-Type Programs Get Second Look," *New York Times,* Apr. 30, 1978; Consortium for Longitudinal Studies, *As the Twig Is Bent: Lasting Effects of Preschool Programs* (Hillsdale, N.J.: Lawrence Erlbaum Associates, 1983); Berrueta-Clement, ed., *Changed Lives;* R. H. McKey et al., *The Impact of Head Start on Children, Families, and Communities,* Final Report of the Head Start Evaluation, Synthesis, and Utilization Project (Washington, D.C.: CSR, 1988); Mary Hatwood Futrell, "Public Schools and Four-Year-Olds," *American Psychologist* 42 (Mar. 1987): 251–53; Janet Currie and Duncan Thomas, "Does Head Start Make a Difference?" *American Economic Review* 85 (1995): 341–64; Walter Gilliam and Ed Zigler, "A Critical Meta-analysis of All Evaluations of State-Funded Preschool from 1977 to 1998: Implications for Policy, Service Delivery and Program Evaluation," *Early Childhood Research Quarterly* 15 (2001): 441–73; Janet Currie and Duncan Thomas, "Early Test Scores, School Quality and Long-Run Effects on Wage and Employment Outcomes," *Research in Labor Economics* 20 (2001): 103–32; Eliana Garces, Duncan Thomas, and Janet Currie, "Longer Term Effects of Head Start," *American Economic Review* 92 (Sept. 2002): 999–1012; Deborah Waber et al., *MRI Study of Normal Brain Development* (Washington, D.C.: National Institute of Health, 1999–).

28. See Steven Barnett, "Benefit-Cost Analysis of Preschool Education," *American Journal of Orthopsychiatry* 63 (1993): 500–508; Frances Campbell and Craig Ramey, "Cognitive and School Outcomes for High Risk African-American Students at Middle Adolescence: Positive Effects of Early Intervention," *American Educational Research Journal* 32 (Winter 1995): 743–72; Arthur Reynolds et al., "Long-term Effects of an Early Childhood Intervention on Educational Achievement and Juvenile Arrest," *Journal of the American Medical Association* 285 (May 9, 2001): 2339–46; Jacques Steinberg, "Gains Found for the Poor in Rigorous Preschool," *New York Times,* May 9, 2001; Katherine Magnuson and Jane Waldfogel, "Early Childhood Care and Education: Effects on Ethnic and Racial Gaps in School Readiness," *Future of Children* 15.1 (Spring 2005): 169–96; Isabell Sawhill, *Opportunity in America* (Princeton, N.J.: Princeton University Press, 2006); Tamar Lewin, "Child Care Helps Most Kids' Learning," *Commercial Appeal,* Nov. 6, 2005.

29. Berrueta-Clement ed., *Changed Lives.* Also see Hechinger, "Preschool Found to Benefit Blacks."

30. Mollison, "Teachers Say Many Kids Not Prepared."

31. The New Commission on the Skills of the American Workforce, *Tough Choices, Tough Times* (Washington, D.C.: National Center on Education and the Economy, 2006). Also see Ann Hulbert, "What Every Child Needs," *New York Times,* Oct. 28, 2007.

32. Brown et al., *Getting Smarter,* 25–26.

33. See Alison Glass, "Early Years Heavily Affect School Success," *Commercial Appeal,* May 18, 2003; "State Money Boosts Ark. Pre-K," *Commercial Appeal,* Feb. 21, 2006; "Illinois Governor Suggests Preschool for All," *New York Times,* Feb. 13, 2006.

34. E. Terrence Jones, *The Metropolitan Chase: Politics and Policies in Urban America* (Upper Saddle River, N.J.: Prentice-Hall, 2002), 177–78.

35. For example, see William Gormley Jr. and Ted Gayer, "Promoting School Readiness in Oklahoma: An Evaluation of Tulsa's Pre-K Program" (paper presented at the Annual Meeting of the American Political Science Association, Chicago, Sept. 3, 2004); "Growing Minds: Schools Getting Involved in Early Learning," *Commercial Appeal,* May 19, 2003.

36. Aimee Edmondson, "After the Tears," *Commercial Appeal,* Apr. 18, 2005.

37. National Education Commission on Time and Learning, *Prisoners of Time* (Washington, D.C.: GPO, 1994). Cited in Edmondson, "Good Preschools for All Could Help Needy Catch Up."

38. Richard Locker, "State Expands pre-K for Fall," *Commercial Appeal,* July 14, 2006; Edmondson, "After the Tears"; Richard Locker, "State Adds Pre-K Classes," *Commercial Appeal,* July 25, 2007.

39. *Commercial Appeal,* Nov. 16, 2004. Also see Richard Locker, "Bredesen stumps for Pre-K Funds," *Commercial Appeal.*

40. See Chris Jones, "Poll Says Preschool Can Affect Crime Rate," *Commercial Appeal,* Aug. 12, 2004.

41. Susan Chira, "Preschool Aid for the Poor: How Big a Head Start?" *New York Times,* Feb. 8, 1990; Eric Hanushek, "The Impact of Differential Expenditures on School Performance," *Educational Researcher* 18, no. 4 (1989): 45–51.

42. Brian Friel, "Scrutiny Mounts for Head Start," *National Journal,* Feb. 19, 2005, 540.

43. See Jencks and Phillips, *The Black-White Test Score Gap,* 7; Chira, "Preschool Aid for the Poor"; Jennifer Lawson, "Among Obstacles Are Lingering Ideas, a Lack of Standards and Short Funds," *Commercial Appeal,* May 20, 2003; Friel, "Scrutiny Mounts for Head Start"; Janet Currie and Duncan Thomas, "Does Head Start Make a Difference?" *American Economic Review* 85 (June 1995): 341–64; Steven Barnett, "Long-Term Effects of Early Childhood Programs on Cognitive and School Outcomes," *Future of Children* 5.3 (1995): 25–50; Janet Currie and Duncan Thomas, "School Quality and the Longer-Term Effects of Head Start" (working paper 6362, National Bureau of Economic Research, Cambridge, Mass., 1998); W. Stephen Barnett and

Sarano Spence Boocock, eds., *Early Care and Education for Children in Poverty: Promises, Programs, and Long-Term Results* (Albany: State University of New York Press, 1998); Douglas Besharov, "Put Politics Aside and Help 'Head Start' Program," *New York Times*, Dec. 28, 1985.

44. Hugh B. Price, *Achievement Matters: Getting Your Child the Best Education Possible* (New York: Kensington Publishing Corp., 2002). Also see Signithia Fordham and John Ogbu, Black Students' School Success: Coping with the Burden of "Acting White," *Urban Review* 18 (1986): 176–206; Sigithia Fordham, *Blacked Out: Dilemmas of Race, Identity, and Success at Capital High* (Chicago: University of Chicago press, 1996); John McWhorter, *Losing the Race: Self-Sabotage in the Black Community* (New York: Sussex Publishers, 2001); Miles Corwin, *And Still We Rise: The Trials and Triumphs of 12 Inner-City Students* (Minneapolis, Minn.: Econo-Clad Books, 2001); Abigail Thernstrom and Stephan Thernstrom, *No Excuses: Closing the Racial Gap in Learning* (New York: Simon and Schuster, 2003); Roland Fryer and Paul Torelli, "Understanding the Prevalence and Impact of 'Acting White,'" (working paper, Harvard University, 2004); Tiffani Chin and Meredith Phillips, "Oppositional to What? Achievement Ideologies, Resistance, and Ethnic Authenticity among Urban Youth" (mimeo, University of California, Los Angeles, 2004); Makebra Anderson, "Why Don't Black Men Achieve As Well Academically?" *Tri-State Defender*, Feb. 19–23, 2005; Elissa Gootman, "Survey Reveals Student Attitudes, Parental Goals and Teacher Mistrust," *New York Times*, Sept. 7, 2007.

45. Richard H. Milner, "Affective and Social Issues among High Achieving African American Students: Recommendations for Teachers and Teacher Education," *Action in Teacher Education* 24.1 (Spring 2002): 81–90.

46. Ronald Ferguson, "A Diagnostic Analysis of Black-White GPA Disparities in Shaker Heights, Ohio" (Brookings Papers on Education Policy, 2001); Ronald Ferguson, "What Doesn't Meet the Eye: Understanding Racial Disparities in Fifteen Suburban School Districts (mimeo, Harvard University, 2002); John Ogbu, *Black American Students in an Affluent Suburb* (Mahwah, N.J.: Lawrence Erlbaum Publishers, 2003).

47. Ogbu, *Black American Students in an Affluent Suburb*. Also see John McWhorter, *Losing the Race: Self-Sabotage in Black America* (New York: Free Press, 2000); John McWhorter, *Winning the Race: Beyond the Crisis in Black America* (New York: Gotham Books, 2005).

48. See Felicia Lee, "Why Are Black Students Lagging?" *New York Times*, Nov. 30, 2002; Phillip Cook and Jens Ludwig, "The Burden of 'Acting White': Do Black Adolescents Disparage Academic Achievement?" in Jencks and Phillips, *The Black-White Test Score Gap*; James Ainsworth-Darnell and Douglas Downey, "Assessing the Oppositional Culture Explanation for Racial/Ethnic Differences in School Performance," *American Sociological Review* 63 (1998): 536–53; *Journal of Blacks in Higher Education* 47 (Spring 2005); *Journal of Blacks in Higher Education* 48 (Summer 2005); *Journal of Blacks in Higher Education* 50 (Winter 2005–6).

49. Karolyn Tyson, William Darity Jr., and Domini Castellino, "Breeding Animosity: The 'Burden of Acting White' and Other Problems of Status Group Hierarchies in

Schools," Sanford Paper Number: SAN04–03, Sept. 2004; Cook and Ludwig, "The Burden of 'Acting White'"; Karolyn Tyson, "Weighing In: Elementary-Age Students and the Debate on Attitudes towards School among Black Students," *Social Forces* 80.4 (2002): 1157–89; Dona Ford and J. John Harris, "Perceptions and Attitudes of Black Students toward School, Achievement, and Other Educational Variables," *Child Development* 67 (1996): 1141–52.

50. See Cook and Ludwig, "The Burden of 'Acting White.'"

51. Ferguson "Comment" in Jencks and Phillips, *The Black-White Test Score Gap*, 394–97. Also see Matthew Lynch, *Closing the Racial Academic Achievement Gap* (Chicago: African American Images, 2006); James Ryan, "Schools, Race, and Money," *Yale Law Review* 109 (1999): 249–315; Chubb and Moe, *Politics, Markets, and America's Schools*, 125–29; Kim Kruse, *The Effects of Low Socioeconomic Environment on a Student's Academic Achievement*, ERIC ED402380 (1996), 165; Lawrence Steinberg, *Beyond the Classroom: Why School Reform Failed and What Parents Need to Do* (New York: Simon and Schuster, 1996); George Galster, "Polarization, Place, and Race," North Carolina Law Review 71 (June, 1993):1421–62.

52. See Nancy Cauthen et al., *Map and Track: State Initiatives for Young Children and Families* (New York: National Center for Children in Poverty, 2000), 13.

53. For example, see A. Biemiller and M. Slonim, "Estimating Root Word Vocabulary Growth in Normative and Advantaged Populations: Evidence for a Common Sequence of Vocabulary Acquisition," *Journal of Educational Psychology* 93 (2001): 498–520; I. L. Beck et al., *Bringing Words to Life* (New York: Guilford Press, 2002); C. Biancarosa Juel et al., Walking with Rosie: A Cautionary Tale of Early Reading Instruction," *Educational Leadership* 60 (2003): 12–18.

54. See Chira, "Preschool Aid for the Poor: How Big a Head Start?" Also see Roland Fryer and Steven Levitt, "Understanding the Black-White Test Score Gap in the First Two Years of School," *Review of Economics and Statistics* 86.2 (May 2004): 447–64.

55. Zigler quoted in Chira, "Preschool Aid for the Poor: How Big a Head Start?"

56. Weikart, *Quality Preschool Programs*, 25.

57. See Nancy Mitchell, "Interaction Can Raise IQ, Studies Find," *Commercial Appeal*, May 18, 2003; Barbara Holden, "Reading Boosts Kids' Brain Function," *Commercial Appeal*, Sept. 18, 2007.

58. See Delores Z. Lambie et al., *Infants: The Ypsilanti-Carnegie Infant Education Program: An Experiment* (Ypsilanti, Mich.: High/Scope Press, Monographs of the High/Scope Educational Research Foundation, #4, 1974); Ann S. Epstein, *The Ypsilanti-Carnegie Infant Education Program: Longitudinal Follow Up* (Ypsilanti, Mich.: High/Scope Press, Monographs of the High/Scope Educational Research foundation, #6, 1979). Also see P. W. Greenwood and F. E. Zimming, *One More Chance: The Pursuit of Planning Intervention Strategies for Chronic Juvenile Offenders* (Santa Monica: Rand Corporation, 1985)

59. See Leah Wells, "Little Income Making Big Differences in Schools," *Commercial Appeal*, May 9, 2007; Barbara Holden, "Reading Boosts Kids' Brain Function," *Commercial Appeal*, Sept. 18, 2007.

60. Quoted in Chris Peck, "Brain Building Starts Innovative Reform," *Commercial Appeal*, May 20, 2003.

61. Deborah Waber et al., *MRI Study of Normal Brain Development*. Also see Lauran Neergaard, "Study Peeks at How Normal Brains Grow," *Yahoo! News*, May 18, 2007, http://news.yahoo.com/.

62. Edmondson, "Parental Apathy, Neglect Challenge Failing School's Children," *Commercial Appeal*, June 3, 2001; C. B. Stendler-Lavatelli, "Environmental Intervention in Infancy and Early Childhood," in Martin Deutcsch et al., eds., *Social Class, Race, and Psychological Development* (New York: Holt Rinehart Winston, 1968), 347–80.

63. Edmondson, "Parental Apathy, Neglect."

64. Ibid.

65. Thernstrom and Thernstrom, *No Excuses*.

66. Ogbu, *Black American Students in an Affluent Suburb*. Also see Annettee Lareau, *Unequal Childhoods: Class, Race, and Family Life* (Berkeley: University of California Press, 2003).

67. Phillips et al., "Family Background," 103–48.

68. Arthur L. Webb, "Our Schools Can Not Fail If Parents Will Do Their Homework," *Tri-State Defender*, May 15–19, 2004.

69. Gerald Bracey, "Schools Are Not 'Failing' Poor Kids," *Commercial Appeal*, Jan. 19, 2002.

70. Noted in Memphis City Schools, "Achieving the Vision: A Five-Year Master Plan for the Memphis City Schools" (internal report, 2006), 35. Also see Anne Henderson et al., *Beyond the Bake Sale* (New York: New Press, 2006); Deborah Waber et al., *MRI Study of Normal Brain Development*.

71. Price, *Achievement Matters: Getting Your Child the Best Education Possible*. Also see Milner, "Affective and Social Issues among High Achieving African American Students"; Sterling M. McMurrin, ed., *Resources for Urban Schools: Better Use and Balance* (Lexington, Ky.: Heath Lexington Books, 1971); James P. Comer, *School Power: Implications of an Intervention Project* (New York: Free Press, 1980).

72. Ogbu, *Black American Students in an Affluent Suburb*, 287–88.

73. All quoted in *Commercial Appeal*, Feb. 29, 2004.

74. David Waters, "Parents Bear Burden of Making Sure Kids Learn," *Commercial Appeal*, Feb. 29, 2004.

75. For example, see Robert Slavin and Nancy Madden, "'Success for All' and African American and Latino Student Achievement," in Chubb and Loveless, *Bridging the Achievement Gap*, 74–90; Abigail Thernstrom and Stephan Thernstrom, "Schools That Work," in Chubb and Loveless, *Bridging the Achievement Gap*, 131–56; David Klein, "High Achievement in Mathematics: Lessons from Three Los Angeles Elementary Schools," in John Chubb and Tom Loveless, *Bridging the Achievement Gap*, 157–70; William Raspberry, "It's Called Baby Steps—and May Giant Strides Follow," *Commercial Appeal*, Nov. 7, 2005; Jennifer Biggs, "A Tale to Tell," *Commercial Appeal*, Apr. 6, 2006.

76. Samuel Casey Carter, *No Excuses: Lessons from 21 High-Performing, High-Poverty Schools* (Washington, D.C.: Heritage Foundation, 2000). But for a critique of the methodology of this book, see Richard Rothstein, "Poverty and Achievement, and Great Misconceptions," *New York Times*, Jan. 3, 2001; Paul Tough, "What It Takes to Make a Student," *New York Times*, Nov. 26, 2006.

77. See Holly Yettick, "Early Head Start Helps Parents Learn to Be All They Can Be to Help Toddlers," *Commercial Appeal*, May 18, 2003.

78. See Mitchell, "Interaction Can Raise IQ, Studies Find."

79. Aimee Edmondson, "City School Board Plans Target Low Test Scores," *Commercial Appeal*, Sept. 12, 2000.

80. Sybil Mitchell, "Mothers of the NILE Restore 'The Village,'" *Tri-State Defender*, Dec. 10-14, 2005.

81. For evidence of the value of individualizing education, see Mike Rose, *Lives on the Boundary* (New York: Penguin, 1989).

82. Quoted in Bob Herbert, "Fewer Students, Greater Gains," *New York Times*, Mar. 11, 2001.

83. Quoted in Michael Winerip, "Miracles of Class Size Unfold Each Day in California," *New York Times*, Oct. 29, 2003.

84. Cited in "Students See Smaller Classes as Best Way to Improve Schools, *New York Times*, Aug. 8, 2001.

85. Alan Krueger and Diane Whitmore, "Would Smaller Classes Help Close the Black-White Achievement Gap," in Chubb and Loveless, *Bridging the Achievement Gap*, 11–46; Cecelia Elena Rouse, "Schools and Student Achievement," *Economic Policy Review* (Mar. 1998): 61–76; "Research Finds Advantages in Classes of 13 to 17 Pupils," *New York Times*, Apr. 30, 1999; Hanushek, Eric, "Some Findings from an Independent Investigation of the Tennessee STAR Experiment," *Educational Evaluation and Policy Analysis* 21 (1999): 143–64. Herbert, "Fewer Students, Greater Gains"; Richard Locker, "Benefits of Smaller Class Sizes Tracked," *Commercial Appeal*, Jan. 29, 1994.

86. Cited in Bob Herbert, "Room to Learn," *New York Times*, May 8, 2000.

87. Peter Maier et al., "First-Year Results of the Student Achievement Guarantee (SAGE) Program," Center for Urban Initiatives and Research, University of Wisconsin at Milwaukee, Dec. 1997; Paul Tough, "What It Takes to Make a Student," *New York Times*, Nov. 26, 2006.

88. Alex Molnar et al., "Wisconsin's SAGE Program and Achievement through Small Classes," in Chubb and Loveless, *Bridging the Achievement Gap*, 91–108; Frederick Mosteller, "The Tennessee Study of Class Size in the Early Grades," *Future of Children* 5.2, 113–27, Summer 1995; Frederick Mosteller et al., "Sustained Inquiry in Education: Lessons from Skill Grouping and Class Size," *Harvard Educational Review* 66.4 (1996): 797–842; Eugene Lewitt and Linda Schumann Baker, "Class Size," *Future of Children* 7.3 (1997): 112–21.

89. U.S. Department of Education, Institute of Education Sciences, Washington, D.C., National Center for Education Statistics, (1999).

90. Caroline Hoxby, "The Effects of Class Size on Student Achievement: New Evidence from Population Variation," *Quarterly Journal of Economics* (Nov. 2000): 1239–85.

91. Thernstrom and Thernstrom, *No Excuses,* cited in Stuart Taylor Jr., "Closing The Racial Gap in Learning: What Does Not Work," *National Journal,* Oct. 25, 2003, 3238.

92. Aimee Edmondson, "Efforts to Cut Class Sizes May Have Hit a Wall," *Commercial Appeal,* Mar. 17, 2002.

93. Abby Goodnough, "Florida Board Backs Retreat on Class Size," *New York Times,* Aug. 20, 2003.

94. Edmondson, "Efforts to Cut Class Sizes May Have Hit a Wall."

95. Heather Peske and Kati Haycock, *Teaching Inequality: How Poor and Minority Students Are Shortchanged on Teacher Quality* (Washington, D.C.: Education Trust, June 2006); William Sanders and June Rivers, *Cumulative and Residual Effects of Teachers on Future Student Academic Achievement* (Knoxville: University of Tennessee Value-Added Research and Assessment Center, 1996), 6; Ronald Ferguson, "Can Schools Narrow the Black-White Test Scores Gap?" in Jencks and Phillips, *The Black-White Test Score Gap,* 318–74; Linda Darling-Hammond, "Teacher Quality and Student Achievement: A Review of State Policy Evidence," University of Washington, Center for the Study of Teaching and Policy, R-99-1 (December 1999).

96. For example, see Brown et al., *Getting Smarter,* 49–57.

97. Alan K. Campbell, "Restoring Teacher's Dignity," *New York Times,* Aug. 28, 1985.

98. Ibid.

99. Quoted in David Broder, "We Know Early Education Pays Off, but Will We Pay for It?" *Commercial Appeal,* Jan. 9, 2002. Also see Jacques Steinberg, "Salary Gaps Still Plaguing Teachers," *New York Times,* Jan. 13, 2000; and Edward McElroy, "Teacher Compensation," http://www.TeachingK-8.com, Aug.–Sept. 2005.

100. Richard Ingersoll, *Why Do High-Poverty Schools Have Difficulty Staffing Their Classrooms with Qualified Teachers?* (Washington, D.C.: Center for American Progress and the Institute for America's Future, 2004); Richard Rothstein, "Teacher Shortages Vanish When the Price Is Right," *New York Times,* Sept. 25, 2002; Natalia Mehlman, "My Brief Teaching Career," *New York Times,* June 24, 2002; David Eggers et al., "Reading, Writing, Retailing," *New York Times,* June 27, 2005; Lou Dobbs, "A Legacy in Search of a President," *CNN.com,* June 20, 2007, http://www.CNN.com/. Sam Dillon, "With Turnover High, Schools Fight for Teachers," *New York Times,* Aug. 27, 2007.

101. Rothstein, "Teacher Shortages Vanish When the Price Is Right." Also see Louis Gerstner et al., *Teaching at Risk: A Call to Action* (New York: Teaching Commission, 2004); Yilu Zhao, "To Find Teachers, Raise Your Hand High and Yell, Me," *New York Times,* Oct. 5, 2002; Abby Goodnough, "With New Rules and Higher Pay, New York Gets Certified Teachers," *New York Times,* Aug. 23, 2002; David Herszenhorn, "New York Offers Housing Subsidy as Teacher Lure," *New York Times,* Apr. 19, 2006; Karen Arenson, "Foundation Hopes to Lure Top Students to Teaching," *New York Times,* Dec. 20, 2007; Lindsay Melvin, "Bridging the Gap: Districts Turn to

Pay Incentives to Keep Teachers at High-Needs Schools," *Commercial Appeal,* Nov. 19, 2007.

102. Matt Miller, "Testing Intentions for Poor Children," *Commercial Appeal,* May 31, 2005.

103. Campbell, "Restoring Teacher's Dignity." Also see McKinsey and Company, *Creating a World-Class Education System in Ohio* (Washington, D.C.: Achieve, 2007), 35–41.

104. Quoted in Philip Howard, "You Can't Buy Your Way Out of a Bureaucracy," *New York Times,* Dec. 3, 2004.

105. Also see Brian Friel, "No Teacher Left Behind," *National Journal,* Sept. 11, 2004, 2712–18.

106. Hugh Price, *Working Together: Mt. Vernon, New York. A Model for School Reform* (New York: National Urban League, 2002).

107. For example, see Richard J. Wood, "Run Public Schools Like Colleges," *New York Times,* July 26, 1989.

108. See Diana Jean Schemo, "When Students' Gains Help Teachers' Bottom Line," *New York Times,* May 9, 2004; Michael Janofsky, "Teacher Merit Pay Tied to Education Gains," *New York Times,* Oct. 4, 2005; Ralph Blumenthal, "Houston Ties teachers' Pay to Test Scores," *New York Times,* Jan. 13, 2006; Diana Jean Schemo, "Tougher Standards Urged for Federal Education Law," *New York Times,* Feb. 14, 2007; Nancy Zuckerbrod, "More Teachers Getting Merit Pay," *Commercial Appeal,* Aug. 19, 2007.

109. Ruma Banerji Kumar, "School 'reconstitution' nothing new," *Commercial Appeal,* Sept. 22, 2003.

110. For example, see Ogbu, *Black American Students in an Affluent Suburb,* 266–267; B. Pederson, "Merit: To Pay or Not Pay? Teachers Grapple with Yet Another Marketplace Reform," *Rethinking Schools* 14.3 (2000): 1, 9–11; L. Cuban and D. B. Tyack, "Lessons from History," *Rethinking Schools* 14.3 (2000): 11; R. Murnane and D. Cohen, "Merit Pay and the Evaluation Problem: Why Most Merit Pay Plans Fail and a Few Survive," *Harvard Educational Review* 56 (1986): 1–17; S. M. Johnson, "Merit Pay for Teachers: A Prescription for Reform," *Harvard Educational Review* 54 (1984): 175–85.

111. For example, see Steinberg, "Salary Gap Still Plaguing Teachers."

112. Todd Purdum, "Rights Groups Sue California Public Schools," *New York Times,* May 18, 2000; Jodi Wilgoren, "Harsh Critique of Teachers Urges Attention to Training," *New York Times,* Oct. 25, 1999.

113. "Official Cites MCS as 'Model for School Reform,'" *Tri-State Defender,* Oct. 2–6, 2004.

114. Ibid.; The New Teacher Project, "How Memphis Is Getting The Teachers It Needs," Washington, D.C.: Philanthropy Roundtable (May 2006).

115. See Richard Rothstein, "Forming the Hand That Holds the Chalk," *New York Times,* Nov. 21, 2001. Also see the recommendations in Gerstner et al., *Teaching at Risk.*

116. See Vivian Gunn Morris, "Teacher Mentoring Paying Off in City Schools," *Commercial Appeal,* Mar. 7, 2006.

117. National Education Commission on Time and Learning, *Prisoners of Time* (Washington, D.C.: GPO, 1994); Quoted in Catherine Manegold, "41% of School Day Is Spent on Academic Subjects, Study Says," *New York Times,* May 5, 1994.

118. Sam Dillon, "School Is Haven When Children Have No Home," *New York Times,* Nov. 27, 2003.

119. Ibid.

120. For example, see Timothy Shriver and Roger Weissberg, "No Emotion Left Behind," *New York Times,* Aug. 16, 2005.

121. See Brown et al., *Getting Smarter,* 15–23.

122. For example, see Harris Cooper et al., "The Effects of Summer Vacation on Achievement Test Scores: A Narrative and Meta-analytic Review," *Review of Educational Research* 66. 3 (1996): 227–68; Barbara Heyns, "Schooling and Cognitive Development: Is There a Season for Learning?" *Child Development* 58 (1987): 1151–60; Doris Entwisle and Karl Alexander, "Winter Setback: The Racial Composition of Schools and Learning to Read," *American Sociological Review* 59 (June 1994): 446–60; Gerald Bracey, "Schools Are Not 'Failing' Poor Kids," *Washington Post,* Jan. 18, 2002.

123. National Commission on Excellence in Education, *A Nation at Risk.* Also a recommendation presented in Brown et al., *Getting Smarter.* In addition, see Jodi Wilgoren, "Calls for Change in the Scheduling of the School Day," *New York Times,* Jan. 10, 2001.

124. See Diana Jean Schemo, "Failing Schools See a Solution in Longer Days," *New York Times,* Mar. 26, 2007.

125. For more information on this program, see Marian Wright Edelman, "Children's Defense Fund's Freedom Summer 2006," *Tri-State Defender,* June 17–21, 2006.

126. See Brown et al., *Getting Smarter,* 18.

127. Marisa Trevino, "Longer School Days Aren't a Panacea," *USA Today,* Apr. 11, 2007.

128. Casey, *No Excuses,* 5.

129. See Diane Ravitch, "What We've Accomplished since World War II," *Principal* 63 (Jan. 1984): ERIC EJ294847. Aimee Edmondson, "Tradition, Politics Keep Underused Schools Alive," *Commercial Appeal,* Feb. 9, 2003; "Parents and Teachers Challenge School Closings in St. Louis," *New York Times,* Sept. 2, 2003.

130. Alan DeYoung, "The Status of American Rural Educational Research: An Integrated Review and Commentary," *Review of Educational Research* 57.2 (Summer 1987): 123–48.

131. David Strang, "The Administrative Transformation of American Education: School District Consolidation, 1938–1980," *Administrative Science Quarterly* 32.3 (Sept. 1987): 352–66; James Conant, *The American High School Today: A First Report to Interested Students* (New York: McGraw Hill, 1959).

132. Jonathan Sher an Stuart Rosenfeld, *Public Education in Sparsely Populated Areas of the United States* (Washington, D.C.: National Institute of Education, 1977).

133. Strang, "The Administrative Transformation of American Education." For an overview, see Loretta Warren Changery, "Implementing a Legislatively Mandated School

District Merger: Lessons Learned," Ph.D. diss., Teachers College, Columbia University, 1994.

134. For a discussion of the role of school consolidation in effective desegregation efforts, see Willis Hawley et al., *Assessment of Current Knowledge About the Effectiveness of School Desegregation Strategies* (Nashville: Center for Education and Human Development Policy, Institute for Public Policy Studies, Vanderbilt University, 1981), 39–40.

135. Strang, "The Administrative Transformation of American Education"; Changery, "Implementing a Legislatively Mandated School District Merger"; E. Young, "Questioning Consolidation," *Tennessee School Board Association Journal* 11.2 (1994): 33–37; Weldon Beckner and Linda O'Neal, "A New View of Smaller Schools," *NASSP Bulletin* 64 (Oct. 1980): 1–7; Steve Kay, "Considerations in Evaluating School Consolidation Proposals," *Small School Forum* 4 (Fall 1982): 8–10; Ravitch, "What We've Accomplished since World War II"; D. K. Wiles, "What Is Useful Information in School Consolidation Debates?" *Journal of Education Finance* 19.3 (1994): 292–318; William Duncombe and John Yinger, "Does School Consolidation Cut Costs?" (Syracuse University, Center for Policy Research Working Paper No. 33, Jan. 2001).

136. For a general discussion of this entire phenomenon, see George C. Howard and Edith Foster Howard, *City-County Educational Relationships in Tennessee* (Knoxville: University of Tennessee Bureau of Public Administration, Feb. 1950), 1–3.

137. For example, see Bill Dries, "Line-Item Budget Control Resides with City Schools," *Commercial Appeal,* Jan. 30, 2000. Nationally, five-sixths of schools are in special districts, while one-sixth are run by municipal governments. See John Levy, *Urban America: Processes and Problems* (Upper Saddle River, N.J.: Prentice Hall, 2000), 272.

138. See Richard Locker and Sherri Drake, "Panel Rejects Special School District," *Commercial Appeal,* Apr. 19, 2000. Also see Ruma Banerji Kumar, "Special Districts Could Levy Taxes: School Consolidation Panel Explores Funding Proposals," *Commercial Appeal,* Apr. 2, 2006. Tennessee has not allowed a new special district since 1982.

139. For example, see *School Consolidation in Tennessee* (Nashville: Association of Independent and Municipal Schools, 1994).

140. See Marcus Pohlmann, Joy Clay, and Kenneth Goings, *School Consolidation: State of Tennessee,* report prepared for Johnnie B. Watson, superintendent, Memphis City Schools, July 2001.

141. See discussion in the *Commercial Appeal,* Feb. 17, 2001.

142. See J. C. Williams, "An Option for Memphis: Merger of the Memphis City Schools with the Shelby County Schools" (paper prepared for the Memphis City Schools, May 29, 1989); "Old Debates Continues on School Consolidation," *Memphis Flyer,* Apr. 18, 2001.

143. Polling data reported in Michael Erskine, "Merge? County and City Are Polls Apart," *Commercial Appeal,* Mar. 24, 2002. Also see "The Other Mayors Speak," *Commer-*

cial Appeal, Feb. 20, 2005; Jimmie Covington, "Merging of City and County Looks Unlikely," *Commercial Appeal,* July 18, 1999.

144. For example, see Tony Jones, "Mayor Wants Community Involvement in Consolidation Debate Here," *Tri-State Defender,* Mar. 3–7, 2001; Blake Fontenay, "Unified School Plan Calls for 5 Divisions," *Commercial Appeal,* Mar. 18, 2003.

145. Willie Herenton, "Want Better Schools? Here's How," *Commercial Appeal,* Mar. 18, 2001; Michael Erskine and Clay Bailey, "Herenton Plan Isn't a Priority in County," *Commercial Appeal,* Jan. 3, 2003; Michael Erskine, "Wharton Poses Joint Operation," *Commercial Appeal,* July 15, 2004; Clay Bailey, "School Spirit," *Commercial Appeal,* Feb. 25, 2005.

146. For example, see Aimee Edmondson, "Funding Plan Flops with City Schools," *Commercial Appeal,* Apr. 23, 2002; Ruma Banerji Kumar, "Schools Could Share," *Commercial Appeal,* Aug. 4, 2004; Michael Erskine, "Schools' Joint Plan Approved," *Commercial Appeal,* July 26, 2005; Alex Doniach, "Merger Chances Boosted," *Commercial Appeal,* Jan. 9, 2008.

147. Tennessee Code Annotated Volume 9, title 49, contains the governing law. See discussion in Williams, "An Option for Memphis," 4–5; Blake Fontenay, "Herenton Plan Appears OK for Ballot," *Commercial Appeal,* Jan. 23, 2003; Arthur Webb, "Does the City School Board Exist? Attorneys Disagree," *Tri-State Defender,* Feb. 8–12, 2003; Paula Wade, "Memphis Can't Surrender Charter," *Commercial Appeal,* Mar. 28, 2002; Blake Fontenay, "Legal Opinion Goes against Herenton on School Merger," *Commercial Appeal,* Apr. 4, 2003.

148. Blake Fontenay, "Council Urges Vote on Schools," *Commercial Appeal,* May 7, 2003.

149. For a good discussion of the pros and cons of local consolidation, see "The Consolidation Option," *Commercial Appeal,* Mar. 2, 2003.

150. See Jimmie Covington, "Rout Asks Mayors to Meet on Schools," *Commercial Appeal,* Feb. 24, 2001.

151. See Richard Locker, "Opinions Differ on School Funding," *Commercial Appeal,* Mar. 11, 2005.

152. For examples, see Heidenreich, *Urban Education,* section 3; McKinsey and Company, "Empower Principals to Function as Instructional Leaders," *Creating a World-Class Education System in Ohio* (Washington, D.C.: Achieve, 2007), 29–33.

153. For example, see Kwame Ture and Charles V. Hamilton, *Black Power* (New York: Random House, 1967), 166–72; Mario Fantini, Marilyn Gittell, and Richard Magat, eds., *Community Control and the Urban School* (New York: Praeger, 1970); David Tyack, "Needed: Reform of a Reform," in Stephen David and Paul Peterson, eds., *Urban Politics and Public Policy: The City in Crisis* (New York: Praeger, 1977), 225–47; Carter, *No Excuses.*

154. For example, see Allan Ornstein, *Metropolitan Schools: Administrative Decentralization vs. Community Control* (Metuchen, N.J.: Scarecrow Press, 1974), especially chap. 4; Joseph Berger, "80 New York City Schools Chosen for Power Sharing," *New York Times,* July 19, 1990; Ruma Banerji Kumar, "Copy N.Y. Schools Here?" *Commercial*

Appeal, Feb. 20, 2005; April Simpson, "Report Finds Unhappiness with City's Parent Units," *New York Times,* June 14, 2006.

155. For example, see Elissa Gootman, "Back to School in a System Being Remade," *New York Times,* Sept. 5, 2006; David Herszenhorn, "In Sweeping Schools Vision, Big Risks for Mayor," *New York Times,* Jan. 18, 2007; Jennifer Medina and David Herszenhorn, "School Year's About to Start, and So, Too, Is a Big Change," *New York Times,* Sept. 3, 2007; Elissa Gootman and Jennifer Medina, "Schools Open to Greet a Year Full of Change," *New York Times,* Sept. 5, 2007.

156. For example, see Stephanie Chambers, *Mayors and Schools: Minority Voices and Democratic Tensions in Urban Education* (Philadelphia: Temple University Press, 2006).

157. See Allan Gold, "Boston's Teachers Pact to Decentralize Schools," *New York Times,* May 23, 1989.

158. See Isabel Wilkerson, "Chicago Schools Try a Radical New Cure," *New York Times,* Oct. 22, 1989; Isabel Wilkerson, "Chicago on Brink of New School System," *New York Times,* Oct. 11, 1989; Dorothy Shipps, "Corporate Influence on Chicago School Reform," in Clarence Stone, ed., *Changing Urban Education* (Lawrence: University of Kansas Press, 1998), 161–83; Anthony Bryk et al., *Chartering Chicago School Reform* (Boulder, Colo.: Westview Press, 1998); Alfred Hess, *School Restructuring, Chicago Style* (Newbury Park, Calif.: Corwin, 1991); Stephanie Chambers, "Urban Education Reform and Minority Political Empowerment," *Political Science Quarterly* 117. 4 (2002–3): 643–65; Stephanie Chambers, *Mayors and Schools: Minority Voices and Democratic Tensions in Urban Education* (Philadelphia: Temple University Press, 2006); Pauline Lipman, *High Stakes Education: Inequality, Globalization, and Urban School Reform* (New York: Routledge, 2004), 32–40.

159. Michael Danielson and Jennifer Hochschild, "Changing Urban Education: Lessons, Cautions, Prospects," in Clarence Stone, ed., *Changing Urban Education* (Lawrence: University Press of Kansas, 1998), 293; Simpson, "Report Finds Unhappiness."

160. See Joseph Berger, "Miami Finds Mixed Results from Power-Sharing Plan in Its Schools," *New York Times,* Mar. 9, 1991; Frederick Hess, *Spinning Wheels: The Politics of Urban School Reform* (Washington, D.C.: Brookings, 1999); Michael Barber and Ruth Dann, eds., *Raising Educational Standards in the Inner Cities: Practical Initiatives in Action* (Cassell: New York, 1996); Ornstein, *Metropolitan Schools,* chap. 4; Wilkerson, "Chicago Schools Try a Radical New Cure"; Peter Applebome, "Chicago School Decentralization Provides Lessons, but No Verdict," *New York Times,* Nov. 8, 1995.

161. E. Terrence Jones, *The Metropolitan Chase: Politics and Policies in Urban America* (Upper Saddle River, N.J.: Prentice-Hall, 2003), 168.

162. Wilbur Rich, *Black Mayors and School Politics* (New York: Garland, 1996), 5, 9. Also see Daniel Duke, "What We Know and Don't Know About Improving Low-Performing Schools," *Phi Delta Kappan* 87.10 (2006): 729–34.

163. For example, see Nancy Zuckerbrod, "Mayors Seek to Take Charge of Schools," *Yahoo! News,* Jan. 9, 2007, http://news.yahoo.com/; Sewell Chan, "Los Angeles

Mayor Sees Bloomberg School Reforms as Model," *New York Times,* Mar. 21, 2006; Mary Cashiola, "Board Out of Their Minds," *Memphis Flyer,* Aug. 21–27, 2003, 14–18.

164. For example, see Edward Fiske, "An Impoverished Urban District Hands Its Schools over to Boston University to Run," *New York Times,* Aug. 16, 1989; Abby Goodnough, "Mayor Plans Tight Control on New York Schools," *New York Times,* Jan. 16, 2003; Abby Goodnough, "Overhaul of New York Schools Sends Top Officials Packing," *New York Times,* Jan. 29, 2003; David Herszenhorn, "As City Goes Back to School, Bloomberg's Plan Faces Test," *New York Times,* Sept. 4, 2003.

165. This intervention discussion has drawn heavily from Peter Eisinger and Richard Hula, "Gunslinger School Administrators: Nontraditional Leadership in Urban School Systems in the United States" (paper presented at the Annual Meeting of the American Political Science Association, Boston, Aug. 29–Sept. 1, 2002). Also see Joseph Viteritti, "Managing the City's Schools," *New York Times,* Nov. 18, 2002.

166. For one of the few studies finding at least marginal gains, see Ken Wong et al., *The Education Mayor: Improving America's Schools* (Washington, D.C.: Georgetown University Press, 2007).

167. For example, see David Kushma, "Class on Running City's Schools Is Now in Session," *Commercial Appeal,* Jan. 30, 2000; Mickie Anderson and Aimee Edmondson, "Should Memphis Look to Chicago Schools?" *Commercial Appeal,* Jan. 30, 2000.

168. See Richard Rothstein, "Mr. Mayor, Schools Chief," *New York Times,* Apr. 17, 2002.

169. Mosteller et al., "Sustained Inquiry in Education."

170. Jeannie Oakes et al., *Educational Matchmaking: Academic and Vocational Tinkering in Comprehensive High Schools* (Santa Monica: Rand, 1992); Anne Wheelock, *Crossing the Tracks: How "Untracking" Can Save America's Schools* (New York: New Press, 1992); Ellen Shell Ruppel, "Off the Track," *Technology Review* (Oct. 6, 1994): 62–64; Jeannie Oakes, "Two Cities' Tracking and within-School Segregation," *Teachers College Record* 96 (1995): 681–90; Leonard Marascuilo and Maryellen McSweeney, "Tacking and Minority Student Attitudes and Performance," in Heidenreich, *Urban Education.*

171. John Goodlad, *A Place Called School: Prospects for the Future* (New York: McGraw-Hill, 1984); Oakes et al., *Educational Matchmaking;* Oakes, "Two Cities' Tracking and within-School Segregation"; Raymond Jerrems, "Racism: Vector of Ghetto Education," in Heidenreich, *Urban Education,* 271–78; Kate Zernike, "Race-Separated Test Scores Divide N.Y. Community," *Commercial Appeal,* Aug. 6, 2000. For some empirical results on tracking, see James Kulik, "An Analysis of the Research on Ability Grouping" (Storrs, Conn.: National Research Center on the Gifted and Talented, University of Connecticut , 1992); Tom Loveless, *The Tracking Wars: State Reform Meets School Policy* (Washington, D.C.: Brookings Institution Press, 1999).

172. For example, see Michael Winerip, "Cheapening the Cap and Gown," *New York Times,* May 3, 2006.

173. Diane Ravitch, "Failing the Wrong Grades," *New York Times,* Mar. 15, 2005. Also see "Closing the Expectations Gap" (Washington, D.C.: Achieve, 2007).

174. See Brian Friel, "High Schools Next on the Federal Agenda," *National Journal,* Mar. 13, 2004, 820–21.

175. National Center for Education Statistics, *Nation's Report Card* (Washington, D.C.: GPO, June 19, 2003).

176. Report discussed in Ruma Banerji Kumar, "Students Get Challenge," *Commercial Appeal,* July 27, 2005; Tamar Lewin, "Many Going to College Aren't Ready, Report Finds," *New York Times,* Aug. 17, 2005. Also see Bob Herbert, "Left Behind, Way Behind," *New York Times,* Aug. 29, 2005; Diana Jean Schemo, "At 2-Year Colleges, Students Eager but Under Prepared," *New York Times,* Sept. 2, 2006.

177. For example, see Committee on Prospering in the Global Economy in the 21st Century, *Rising above the Gathering Storm: Energizing and Employing America for a Brighter Economic Future* (Washington, D.C.: National Academies Press, 2007); Dan Freedman, "U.S. Students Score in the Middle on International Tests," *Commercial Appeal,* Dec. 5, 2001; Karen Arenson, "Math and Science Tests Find 4th and 8th Graders in U.S. Still Lag Many Peers," *New York Times,* Dec. 15, 2004; Thomas Friedman, "What, Me Worry?" *New York Times,* Apr. 29, 2005; Louis Harris, *Metropolitan Life Survey of the American Teacher, 1985–1995* (New York: Met Life, 1995); Education Week, *Quality Counts 98* (Washington, D.C., 1998), 17:17; Nicholas Kristof, "Watching the Jobs Go By," *New York Times,* Feb. 11, 2004; Thomas Friedman, "Losing Our Edge?" *New York Times,* Apr. 22, 2004; Brent Staples, "Why the United States Should Look to Japan for Better Schools," *New York Times,* Nov. 21, 2005; Associated Press, "Other Countries' Students Surpass U.S.'s on Tests," *New York Times,* Dec. 5, 2007; Sam Dillon, "Study Compares States' Math and Science Scores With Other Countries" *New York Times,* Nov. 14, 2007.

178. Carter, *No Excuses.* Also see Abigail Thernstrom, "Testing, the Easy Target," *New York Times,* June 10, 1999.

179. For example, see Laurence Toenjes et al., "High-Stakes Testing, Accountability, and Student Achievement in Texas and Houston," in Chubb and Loveless, *Bridging the Achievement Gap,* 109–30; Matthew Gandal et al., *Do Graduation Tests Measure Up?* (Washington, D.C.: Achieve, 2004). Latter cited in Diana Jean Schemo, "Study Finds Senior Exams Are Too Basic," *New York Times,* June 10, 2004. Also see Michael Janofsky, "Students Say High Schools Let Them Down," *New York Times,* July 16, 2005; see Michael Janofsky, "Report Says States Aim Low in Science Classes," *New York Times,* Dec. 8, 2005; Lilly Rockwell, "Dropouts Say They're Just Bored," *Commercial Appeal,* Mar. 3, 2006.

180. Robert Pear, "Governors of 13 States Plan to Raise Standards in High Schools," *New York Times,* Feb. 28, 2005; Greg Winter, "Governors Seek Rise in High School Standards," *New York Times,* Feb. 23, 2005; Brian Friel, "High Schools Are on the Agenda," *National Journal,* Mar. 5, 2005, 695–96. For the rationale of Bill Gates, see Friedman, "What, Me Worry?" Also see American Diploma Project, *Ready or Not: Creating a High School Diploma That Count* (Washington, D.C.: Achieve, 2004), reported in Karen Arenson, "Study Says U.S. Should Replace States' High School Standards," *New York Times,* Feb. 10, 2004; Ben Feller, "Student Exit Tests Are 'Here to Stay,'" *Commercial Appeal,* Aug. 14, 2003; Kate McGreevy, "States Raising the

Bar on High School Graduation Standards," *School Reform News*, June 2006, 10. Bill Gates and Eli Broad also launched their "Ed in '08" campaign to raise public awareness of educational issues. See David Herszenhorn, "Billionaires Start $60 Million Schools Effort," *New York Times*, Apr. 25, 2007. Also see an application of these principles to the state of Ohio in McKinsey and Company, *Creating a World-Class Education System in Ohio* (Washington, D.C.: Achieve, 2007), 25–28, 43–47, 57–66.

181. For example, see Jennifer Medina, "More Students Finish School, Given the Time," *New York Times*, Aug. 21, 2007.

182. See Dan Balz, "Gates Urges Governors to Restructure High Schools," *Commercial Appeal*, Feb. 27, 2005. Among other things, the 2005 National Education Summit on High Schools produced "Closing the Expectations Gap: An Annual 50-State Progress Report on the Alignment of High School Policies with the Demands of College and Work" (Washington, D.C.: Achieve, 2007). As an example of such reform alternatives, see "Florida Bill Asks High Schoolers to Declare Major," *New York Times*, Mar. 26, 2006.

183. Schools failing to make adequate yearly progress after one year are put on notice; after two years they are labeled "in need of improvement" and must offer school choice with transportation; after three years they must offer tutoring and school choice; after four years they are placed in "corrective action," which can require new curricula, extended school days, and new employees; after five years they receive a "restructuring plan"; and after six years they must be "restructured" by such means as reopening as a charter school, replacing most or all of the staff, state takeover, or privatization. See Patrick McGuinn, *No Child Left Behind and the Transformation of Federal Education Policy, 1965–2005* (Lawrence: University Press of Kansas, 2006); Frederick Hess, *No Child Left Behind* (New York: Peter Lang, 2006); Paul Peterson, *No Child Left Behind? The Politics and Practice of School Accountability* (Washington, D.C.: Brookings Institute Press, 2003).

184. Brian Friel, "Making the Grade?" *National Journal*, Sept. 13, 2003, 2765.

185. Sam Dillon, "1 in 4 Schools Fall Short under Bush Law," *New York Times*, Jan. 27, 2004; John Cronin, G. Gage Kingsbury, Martha McCall, and Branin Bowe, *The Impact of the No Child Left Behind Act on Student Achievement and Growth: 2005 Edition* (Lake Oswego, Ore.: Northwest Evaluation Association, 2005), cited in Greg Winter, "Study Finds Shortcoming in New Law on Education," *New York Times*, Apr. 13, 2005.

186. Diana Jean Schemo, "New Federal Rule Tightens Demands on Failing Schools," *New York Times*, Nov. 27, 2002; Sam Dillon, "Most States Fail Demands in Education Law," *New York Times*, July 25, 2006.

187. Ruma Banerji Kumar, "More Schools Miss the Mark," *Commercial Appeal*, Sept. 5, 2003; James Brosnan, "2 years after NCLB," *Commercial Appeal*, Jan. 8, 2004.

188. Gerald Bracey, "No Child Left Behind: Trojan Horse for Schools," *Commercial Appeal*, June 22, 2003.

189. Quoted in Diana Jean Schemo, "Law Overhauling School Standards Is Seen As Skirted," *New York Times*, Oct. 14, 2002.

190. See Wendi Thomas, "Tutors Get Schools off 'Bad' List," *Commercial Appeal,* Aug. 15, 2004.

191. From Wiley Henry, "Dr. Johnson Recommends Clean Sweep of 3 Schools," *Tri-State Defender,* Apr. 16–20, 2005. Also see Ruma Banerji Kumar, "New Faces at Troubled Schools?" *Commercial Appeal,* May 8, 2004; Wayne Risher, "Fresh Start Gears up at 5 Schools," *Commercial Appeal,* May 18, 2004; Lora Jobe, "Time to Quit Waiting to Help Schools," *Commercial Appeal,* Sept. 21, 2003; Michael Hooks Jr., "Reconstitution Aims to Help Kids, Not Hurt Educators," *Commercial Appeal,* Sept. 21, 2003. Meanwhile, states like Maryland did move to take over failing schools. See Diana Jean Schemo, "Maryland Acts to Take Over Failing Baltimore Schools," *New York Times,* Mar. 30, 2006.

192. Ruma Banerji Kumar, "Warning Signs May Have Been Missed," *Commercial Appeal,* Dec. 9, 2003.

193. Kumar, "New Faces at Troubled Schools?" Wiley Henry, "One Day at a Time," *Tri-State Defender,* May 22–26, 2004; Urban Child Institute, *The State of Children in Memphis and Shelby County* (Memphis: Urban Child Institute, 2006). For a discussion of the mobility ("transciency") problem per se, see Harry Miller, *Social Foundations of Education* (New York: Holt Rinehart Winston, 1978), 112–14. Also for examples of how children can bounce from the home of one relative to the next, see Ian Urbina, "Trying to Keep Child Care in the Family," *New York Times,* July 26, 2006; Erik Eckholm, "To Avoid Student Turnover, Parents Get Rent Help," *New York Times,* June 24, 2008.

194. See Sam Dillon, "School Law Stirs Efforts to End Minority Gap," *New York Times,* May 27, 2005.

195. See *National Journal,* May 13, 2000, 1537; Peter Applebome, "Revamped Kentucky Schools Are a Study in Pros and Cons," *New York Times,* Mar. 25, 1996.

196. National Assessment of Educational Progress (NAEP) results, reported in Sam Dillon, "Young Students Post Solid Gains in Federal Tests," *New York Times,* July 15, 2005; Sam Dillon, "Education Law Gets First Test in U.S. Schools," *New York Times,* Oct. 20, 2005; Sam Dillon, "Schools Slow in Closing Gaps between Races," *New York Times,* Nov. 20, 2006; Paul Tough, "What It Takes to Make a Student," *New York Times,* Nov. 26, 2006; Sam Dillon, "New Study Finds Gains since No Child Left Behind," *New York Times,* June 6, 2007; Alan Finder, "Math and Reading SAT Scores Drop," *New York Times,* Aug. 28, 2007; Sam Dillon, "Scores Show Mixed Results for Bush Education Law," *New York Times,* Sept. 25, 2007; Sam Dillon, "Math Rises, but Reading Is Mixed," *New York Times,* Sept. 26, 2007.

197. Cited in Sam Dillon, "Some School Districts Challenge Bush's Signature Education Law," *New York Times,* Jan. 2, 2004. See http://www.publicagenda.org.

198. Sara Rimer, "Failing and Frustrated School Tires Even F's," *New York Times,* Dec. 3, 2002.

199. Pauline Lipman, "Making the Global City, Making Inequality: The Political Economy and Cultural Politics of Chicago School Policy," *American Educational Research Journal* 39.2 (Summer 2002): 379–419; Michael Winerip, "Going for Depth Instead of Prep," *New York Times,* June 11, 2003; National Center for Fair and Open Testing,

How Standardized Testing Damages Education (see http://www.fairtest.org/facts/howharm.htm).

200. Quoted in Brian Friel, "Don't Know Much About History," *National Journal,* Aug. 2, 2003, 2500; Sam Dillon, "Schools Cut Back Subjects to Push Reading and Math," *New York Times,* Mar. 26, 2006; Sam Dillon, "Modest Gains Seen in U.S. Students' History Scores," *New York Times,* May 16, 2007.

201. Michael Winerip, "An Embedded Reporter in the Trenches of P.S. 48," *New York Times,* Apr. 2, 2003.

202. Richard Lomax, *The Impact of Standardized Testing on Minority Students* (Chestnut Hill, Mass.: NSF Study, Center for the Study of Testing, Evaluation, and Educational Policy, Boston College, 1992). Report discussed in Susan Chira, "Study Finds Standardized Tests May Hurt Education Efforts," *New York Times,* Oct. 16, 1992. Also see Sam Dillon, "Test Shows Drop in Science Achievement for 12th Graders," *New York Times,* May 25, 2006; "No Child Left Behind? Ask the Gifted," *New York Times,* Apr. 5, 2006.

203. Greg Winter, "City Districts Show Gains in Series of School Tests," *New York Times,* Mar. 26, 2003; Greg Winter, "More Schools Rely on Tests, but Big Study Raises Doubts," *New York Times,* Dec. 28, 2002; Diana Jean Schemo, "Test Shows Students' Gains in Math Falter by Grade 12," *New York Times,* Aug. 3, 2001.

204. See Richard Rothstein, "Dropout Rate Is Climbing and Likely to Go Higher," *New York Times,* Oct. 9, 2002; John Bridgeland et al., *The Silent Epidemic: Perspectives of High School Dropouts* (Seattle, Wash.: Bill and Melinda Gates Foundation Report, Mar. 2006); Thomas Poetter et al., *No Child Left Behind and the Illusion of Reform* (Lanham, Md.: University Press of America, 2006); Deborah Meier, *Many Children Left Behind: How the No Child Left Behind Act Is Damaging Our Children and Our Schools* (Boston: Beacon Press, 2004); Halimah Abdullah, "The Math Looks Rough for Schools," *Commercial Appeal,* Mar. 4, 2006; Nathan Thornburgh, "Dropout Nation," *Time,* Apr. 17, 2006; Tamar Lewin, "Boys Are No Match for Girls in Completing School," *New York Times,* Apr. 19, 2006; Diana Jean Schemo, "A Third of U.S. Dropouts Never Reach 10th Grade," *New York Times,* June 21, 2006; Jennifer McMurrer, *Choices, Changes, and Challenges: Curriculum and Instruction in the NCLB Era* (Washington, D.C.: Center on Education Policy, 2007).

205. David Herszenhorn, "Studies in Chicago Fault Holding Back of 3rd Graders," *New York Times,* Apr. 7, 2004; Also see Gary Orfield et al., "Schools More Separate: Consequences of a Decade of Resegregation," Civil Rights Project Report, Harvard University, July 18, 2001.

206. Madaus quoted in Chira, "Study Finds Standardized Tests May Hurt Education Efforts." Also see William Raspberry, "Academic Tests Fail to Meet Worthy Goals," *Commercial Appeal,* Sept. 28, 1999; Richard Rothstein, "The Growing Revolt Against the Testers," *New York Times,* May 30, 2001; National Center for Fair and Open Testing, *Failing Our Children* (see http://www.fairtest.org/Failing Our Children.htm).

207. Steven Ross, "Evaluate Schools by Multiple Measures," *Commercial Appeal,* Jan. 4, 2004.

208. See Michael Winerip, "Holding Back a Pupil: A Bad Idea Despite Intent," *New York Times,* May 21, 2003.

209. For example, see Joseph Berger, "This Is a Test, Results May Vary," *New York Times,* June 13, 2007.

210. See Sam Dillon, "Good Schools or Bad? Ratings Baffle Parents," *New York Times,* Sept. 5, 2004; Ford Fessenden, "How to Measure Student Proficiency?" *New York Times,* Dec. 31, 2003; Diana Henriques, "Rising Demands for Testing Push Limits of Its Accuracy," *New York Times,* Sept. 2, 2003; National Center for Fair and Open Testing, *Testing Our Children* (see http://www.fairtest.org/states/tn.htm); National Center for Fair and Open Testing, *The Limits of Standardized Tests for Diagnosing and Assisting Student Learning* (see http://www.fairtest.org/facts/LimitsofTests. htm); National Center for Fair and Open Testing, *What's Wrong With Standardized Tests?* (see http://www.fairtest.org/facts/whatwron.htm); National Center for Fair and Open Testing, *Norm-Referenced Achievement Tests* (see http://www.fairtest. org/facts/nratests.html); Diane Ravitch, "Every State Left Behind," *New York Times,* Nov. 7, 2005; Diana Jean Schemo, "Grades Rise, but Reading Skills Do Not," *New York Times,* Feb. 23, 2007.

211. GAO Report quoted in Diana Jean Schemo, "Problems Seen for Expansion of Testing of U.S. Students," *New York Times,* Oct. 5, 2004, for local examples, see Ruma Banerji Kumar and Halimah Abdullah, "NCLB Test Scores Look Good—On Paper," *Commercial Appeal,* Mar. 5–7, 2005; Halimah Abdullah, "Some Students Slip 'Behind' the Shadows," *Commercial Appeal,* Mar. 7, 2006.

212. For example, see Malcolm Gay, "State Takes Control of Troubled Public Schools in St. Louis," *New York Times,* Mar. 23, 2007.

213. Quoted in Diana Jean Schemo, "Effort by Bush on Education Faces Obstacles in the States," *New York Times,* Aug. 18, 2004.

214. Quoted in Friel, "Making the Grade?" 2765.

215. Diana Jean Schemo, "Effort by Bush on Education Faces Obstacles in the States," *New York Times,* Aug. 18, 2004; Ben Feller, "Hundreds of Schools Wipe Slate: But Some Stop Short of Drastic Measures Called for by Law," *Commercial Appeal,* May 10, 2006.

216. See Diana Jean Schemo, "Houston Schools Ease Rules on High School Promotion," *New York Times,* Apr. 9, 2004; "The School Testing Dodge," *New York Times,* July 2, 2006; Winerip, "Cheapening the Cap and Gown"; Ford Fessenden," Schools Under Scrutiny Over Cheating," *New York Times,* Sept. 9, 2007.

217. See Diana Jean Schemo, "States' End Run Dilutes Burden for Special Ed," *New York Times,* June 7, 2004; Schemo, "Effort by Bush on Education Faces Obstacles in the States"; Nicole Ziegler et al., "States Omit Minorities' School Scores," Associated Press, Apr. 18, 2006, http://hews.yahoo.com/; "School Reform in Danger," *New York Times,* May 8, 2006; Schemo, "Law Overhauling School Standards Is Seen As Skirted"; Sam Dillon, "Students Ace State Tests, but Earn D's and F's from U.S.," *New York Times,* Nov. 26, 2005; "The School Testing Dodge," *New York Times,* July 2, 2006; Tamar Lewin, "State School Standards Vary Widely in Study," *New York Times,* June 7, 2007; Tamar Lewin, "States Found to Vary Widely on Education,"

New York Times, June 8, 2007; Elizabeth Weil, "When Should a Kid Start Kindergarten," *New York Times,* June 3, 2007; Stephanie Germeraad, *Graduation Matters: How NCLB Allows States to Set the Bar Too Low for Improving High School Graduation Rates* (Washington, D.C.: Education Trust, 2007); Brian Friel, "No Teacher Left Behind," *National Journal,* Sept. 11, 2004, 2714, 2716; Diana Jean Schemo, "Report Cites Low Teacher Standards," *New York Times,* June 13, 2002; Kate Zernike, "Less Training, More Teachers: New Math for Staffing Classes," *New York Times,* Aug. 20, 2000; Ruma Banerji Kumar, "Teachers under Pressure to Become 'Highly Qualified,'" *Commercial Appeal,* Mar. 8, 2006. Paige and Bucholz quoted in Diana Jean Schemo, "States Get Federal Warning on School Standards," *New York Times,* Oct. 24, 2002.

218. NAEP stands for the National Assessment of Educational Progress. It has recently been renamed the Nation's Report Card. TCAP is the Tennessee Comprehensive Assessment Program. See Dakarai Aarons, "Report Card," *Commercial Appeal,* Sept. 26, 2007.

219. Paige and Bucholz quoted in Diana Jean Schemo, "States Get Federal Warning on School Standards," *New York Times,* Oct. 24, 2002.

220. Quoted in "Rescuing Educational Reform," *New York Times,* Mar. 2, 2004.

221. See "Bad News from Connecticut," *New York Times,* July 29, 2005; Dillon, "Some School Districts Challenge Bush's Signature Education Law"; "Schools Consider Lawsuits over No Child Left Behind Act, *Tri-State Defender,* Nov. 6–10, 2004.

222. See Sam Dillon, "Districts and Teachers' Union Sue Over Bush Law," *New York Times,* Apr. 21, 2005; William Schneider, "No Lawsuit Left Behind," *National Journal,* Apr. 30, 2005, 1348; Noreen Gillespie, "Connecticut Sues No Child Left Behind," *Commercial Appeal,* Aug. 23, 2005; Jesse McKinley, "California Court Reinstates Statewide Exit Exam for High Schools," *New York Times,* May 25, 2006; Michael Janofsky, "Judge Rejects Challenge to Bush Education Law," *New York Times,* Nov. 24, 2005.

223. See Dillon, "Some School Districts Challenge Bush's Signature Education Law."

224. Sam Dillon, "Utah House Rebukes Bush with Its Vote on School Law, *New York Times,* Feb. 11, 2004; Sam Dillon, "Utah Bill Mounts Challenge to Federal Education Law," *New York Times,* Feb. 16, 2005; Sam Dillon, "Utah Vote Rejects Parts of Education Law," *New York Times,* Apr. 20, 2005.

225. Quoted in Sam Dillon, "New U.S. Secretary Showing Flexibility on 'No Child' Act," *New York Times,* Feb. 14, 2005. For a section-by-section critique of the No Child Left Behind Act, see National Center for Fair and Open Testing, Initial Fair Test Analysis of ESEA as passed by Congress, Dec. 2002 (see http://www.fairtest.org/nattest/ ESEA.htm).

226. See Sam Dillon, "Report Faults Bush Initiative on Education," *New York Times,* Feb. 24, 2005.

227. See Sam Dillon, "President's Initiative to Shake Up Education Is Facing Protests," *New York Times,* Mar. 8, 2004; Diana Jean Schemo, "14 States Ask U.S. to Revise Some Education Law Rules," *New York Times,* Mar. 25, 2004; Brian Friel, "Damage Control for 'No Child Left Behind,'" *National Journal,* June 5, 2004, 1786–87.

228. For example, see Sam Dillon, "U.S. to Ease Some Provisions of School Law," *New York Times,* Mar. 14, 2004; Diana Jean Schemo, "Rules Eased on Upgrading U.S. Schools," *New York Times,* Mar. 16, 2004; Sam Dillon, "New U.S. Secretary Showing Flexibility on 'No Child' Act"; Sam Dillon, "Facing State Protests, U.S. Offers More Flexibility on School Rules," *New York Times,* Mar. 8, 2005; Susan Saulny, "U.S. Provides Rules to States for Testing Special Pupils," *New York Times,* May 11, 2005; Sam Dillon, "Education Law Is Loosened for Failing Chicago Schools," *New York Times,* Sept. 2, 2005; "Some States to Get Wider Latitude in Measuring Students' Gains," *New York Times,* Nov. 19, 2005; Robert Holland, "Intense Battle Looms over NCLB," *School Reform News,* Feb. 2006, 3; Diana Jean Schemo, "Flexibility Granted to 2 States in No Child Left Behind," *New York Times,* May 18, 2006; Sam Dillon, "U.S. Eases 'No Child' as Applied to Some States," *New York Times,* March 19, 2008.

229. For example, see Thomas Hargrove and Guido Stempel III, "Few Support Test Law's Renewal," *Commercial Appeal,* June 3, 2007. Also see Gallup Poll results, reported in *U.S. News and World Report,* Aug. 23, 2006; Brian Freel, "Stay the Course?" *National Journal,* Oct. 7, 2006, 28–32; Andrew Kohut, *No Child Left Behind Gets Mixed Grades* (Washington, D.C.: Pew Research Center, 2007); Diana Jean Schemo, "20 States Ask for Flexibility in School Law," *New York Times,* Feb. 22, 2006; Diana Jean Schemo, "Democrats Push for Changes to No Child Left Behind Law," *New York Times,* Jan. 9, 2007; Lisa Caruso, "Teacher Tensions," *National Journal,* Jan. 27, 2007, 27–28; Sam Dillon, "Battle Grows Over Renewing Landmark Education Law," *New York Times,* Apr. 7, 2007; Diana Jean Schemo," Secretary of Education Criticizes Proposal," *New York Times,* Sept. 6, 2007; Lisa Caruso, "Schoolyard Quarrel," *National Journal,* Sept. 15, 2007, 38–43; Diana Jean Schemo," Teachers and Rights Groups Oppose Education Measure," *New York Times,* Sept. 11, 2007.

230. Lola Bolden, "Teachers Are Solution, Not Problem," *Commercial Appeal,* June 22, 2003. Also see Aimee Edmondson, "Teachers Slam TCAP," *Commercial Appeal,* Sept. 24, 2003; Ruma Banerji Kumar, "Dire Stakes Directing Her Class Now, a Veteran Sighs," *Commercial Appeal,* Sept. 23, 2003.

231. Ruma Banerji Kumar, "Montessori Grappling with Feds," *Commercial Appeal,* May 31, 2005.

232. LaVerne Dickerson, "Focus on 'Accountability' Turns Testing on Its Head," *Commercial Appeal,* June 22, 2003. Also see William White II, "Putting Testing to the Test," *Commercial Appeal,* Sept. 21, 2003.

233. Richard Rothstein, "Decrees on Fixing Schools May Fail the Reality Test," *New York Times,* Oct. 3, 2001; David Herszenhorn, "In Reversal, Chicago Eases Promotions," *New York Times,* Mar. 25, 2004.

234. Quoted in Schemo, "Houston Schools Ease Rules on High School Promotion." Locally, see Halimah Abdullah, "A for Attendance," *Commercial Appeal,* Oct. 3, 2005.

235. See Friel, "Making the Grade?" *National Journal,* Sept. 13, 2003, 2767; Sam Dillon, "Cuts Put Schools and Law to the Test," *New York Times,* Aug. 31, 2003.

236. Quoted in Michael Winerip, "In 'No Child Left Behind,' a Problem with the Math," *New York Times,* Oct. 1, 2003.

237. Schemo, "Effort by Bush on Education Faces Obstacles in the States"; Dillon, "1 in 4 Schools Fall Short under Bush Law"; Julia Silverman, "Some Now Transferring Back after Switching Schools under Bush Plan," *Commercial Appeal*, Jan. 29, 3003; Susan Saulny, "Tutor Program Offered by Law Is Going Unused," *New York Times*, Feb. 12, 2006; Susan Saulny, "Few Students Seek Free Tutoring or Transfers from Failing Schools," *New York Times*, Apr. 6, 2006.

238. For example, see Susan Saulny, "A Lucrative Brand of Tutoring Grows Unchecked," *New York Times*, Apr. 4, 2005; Brian Friel, "A Test for Tutoring," *National Journal*, Apr. 16, 2005, 1161–62; Sam Dillon, "For Children Being Left Behind, Private Tutors Face Rocky Start," *New York Times*, Apr. 16, 2004; Brian Freel, "Tutors Face Their Own Exams," *National Journal*, Apr. 30, 2005, 1318–19; Ruma Banerji Kumar, "Making Cash, Not the Grade," *Commercial Appeal*, Mar. 6, 2006.

239. For example, see Schemo, "New Federal Rule Tightens Demands on Failing Schools."

240. See Diana Jean Schemo, "Rule on Failing Schools Draws Fire," *New York Times*, Nov. 28, 2002; Diana Jean Schemo, "Republicans Propose National School Voucher Program," *New York Times*, July 19, 2006; Diana Jean Schemo, "Bush Proposes Broadening the No Child Left Behind Act," *New York Times*, Jan. 25, 2007.

241. Brian Friel, "For-Profit Educators Unite," *National Journal*, Feb. 7, 2004, 394; Tamar Lewin, "Chock Full of Choice," *New York Times*, June 29, 2002; Julia Silverman, "Public Schools Courting Home-schoolers," *Commercial Appeal*, Apr. 8, 2005.

242. See National Commission on Excellence in Education, *A Nation at Risk* (Washington, D.C.: GPO, 1983); "Growing Trend: Parental Choice in Public Schools," *New York Times*, July 11, 1988; Carol Steinbach and Neal Peirce, "Multiple Choice," *National Journal*, July 1, 1989, 1692–95; Don Wycliff, "Right to Choose School Gains in Cities," *New York Times*, June 9, 1990; Applebome, "School Choice Changing Face of U.S. Education"; Richard Kahlenberg, *All Together Now: Creating Middle Class Schools through Public School Choice* (Baltimore, Md.: Brookings Institute Press, 2003); Patrick Wolf and Stephen Macedo, eds., *Educating Citizens: International Perspectives on Civic Values and School Choice* (Baltimore, Md.: Brookings Institute Press, 2004); John Betts and Tom Loveless, eds., *Getting Choice Right: Ensuring Equity and Efficiency in Education Policy* (Baltimore, Md.: Brookings Institute Press, 2005); Robert Enlow, *The ABCs of School Choice, 2006–2007* (Indianapolis: Milton and Rose D. Friedman Foundation, 2007).

243. For example, see Susan Saulny, "The Gilded Age of Home Schooling," *New York Times*, June 5, 2006; Zinnie Chen Sampson, "More Black Families Home Schooling," Associated Press report, *Yahoo! News*, Dec. 13, 2005, http://news.yahoo.com/. David Crary, "Public Schools Targeted for Kids' Removal," *Commercial Appeal*, Sept. 3, 2006; Susan Saulny, "Home Schoolers Content to Take Children's Lead," *New York Times*, Nov. 26, 2006.

244. For general discussion, see Michelle Fine, ed., *Chartering Urban School Reform: Reflections on Public High Schools in the Midst of Change* (New York: Teachers College Press, 1994); Diane Ravitch and Joseph P. Viteritti, *New Schools for a New Century: The Redesign of Urban Education* (New Haven: Yale University Press, 1997).

245. See Steinbach and Peirce, "Multiple Choice"; Amy Stuart Wells, "Once a Desegregation Tool, Magnet School Becoming School of Choice," *New York Times,* Jan. 9, 1991; L. M. Hoffman, *Overview of Public Elementary and Secondary Schools and Districts: School Year 2001–02* (Washington, D.C.: National Center for Education Statistics and Common Core of Data, 2003); Lewin, "Chock Full of Choice."

246. Gary Orfield et al, *Dismantling Desegregation,* 241. For another impressive example, see discussion of Fairfax County's Thomas Jefferson High School for Science and Technology in Tyler Currie, "The Quest," *Washington Post,* Aug. 7, 2005.

247. See Steinbach and Peirce, "Multiple Choice"; Amy Stuart Wells, "Once a Desegregation Tool, Magnet School Becoming School of Choice," *New York Times,* Jan. 9, 1991; Lewin, "Chock Full of Choice."

248. *Parents Involved in Community Schools v. Seattle School District No. 1,* 127 S.Ct. 2738 (2007); *Meredith v. Jefferson County Board of Education,* 126 S.Ct. 2351 (2007).

249. See E. M. Gramlich and P. P. Koshel, *Educational Performance Contracting: An Evaluation of an Experiment* (Washington, D.C.: Brookings Institute, 1975).

250. See Lewin, "Chock Full of Choice."

251. Friel, "For-Profit Educators Unite."

252. Jacques Steinberg, "42 Failing Schools in Philadelphia to Be Privatized," *New York Times,* Apr. 18, 2002.

253. Jacques Steinberg, "In Largest Schools Takeover, State Will Run Philadelphia's," *New York Times,* Dec. 22, 2001; "Plan to Privatize School Offices Is Dropped," *New York Times,* Nov. 21, 2001; Steinberg, "42 Failing Schools in Philadelphia to Be Privatized."

254. Steinberg, "42 Failing Schools in Philadelphia to Be Privatized"; Jacques Steinberg, "At 42 Newly Privatized Philadelphia Schools, Uncertainty Abounds," *New York Times,* Apr. 18, 2002; Jacques Steinberg, "Philadelphians Jittery Over Plan to Privatize 20 Schools," *New York Times,* May 20, 2002; Sara Rimer, "Philadelphia Drops a Manager of Five Elementary Schools," *New York Times,* Apr. 18, 2003; Jacques Steinberg, "For-Profit School Venture Has Yet to Turn a Profit," *New York Times,* Apr. 8, 2002; Diana Henriques and Jacques Steinberg, "Woes for Company Running Schools," *New York Times,* May 14, 2002; Jacques Steinberg, "Panel to Safeguard School Management Contracts," *New York Times,* May 16, 2002; "Big Charter School in Boston Breaks Its Ties with Edison," *New York Times,* May 17, 2002; Jacques Steinberg and Diana Henriques, "Edison Schools Gets Reprieve," *New York Times,* June 5, 2002; Jacques Steinberg and Diana Henriques, "Complex Calculations on Academics," *New York Times,* July 16, 2002.

255. See Ray Budde, "The Evolution of the Charter Concept," *Phi Delta Kappan* (Sept. 1996): 72–73. That entire issue of Phi Delta Kappan is devoted to charter schools.

256. See discussion of San Diego's charter efforts in Helen Gao, "Education Makeovers: 3 Underachieving Schools Are Switching to Charters," *San Diego Union-Tribune,* Aug. 15, 2005. As for underfunding, see Sam Dillon, "Backer of Charter Schools Finds They Trail in Financing," *New York Times,* Aug. 23, 2005.

257. Sam Dillon, "Charter Schools Alter Map of Public Education in Dayton," *New York Times,* Mar. 27, 2005. Also see McKinsey and Company, *Creating a World-Class Education System in Ohio* (Washington, D.C.: Achieve, 2007), 67–75.

258. "With New Ideas and Fresh Hope, a Charter School in the Bronx Goes to Work," *New York Times,* Aug. 23, 2000.

259. See Neil MacFarquhar, "Public, but Independent, Schools Inspire Public Hope and Hostility," *New York Times,* Dec. 27, 1996; Lewin, "Chock Full of Choice"; Sara Rimer, "Study Finds Charter Schools Lack Experienced Teachers," *New York Times,* Apr. 8, 2003.

260. For example, see Sam Dillon, "Maverick Leads Charge for Charter Schools," *New York Times,* July 24, 2007.

261. Nathan and Tantillo quoted in MacFarquhar, "Public, but Independent, Schools Inspire Public Hope and Hostility." Also see Joe Nathan, *Charter Schools: Creating Hope and Opportunity in American Education* (San Francisco: Jossey-Bass, 1996). As an example of innovation, ten New York City charter schools recently agreed to participate in a merit-pay experiment funded largely by the U.S. Dept. of Education. See David Herszenhorn, "City Nonprofit Group Gets Money for Merit Pay at Charter Schools," *New York Times,* June 7, 2007.

262. Thernstrom and Thernstrom, *No Excuses.* Also see Robin Barnes, "Black America and School Choice: Charting a New Course," *Yale Law Journal* 106.8 (June 1997): 2403–2433. For another example of a successful inner-city school, see Joseph Berger's analysis of Harlem's George Jackson Academy in Joseph Berger, "A School Frees Low-Income Boys from the Pressures of the Streets," *New York Times,* May 16, 2007.

263. Bruce Fuller et al., *Charter Schools and Inequality* (Berkeley, Calif.: Policy Analysis for California Education, 2003).

264. For example, see Josh Barbanel, "Charter Schools Grow in Suburbs, Uneasily," *New York Times,* May 3, 2003.

265. See MacFarquhar, "Public, But Independent, Schools Inspire Public Hope and Hostility"; Sam Dillon, "Voters to Decide on Charter Schools," *New York Times,* Oct. 25, 2004; Sam Dillon and Diana Jean Schemo, "Charter Schools Fall Short in Public Schools Match Up," *New York Times,* Nov. 23, 2004.

266. See David Herszenhorn, "Patrons' Sway Leads to Friction in Charter School," *New York Times,* June 28, 2007.

267. See Sam Dillon, "Collapse of 60 Charter Schools Leaves Californians Scrambling," *New York Times,* Sept. 17, 2004.

268. See Barbanel, "Charter Schools Grow in Suburbs, Uneasily"; Sam Dillon, "Washington Voters Down New Format for Schools," *New York Times,* Nov. 4, 2004.

269. Quoted in Kate Zernike, "Suburbs Face Tests As Charter Schools Continue to Spread," *New York Times,* Dec. 16, 2000.

270. See Milton Friedman, "The Voucher Idea," *New York Times Magazine,* Sept. 23, 1973, 22–72; Henry Levin, "Why Ghetto Schools Fail," in Heidenreich, *Urban Education,* 257–62; *Education Week,* July 10, 1996; Theodore Forstmann and Bruce Korver,

"How to Energize Education," *New York Times,* Jan. 3, 1998; Charles Wheelan, "Turning the Tables on School Choice," *New York Times,* May 25, 1999; Jodi Wilgoren, "Young Blacks Turn to Vouchers As Civil Rights Issue," *New York Times,* Oct. 9, 2000; Milton Friedman, "The Market Can Transform Our Schools," *New York Times,* July 2, 2000." Also see Paul E. Peterson and Jay P. Greene, "Race Relations and Central City Schools: It's Time for an Experiment with Vouchers," *Brookings Review* 16.2 (Spring 1998): 33–37; Michael Janofsky, "Parents Lead Way As States Debate School Vouchers," *New York Times,* Jan. 31, 2000; Michael Leo Owens, "Why Blacks Support Vouchers," *New York Times,* Feb. 26, 2002; Brian Friel, "Public or Private Schools? It's Your Choice," *National Journal,* Jan. 8, 2005, 34.

271. See Susan Goerlich Zief et al., *Systematic Review of the Research on Market-Based Choice Plans* (Washington, D.C.: GPO, 2005); Paul Peterson, "School Choice: A Report Card," *Virginia Journal of Social Policy and the Law* 6.1 (1998): 47–80; Damien Cave and Josh Benson, "Voucher Issue a Touchy Topic in Newark Race," *New York Times,* Apr. 17, 2006.

272. Paul Peterson and Martin West, "Power of the Voucher," *New York Sun,* Apr. 11, 2005; Sam Dillon, "Florida Supreme Court Blocks School Vouchers," *New York Times,* Jan. 6, 2006; Robin Pogrebin, "GOP Lawmakers Deal a Setback to Governor Bush in Florida," *New York Times,* May 13, 2006; Associated Press, "Broad Voucher Plan Is Approved in Utah," *New York Times,* Feb. 11, 2007.

273. Applebome, "School Choice Changing Face of U.S. Education"; Liu, "Real Options for School Choice"; Janofsky, "Parents Lead Way As States Debate School Vouchers"; Jodi Wilgoren, "School Voucher Proponents Redefining Their Terms," *Commercial Appeal,* Dec. 25, 2000; David Bositis, "School Vouchers along the Color Line," *New York Times,* Aug. 15, 2001; Owens, "Why Blacks Support Vouchers"; Richard Rothstein, "Yes, Vouchers Are Dead, and Alternatives Flawed," *New York Times,* June 20, 2001.

274. See "House Approves a Voucher Plan for Poor Washington Students," *New York Times,* Sept. 6, 2003; Friel, "Public or Private Schools?" 33–35.

275. Goodwin Liu, "Real Options for School Choice," *New York Times,* Dec. 4, 2002.

276. See Friel, "Public or Private Schools?" 34–35; William Raspberry, "Point-and-Click Solutions," *Commercial Appeal,* Mar. 12, 2000; John Levy, *Urban America: Processes and Problems* (Upper Saddle River, N.J.: Prentice Hall, 2000), 287–88.

277. Christopher Jencks et al., *Education Vouchers,* Cambridge, Mass.: Center for the Study of Public Policy, 1970.

278. See Diana Jean Schemo, "Public Schools Perform Near Private Ones in Study," *New York Times,* July 15, 2006. For evidence of some marginal advantages of Catholic schools teaching minority youths, see Andrew Greeley, *Catholic High Schools and Minority Students* (Edison, N.J.: Transaction Publishers, 2002).

279. Follick, "Florida Supreme Court Takes Up Vouchers."

280. *Zelman v. Simmons-Harris* 534 U.S. 1077 (2002). Also see *Jackson v. Benson* 525 U.S. 997 (1998).

281. See Samuel Freedman, "Newark's School Choices Grow Bleaker," *New York Times*, June 21, 2006. For a more comprehensive evaluation, see William Howell and Paul Peterson, *The Education Gap: Vouchers and Urban Schools* (Baltimore: Brookings Institute Press, 2005).

282. For example, see Zief et al., *Systematic Review of the Research on Market-Based Choice Plans*.

283. Mark Schneider et al., *Choosing Schools: Consumer Choice and the Quality of American Schools* (Princeton, N.J.: Princeton University Press, 2000); Paul Teske and Mark Schneider, "What Research Can Tell Policymakers About School Choice," *Journal of Policy Analysis and Management* 20.4 (2001): 609–31; Mark Schneider and Jack Buckley, "What Do Parents Want from Schools?" (paper presented at the annual meeting of the Midwest Political Science Association, Chicago, Apr. 2002); Martin West and Paul Peterson, "The Efficacy of Choice Threats within School Accountability Systems" (paper presented at the Annual Conference of the Royal Economic Society, University of Nottingham, Mar. 2005); Peterson and West, "Power of the Voucher"; Joseph Viteritti, "Schoolyard Revolutions: How Research on Urban School Reform Undermines Reform," *Political Science Quarterly* 118.2 (2003): 233–59; William Howell et al., "Test-Score Effects of School Vouchers in Dayton, Ohio, New York City, and Washington, D.C.: Evidence from Randomized Field Studies" (paper presented at the annual meeting of the American Political Science Association, Washington, D.C., Sept. 2000); Christopher and Sarah Theule Lubienski, "A New Look at Public and Private Schools: Student Background and Mathematics Achievement, *Phi Delta Kappan* 86.9 (2005): 696–99; Sarah Theule Lubienski, "Examining Instruction, Achievement and Equity with NAEP Mathematics Data," *Education Policy Analysis Archives* 14.14 (2006): 1–39.

284. Quoted in Wycliff, "Right to Choose School Gains in Cities." Also see Jodi Wilgoren, "Schools Are Now Marketers Where Choice Is Taking Hold," *New York Times*, Apr. 20, 2001.

285. For example, see Steinbach and Peirce, "Multiple Choice"; Wells, "Once a Desegregation Tool, Magnet School Becoming School of Choice"; Orfield, *Dismantling Desegregation*, 256–61.

286. Caroline Hoxby, *Achievement in Charter Schools and Regular Public Schools in the United States: Understanding the Differences* (Harvard University paper, http://post.economics.harvard.edu/faculty/hoxby/papers/hoxbycharter_dec.pdf); Caroline Hoxby, *A Straightforward Comparison of Charter Schools and Regular Schools in the United States* (Harvard University paper, http://post.economics.harvard.edu/faculty/hoxby/papers/charters_040909.pdf); Francis Shen and Kenneth Wong, "Charter Law and Charter Outcomes: Re-Examining the Charter School Marketplace" (paper presented at the National Conference on Charter School Research, Nashville, Tenn., Sept. 2006); Bryan Hassel, *Charter School Achievement: What We Know* (Washington, D.C.: Charter School Leadership Council, 2005).

287. See Timothy Egan, "Failures Raise Questions for Charter Schools," *New York Times*, Apr. 5, 2002; Greg Toppo, "Charter School Students Are Scoring Poorly," *Commercial*

Appeal, Sept. 3, 2002; Diana Jean Schemo, "Nation's Charter Schools Lagging Behind, U.S. Test Scores Reveal," *New York Times,* Apr. 17, 2004; "Bad News on the Charter Front," *New York Times,* Aug. 18, 2004; Diana Jean Schemo, "A Second Report Shows Charter School Students Not Performing as Well as Other Students," *New York Times,* Dec. 16, 2004; Francis Clines, "Re-Educating the Voters About Texas' Schools," *New York Times,* June 3, 2003; Dillon and Diana Jean Schemo, "Charter Schools Fall Short in Public Schools Match Up"; K. R. Howe and S. S. Foster, *An Assessment of Colorado's Charter Schools: Implications for Policy* (Boulder, Colo.: EPIC Policy Center, 2005); A. R. Contreras, "Charter School Movement in California and Elsewhere," *Education and Urban Society* 27.2 (1995): 213–28; T. L. Good and J. S. Braden, *The Great School Debate: Choice, Vouchers, and Charters* (Mahwah, N.J.: Lawrence Erlbaum, 2000), 137, 173–74; Rimer, "Study Finds Charter Schools Lack Experienced Teachers"; Michael Winerip, "When It Goes Wrong at a Charter School," *New York Times,* Mar. 5, 2003; "Exploding the Charter School Myth," *New York Times,* Aug. 27, 2006; Diana Jean Schemo, "Study of Test Scores Finds Charter Schools Lagging," *New York Times,* Aug. 23, 2006.

288. See Steinberg and Henriques, "Complex Calculations on Academics"; Schemo, "A Second Report Shows Charter School Students Not Performing as Well as Other Students"; Edward Wyatt, "Higher Scores Aren't Cure-All, a For-Profit School Discovers," *New York Times,* Mar. 13, 2001.

289. Gramlich and Koshel, *Educational Performance Contracting.*

290. See Tamar Lewin, "School Voucher Study Finds Satisfaction," *New York Times,* Sept. 18, 1997; Janofsky, "Parents Lead Way As States Debate School Vouchers"; Sam Dillon, "Voucher Use in Washington Wins Praise of Parents," *New York Times,* June 22, 2007.

291. William Howell and Paul Peterson, *The Education Gap: Vouchers and Urban Schools* (Washington, D.C.: Brookings Institution, 2002); Edward Wyatt, "Study Finds Higher Test Scores among Blacks with Vouchers," *New York Times,* Aug. 29, 2000; Paul Peterson and William Howell, "Voucher Programs and the Effect of Ethnicity on Test Scores," in Chubb and Loveless, *Bridging the Achievement Gap,* 47–73.

292. Quoted in Friel, "Public or Private Schools?" 35; Richard Rothstein, "Judging Vouchers' Merits Proves to Be Difficult Task," *New York Times,* Dec. 13, 2000; Tamar Lewin, "Few Clear Lessons from Nation's First School-Choice Program," *New York Times,* Mar. 27, 1999; Richard Rothstein, "Failed Schools? The Meaning Is Unclear," *New York Times,* July 3, 2002; Michael Winerip, "What a Voucher Study Truly Showed, and Why," *New York Times,* May 7, 2003; Sam Dillon, "Report Defends Vouchers but Fails to Quell Debate," *New York Times,* June 13, 2003; Patrick Wolf, "Looking Inside the Black Box: What School Factors Explain Voucher Gains in Washington, D.C." (paper presented at the annual meeting of the American Political Science Association, Philadelphia, Aug. 2003); Kevin Smith, "Data Don't Matter? Academic Research and School Choice," *Perspectives on Politics* 3.2 (June 2005): 285–99; Good and Braden, *The Great School Debate,* 99, 110.

293. Brian Gill et al., *Rhetoric Versus Reality: What We Know and What We Need to Know About Vouchers and Charter Schools* (Santa Monica: Rand, 2001); Jeanne

Powers and Peter Cookson, "The Politics of School Choice Research: Fact, Fiction, and Statistics ," *Educational Policy* 13.1 (1999): 104–22.

294. Quoted in Janofsky, "Parents Lead Way As States Debate School Vouchers." Also see Barbara Miner, "The False Promise of School Vouchers," *Tri-State Defender,* Mar. 8–13, 2002.

295. See "Reinventing High School," *New York Times,* Feb. 1, 2005; John Weidman, "Facilitating the Transition from School to Work," in B. Jones and K. Borman, eds., *Investing in U.S. Schools: Directions for Educational Policy* (Norwood, N.J.: Ablex, 1994), 37–49.

296. Aimee Edmondson, "Board Approves State's 1st Charter School," *Commercial Appeal,* Jan. 28, 2003; Karin Miller, "First Charter Schools Prepare for Challenge," *Commercial Appeal,* Aug. 3, 2003; "Panel Expands Charter Schools," *Commercial Appeal,* Apr. 28, 2005. As of October 2006, Memphis had ten charter schools and had applied for its eleventh.

297. See Halimah Abdullah, "Charter School Re-rejected," *Commercial Appeal,* Dec. 17, 2005.

298. Aimee Edmondson, "Watson Working to Create Memphis KIPP," *Commercial Appeal,* Mar. 6, 2001; Aimee Edmondson, "KIPP Middle School Is Ready to Go Year-round, Saturdays," *Commercial Appeal,* June 13, 2002; Kevin McKenzie, "After Its First Year, Innovative KIPP School Gets High Marks," *Commercial Appeal,* July 22, 2003; Jodi Wilgoren, "After Success with Poor, Schools Try Cloning," *New York Times,* Aug. 16, 2000; Bob Herbert, "KIPP Schools Offer a Chance to Work Hard and to Learn," *New York Times,* Dec. 16, 2002.

299. Ruma Banerji, "Year-round Classes May Be Thing of Past," *Commercial Appeal,* Apr. 15, 2003.

300. For example, see the articles on Cherokee Elementary's "Co-nect" program, in the *Commercial Appeal,* June 4, 2001; and W. L. Sanders et al., *Value-Added Achievement Results for Three Cohorts of Roots and Wings Schools in Memphis: 1995–1999 Outcomes* (Memphis: University of Memphis Center for Research in Educational Policy, 2000). Also see Mayor W. W. Herenton's critical comments concerning the House reforms in Aimee Edmondson, "Mayor Backs Watson to Lead Schools," *Commercial Appeal,* Aug. 30, 2000.

301. For example, see Jimmie Covington, "Memphis Magnet Strong Attraction to Children, Parents," *Commercial Appeal,* Apr. 23, 1978; Jimmie Covington, "Parents Begin 'Camping in' for Space in Optional Schools," *Commercial Appeal,* Feb. 1, 1989; Michael Erskine, "Told There Are No Limits, Delano Students Excel," *Commercial Appeal,* June 6, 2001.

302. For example, see Toni Hampton, "Choosy Parents Use Community Report Card," *Commercial Appeal,* Apr. 25, 2006.

303. For example, see John Branston, "School Choice in Memphis," *Memphis Flyer,* Nov. 4–10, 2004, 9; Michael Erskine, "Energizing leader 'Dr. T' credits success to elite kids," *Commercial Appeal,* June 7, 2001.

Chapter 7
Conclusions

1. William Julius Wilson, "Commentary" in Jencks and Phillips, *The Black-White Test Score Gap*, 510.

2. See Michael Danielson and Jennifer Hochschild, "Changing Urban Education: Lessons, Cautions, and Prospects," in Clarence Stone, ed., *Changing Urban Education* (Lawrence: University Press of Kansas, 1998).

3. Greg Duncan and Jeanne Brooks-Gunn, eds., *Consequences of Growing Up Poor* (New York: Russell Sage, 1997), 608.

4. Testimony of Harry Holzer, before the House Ways and Means Committee's hearing on the Economic and Societal Costs of Poverty, Jan. 24, 2007. See Erik Eckholm, "Childhood Poverty Is Found to Portend High Adult Costs," *New York Times,* Jan. 25, 2007.

5. "What Lasting Difference Will a 'Living Wage' Really Make?, *Tri-State Defender,* July 10–14, 2006.

6. Steven Greenhouse, "Can't Wal-Mart, a Retail Behemoth, Pay More?" *New York Times,* May 4, 2005.

7. For example, see Ann Flanagan and David Grissmer, "The Role of Federal Resources in Closing the Achievement Gap," in John Chubb and Tom Loveless, eds., *Bridging the Achievement Gap* (Washington, D.C.: Brookings, 2002), 199–226.

8. For example, see the Tri-State Defender editorial, "What Lasting Difference Will a 'Living Wage' Really Make? *Tri-State Defender,* July 10–14, 2006.

9. See Bruce Stokes, "Jobless, the Danish Way," *National Journal,* Mar. 4, 2006, 28–34.

10. Stokes, "Jobless, the Danish Way," 30. Paul Krugman calls for an American variant in Paul Krugman, "Divided Over Trade," *New York Times,* May 14, 2007.

11. For a recent discussion, see Daniel Glover, "Prevailing Views on Prevailing Wages," *National Journal,* Oct. 8, 2005, 3108.

12. See Magen Howard, "Petitions Push City for Hourly Minimum Pay," *Commercial Appeal,* July 24, 2005.

13. For example, see Dalton Conley, "Turning the Tax Tables to Help the Poor," *New York Times,* Nov. 15, 2004.

14. Center for American Progress, *From Poverty to Prosperity: A National Strategy to Cut Poverty in Half* (Washington, D.C. Center for American Progress, 2007). For reactions, see Erik Eckholm, "Group Proposes Detailed Plan to Reduce Poverty in Half," *New York Times,* Apr. 25, 2007.

15. For example, see Paul Hill, Christine Campbell, and James Harvey, *It Takes a City: Getting Serious about Urban School Reform* (Washington, D.C.: Brookings Institute, 2000), 25.

16. Madaus quoted in Chira, "Study Finds Standardized Tests May Hurt Education Efforts."

17. James Ryan, "Schools, Race, and Money," *Yale Law Review* 109 (1999): 327.

18. For example, see Associated Press, "Schools Offering Day Care Centers," *New York Times,* Aug. 25, 2007.

19. Samuel Casey Carter, *No Excuses: Lessons from 21 High-Performing, High-Poverty Schools* (Washington, D.C.: Heritage Foundation, 2000).

20. Alex Molnar, et al., "Wisconsin's SAGE Program and Achievement through Small Classes," in Chubb and Loveless, *Bridging the Achievement Gap,* 91–108; Frederick Mosteller, "The Tennessee Study of Class Size in the Early Grades," *Future of Children* 5.2 (Summer 1995): 113–27; Frederick Mosteller et al., "Sustained Inquiry in Education: Lessons from Skill Grouping and Class Size," *Harvard Educational Review* 66.4 (1996): 797–842; Eugene Lewitt and Linda Schumann Baker, "Class Size," *Future of Children* 7.3 (1997): 112–21.

21. Heather Peske and Kati Haycock, *Teaching Inequality: How Poor and Minority Students Are Shortchanged on Teacher Quality* (Washington, D.C.: Education Trust, June 2006); Sanders and Rivers, *Cumulative and Residual Effects of Teachers,* 6; Ronald Ferguson, "Can Schools Narrow the Black-White Test Scores Gap?" in Jencks and Phillips, *The Black-White Test Score Gap,* 318–74; Linda Darling-Hammond, "Teacher Quality and Student Achievement: A Review of State Policy Evidence," University of Washington, Center for the Study of Teaching and Policy, R-99-1 (December 1999). Also see Michele Foster, *Black Teachers on Teaching* (New York: New Press, 1997).

22. Quoted in Sam Dillon, "Imported from Britain: Ideas to Improve Schools," *New York Times,* Aug. 15, 2007.

23. For example, see Harris Cooper et al., "The Effects of Summer Vacation on Achievement Test Scores: A Narrative and Meta-analytic Review," *Review of Educational Research* 66.3 (1996): 227–68; Barbara Heyns, "Schooling and Cognitive Development: Is There a Season for Learning?" *Child Development* 58 (1987): 1151–60; Doris Entwisle and Karl Alexander, "Winter Setback: The Racial Composition of Schools and Learning to Read," *American Sociological Review* 59 (June 1994): 446–60; Gerald Bracey, "Schools Are Not 'Failing' Poor Kids," *Washington Post,* Jan. 18, 2002.

24. Casey, *No Excuses,* 5.

25. Quoted in Leonard Pitts Jr., "What Works: Think Big about the Little Ones," *Commercial Appeal,* Jan. 29, 2007. Also see, for example, Daniel Aladjem and Kathryn Borman, eds., *Examining Comprehensive School Reform* (Washington, D.C.: Urban Institute Press, 2006).

26. See Marcus Pohlmann, Joy Clay, and Kenneth Goings, *School Consolidation: State of Tennessee,* report prepared for Johnnie B. Watson, superintendent, Memphis City Schools, July 2001.

27. See Blake Fontenay, "Unified School Plan Calls for 5 Divisions," *Commercial Appeal,* Mar. 18, 2003.

28. For examples, see Heidenreich, *Urban Education,* section 3.

29. Michael Danielson and Jennifer Hochschild, "Changing Urban Education: Lessons, Cautions, Prospects," in Clarence Stone, ed., *Changing Urban Education* (Lawrence: University Press of Kansas, 1998), 293; Simpson, "Report Finds Unhappiness."

30. For example, see Tony Jones, "Mayor Wants Community Involvement in Consolidation Debate Here," *Tri-State Defender,* Mar. 3–7, 2001; Blake Fontenay, "Unified School Plan Calls for 5 Divisions," *Commercial Appeal,* Mar. 18, 2003.

31. See Allan Ornstein et al., *Reforming Metropolitan Schools* (Pacific Palisades, Calif.: Goodyear Publishing, 1975), chap. 5. Amy Stuart Wells and Robert Crain, *Stepping Over the Color Line: African-American Students in White Suburban Schools* (New Haven: Yale University Press, 1997); Janet Ward Schofield, "Review of Research on School Desegregation's Impact on Elementary and Secondary School Students," in James Banks, ed., *Handbook of Research on Multicultural Education* (New York: Macmillan, 1995); Rita Mahard and Robert Crain, "Research on Minority Achievement in Desegregated Schools," in Christine Rossell and Williss Hawley, eds., *The Consequences of School Desegregation* (Philadelphia: Temple University Press, 1983), 103–25; Sara Rimer, "Schools Try Integration by Income, Not Race," *New York Times,* May 8, 2003; Alan Finder, "As Test Scores Jump, Raleigh Credits Integration by Income," *New York Times,* Sept. 25, 2005; "Ever Higher Society."

32. Mark Schneider et al., *Choosing Schools: Consumer Choice and the Quality of American Schools* (Princeton, N.J.: Princeton University Press, 2000); Paul Teske and Mark Schneider, "What Research Can Tell Policymakers About School Choice," *Journal of Policy Analysis and Management* 20.4 (2001): 609–31; Mark Schneider and Jack Buckley, "What Do Parents Want from Schools?" (paper presented at the annual meeting of the Midwest Political Science Association, Chicago, Apr. 2002); Martin West and Paul Peterson, "The Efficacy of Choice Threats within School Accountability Systems" (paper presented at the Annual Conference of the Royal Economic Society, University of Nottingham, Mar. 2005); Peterson and West, "Power of the Voucher"; Joseph Viteritti, "Schoolyard Revolutions: How Research on Urban School Reform Undermines Reform," *Political Science Quarterly* 118.2 (2003): 233–59; William Howell et al., "Test-Score Effects of School Vouchers in Dayton, Ohio, New York City, and Washington, D.C.: Evidence from Randomized Field Studies" (paper presented at the annual meeting of the American Political Science Association, Washington, D.C., Sept. 2000); Christopher and Sarah Theule Lubienski, "A New Look at Public and Private Schools: Student Background and Mathematics Achievement, *Phi Delta Kappan* 86.9 (2005): 696–99; Sarah Theule Lubienski, "Examining Instruction, Achievement and Equity with NAEP Mathematics Data," *Education Policy Analysis Archives* 14.14 (2006): 1–39; Friel, "Public or Private Schools?" 35; Richard Rothstein, "Judging Vouchers' Merits Proves to Be Difficult Task," *New York Times,* Dec. 13, 2000; Tamar Lewin, "Few Clear Lessons from Nation's First School-Choice Program," *New York Times,* Mar. 27, 1999; Rothstein, "Failed Schools?"; Michael Winerip, "What a Voucher Study Truly Showed, and Why," *New York Times,* May 7, 2003; Sam Dillon, "Report Defends Vouchers but Fails to Quell Debate," *New York Times,* June 13, 2003; Patrick Wolf, "Looking Inside the Black Box: What School Factors Explain Voucher Gains in Washington, D.C." (paper presented at the annual meeting of the American Political Science Association, Philadelphia, Aug. 2003); Kevin Smith, "Data Don't Matter? Academic Research and School Choice," *Perspectives on Politics* 3.2 (June 2005): 285–99; Good and Braden, *The Great School*

Debate, 99, 110; Brian Gill et al., *Rhetoric Versus Reality: What We Know and What We Need to Know About Vouchers and Charter Schools* (Santa Monica: Rand, 2001); Jeanne Powers and Peter Cookson, "The Politics of School Choice Research: Fact, Fiction, and Statistics ," *Educational Policy* 13.1 (1999): 104–22; Janofsky, "Parents Lead Way As States Debate School Vouchers." Also see Barbara Miner, "The False Promise of School Vouchers," *Tri-State Defender,* Mar. 8–13, 2002.

33. Interviews with David Sojourner, longtime director of Student Information of the Memphis City Schools.

34. Ruma Banerji Kumar, "Schools Could Get Sweeping Changes," *Commercial Appeal,* Jan. 20, 2006.

35. See Ruma Banji Kumar, "Keeping the Faith," *Commercial Appeal,* Dec. 10, 2004.

36. See Ruma Banji Kumar, "Schools See Work Pay Off," *Commercial Appeal,* Aug. 2, 2005.

37. See Ruma Banerji Kumar, "Retired Teachers Bring an Expert's Touch to Classroom," *Commercial Appeal,* Mar. 13, 2006.

38. See Halimah Abdullah, "Early-Education Classes Cross Language, Income Barriers," *Commercial Appeal,* Sept. 26, 2005.

39. Quoted in Jon Sparks and Bill Dries, "Herenton Hits Racial Nerve on Schools," *Commercial Appeal,* Feb. 25, 2005.

40. See Anna Bernasek, "What's the Return on Education?" *New York Times,* Dec. 11, 2005.

41. Quoted in Jodi Wilgoren, "National Study Examines Reasons Why Pupils Excel," *New York Times,* July 27, 2000.

42. David Grissmer et al., *Improving Student Achievement* (Santa Monica: Rand Corporation, 2000).

43. See Paul Tough, "The Harlem Project," *New York Times,* June 20, 2004.

44. David Broder, "National Education Fix Needs Some Big Ideas," *Commercial Appeal,* Aug. 29, 2005.

45. See James Ryan, "Schools, Race, and Money," *Yale Law Review* 109 (1999): 249–311.

46. For example, see Orfield and Eaton, *Dismantling Desegregation,* 54; Leah Wells, "Little Income Makes Big Difference in Schools," *Commercial Appeal,* May 9, 2007.

47. See Douglas Rooks, "EPS: The Bedrock for School Funding Decisions," *Choices: Ideas for Shared Prosperity* 13.4 (May 2007): 1–6.

48. Gallup Poll, Aug. 24, 2006.

49. Quoted in Debra Nussbaum, "Connecting with the Voters on Bond Issues," *New York Times,* June 17, 2007.

50. For example, see "Keeping the Faith with AmeriCorps," *New York Times,* June 17, 2006.

51. For example, see McKinsey and Company, *Creating a World-Class Education System in Ohio* (Washington, D.C.: Achieve, 2007), 49–56.

52. For example, see Henry Louis Gates Jr., "Breaking the Silence," *New York Times*, Aug. 1, 2004.

53. Arthur Levine, *Educating School Teachers* (Washington D.C.: Education Schools Project, Report #2, Sept. 2006). See Alan Finder, "Report Critical of Training of Teachers," *New York Times*, Sept. 19, 2006.

54. For example, see Sam Dillon, "Long Reviled, Merit Pay Gains among Teachers," *New York Times*, June 18, 2007; Nancy Zuckerbrod, "Rules for Teachers Fail Test," *Commercial Appeal*, June 27, 2007.

55. "Crisis in Education: Investing in the Children of Memphis and Shelby County," report of the Memphis NAACP, submitted to Federal District Judge Robert McCrae, Memphis, Oct. 10, 1988, pp. 6–13.

Bibliography

Abramson, Paul, John Aldrich, and David Rhode. *Change and Continuity in the 1980 Election.* Washington, D.C.: Congressional Quarterly Press, 1982.

Adams, Michelle Miller. *Owning Up: Poverty, Assets and the American Dream.* Washington, D.C.: Brookings Institution Press, 2002.

Adkins, Walter. "Beale Street Goes to the Polls." Ph.D. diss., Ohio State University Press, 1935.

Adrian, Charles, and Oliver Williams. *Four Cities.* Philadelphia: University of Pennsylvania Press, 1961.

Alford, Robert, and Eugene Lee. "Voting Turnout in American Cities." *American Political Science Review* 62.3 (1968): 796–813.

Alger, Horatio. *Luck and Pluck; Or, the Progress of Walter Conrad.* New York: Pavillion Press, 2003.

———. *Ragged Dick; Or, Street Life in New York with the Boot Blacks.* New York: Signet Classics, 1990.

———. *Tattered Tom; Or, the Story of a Street Arab.* Philadelphia: Polyglot Press, 2002.

Alinsky, Saul. *Rules for Radicals.* New York: Random House, 1971.

Allanach, Ron. "A Tale of Two Schools." *Principal Leadership: Middle School Ed.* 2.9 (May 2002): 6–9.

Allen, Robert. *Our Fair City.* New York: Vanguard, 1947.

American Diploma Project. *Ready or Not: Creating a High School Diploma That Counts.* Washington, D.C.: Achieve, 2004.

Anderson, James. *The Education of Blacks in the South, 1860–1935.* Chapel Hill: University of North Carolina Press, 1988.

Anyon, Jean. *Ghetto Schooling: A Political Economy of Urban Educational Reform.* New York: Teachers College Press, 1997.

Applebaum, Eileen, Annette Bernhardt, and Richard Murnane, *Low-Wage America: How Employers Are Reshaping Opportunity in the Workplace.* New York: Russell Sage, 2006.

Applebome, Peter. "School Choice Changing Face of U.S. Education." *Commercial Appeal,* Sept. 4, 1996.

Archibald, Douglas, and Fred Newman. *Beyond Standardized Testing: Assessing Authentic Achievement in the Secondary School.* Reston, Va.: National Association of Secondary School Principals, undated.

Arnott, Margaret, and Charles Raab. *Governance of Schooling: Comparative Studies of Devolved Management.* New York: Routledge Falmer, 2000.

Artilles, Alfredo, and Grace Zamora-Duran, eds. *Reducing Disproportionate Representation of Culturally Diverse Students in Special and Gifted Education.* Reston, Va.: Council for Exceptional Children, 1997.

Astin, Alexander. *The Myth of Equal Access to Higher Education.* Atlanta: Southern Education Foundation, 1975.

Baker, Elizabeth Lassiter, and Linda Brown Porter. *A Parent's Guide to Memphis Area Private Schools: 1973 Edition.* Memphis: Barton Press, 1973.

Bane, Mary Jo, and David Ellwood. *Welfare Realities: From Rhetoric to Reform.* Cambridge, Mass.: Harvard University, 1994.

Banks, James, ed. *Handbook of Research on Multicultural Education.* New York: Macmillan, 1995.

Bankston III, Carl, and Stephen Caldas. *A Troubled Dream: The Promise and Failure of School Desegregation in Louisiana.* Nashville: Vanderbilt University Press, 2001.

Barber, Michael, and Ruth Dann, eds. *Raising Educational Standards in the Inner Cities: Practical Initiatives in Action.* New York: Cassell, 1996.

Barnett, W. Stephen, and Sarano Spence Boocock, eds. *Early Care and Education for Children in Poverty: Promises, Programs, and Long-Term Results.* Albany: State University of New York Press, 1998.

Barton, Paul, and Richard Coley, *The Family: America's Smallest School.* Princeton: Educational Testing Service, 2007.

Beifuss, Joan. *At the River I Stand.* Memphis: B & W Books, 1985.

Bell, Daniel. *The Coming of the Post-Industrial Society.* New York: Basic Books, 1975.

Benveniste, Luis, Martin Carnoy, and Richard Rothstein. *All Else Equal: Are Public and Private Schools Different?* New York: Taylor and Francis Publishing, 2002.

Berkeley, Kathleen. *"Like a Plague of Locusts": Immigration and Social Change in Memphis, Tennessee.* Los Angeles: UCLA Press, 1980.

Berlin, Ira. *Slaves without Masters.* New York: Pantheon, 1974.

Berliner, David, and Bruce Biddle. *The Manufactured Crisis: Myths, Fraud, and the Attack on America's Public Schools.* Reading, Mass.: Addison-Wesley, 1995.

Bernstein, Jared, et al. *Pulling Apart: State-by-State Analysis of Income Trends.* Washington, D.C.: Economic Policy Institute, Center on Budget and Policy Priorities, 2006.

Berrueta-Clement, John. ed. *Changed Lives: The Effects of the Perry Preschool Program on Youths Through Age 19 (Monographs of the High/Scope Educational Research Foundation #8).* Ypsilanti, Mich.: High/Scope Press, 1984.

Berry, Gordon. *Strategies for Successful Teaching in Urban Schools: Ideas and Techniques from Central City Teachers.* Palo Alto: R & E Research Associates, 1982.

Berube, Maurice. *American School Reform: Progressive, Equity, and Excellence Movements, 1883–1993.* Westport, Conn.: Praeger, 1994.

Biles, Roger. *Memphis in the Great Depression.* Knoxville: University of Tennessee Press, 1986.

Black, Earl, and Merle Black. *Politics and Society in the South.* Cambridge, Mass.: Harvard University Press, 1987.

Bloom, Benjamin. *Stability and Change in Human Characteristics.* New York: John Wiley, 1964.

Bollens, John, and Henry Schmandt. *The Metropolis.* New York: Harper Collins, 1982.

Bond, Horace Mann. *The Education of the Negro in the American Social Order.* Englewood Cliffs, N.J.: Prentice-Hall, 1934.

———. *Negro Education in Alabama: A Study in Cotton and Steel.* New York: Associate Publishers, 1939.

Bowles, Samuel. "Unequal Education and the Reproduction of the Hierarchical Division of Labor." In *The Capitalist System: A Radical Analysis of American Society,* ed. Richard Edwards. Englewood Cliffs, N.J.: Prentice-Hall, 1972, 218–29.

Bowles, Samuel, et al. *Unequal Chances: Family Background and Economic Success.* Princeton, N.J.: Princeton University Press, 2005.

Brantlinger, Ellen. *Dividing Classes: How the Middle Class Negotiates and Rationalizes School Advantage.* New York: Taylor and Francis Publishing, 2003.

Brown, Cynthia, et al. *Getting Smarter, Becoming Fairer.* Washington, D.C.: Center for American Progress, 2005.

Brownell, Blaine, and David Goldfield. *The City in Southern History.* Port Washington, N.Y.: Kennikat Press, 1977.

Browning, Rufus, Dale Rogers Marshall, and David Tabb. "Minority Mobilization in Ten Cities: Failures and Success." In *Black Electoral Politics,* ed. Lucius Barker. New Brunswick, N.J.: Transaction Books, 1990, 8–32.

———. *Racial Politics in American Cities.* New York: Longman Publishers, 2002.

Bryk, Anthony, et al. *Chartering Chicago School Reform.* Boulder, Colo.: Westview Press, 1998.

Bullard, Robert, ed. *In Search of the New South: The Black Urban Experience in the 1970s and 1980s.* Tuscaloosa: University of Alabama Press, 1989.

Butchart, Ronald. *Northern Schools, Southern Blacks, and Reconstruction: Freedmen's Education, 1862–1875.* Westport, Conn.: Greenwood Press, 1980.

Capers, Gerald, Jr. *The Biography of a River Town. Memphis: Its Historic Age.* Chapel Hill: University of North Carolina Press, 1939.

Carnoy, Martin. *Faded Dreams: The Politics and Economics of Race in America.* New York: Cambridge University Press, 1994.

Carter, Robert. "Reimagining Race in Education: A New Paradigm from Psychology." *Teachers College Record* 102.5 (2000): 864–97.

Carter, Samuel Casey. *No Excuses: Lessons from 21 High Performing, High Poverty Schools.* Washington, D.C.: Heritage Foundation, 2001.

Cashin, Sheryll. *The Failures of Integration: How Race and Class Are Undermining the American Dream.* New York: Public Affairs Books, 2005.

Castells, Manuel. *The Information Age: Economy, Society, and Culture.* New York: Oxford University Press, 2000.

Castells, Manuel, et al. *Critical Education in the New Information Age.* Lanham, Md.: Rowman and Littlefield, 1999.

Cauthen, Nancy, et al. *Map and Track: State Initiatives for Young Children and Families.* New York: National Center for Children in Poverty, 2000.

Chambers, Stephanie. *Mayors and Schools: Minority Voices and Democratic Tensions in Urban Education.* Philadelphia: Temple University Press, 2006.

Chubb, John, and Terry Moe. *Politics, Markets, and American Schools.* Washington, D.C.: Brookings, 1990.

Chubb, John, and Tom Loveless, eds. *Bridging the Achievement Gap.* Washington D.C.: Brookings Institution Press, 2002.

Chudacoff, Howard. *The Evolution of American Urban Society.* Englewood Cliffs, N.J.: Prentice-Hall, 1981.

Church, Annette, and Roberta Church. *The Robert R. Churches.* Ann Arbor: University of Michigan Press, 1974.

Claydon, Leslie. *Renewing Urban Teaching.* New York: Cambridge University Press, 1973.

Coleman, James, and Sara Kelly. "Education." In *The Urban Predicament,* ed. William Gorham and Nathan Glazer. Washington, D.C.: Urban Institute, 1976, 231–80.

Comer, James. *School Power: Implications of an Intervention Project.* New York: Free Press, 1980.

———. *Waiting for a Miracle.* New York: Penguin Putnam, 1997.

Conant, James. *The American High School Today: A First Report to Interested Students.* New York: McGraw Hill, 1959.

Consortium for Longitudinal Studies. *As the Twig Is Bent: Lasting Effects of Preschool Programs.* Hillsdale, N.J.: Lawrence Erlbaum Associates, 1983.

Cornelius, Janet Duitsman. *When I Can Read My Title Clear: Literacy, Slavery, and Religion in the Antebellum South.* Columbia, S.C.: University of South Carolina Press, 1991.

Corwin, Miles. *And Still We Rise: The Trials and Triumphs of 12 Inner-City Students.* Minneapolis, Minn.: Econo-Clad Books, 2001.

Council of Great City Schools. *Closing the Achievement Gaps in Urban Schools: A Survey of Academic Progress and Promising Practices in the Great City Schools.* Washington, D.C.: Council of Great City Schools, 1999.

Cowan, Thomas. *Values and Policy in Shelby County, Tennessee.* Memphis: Christian Brothers College Study, 1979.

Cronin, John, et al. *The Impact of the No Child Left Behind Act on Student Achievement and Growth: 2005 Edition.* Lake Oswego, Oreg.: Northwest Evaluation Association, 2005.

Cross, Theodore, and Robert Bruce Slater. *The Alarming Decline in Academic Performance of African American Men.* New York: Journal of Blacks in Higher Education, 2000.

Cuban, Larry, and Michael Usdan, eds. *Powerful Reforms and Shallow Roots: Improving America's Urban Schools.* New York: Teachers College Press, 2003.

Danziger, Shelton, and Peter Gottschalk. *Diverging Fortunes: Trends in Poverty and Inequality.* Washington, D.C.: Russell Sage Foundation and the Population Bureau, The American People Series, 2004.

———. *America Unequal.* Cambridge, Mass.: Harvard University Press, 1995.

David, Stephen, and Paul Peterson, eds. *Urban Politics and Public Policy: The City in Crisis.* New York: Praeger, 1977.

DeMott, Benjamin. *The Imperial Middle: Why Americans Can't Think Straight About Class.* New York: William Morrow, 1990.

Deutcsch, Martin, et al., eds. *Social Class, Race, and Psychological Development.* New York: Holt Rinehart Winston, 1968.

Dollard, John. *Caste and Class in a Southern Town.* New Haven: Yale University Press, 1938.

DuBois, W. E. B. *The Souls of Black Folk.* Chicago: McClung, 1903.

Duncan, Greg, and Jeanne Brooks-Gunn, eds. *Consequences of Growing Up Poor.* New York: Russell Sage, 1997.

Edmondson, Aimee. "Parental Apathy, Neglect Challenge Failing School's Children." *Commercial Appeal,* June 3, 2001.

———. "Expert Sure It's Not the Schools: Pre-K Patterns Tie Their Hands." *Commercial Appeal,* May 19, 2003.

Egerton, John. *Speak Now Against the Day.* New York: Knopf, 1994.

Elazar, Daniel. *American Federalism.* New York: Crowell, 1972.

Ellis, John. "Disease and the Destiny of a City: The 1878 Yellow Fever Epidemic in Memphis." *West Tennessee Historical Papers* 28 (1974): 75–89.

Fantini, Mario, Marilyn Gittell, and Richard Magat. *Community Control and the Urban School.* New York: Praeger Publishers, 1970.

Fasold, Mark. "Disparate Impact Analyses of TAAS Scores and School Quality." *Hispanic Journal of Behavioral Sciences* 22.4 (2000): 460–81.

Field, Frank, ed. *Education and the Urban Crisis.* London: Routledge & Kegan Paul, 1977.

Fine, Michelle, ed. *Chartering Urban School Reform: Reflections on Public High Schools in the Midst of Change.* New York: Teachers College Press, 1994.

Finn, Chester, Brunno Manno, and Gregg Vanourek. *Charter Schools in Action: Renewing Public Education.* Princeton, N.J.: Princeton University Press, 2000.

Firestone, William, et al. *Education Reform from 1983 to 1990: State Action and District Response.* New Brunswick, N.J.: Consortium for Policy Research in Education, 1991.

Fiske, Edward, and Helen Ladd. *When Schools Compete: A Cautionary Tale.* Washington D.C.: Brookings Institution Press, 2000.

Fordham, Sigithia. *Blacked Out: Dilemmas of Race, Identity, and Success at Capital High.* Chicago: University of Chicago Press, 1996.

Frankenberg, Erica, et al. *A Multiracial Society with Segregated Schools: Are We Losing the Dream?* Cambridge Mass.: Civil Rights Project of Harvard University, 2003.

Franklin, John Hope. *From Slavery to Freedom: A History of Negro Americans.* New York: Knopf, 1980.

Friedman, Milton. *Capitalism and Freedom.* Chicago: University of Chicago Press, 1962.

Friedman, Thomas. *The World Is Flat: A Brief History of the Twenty-First Century.* New York: Farrar, Straus, and Giroux, 2005.

Fullan, Michael, and Suzanne Stiegelbauer. *The New Meaning of Educational Change.* New York: Teacher's College Press, 1991.

Fuller, Bruce, et al. *Charter Schools and Inequality.* Berkeley: Policy Analysis for California Education, 2003.

Fuller, T. O. *The Inter-Racial Blue Book.* Memphis: Inter-Racial League, 1925.

Gandal, Matthew, et al. *Do Graduation Tests Measure Up?* Washington, D.C.: Achieve, 2004.

Garibaldi, Antoine, and Wormier Reed, eds. *The Education of African-Americans.* New York: Auburn House, 1991.

Garner, Norman. *Teaching in the Urban Community School.* London: Ward Lock Educational, 1973.

Gilder, George. *Wealth and Poverty.* New York: Basic Books, 1981.

Gill, Brian, et al. *Rhetoric versus Reality: What We Know and What We Need to Know about Vouchers and Charter Schools.* Santa Monica: Rand, 2001.

Glaab, Charles, and Theodore Brown. *A History of Urban America.* New York: Macmillan, 1976.

Goldfield, David. *Cotton Fields and Skyscrapers.* Baltimore: Johns Hopkins University Press, 1989.

Good, Thomas, and Jennifer Braden. *The Great School Debate: Choice, Vouchers, and Charters.* Mahwah, N.J.: Lawrence Erlbaum, 2000.

Goodenow, Ronald, and Diane Ravitch, eds. *Schools in Cities: Consensus and Conflict in American Educational History.* New York: Holmes and Meier, 1983.

Goodlad, John. *A Place Called School: Prospects for the Future.* New York: McGraw-Hill, 1984.

Gordon, June. *The Color of Teaching. Educational Change and Development Series.* New York: Routledge Falmer, 2000.

Grace, Gerald. *Teachers, Ideology and Control: A Study in Urban Education.* London: Routledge & Kegan Paul, 1978.

Gramlich, Edward, and Patricia Koshel. *Educational Performance Contracting: An Evaluation of an Experiment.* Washington, D.C.: Brookings Institute, 1975.

Grant, Robert. *The Black Man Comes to the City.* Chicago: Nelson Hall, 1972.

Greenwood, Peter, and Franklin Zimming. *One More Chance: The Pursuit of Planning Intervention Strategies for Chronic Juvenile Offenders.* Santa Monica: Rand Corp., 1985.

Gregory, Shelia. "Strategies for Improving the Racial Climate for Students of Color in Predominately White Intuitions." *Equality and Excellence in Education* 33.3 (2000): 39–47.

Grogan, Margaret. "A Black Woman Superintendent Tells." *Urban Education* 35.5 (2000): 597–602.

Guinier, Lani, et al. *Becoming Gentlemen: Women, Law Schools and Institutional Change.* Boston: Beacon Press, 1997.

Hacker, Andrew. *Two Nations: Black and White, Separate, Hostile, Unequal.* New York: Scribner's, 1992.

Hammel, Raymond, and John Nagle. *Urban Education in America: Problems and Prospects.* New York: Oxford University Press, 1973.

Hannaway, Jane, and Martin Carnoy, eds. *Decentralization and School Improvement: Can We Fulfill the Promise?* San Francisco: Josey-Bass, 1993.

Harkins, John. *Metropolis of the American Nile.* Oxford, Miss.: Guild Bindery Press, 1982.

Harlan, Louis. *Separate and Unequal: School Campaigns and Racism in the Southern Seaboard States, 1901–1915.* Chapel Hill: University of North Carolina Press, 1958.

Harrigan, John. *Empty Dreams, Empty Pockets: Class Bias in American Politics.* New York: Macmillan, 1993.

Harrington, Michael. *The New American Poverty.* New York: Penguin, 1985.

Harris, Louis. *Metropolitan Life Survey of the American Teacher, 1985–1995.* New York: Met Life, 1995.

Hassel, Bryan. *The Charter School Challenge: Avoiding the Pitfalls, Fulfilling the Promise.* Washington D.C.: Brookings Institution Press, 1999.

Heidenreich, Richard, ed. *Current Readings in Urban Education.* Arlington, VA.: College Readings, 1972.

———. *Urban Education.* Arlington, Va.: College Readings, 1972.

Henderson, Anne, et al. *Beyond the Bake Sale.* New York: New Press, 2006.

Hennig, Jeffrey, et al. *The Color of School Reform: Race, Politics, and the Challenge of Urban Education.* Princeton, N.J.: Princeton University Press, 1999.

Henry, Michael. *Race, Poverty, and Domestic Policy.* New Haven, Conn.: Yale University Press, 2004.

Henry, Sue Ellen, and Abe Feuerstein. "Now We Go to Their School: Desegregation and Its Contemporary Legacy." *Journal of Negro Education* 68.2 (1999): 164–81.

Hess, Alfred. *School Restructuring, Chicago Style.* Newbury Park, Calif.: Corwin, 1991.

Hess, Frederick. *Spinning Wheels: The Politics of Urban School Reform.* Washington D.C.: Brookings Institution Press, 1998.

———. *Revolution at the Margins: The Impact of Competition on Urban School Systems.* Washington D.C.: Brookings Institution Press, 2001.

Hill, Paul, Christine Campbell, and James Harvey. *It Takes a City: Getting Serious about Urban School Reform.* Washington D.C.: Brookings Institution Press, 1999.

Hill, Paul, and Mary Beth Celio. *Fixing Urban Schools.* Washington D.C.: Brookings Institution Press, 1998.

Hill, Paul, and Robin Lake. *Charter Schools and Accountability in Public Education.* Washington D.C.: Brookings Institution Press, 2001.

Hochschild, Jennifer. *Facing Up to the American Dream: Race, Class, and the Soul of a Nation.* Princeton: Princeton University Press, 1995.

Hochschild, Jennifer, and Nathan Scovronick. *The American Dream and the Public Schools.* New York: Oxford University Press, 2002.

Hodgkinson, Harold. "Educational Demographics: What Teachers Should Know." *Educational Leadership* 58.4 (Dec. 2000–Jan. 2001): 6–11.

Hollins, Etta, Joyce King, and Warren Hayman, eds. *Teaching Diverse Populations: Formulating a Knowledge Base.* Albany: State University of New York Press, 1994.

Holloway, Harry. *The Politics of the Southern Negro.* New York: Random House, 1969.

Holzer, Harry, et al. *Reconnecting Disadvantaged Young Men.* New York: Urban Institute, 2006.

Honey, Michael. *Southern Labor and Black Civil Rights.* Champaign: University of Illinois Press, 1993.

Horn, Wade, and Andrew Bush. *Fathers, Marriage, and Welfare Reform.* New York: Hudson Institute, 1997.

Howe, Kenneth, and Samana Foster. *An Assessment of Colorado's Charter Schools: Implications for Policy.* Boulder, Colo.: EPIC Policy Center, 2005.

Howell, William, and Paul Peterson. *The Education Gap: Vouchers and Urban Schools.* Washington D.C.: Brookings Institution Press, 2001.

Hughes, Mark Allen. *Poverty in Cities.* New York: National League of Cities, 1989.

Hunt, J. McVicker. *Intelligence and Experience.* New York: Ronald Press, 1961.

Ignatiev, Noel. *How the Irish Became White.* New York: Routledge Press, 1996.

Ingersoll, Richard. *Why Do High-Poverty Schools Have Difficulty Staffing Their Classrooms with Qualified Teachers?* Washington, D.C.: Center for American Progress and the Institute for America's Future, 2004.

Irons, Peter. *Jim Crow's Children: The Broken Promise of the Brown Decision.* New York: Viking Press, 2002.

Jackson, Kenneth. *Crabgrass Frontier: The Suburbanization of the United States.* New York: Oxford University Press, 1985.

Jencks, Christopher, and Meredith Phillips, eds. *The Black-White Test Score Gap.* Washington D.C.: Brookings Institution Press, 1998.

Jencks, Christopher, and Paul Peterson, eds. *The Urban Underclass.* Washington, D.C.: Brookings Institution Press, 1991.

Jencks, Christopher, et al. *Inequality: A Reassessment of the Effect of Family and Schooling in America.* New York: Basic Books, 1972.

Jones, Bruce, and Katherine Borman, eds. *Investing in U.S. Schools: Directions for Educational Policy.* Norwood, N.J.: Ablex, 1994.

Jones, Dionne, ed. *African American Males: A Critical Link in the African American Family.* Edison, N.J.: Transaction Publications, 1994.

Jones, E. Terrence. *The Metropolitan Chase: Politics and Policies in Urban America.* Upper Saddle River, N.J.: Prentice-Hall, 2002.

Judd, Dennis. *The Politics of American Cities.* New York: Harper Collins, 1988.

Kahlenberg, Richard. *All Together Now: Creating Middle Class Schools through Public School Choice.* Washington D.C.: Brookings Institution Press, 2003.

———. *A Nation at Risk: Preserving Public Education as an Engine for Social Mobility.* Washington D.C.: Brookings Institution Press, 2000.

Kantor, Harvey, and Barbara Brengel. *Urban Education and the 'Truly Disadvantaged': The Historical Roots of the Contemporary Crisis.* Princeton, N.J.: Princeton University Press, 1993.

Katz, Michael, ed. *School Reform: Past and Present.* Boston: Little, Brown and Co., 1971.

Katzman, Martin. *The Political Economy of Urban Schools.* Cambridge, Mass.: Harvard University Press, 1971.

Keating, John, and O. F. Fedder. *History of Memphis.* Syracuse, N.Y., 1886.

Kesselman, Mark, ed. *The Politics of Globalization.* New York: Houghton Mifflin, 2007.

Key, V. O. *Southern Politics in State and Nation.* New York: Knopf, 1949.

Kirby, Michael. *Memphis Poll 1993.* Memphis: Finance Division, 1993.

Kousser, Morgan. *The Shaping of Southern Politics: Suffrage Restriction and the Establishment of the One Party South, 1880–1910.* New Haven: Yale University Press, 1974.

Kozol, Jonathan. *Death at an Early Age.* Boston: Houghton Mifflin, 1967.

———. *Free Schools.* Boston: Houghton Mifflin, 1972.

———. *Illiterate America.* Garden City, N.Y.: Anchor Press/Doubleday, 1985.

———. *The Night Is Dark and I Am Far from Home.* Boston: Houghton Mifflin, 1975.

———. *Ordinary Resurrections: Children in the Years of Hope.* New York: Crown Publishers, 2000.

———. *Savage Inequalities: Children in America's Schools.* New York: Crown Publishers, 1991.

Kretovics, Joseph, and Edward J. Nussel, eds. *Transforming Urban Education.* Boston: Allyn and Bacon, 1994.

Kristol, Irving. *Two Cheers for Capitalism.* New York: Basic Books, 1978.

Krug, Edward. *Salient Dates in American Education, 1635–1964.* New York: Harper & Row, 1966.

Kweit, Robert, and Mary Grisez Kweit. *People and Politics in Urban America.* Pacific Grove, Calif.: Brooks-Cole, 1990.

Laffer, Arthur, and James Seymour. *The Economics of the Tax Revolt.* Orlando, Fla.: Harcourt, Brace, Jovanovich, 1979.

Lambie, Delores, et al. *Infants: The Ypsilanti-Carnegie Infant Education Program: An Experiment.* Ypsilanti, Mich.: High/Scope Press, Monographs of the High/Scope Educational Research Foundation #4, 1974.

Lamon, Lester. *Black Tennesseans, 1900–1930.* Knoxville: University of Tennessee Press, 1977.

Learmonth, James, and Lauren Maidment, eds. Teaching and Learning in Cities. United Kingdom: Whitebread Education Partnership, 1993.

Lee, George. *Beale Street.* New York: R. O. Ballou, 1934.

Lehman, Nicholas. *The Promised Land.* New York: Alfred Knopf, 1991.

Levin, Murry. *Teach Me! Kids Will Learn When Oppression Is the Lesson.* New York : Monthly Review Press, 1998.

Levine, Daniel, and Robert Havighurst, eds. *The Future of Big-City Schools: Desegregation Policies and Magnet Alternatives.* California: McCutchan Publishing Corp., 1977.

Levine, David. "The Crisis in Urban Education." *Perspectives on Urban America.* Ed. Melvin Urofsky. Garden City, N.Y.: Peter Smith, 1973.

Levy, Frank. *Dollars and Dreams: The Changing American Income Distribution.* New York: Norton, 1988.

Levy, John. *Urban America: Processes and Problems.* Upper Saddle River, N.J.: Prentice Hall, 2000.

Lewinsohn, Paul. *Race, Class and Party: A History of Negro Suffrage and White Politics in the South.* New York: Russell and Russell, 1963.

Lichtenstein, Nelson, ed. *Wal-Mart: The Face of Twenty-First-Century Capitalism.* New York: New Press, 2005.

Lightfoot, Alfred. *Urban Education in Social Perspective.* Chicago: Rand McNally College Publishing Co., 1978.

Lipman, Pauline. "Making the Global City, Making Inequality: The Political Economy and Cultural Politics of Chicago School Policy." *American Educational Research Journal* 39.2 (2002): 379–419.

———. *High Stakes Education: Inequality, Globalization, and Urban School Reform.* New York: Taylor and Francis Books, 2004.

Logan, Rayford. *The Betrayal of the Negro.* London: Collier and McMillan, 1965.

Loveless, Tom. *Conflicting Missions? Teachers Unions and Educational Reform.* Washington D.C.: Brookings Institution Press, 2000.

———. *The Tracking Wars: State Reform Meets School Policy.* Washington, D.C.: Brookings Institution Press, 1999.

Lowe, Jeanne. *Cities in a Race with Time.* New York: Random House, 1967.

Lutz, Frank, ed. *Toward Improved Urban Education.* Worthington: Charles A. Jones Publishing Co., 1970.

Lynn, Barry. *End of the Line: The Rise and Coming Fall of the Global Corporation*. New York: Doubleday, 2005.

Maier, Peter, et al. *First-Year Results of the Student Achievement Guarantee (SAGE) Program, Center for Urban Initiatives and Research*. Milwaukee: University of Wisconsin at Milwaukee, 1997.

Majors, Richard. *Educating Our Black Children: New Directions and Radical Approaches*. New York: Routledge Falmer, 2001.

Manegold, Catherine. "41% of School Day Is Spent on Academic Subjects, Study Says." *New York Times,* May 5, 1994.

Marcus, Sheldon, and Harry Rivlin, eds. *Conflicts in Urban Education*. New York: Basic Books, 1970.

Massey, Douglas, and Nancy Denton. *American Apartheid: Segregation and the Making of the Underclass*. Cambridge, Mass.: Harvard University Press, 1993.

Mayer, Susan, and Paul Peterson. *Earning and Learning: How Schools Matter*. Washington D.C.: Brookings Institution Press, 1999.

McAdams, Donald. *Fighting to Save Our Urban Schools . . . and Winning! Lessons from Houston*. New York: Teachers College Press, 2000.

McClafferty, Karen, Carlos Abberts Torres, and Theodore Mitchell, eds. *Challenges of Urban Education: Sociological Perspectives for the Next Century*. New York: State University of New York Press, 2000.

McFate, Katherine, ed. *The Metropolitan Area Fact Book*. Washington, D.C.: Joint Center for Political Studies, 1989.

McLanahan, Sara, and Gary Sandefur. *Growing up with a Single Parent*. Cambridge, Mass.: Harvard University Press, 1994.

McMurrin, Sterling, ed. *Resources for Urban Schools: Better Use and Balance*. Lexington, Ky.: Heath Lexington Books, 1971.

McWhorter, John. *Losing the Race: Self-Sabotage in the Black Community*. New York: Sussex Publishers, 2001.

———. *Winning the Race: Beyond the Crisis in Black America*. New York: Gotham Books, 2005.

Meier, August, and Elliot Rudwick. *From Plantation to Ghetto*. New York: Hill and Wang, 1969.

Melton, Gloria Brown. "Blacks in Memphis, Tennessee, 1920–1955." Ph.D. diss., Washington State University, 1982.

Memphis and Shelby County Office of Planning and Development. *Southeast Memphis, Annexation Area, 1987*. Memphis: Memphis and Shelby County Office of Planning and Development, 1987.

Menacker, Julius. *Vitalizing Guidance in Urban Schools*. New York: Dodd, Mead & Co., 1974.

Miller, Harry. *Social Foundations of Education: An Urban Focus*. New York: Holt, Rinehart and Winston, 1978.

Miller, L. Scott. *An American Imperative: Accelerating Minority Educational Advancement*. New Haven, Conn.: Yale University Press, 1995.

Miller, William. *Mr. Crump of Memphis*. Baton Rouge: Louisiana State University Press, 1964.

———. *Memphis during the Progressive Era*. Memphis: Memphis State University Press, 1957.

Milner, Richard. "Affective and Social Issues among High Achieving African American Students: Recommendations for Teachers and Teacher Education." *Action in Teacher Education* 24.1 (2002): 81–89.

Mincy, Ronald. *Black Males Left Behind*. New York: Urban Institute, 2006.

Mirel, Jeffrey. *The Rise and Fall of an Urban School System: Detroit, 1907–81*. Ann Arbor: University of Michigan Press, 1993.

Moe, Terry. *Schools, Vouchers and the American Public*. Washington D.C.: Brookings Institution Press, 2000.

Morphet, Edgar, David Jesser, and Arthur Ludka, eds. *Revitalizing Education in the Big Cities*. Denver: Improving State Leadership in Education, 1972.

Morris, Jerome. "What Is the Future of Predominantly Black Urban Schools? The Politics of Race in Urban Education Policy." *Phi Delta Kappan* 81.4 (1999): 316–19.

Morris, Robert. *Reading, 'Riting, and Reconstruction: The Education of Freedmen in the South, 1861–1870*. Chicago: University of Chicago Press, 1981.

Murphy, Joseph, and Phillip Hallinger. *Restructuring Schooling: Learning from On-Going Efforts*. Newbury Park, Calif.: Corwin Press, 1993.

Murtadha-Watts, Khuala. "Cleaning up and Mutinous in the Wake of Urban School Administration Tempest." *Urban Education* 35.5 (2000): 603–15.

Mydral, Gunnar. *An American Dilemma*. New York: Harper, 1944.

Nathan, Joe. *Charter Schools: Creating Hope and Opportunity in American Education*. San Francisco: Jossey-Bass, 1996.

National Education Commission on Time and Learning. *Prisoners of Time*. Washington, D.C.: GPO, 1994.

National Urban League. *The State of Black America*. New York: National Urban League, various years.

Newman, Katherine. *Declining Fortunes: The Withering of the American Dream*. New York: Basic Books, 1993.

Oakes, Jeannie, et al. *Educational Matchmaking: Academic and Vocational Tinkering in Comprehensive High Schools*. Santa Monica: Rand, 1992.

Ogbu, John. *Black American Students in an Affluent Suburb*. Mahwah, N.J.: Lawrence Erlbaum Publishers, 2003.

Ohio University. *The Impact of Head Start: An Evaluation of the Effect of Head Start on Children's Cognitive and Affective Development*. Athens, Ohio: Westinghouse Learning Corporation, 1969.

Oliver, Melvin, and Tom Shapiro. *Black Wealth/White Wealth*. New York: Routledge, 1997.

Orfield, Gary. *Dropouts in America.* Boston: Harvard University Press, 2004.

——. "School Desegregation After Two Generations: Race, Schools, and Opportunity in Urban Society,."" In *Race in America,* ed. Herbert Hill and James Jones. Madison: University of Wisconsin Press, 1993, 234–62.

Orfield, Gary, et al. "Schools More Separate: Consequences of a Decade of Resegregation." Harvard University, Civil Rights Project Report, 2001.

Orfield, Gary, and Mindy Kornhaber. *Raising Standards or Raising Barriers: Inequality and High Stakes Testing in Public Education.* Washington D.C.: Brookings Institution Press, 2001.

Orfield, Gary, and Susan Eaton. *Dismantling Desegregation: The Quiet Reversal of Brown v. Board of Education.* New York: Norton, 1996.

Ornstein, Allan. *Urban Education: Student Unrest, Teacher Behaviors, and Black Power.* Columbus: Charles E. Merrill Publishing Co., 1972.

——. *Metropolitan Schools: Administrative Decentralization vs. Community Control.* Metuchen, N.J.: Scarecrow Press, 1974.

Ornstein, Allan, Daniel Levine, and Doxey Wilkerson. *Reforming Metropolitan Schools.* Pacific Palisades, Calif.: Goodyear Publishing Co., 1975.

Orr, Marion. *Black Social Capital: The Politics of School Reform in Baltimore,1986–1998.* Lawrence: University Press Kansas, 1999.

Papadimitriou, Dimitri, and Edward Wolff. *Poverty and Prosperity in the USA in the Late 20th Century.* New York: Palgrave Macmillan, 1993.

Payne, Charles. *Getting What We Asked For: The Ambiguity of Success and Failure in Urban Education.* Westport, Conn.: Greenwood Press, 1984.

Perlman, Joel, and Robert Margo. *Women's Work? Schoolteachers, 1670–1920.* Chicago: University of Chicago Press, 2001.

Perrucci, Robert, and Earl Wysong. *The New Class Society: Goodbye American Dream?* New York: Rowman and Littlefield, 2002.

Peterson, Paul, and David Campbell. *Charters, Vouchers and Public Education.* Washington D.C.: Brookings Institution Press, 2001.

Peterson, Paul, and Jay Greene. "Race Relations and Central City Schools: It's Time for an Experiment with Vouchers." *Brookings Review* 16.2 (1998): 33–37.

Peterson, Paul, and Bryan Hassel. *Learning from School Choice.* Washington D.C.: Brookings Institution Press, 1998.

Phillips, Kevin. *Boiling Point: Democrats, Republicans, and the Decline of Middle-Class Prosperity.* New York: Harper Publishers, 1993.

——. *The Politics of Rich and Poor.* New York: Harper, 1990.

Phillips, Robert, and John Furlong. *Education, Reform and the State: Twenty Five Years of Politics, Policy and Practice.* Taylor and Francis Publishing, 2001.

Pohlmann, Marcus. *Black Politics in Conservative America.* New York: Longman, 2007.

——. *Governing the Postindustrial City.* New York: Longman Press, 1993.

——. *Political Power in the Postindustrial City.* New York: Stonehill, 1986.

Pohlmann, Marcus, and Michael Kirby. *Racial Politics at the Crossroads: Memphis Elects Dr. W.W. Herenton.* Knoxville: University of Tennessee Press, 1996.

Polite, Vernon, and James Earl Davis. *African American Males in School and Society: Practices and Policies for Effective Education.* New York: Teachers College Press, 1999.

Popham, James. *America's Failing Schools: How the Parents and Teachers Can Cope with No Child Left Behind.* New York, N.Y.: Taylor and Francis Publishing, 2004.

Portz, John, Lana Stein, and Robin Jones. *City Schools and City Politics: Institutions and Leadership in Pittsburgh, Boston, and St. Louis.* Lawrence: University Press of Kansas, 1999.

πPrice, Hugh. *Achievement Matters: Getting Your Child the Best Education Possible.* New York: Kensington Publishing Corp., 2002.

——. *Working Together: Mt. Vernon, New York: A Model for School Reform.* New York: National Urban League, 2002.

Price, Margaret. *The Negro Vote in the South.* Atlanta: Southern Regional Council, 1957.

Rabinowitz, Howard. *Race Relations in the South, 1865–1890.* New York: Oxford University Press, 1978.

Rank, Mark. *One Nation, Underprivileged: Why American Poverty Affects Us All.* New York: Oxford University Press, 2004.

Ravitch, Diane. *Brookings Papers on Education Policy.* Washington, D.C.: Brookings Institute, various years.

——. *Lessons from New York: The Redesign of Urban Education.* Washington, D.C.: Johns Hopkins University Press, 2000.

——. *The Troubled Crusade: American Education, 1945–1980.* New York: Basic Books, 1983.

Ravitch, Diane, and Ronald Goodenow, eds. *Educating an Urban People: The New York City Experience.* New York: Teachers College Press, 1981.

Ravitch, Diane, and Joseph Viteritti. *New Schools for a New Century: The Redesign of Urban Education.* New Haven: Yale University Press, 1997.

Reed, Douglas. *On Equal Terms: The Constitutional Politics of Educational Opportunity.* Princeton: Princeton University Press, 2001.

Reich, Robert. *The Work of Nations: Preparing Ourselves for 21st Century Capitalism.* New York: Knopf, 1991.

Rich, Wilbur. *Black Mayors and School Politics: The Failure of Reform in Detroit, Gary, and Newark.* New York: Garland Press, 1996.

Rist, Ray. *The Urban School: A Factory for Failure.* Edison, N.J.: Transaction Publications, 2002.

Rose, Mike. *Lives on the Boundary.* New York: Penguin, 1989.

Rothstein, Richard. *The Way We Were?: The Myths and Realities of America's Student Achievement.* Washington D.C.: Brookings Press, 1998.

Rubin, Beth, and Elena Silva. *Critical Voices in School Reform: Students Living through Change.* New York, N.Y.: Taylor and Francis Publishing, 2003.

Ryan, James. "Schools, Race, and Money." *Yale Law Review* 109 (1999): 249–315.

Sanders, William, and June Rivers. *Cumulative and Residual Effects of Teachers on Future Student Academic Achievement*. Knoxville: University of Tennessee Value-Added Research and Assessment Center, 1996.

Sanders, William, et al. *Value-Added Achievement Results for Three Cohorts of Roots and Wings Schools in Memphis: 1995–1999 Outcomes*. Memphis: University of Memphis Center for Research in Educational Policy, 2000.

Sassen, Saskia. *The Global City*. Princeton, N.J.: Princeton University Press, 1999.

Sawhill, Isabell, and John Morton. *Economic Mobility: Is the American Dream Alive and Well?* Washington, D.C.: Economic Mobility Project, 2007.

Schiller, Bradley. "Education and Ability." In *The Economics of Poverty and Discrimination*. Upper Saddle River, N.J.: Prentice-Hall, 2001, 172–86.

Schneider, Mark, et al. *Choosing Schools: Consumer Choice and the Quality of American Schools*. Princeton, N.J.: Princeton University Press, 2000.

Schor, Juliet. *The Overworked American: The Unexpected Decline of Leisure*. New York: Basic Books, 1991.

Scott, Robert E. *The High Price of "Free" Trade*. Washington, D.C.: Economic Policy Institute, 2003.

Seashore, Karen, Louis Seashore, and Matthew Miles. *Improving the Urban High School: What Works and Why*. New York : Teachers College Press, 1990.

Semel, Susan, and Alan Sadovnik, eds. *Schools of Tomorrow, Schools of Today: What Happened to Progressive Education*. New York: Peter Lang, 1999.

Sheldon, Marcus, and Harry Rivlin, eds. *Conflicts in Urban Education*. New York: Basic Books, 1970.

Sheldon, Marcus, and Philip Vairo. *Urban Education: Crisis or Opportunity?* New Jersey: Scarecrow Press, 1972.

Sher, Jonathan, and Stuart Rosenfeld. *Public Education in Sparsely Populated Areas of the United States*. Washington, D.C.: National Institute of Education, 1977.

Shipps, Dorothy. *School Reform, Corporate Style: Chicago, 1880–2000*. Lawrence: University of Kansas Press, 2006.

Shirley, Dennis. *Community Organizing for Urban School Reform*. Austin: University of Texas Press, 1997.

Shore, Rima. *Rethinking the Brain: New Insights into Early Development*. New York: Families and Work Institute, 1997.

Shulman, Beth. *The Betrayal of Work: How Low-Wage Jobs Fail 30 Million Americans and Their Families*. New York: New Press, 2003.

Sigafoos, Robert. *Cotton Row to Beale Street*. Memphis: Memphis State University Press, 1979.

Sigelman, Lee, and Susan Welch. *Black Americans' Views of Racial Inequality: The Dream Deferred*. New York: Cambridge University Press, 1991.

Sklar, Holly. *Chaos or Community?: Seeking Solutions, Not Scapegoats for Bad Economics*. Boston: South End, 1995.

Smith, Richard. "The Economics of Educational Discrimination in the United States South, 1870–1910." Ph.D. diss., University of Wisconsin, 1973.

Sousa, David. *How the Brain Learns.* Thousand Oaks, Calif.: Corwin Press, 2000.

Spangenberg, Gail, and Edward Meade. *A Tale of Three Cities: Boston, Birmingham, Hartford.* New York: Ford Foundation Series on Higher Education in the Cities, 1981.

Sternleib, George, and James Hughes. *Income and Job.* New Brunswick, N.J.: Center for Urban Policy Research, 1984.

Stiglitz, Joseph. *Globalization and Its Discontents.* London: Allen Lane, 2002.

Stone, Clarence, ed. *Changing Urban Education.* Lawrence: University of Kansas Press, 1998.

Stone, Clarence, et al. *Building Civic Capacity: The Politics of Reforming Urban Schools.* Lawrence: University of Kansas Press, 2001.

Sugarman, Stephen, and Frank Kemerer. *School Choice and Social Controversy.* Washington D.C.: Brookings Institution Press, 1999.

Taueber, Karl, and Alma Taueber. *Negroes in the Cities.* Chicago: Aldine, 1965.

Taylor, Alrutheus. *The Negro in Tennessee, 1865–1880.* New York: Associated Publishers, 1941.

Taylor, Denny, and Catherine Dorsey-Gaines. *Growing Up Literate: Learning from Inner-City Families.* Portsmouth: Heinemann, 1988.

Thernstrom, Abigail, and Stephan Thernstrom. *No Excuses: Closing the Racial Gap in Learning.* New York: Simon and Schuster, 2003.

Thompson, Daniel. *Negro Leadership Class.* Englewood Cliffs, N.J.: Prentice-Hall, 1963.

Thornbury, Robert. *The Changing School.* London: Methuen and Co. Ltd., 1978.

Tucker, David. *Memphis since Crump.* Knoxville: University of Tennessee Press, 1980.

Ture, Kwame, and Charles Hamilton. *Black Power.* New York: Random House, 1967.

Tyack, David. *The One Best System: A History of American Urban Education.* Cambridge, Mass.: Harvard University Press, 1974.

Tyack, David, and Larry Cuban. *Tinkering toward Utopia: A Century of Public School Reform.* Cambridge, Mass.: Harvard University Press, 1995.

Uchitelle, Louis. *The Disposable American: Layoffs and Their Consequences.* New York: Knopf, 2006.

Viteritti, Joseph. *Choosing Equality: School Choice, the Constitution, and Civil Society.* Washington D.C.: Brookings Institution Press, 1999.

Wang, Margaret, and Edmund Gordon, eds. *Education Resilience in Inner-City America: Challenges and Prospects.* New Jersey: Lawrence Erlbaum Associates, Publishers, 1994.

Wanninski, Jude. *The Way the World Works.* New York: Basic Books, 1978.

Warner, Sam Bass. *Streetcar Suburbs.* Cambridge, Mass.: Harvard University Press, 1962.

——. *The Urban Wilderness.* New York: Harper and Row, 1972.

Weikart, David. "Quality Preschool Programs: A Long-Term Social Investment." Occasional Paper #5, Ford Foundation Project on Social Welfare and the American Future, New York, 1989.

Weinberg, Meyer. *A Chance to Learn: A History of Race and Education in the United States.* New York: Cambridge University Press, 1977.

Weiner, Lois. *Urban Teaching: The Essentials.* New York: Teachers College Press, 1999.

Weis, Lois, and Michelle Fine, ed. *Construction Sites: Excavating Race, Class, and Gender among Urban Youth.* New York: Teachers College Press, 2000.

West, Anne, and Hazel Pennell. *Underachievement in Schools.* London: Routledge Falmer, 2003.

Wheelock, Anne. *Crossing the Tracks: How "Untracking" Can Save America's Schools.* New York: New Press, 1992.

Williamson, Joel. *The Crucible of Race.* New York: Oxford, 1984.

Wilson, Catherine. *Telling a Different Story: Teaching and Literacy in an Urban Preschool.* New York: Teachers College Press, 2000.

Wilson, William Julius. *The Truly Disadvantaged.* Chicago: University of Chicago Press, 1987.

———. *When Work Disappears: The World of the New Urban Poor.* New York: Knopf, 1996.

Wilson, Catherine. *Telling a Different Story: Teaching and Literacy in an Urban Preschool.* New York: Teachers College Press, 2000.

Wright, William. *Memphis Politics: An Example of Racial Bloc Voting.* New York: McGraw-Hill, 1962.

Young, John Preston. *Standard History of Memphis.* Knoxville: H. W. Crew, 1912.

Index